CALIFORNIA

GO MATH

Middle School Grade 8

Edward B. Burger

Juli K. Dixon

Timothy D. Kanold

Matthew R. Larson

Steven J. Leinwand

Martha E. Sandoval-Martinez

Printed in the U.S.A.

ISBN 978-0-544-20698-4

17 0877 25 24 23 22 21

4500819080   E F G

Authors

Edward B. Burger, Ph.D., is the President of Southwestern University, a former Francis Christopher Oakley Third Century Professor of Mathematics at Williams College and a former vice provost at Baylor University. He has authored or coauthored more than sixty-five articles, books, and video series; delivered over five hundred addresses and workshops throughout the world; and made more than fifty radio and television appearances. He is a Fellow of the American Mathematical Society as well as having earned many national honors, including the Robert Foster Cherry Award for Great Teaching in 2010. In 2012, Microsoft Education named him a "Global Hero in Education."

Juli K. Dixon, Ph.D., is a Professor of Mathematics Education at the University of Central Florida. She has taught mathematics in urban schools at the elementary, middle, secondary, and post-secondary levels. She is an active researcher and speaker with numerous publications and conference presentations. Key areas of focus are deepening teachers' content knowledge and communicating and justifying mathematical ideas. She is a past chair of the NCTM Student Explorations in Mathematics Editorial Panel and member of the Board of Directors for the Association of Mathematics Teacher Educators.

Timothy D. Kanold, Ph.D., is an award-winning international educator, author, and consultant. He is a former superintendent and director of mathematics and science at Adlai E. Stevenson High School District 125 in Lincolnshire, Illinois. He is a past president of the National Council of Supervisors of Mathematics (NCSM) and the Council for the Presidential Awardees of Mathematics (CPAM). He has served on several writing and leadership commissions for NCTM during the past decade. He presents motivational professional development seminars with a focus on developing professional learning communities (PLC's) to improve the teaching, assessing, and learning of students. He has recently authored nationally recognized articles, books, and textbooks for mathematics education and school leadership, including *What Every Principal Needs to Know about the Teaching and Learning of Mathematics.*

Matthew R. Larson, Ph.D., is the K-12 mathematics curriculum specialist for the Lincoln Public Schools and served on the Board of Directors for the National Council of Teachers of Mathematics from 2010-2013. He is a past chair of NCTM's Research Committee and was a member of NCTM's Task Force on Linking Research and Practice. He is the author of several books on implementing the Common Core Standards for Mathematics. He has taught mathematics at the secondary and college levels and held an appointment as an honorary visiting associate professor at Teachers College, Columbia University.

Steven J. Leinwand is a Principal Research Analyst at the American Institutes for Research (AIR) in Washington, D.C., and has over 30 years in leadership positions in mathematics education. He is past president of the National Council of Supervisors of Mathematics and served on the NCTM Board of Directors. He is the author of 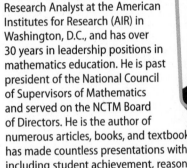 numerous articles, books, and textbooks and has made countless presentations with topics including student achievement, reasoning, effective assessment, and successful implementation of standards.

Martha E. Sandoval-Martinez is a mathematics instructor at El Camino College in Torrance, California. She was previously a Math Specialist at the University of California at Davis and former instructor at Santa Ana College, Marymount College, and California State University, Long Beach. In her current and former positions, she has worked extensively to improve fundamental pre-algebra and algebra skills in students who have historically struggled with mathematics.

UNIT 1 — Real Numbers, Exponents, and Scientific Notation

MODULE 1 — Real Numbers

CA CC

MODULE 2 — Exponents and Scientific Notation

CA CC

UNIT 2 Proportional and Nonproportional Relationships and Function

MODULE 3 Proportional Relationships

MODULE 4 Nonproportional Relationships

Writing Linear Equations

MODULE **5**

Functions

MODULE **6**

UNIT 3 Solving Equations and Systems of Equations

Solving Linear Equations

CA CC

MODULE 8

Solving Systems of Linear Equations

CA CC

UNIT 4 Transformational Geometry

 MODULE 9 **Transformations and Congruence**

CA CC

MODULE 10 **Transformations and Similarity**

CA CC

MODULE 11 Angle Relationships in Parallel Lines and Triangles

MODULE 12 The Pythagorean Theorem

MODULE 13 Volume

UNIT 6 Statistics

MODULE 14 Scatter Plots

MODULE 15 Two-Way Tables

California Common Core Standards for Mathematics

Correlation for *HMH California Go Math* Grade 8

Standard	Descriptor	Taught	Reinforced
8.NS THE NUMBER SYSTEM			
Know that there are numbers that are not rational, and approximate them by rational numbers.			
8.NS.1	Know that numbers that are not rational are called irrational. Understand informally that every number has a decimal expansion; for rational numbers show that the decimal expansion repeats eventually, and convert a decimal expansion which repeats eventually into a rational number.	SE: 7–9, 12, 15–17, 18	SE: 13-14, 19–20, 27, 28
8.NS.2	Use rational approximations of irrational numbers to compare the size of irrational numbers, locate them approximately on a number line diagram, and estimate the value of expressions (e.g., π^2).	SE: 10–12, 21–23, 24	SE: 14, 25–26, 27, 28

Standard	Descriptor	Taught	Reinforced
8.EE EXPRESSIONS AND EQUATIONS			
Work with radicals and integer exponents.			
8.EE.1	Know and apply the properties of integer exponents to generate equivalent numerical expressions.	SE: 33–37	SE: 39–40, 59, 60
8.EE.2	Use square root and cube root symbols to represent solutions to equations of the form $x^2 = p$ and $x^3 = p$, where p is a positive rational number. Evaluate square roots of small perfect squares and cube roots of small perfect cubes. Know that $\sqrt{2}$ is irrational.	SE: 9–11, 12	SE: 13–14, 27, 28
8.EE.3	Use numbers expressed in the form of a single digit times an integer power of 10 to estimate very large or very small quantities, and to express how many times as much one is than the other.	SE: 41–43, 44, 47–49, 50	SE: 45–46, 51–52, 59, 60
8.EE.4	Perform operations with numbers expressed in scientific notation, including problems where both decimal and scientific notation are used. Use scientific notation and choose units of appropriate size for measurements of very large or very small quantities (e.g., use millimeters per year for seafloor spreading). Interpret scientific notation that has been generated by technology.	SE: 53–55, 56	SE: 57–58, 59, 60
Understand the connections between proportional relationships, lines, and linear equations.			
8.EE.5	Graph proportional relationships, interpreting the unit rate as the slope of the graph. Compare two different proportional relationships represented in different ways.	SE: 85–87, 88, 170, 172	SE: 89–90, 91, 92, 173–174
8.EE.6	Use similar triangles to explain why the slope m is the same between any two distinct points on a non-vertical line in the coordinate plane; derive the equation $y = mx$ for a line through the origin and the equation $y = mx + b$ for a line intercepting the vertical axis at b.	SE: 73–75, 76, 103, 105, 106, 366–367	SE: 77–78, 91, 92, 108, 123, 124, 370

Standard	Descriptor	Taught	Reinforced
Analyze and solve linear equations and pairs of simultaneous linear equations.			
8.EE.7	Solve linear equations in one variable.	SE: 199–201, 202, 205–207, 208, 357, 360, 365–366, 368; *See also parts a and b below.*	SE: 203–204, 209–210, 223, 224, 361–362, 369–370; *See also parts a and b below.*
8.EE.7a	Give examples of linear equations in one variable with one solution, infinitely many solutions, or no solutions. Show which of these possibilities is the case by successively transforming the given equation into simpler forms, until an equivalent equation of the form $x = a$, $a = a$, or $a = b$ results (where a and b are different numbers).	SE: 217–219, 220	SE: 221–222, 223, 224
8.EE.7b	Solve linear equations with rational number coefficients, including equations whose solutions require expanding expressions using the distributive property and collecting like terms.	SE: 199–201, 202, 205–207, 208, 211–213, 214, 359, 360	SE: 203–204, 209–210, 215–216, 223, 224, 361–362
8.EE.8	Analyze and solve pairs of simultaneous linear equations.	SE: 230–233, 234; *See also parts a–c below.*	SE: 235–236, 267, 268; *See also parts a–c below.*
8.EE.8a	Understand that solutions to a system of two linear equations in two variables correspond to points of intersection of their graphs, because points of intersection satisfy both equations simultaneously.	SE: 229–234	SE: 235-236, 267, 268
8.EE.8b	Solve systems of two linear equations in two variables algebraically, and estimate solutions by graphing the equations. Solve simple cases by inspection.	SE: 237–241, 242, 245–249, 250, 253–256, 258, 261–263, 264	SE: 243–244, 251–252, 259–260, 265–266, 267, 268
8.EE.8c	Solve real-world and mathematical problems leading to two linear equations in two variables.	SE: 232–233, 234, 240–241, 242, 248–249, 250, 256–257, 258	SE: 235–236, 243–244, 251–252, 259–260, 266, 268

8.F FUNCTIONS

Define, evaluate, and compare functions.

Standard	Descriptor	Taught	Reinforced
8.F.1	Understand that a function is a rule that assigns to each input exactly one output. The graph of a function is the set of ordered pairs consisting of an input and the corresponding output.	SE: 155–159, 160, 163	SE: 161–162, 166–167, 181, 182
8.F.2	Compare properties of two functions each represented in a different way (algebraically, graphically, numerically in tables, or by verbal descriptions).	SE: 87, 88, 118–120, 169–171, 172	SE: 89–90, 122, 123, 124, 173–174, 181, 182
8.F.3	Interpret the equation $y = mx + b$ as defining a linear function, whose graph is a straight line; give examples of functions that are not linear.	SE: 97–99, 100, 109–111, 112, 115, 119, 164–165,166	SE: 101–102, 113–114, 121, 123, 124, 167–168, 181, 182

Use functions to model relationships between quantities.

Standard	Descriptor	Taught	Reinforced
8.F.4	Construct a function to model a linear relationship between two quantities. Determine the rate of change and initial value of the function from a description of a relationship or from two (x, y) values, including reading these from a table or from a graph. Interpret the rate of change and initial value of a linear function in terms of the situation it models, and in terms of its graph or a table of values.	SE: 79–81, 82, 85, 88, 104, 106, 110–111, 112, 116–117, 119, 129–131, 132, 135–137, 138, 169–170, 171, 172	SE: 78, 93–84, 89, 91, 92, 107–108, 113–114, 121–122, 123, 124, 133–134, 139–140, 149, 150, 173–174
8.F.5	Describe qualitatively the functional relationship between two quantities by analyzing a graph (e.g., where the function is increasing or decreasing, linear or nonlinear). Sketch a graph that exhibits the qualitative features of a function that has been described verbally.	SE: 175–177, 178	SE: 179–180, 181, 182

Standard	Descriptor	Taught	Reinforced
8.G GEOMETRY			
Understand congruence and similarity using physical models, transparencies, or geometry software.			
8.G.1a	Verify experimentally the properties of rotations, reflections, and translations: Lines are taken to lines, and line segments to line segments of the same length.	SE: 281–283, 284, 287–289, 290, 293–295, 296	SE: 285–286, 291–292, 297–298, 311, 312
8.G.1b	Verify experimentally the properties of rotations, reflections, and translations: Angles are taken to angles of the same measure.	SE: 281–283, 284, 287–289, 290, 293–295, 296	SE: 285–286, 291–292, 297–298, 311, 312
8.G.1c	Verify experimentally the properties of rotations, reflections, and translations: Parallel lines are taken to parallel lines.	SE: 281–283, 284, 287–289, 290, 293–295, 296	SE: 385–286, 291–292, 297–298, 311, 312
8.G.2	Understand that a two-dimensional figure is congruent to another if the second can be obtained from the first by a sequence of rotations, reflections, and translations; given two congruent figures, describe a sequence that exhibits the congruence between them.	SE: 305–307, 308	SE: 309–310, 311, 312
8.G.3	Describe the effect of dilations, translations, rotations, and reflections on two-dimensional figures using coordinates.	SE: 283–284, 289–290, 295–296, 299–302, 318–319, 320, 323–325, 326	SE: 285–286, 291–292, 297–298, 303–304, 321–322, 327–328, 335, 336
8.G.4	Understand that a two-dimensional figure is similar to another if the second can be obtained from the first by a sequence of rotations, reflections, translations, and dilations; given two similar two-dimensional figures, describe a sequence that exhibits the similarity between them.	SE: 317–318, 319–320, 329–331, 332	SE: 321–322, 333–334, 335, 336
8.G.5	Use informal arguments to establish facts about the angle sum and exterior angle of triangles, about the angles created when parallel lines are cut by a transversal, and the angle-angle criterion for similarity of triangles.	SE: 349–352, 355–357, 358, 360, 363–364	SE: 353–354, 361–362, 369–370, 371, 372

Standard	Descriptor	Taught	Reinforced
Understand and apply the Pythagorean Theorem.			
8.G.6	Explain a proof of the Pythagorean Theorem and its converse.	SE: 377–378, 383–385, 386	SE: 382, 387–388
8.G.7	Apply the Pythagorean Theorem to determine unknown side lengths in right triangles in real-world and mathematical problems in two and three dimensions.	SE: 378–380	SE: 381–382, 395, 396
8.G.8	Apply the Pythagorean Theorem to find the distance between two points in a coordinate system.	SE: 389–392	SE: 393–394, 395, 396
Solve real-world and mathematical problems involving volume of cylinders, cones, and spheres.			
8.G.9	Know the formulas for the volumes of cones, cylinders, and spheres and use them to solve real-world and mathematical problems.	SE: 401–403, 404, 407–409, 410, 413–415, 416	SE: 405–406, 411–412, 417–418, 419, 420

8.SP STATISTICS AND PROBABILITY			
Investigate patterns of association in bivariate data.			
8.SP.1	Construct and interpret scatter plots for bivariate measurement data to investigate patterns of association between two quantities. Describe patterns such as clustering, outliers, positive or negative association, linear association, and nonlinear association.	SE: 144–145, 146, 435–437, 438, 441–442, 444	SE: 147–148, 149, 150, 439–440, 445–446, 447, 448
8.SP.2	Know that straight lines are widely used to model relationships between two quantitative variables. For scatter plots that suggest a linear association, informally fit a straight line, and informally assess the model fit by judging the closeness of the data points to the line.	SE: 141–142, 146, 441–442, 444	SE: 147–148, 445–446, 447, 448
8.SP.3	Use the equation of a linear model to solve problems in the context of bivariate measurement data, interpreting the slope and intercept.	SE: 142–143, 146, 442–444	SE: 147–148, 445–446, 447, 448
8.SP.4	Understand that patterns of association can also be seen in bivariate categorical data by displaying frequencies and relative frequencies in a two-way table. Construct and interpret a two-way table summarizing data on two categorical variables collected from the same subjects. Use relative frequencies calculated for rows or columns to describe possible association between the two variables.	SE: 453–455, 456, 459–463, 464	SE: 457–458, 465–466, 467, 468

Standard	Descriptor	Citations
MP MATHEMATICAL PRACTICES STANDARDS		*The mathematical practices standards are integrated throughout the book. See, for example, the citations below.*
MP.1	**Make sense of problems and persevere in solving them.**	SE: 14, 122, 180, 204, 213, 221, 244, 256–257, 310, 382, 294, 417, 457–458
MP.2	**Reason abstractly and quantitatively.**	SE: 14, 40, 82, 105, 113, 155–156, 200–204, 216, 256–257, 356–357, 377–378
MP.3	**Construct viable arguments and critique the reasoning of others.**	SE: 20, 102, 148, 210, 260, 304, 354, 412, 446
MP.4	**Model with mathematics.**	SE: 75, 131–132, 206–207, 256–257, 365–366, 415, 459–463
MP.5	**Use appropriate tools strategically.**	SE: 22, 55, 199, 229–233, 287, 317, 349–350, 355, 377, 401
MP.6	**Attend to precision.**	SE: 58, 108, 145, 175–179, 216, 236, 252, 354, 406, 439
MP.7	**Look for and make use of structure.**	SE: 10–11, 33–36, 47, 135–137, 155–156, 210, 299–302, 383, 436, 441–443
MP.8	**Look for and express regularity in repeated reasoning.**	SE: 8, 33–36, 47, 109, 199, 237, 245, 253, 299–302, 390, 442

Succeeding with HMH California Go Math

Actively participate in your learning with your write-in Student Edition. Explore concepts, take notes, answer questions, and complete your homework right in your textbook!

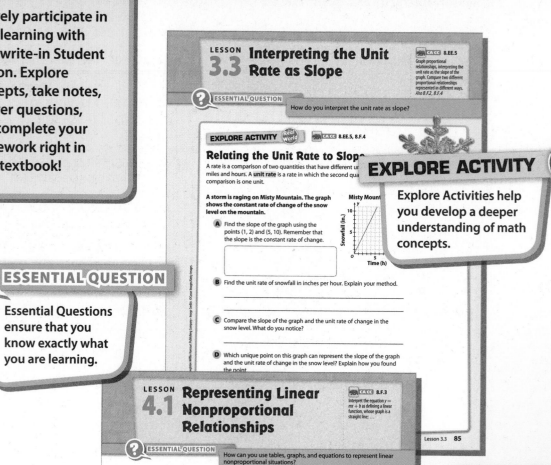

LESSON 3.3 Interpreting the Unit Rate as Slope

CACC 8.EE.5
Graph proportional relationships, interpreting the unit rate as the slope of the graph. Compare two different proportional relationships represented in different ways. Also 8.F.2, 8.F.4

? ESSENTIAL QUESTION How do you interpret the unit rate as slope?

EXPLORE ACTIVITY Real World **CACC 8.EE.5, 8.F.4**

Relating the Unit Rate to Slope

A rate is a comparison of two quantities that have different u... miles and hours. A **unit rate** is a rate in which the second qua... comparison is one unit.

A storm is raging on Misty Mountain. The graph shows the constant rate of change of the snow level on the mountain.

A Find the slope of the graph using the points (1, 2) and (5, 10). Remember that the slope is the constant rate of change.

B Find the unit rate of snowfall in inches per hour. Explain your method.

C Compare the slope of the graph and the unit rate of change in the snow level. What do you notice?

D Which unique point on this graph can represent the slope of the graph and the unit rate of change in the snow level? Explain how you found the point.

Lesson 3.3 85

EXPLORE ACTIVITY Real World

Explore Activities help you develop a deeper understanding of math concepts.

? ESSENTIAL QUESTION

Essential Questions ensure that you know exactly what you are learning.

LESSON 4.1 Representing Linear Nonproportional Relationships

CACC 8.F.3
Interpret the equation y = mx + b as defining a linear function, whose graph is a straight line; ...

? ESSENTIAL QUESTION How can you use tables, graphs, and equations to represent linear nonproportional situations?

Representing Linear Relationships Using Tables

You can use an equation to describe the relationship between two quantities in a real-world situation. You can use a table to show some values that make the equation true.

EXAMPLE 1 Real World **CA CC Prep for 8.F.3**

The equation $y = 3x + 2$ gives the total charge for one person, y, renting a pair of shoes and bowling x games at Baxter Bowling Lanes based on the prices shown. Make a table of values for this situation.

STEP 1 Choose several values for x that make sense in context.

x (number of games)	1	2	3	4
y (total cost in dollars)				

STEP 2 Use the equation $y = 3x + 2$ to find y for each value of x.

x (number of games)	1	2	3	4
y (total cost in dollars)	5	8	11	14

Substitute 1 for x.
$y = 3(1) + 2 = 5.$

BAXTER bowling lanes
$3 per game
$2 shoe rental

YOUR TURN

Your Turn exercises check your understanding of new concepts.

YOUR TURN

1. Francisco makes $12 per hour doing part-time work on Saturdays. He spends $4 on transportation to and from work. The equation $y = 12x - 4$ gives his earnings y, after transportation costs, for working x hours. Make a table of values for this situation.

x (number of hours)				
y (earnings in dollars)				

Personal Math Trainer
Online Practice and Help
my.hrw.com

Lesson 4.1 97

Math On the Spot
my.hrw.com

Math On the Spot

(⏻) my.hrw.com

Scan QR codes with your smart phone to watch Math On the Spot tutorial videos for every example in the book!

Unit Project

Unit Project 🔶 CACC 8.G.1, 8.G.3

Transforming the World

For this project, create a presentation that shows real-world examples of transformations. Include three rotations, three translations, and three reflections. Your project can show photographs or drawings that you have found during your research. Your examples do not have to illustrate exact transformations. For example, you can include a photo of ___ that closely resembles, but does not ___ ___tional pattern.

___ ___ object, the transformation
___ ___ you found the obje___
___ questions you h___
___acher.

Apply new skills and concepts to solve real-world problems in Unit Projects and Math in Careers Activities.

MATH IN CAREERS | ACTIVITY

Contractor Fernando is expanding his dog's ___
original yard has a fence represented by rectan___
coordinate plane. Fernando hires a contractor ___
fence that should enclose 6 times as much area a___
The shape of the yard must remain the same. The ___
the fence shown by rectangle L'M'N'O'. Determine ___
Fernando's requirements for the new fence. Expl___

340 Unit 4

Reading Start-Up

Visualize Vocabulary

Use the ✔ words to complete the diagram.

Reviewing Proportions

2:6, 3 to 4

5 25 35
— — —
10 50 70

12 in
——
1 f___
$1.2___
per ounce

Understand Vocabulary

Match the term on the left to the definition on the right.

1. unit rate

2. constant of proportionality

3. proportional relationship

A. A constant ratio of two variables related proporti___

B. A rate in which the second qu___ in the comparison is one unit.

C. A relationship between two quantities in which the ratio of one quantity to the other quantity is constant.

Vocabulary

Review Words
- constant *(constante)*
- ✔ equivalent ratios *(razones equivalentes)*
- proportion *(proporción)*
- rate *(tasa)*
- ✔ ratios *(razón)*
- ✔ unit rates *(tasas unitarias)*

Reading Start-Up

Get vocabulary, language, and note-taking support throughout the book.

Active Reading

Key-Term Fold Before beginning the module, create a key-term fold to help you learn the ___ ___rite the highlighted ___ ___e of the flap. Write ___ on the other side ___ fold to quiz yourself ___is module.

Module 3   **71**

UNIT 5
MIXED REVIEW

Assessment Readiness

Personal Math Trainer
Online Practice and Help
my.hrw.com

1. Consider the system of equations $\begin{cases} 3x + 3y = 6 \\ 6x - y = -16 \end{cases}$.
   Will the solution method eliminate a variable from the system?
   Select Yes or No.

   A. Multiply the first equation by 2 and subtract the equations.   ○ Yes   ○ No

   B. Multiply the second equation by 3 and add the equations.   ○ Yes   ○ No

   C. Multiply the first equation by 6 and the second equation by 3 and add the equations.   ○ Yes   ○ No

2. Angle ABC is an exterior angle of ∠BCD.
   Choose True or False for each statement.

   A. m∠D = 40°   ○ True   ○ False
   B. m∠ABC = 110°   ○ True   ○ False
   C. m∠CBD = 70°   ○ True   ○ False

3. A straight road connects the towns of Winridge and Upper Lansbury. On a map on which each unit represents 10 miles, the coordinates of Winridge are (8, 4) and the coordinates of Upper Lansbury are (6, 10). If Ty drives from Winridge to Upper Lansbury at an average speed of 40 miles per hour, will the trip take more than an hour? Explain your reasoning.

4. Earth has a radius of 6371 kilometers, and the Moon has a radius of 1737 kilometers. How many times larger is Earth's volume than the Moon's volume? Explain how you determined the answer.

Performance Tasks

★ **5.** A paper cup is shaped like ___ 4.6 centimeters, and the sl___

   a. What is the height h of ___ centimeter? Explain ho___

   b. What is the volume of the cup to the ne___

Assessment Readiness

Prepare for new high-stakes tests with SBAC aligned practice items and Performance Tasks.

★★ **6.** An architect uses drafting software to draw ∠AB___ the patio of a house.

   a. Determine the exact length of each side of th___ in the drawing.

   b. Is the triangle a right triangle? Justify your answer.

   c. The architect uses the software to determine that ∠C measures 56.3°. What are the measures of the other two angles of the triangle? Explain how you determined the answers.

★★★ **7.** The diagram shows how several steel beams intersect to form part of the structure of a building. In the diagram line p is parallel to line q. What is the length of the beam with endpoints at A and B? Justify each step of your work. (*Hint:* First show similar triangles.)

CA11

GO DIGITAL
my.hrw.com

Enhance Your Learning!

The eStudent Edition provides additional multimedia resources to enhance your learning. You can write in answers, take notes, watch videos, explore concepts with virtual manipulatives, and get homework help!

Real-World Videos show you how specific math topics can be used in all kinds of situations.

Math On the Spot

⏻ my.hrw.com

Math On the Spot video tutorials provide step-by-step instruction of the math concepts covered in each example.

Personal Math Trainer lets you practice, take quizzes and tests, and get homework help with instant feedback!

Personal Math Trainer provides a variety of learning aids that develop and improve your understanding of math concepts, including videos, guided examples, and step-by-step solutions.

Personal Math Trainer

Online Practice and Help

my.hrw.com

Animated Math activities and virtual manipulatives let you interactively explore and practice key math concepts and skills.

Animated Math

my.hrw.com

Standards for Mathematical Practice

The topics described in the Standards for Mathematical Content will vary from year to year. However, the *way* in which you learn, study, and think about mathematics will not. The Standards for Mathematical Practice describe skills that you will use in all of your math courses. These pages show some features of your book that will help you gain these skills and use them to master this year's topics.

MP.1 Make sense of problems and persevere in solving them.

Mathematically proficient students start by explaining to themselves the meaning of a problem… They analyze givens, constraints, relationships, and goals. They make conjectures about the form… of the solution and plan a solution pathway…

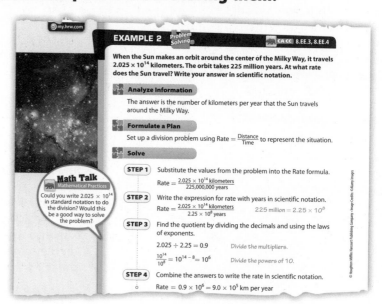

EXAMPLE 2 Problem Solving   CA CC 8.EE.3, 8.EE.4

When the Sun makes an orbit around the center of the Milky Way, it travels 2.025×10^{14} kilometers. The orbit takes 225 million years. At what rate does the Sun travel? Write your answer in scientific notation.

Analyze Information

The answer is the number of kilometers per year that the Sun travels around the Milky Way.

Formulate a Plan

Set up a division problem using Rate $= \frac{Distance}{Time}$ to represent the situation.

Solve

STEP 1 Substitute the values from the problem into the Rate formula.
Rate $= \frac{2.025 \times 10^{14} \text{ kilometers}}{225,000,000 \text{ years}}$

STEP 2 Write the expression for rate with years in scientific notation.
Rate $= \frac{2.025 \times 10^{14} \text{ kilometers}}{2.25 \times 10^{8} \text{ years}}$ 225 million $= 2.25 \times 10^{8}$

STEP 3 Find the quotient by dividing the decimals and using the laws of exponents.
$2.025 \div 2.25 = 0.9$ *Divide the multipliers.*
$\frac{10^{14}}{10^{8}} = 10^{14-8} = 10^{6}$ *Divide the powers of 10.*

STEP 4 Combine the answers to write the rate in scientific notation.
Rate $= 0.9 \times 10^{6} = 9.0 \times 10^{5}$ km per year

Math Talk
Mathematical Practices
Could you write 2.025×10^{14} in standard notation to do the division? Would this be a good way to solve the problem?

Problem-solving examples and exercises lead students through problem solving steps.

MP.2 Reason abstractly and quantitatively.

Mathematically proficient students… bring two complementary abilities to bear on problems…: the ability to decontextualize— to abstract a given situation and represent it symbolically… and the ability to contextualize, to pause… in order to probe into the referents for the symbols involved.

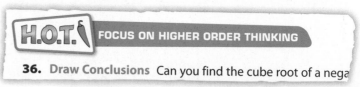

H.O.T. FOCUS ON HIGHER ORDER THINKING

36. Draw Conclusions Can you find the cube root of a nega

Unit Project   CA CC 8.F.4, 8.SP.1, 8.

Focus on Higher Order Thinking exercises in every lesson and a **Project** in every unit require you to use logical reasoning, represent situations symbolically, use mathematical models to solve problems, and state your answers in terms of a problem context.

MP.3 Construct viable arguments and critique the reasoning of others.

Mathematically proficient students... justify their conclusions, [and]... distinguish correct... reasoning from that which is flawed.

Reflect

2. **Make a Conjecture** Use your results from parts **E**, **H**, and a conjecture about translations.

Essential Question Check-in and **Reflect** in every lesson ask you to evaluate statements, explain relationships, apply mathematical principles, make conjectures, construct arguments, and justify your reasoning.

MP.4 Model with mathematics.

Mathematically proficient students can apply... mathematics... to... problems... in everyday life, society, and the workplace.

Real-world examples and **mathematical modeling** apply mathematics to other disciplines and real-world contexts such as science and business.

MP.5 Use appropriate tools strategically.

Mathematically proficient students consider the available tools when solving a... problem... [and] are... able to use technological tools to explore and deepen their understanding...

Exploration Activities in lessons use concrete and technological tools, such as manipulatives or graphing calculators, to explore mathematical concepts.

MP.6   Attend to precision.

Mathematically proficient students… communicate precisely… with others and in their own reasoning… [They] give carefully formulated explanations…

19. Communicate Mathematical Ideas Explain how you can fir height of a cylinder if you know the diameter and the volum an example with your explana

> **Key Vocabulary**
>
> **slope** *(pendiente)*
> A measure of the steepness of a line on a graph; the rise divided by the run.

Precision refers not only to the correctness of calculations but also to the proper use of mathematical language and symbols. **Communicate Mathematical Ideas** exercises and **Key Vocabulary** highlighted for each module and unit help you learn and use the language of math to communicate mathematics precisely.

MP.7   Look for and make use of structure.

Mathematically proficient students… look closely to discern a pattern or structure… They can also step back for an overview and shift perspectives.

Follow the steps to informally prove the Triangle Sum Theorem. You should draw each step on your own paper. The figures below are provided for you to check your work.

A Draw a triangle and label the angles as ∠1, ∠2, and ∠3 as shown.

B Draw line *a* through the base of the triangle.

C The Parallel Postulate states that through a point not on a line ℓ, there is exactly one line parallel to line ℓ. Draw line *b* parallel to line *a*, through the vertex opposite the base of the triangle.

D Extend each of the non-base sides of the triangle to form transversal *s* and transversal *t*. Transversals *s* and *t* intersect parallel lines *a* and *b*.

E Label the angles formed by line *b* and the transversals as ∠4 and ∠5.

F Because ∠4 and _____ are alternate interior

Throughout the lessons, you will observe regularity in mathematical structures in order to make generalizations and make connections between related problems. For example, you can apply your knowledge of geometric theorems to determine when an auxiliary line would be helpful.

MP.8   Look for and express regularity in repeated reasoning.

Mathematically proficient students… look both for general methods and for shortcuts… [and] maintain oversight of the process, while attending to the details.

Use your pattern to complete this equation: $(7^2)^4 = 7^{\boxed{}}$.

B Describe any patterns you see. Use your pattern to deter of 1 pencil.

20. Look for a Pattern Describe the pattern in the equation. The equation.

$$0.3x + 0.03x + 0.003x + 0.0003x + \ldots = 3$$

You will look for repeated calculations and mathematical patterns in examples and exercises. Recognizing patterns can help you make generalizations and obtain a better understanding of the underlying mathematics.

GRADE 7 PART 1

Review Test

Personal
Math Trainer

Online Practice
and Help

my.hrw.com

1. Evaluate $a + b$ for $a = 34$ and $b = -6$.

_____

2. A triangle has sides with lengths of $5x - 7$, $3x - 4$, and $2x - 6$. What is the simplified expression for the perimeter of the triangle?

_____

3. Which of the following ratios forms a proportion? Select Yes or No.

A. $\frac{28}{49} \overset{?}{=} \frac{4}{7}$ ○ Yes ○ No

B. $\frac{4}{7} \overset{?}{=} \frac{16}{28}$ ○ Yes ○ No

C. $\frac{4}{7} \overset{?}{=} \frac{16}{35}$ ○ Yes ○ No

D. $\frac{4}{7} \overset{?}{=} \frac{20}{35}$ ○ Yes ○ No

4. For a sale, a store decreases its prices on all items by 25%. An item that cost \$120 before the sale now costs $\$120 - 0.25(\$120)$. Use the Distributive Property to write an equivalent expression for the item's cost now.

_____

5. Write an equation that models the situation and find its solution.

It's going to be Lindsay's birthday soon, and her friends Mary, Mikhail, Anne, Kim, Makoto, and Isabel have contributed equal amounts of money to buy her a present. They have \$36.00 to spend between them. Determine how much each contributed.

_____

_____

6. Solve $4(a + 4) - 2 = 34$.

_____

7. Four sisters bought a present for their father. They received a 10% discount on the original price of the gift. After the discount was taken, each sister paid \$9.00. What was the original price of the gift?

_____

8. Justin is redoing his bathroom floor with tiles measuring 6 in. by 13 in. The floor has an area of 8,500 in². What is the least number of tiles he will need?

_____

9. One winter day, the temperature ranged from a high of 20 °F to a low of −25 °F. By how many degrees did the temperature change?

_____

10. Terry drove 310 miles in 5 hours at a constant speed. How long would it take him to drive 403 miles at the same speed?

_____

11. 128 is 74% of what number? If necessary, round your answer to the nearest hundredth.

_____

12. Tell whether the data show a direct variation. If so, identify the constant of variation.

Number of Baskets	Cost
5	$15
7	$21
9	$27
13	$39
15	$45

_____

_____

13. The graph shows the distance Jamie walks over time. Does she walk at a constant or variable speed? How fast is Jamie walking?

_____

_____

14. Darryl is reading a book at the rate of 4.5 pages per minute. What ordered pair on a graph of his reading rate would represent the number of minutes it would take him to read 90 pages?

_____

15. The water level in a plastic pool changed by –8 gallons each hour due to a small hole in the bottom. After 6 hours, the pool contained 132 gallons. How much water was in the pool originally?

_____

16. The ratio of adults to children attending a new exhibit at the museum was found to be 8:5. Based on this ratio, if 390 people attended one day, how many would be children?

_____

Performance Task

17. The graph shows the relationship between the total cost and the number of pounds of rice purchased.

Part A: What does (6, 18) represent?

_____

Part B: Which point represents the unit price?

_____

Part C: How many pounds would you have to buy for the total to be $12? Explain how to find the answer.

_____

_____

_____

_____

GRADE 7 PART 2

Review Test

Personal
Math Trainer

Online Practice
and Help

my.hrw.com

1. What are the actual dimensions of the Check-out Area?

Floor plan of library

Scale: 1 cm : 5 m

_____

2. For a history fair, a school is building a circular wooden stage that will stand 2 feet off the ground. Find the area of the stage if the radius of the stage is 19 feet. Use 3.14 for π.

_____

3. Find the area of the circle to the nearest tenth. Use 3.14 for π.

4.4 mm

_____

4. What is the solution of the inequality $-0.4x - 1.2 > 0.8$?

_____

5. Find m$\angle LMN$.

_____

6. Ralph is an electrician. He charges an initial fee of $32, plus $33 per hour. If Ralph earned $197 on a job, how long did the job take?

_____

7. Find the volume of the cylinder. Use 3.14 for π. Round your answer to the nearest tenth.

3.9 m

15 m

_____

8. State a method that could be used to simulate how many boys and how many girls are in a random sample of 20 students from a school population that is half boys and half girls.

_____

_____

_____

_____

_____

9. Roberto plays on the school baseball team. In the last 9 games, Roberto was at bat 32 times and got 11 hits. What is the experimental probability that Roberto will get a hit during his next time at bat? Express your answer as a fraction in simplest form.

_____

10. A coin-operated machine sells plastic rings. It contains 14 pink rings, 10 green rings, 9 purple rings, and 13 black rings. Sarah puts a coin into the machine. Find the theoretical probability she gets a pink ring. Express your answer as a decimal. If necessary, round your answer to the nearest thousandth.

_____

11. A manufacturer inspects a sample of 400 personal video players and finds that 399 of them have no defects. The manufacturer sent a shipment of 2000 video players to a distributor. Predict the number of players in the shipment that are likely to have no defects.

_____

12. An experiment consists of rolling two fair number cubes. What is the probability that the sum of the two numbers will be 8? Express your answer as a fraction in simplest form.

_____

13. The student council president wants to find out the opinion of the students on the issue of school lunch options. The president sends out a survey to a random sample of students in the school. What type of sample is this? Explain.

_____

_____

_____

14. A map of Australia has a scale of 1 cm : 110 km. If the distance between Darwin and Alice Springs is 1444 kilometers, how far apart are they on the map, to the nearest tenth of a centimeter?

_____

15. Using the following data, state the errors in the box-and-whisker plot.

33, 27, 6, 34, 31, 59, 26, 1, 30

_____

_____

_____

_____

Performance Task

16. The number of goals scored by a hockey team in each of its first 10 games is 2, 4, 0, 3, 4, 1, 3, 1, 1, and 5.

a. Find the mean number of goals scored.

_____

b. Find the mean absolute deviation (MAD) of the number of goals scored.

_____

c. A second team in the same division scores a mean of 4.5 goals in its first 10 games, with the same MAD as the team above. Compare the difference in the teams' mean number of goals with the MAD in the number of goals scored.

_____

_____

GRADE 8 PART 1

Benchmark Test

Personal
Math Trainer

Online Practice
and Help

my.hrw.com

1. Multiply. Write the product as one power.
   $a^8 \cdot a^5$

   _____

2. Simplify $(6^{-4})^6$.

   _____

3. A square mosaic is made of small glass squares. If there are 196 small squares in the mosaic, how many are along an edge?

   _____

4. Simplify $2\sqrt{-19 + 44}$.

   _____

5. A passenger plane travels at about 7.97×10^2 feet per second. The plane takes 1.11×10^4 seconds to reach its destination.

   About how far must the plane travel to reach its destination? Write your answer in scientific notation.

   _____

6. Approximate $\sqrt{158}$ to the nearest hundredth.

   _____

7. Write a rule, in slope-intercept form, for the linear function represented in the table.

x	y
−3	12
−2	10
3	0
5	−4

8. A remote-control airplane descends at a rate of 2 feet per second. After 3 seconds it is 67 feet above the ground. Write the equation in point-slope form that models the situation. Then, find the height of the plane after 8 seconds.

   _____

9. A bicyclist heads east at 19 km/h. After she has traveled 24.2 kilometers, another cyclist sets out in the same direction going 30 km/h. About how long will it take the second cyclist to catch up to the first cyclist?

   _____

10. What is the equation of the graph in slope-intercept form?

    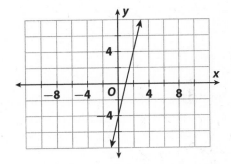

    _____

11. Solve $-2z + 3 + 7z = -12$.

    _____

12. How many solutions does the equation $c = -c + 2$ have?

    _____

13. What is the solution of the system of equations?

$y = 3x + 1$

$y = 5x - 1$

_____

14. Which of these functions is linear? Select Yes or No.

A. $y = x^2 - x$ ⃝ Yes ⃝ No

B. $y = 1 - x$ ⃝ Yes ⃝ No

C. $y = \frac{x}{3}$ ⃝ Yes ⃝ No

D. $y = \frac{2}{3}x - 2x$ ⃝ Yes ⃝ No

15. Which function has the greatest rate of change? Explain.

A. $y = -5x$

B. $\{(-1, -2), (1, 2), (3, 6), (5, 10), (7, 14)\}$

C. A fitness club charges a $200 membership fee plus monthly fees of $25.

D. $y = 3x - 16$

_____

_____

16. The graph below shows an airplane's speed over a period of time. Describe the events.

_____

_____

_____

_____

17. Identify $\sqrt{\frac{169}{64}}$ as *rational* or *irrational*. Explain your reasoning.

_____

Performance Task

18. Ashley reads 2 pages/minute for 10 minutes, takes a 10 minute break, and then reads at the same rate for 10 more minutes. Adam reads at the same rate the entire time. The equation for the number of pages he reads is $y = 1.2x$. How are these functions similar? How are they different?

_____

_____

_____

_____

_____

_____

_____

_____

_____

_____

GRADE 8 PART 2

Benchmark Test

Personal
Math Trainer

Online Practice
and Help

my.hrw.com

1. In the gift shop of the History of Flight museum, Elisa bought a kit to make a model of a jet airplane. The actual plane is 21 feet long with a wingspan of 17.5 feet. If the finished model will be 12 inches long, what will the wingspan be?

_____

2. Find the angle measures in the isosceles triangle.

3. What is the solution of the system of equations?
$y = 3x - 1$
$y = 5x + 1$

_____

4. Melanie is making a piece of jewelry that is in the shape of a right triangle. The two shorter sides of the piece of jewelry are 9 mm and 12 mm. Find the perimeter of the piece of jewelry.

_____

5. Find the distance, to the nearest tenth, from $T(4, -2)$ to $U(-2, 3)$.

_____

6. Which of the following is a congruence transformation? Select Yes or No.

   A. A reflection over the *x*-axis.
   ○ Yes ○ No

   B. A dilation with scale factor 0.5.
   ○ Yes ○ No

   C. A translation 1 unit left.
   ○ Yes ○ No

   D. A dilation with scale factor 1.
   ○ Yes ○ No

7. Harry and Selma start driving from the same location. Harry drives 42 miles north while Selma drives 144 miles east. How far apart are Harry and Selma when they stop?

_____

8. Which triangle with side lengths given below is a right triangle? Select Yes or No.

   A. 10, 15, 20   ○ Yes ○ No

   B. 10, 24, 25   ○ Yes ○ No

   C. 9, 40, 41   ○ Yes ○ No

   D. 11, 60, 61   ○ Yes ○ No

9. Angles *B* and *F* are corresponding angles formed by a transversal intersecting two parallel lines. Angle *B* has a measure of 44°. What is the measure of Angle *F*?

_____

10. What transformation preserves similarity between the preimage and image, but does not preserve congruence?

_____

_____

11. An artist is creating a large conical sculpture for a park. The cone has a height of 16 m and a diameter of 25 m. Find the volume of the sculpture to the nearest hundredth.

_____

12. A cylindrical barrel has a radius of 7.6 ft and a height of 10.8 ft. Tripling which dimension(s) will triple the volume of the barrel? Select Yes or No.

A. height   ◯ Yes   ◯ No

B. radius   ◯ Yes   ◯ No

C. diameter   ◯ Yes   ◯ No

13. What linear equation best models the data in the scatter plot? Write your answer in $y = mx + b$ form, and round m and b to the nearest integer.

_____

14. On Monday, a work group eats at Ava's café, where a lunch special is $8 and a dessert is $2. The total is $108. On Friday, the group eats at Bo's café, where a lunch special is $6 and a dessert is $3. The total is $90. Each time, the group orders the same number of lunches and the same number of desserts. How many lunches and desserts are ordered?

_____

15. Dilate the figure by a scale factor of 0.5 with the origin as the center of dilation.

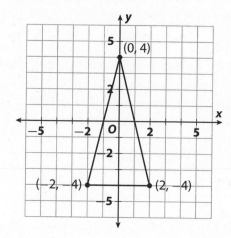

Performance Task

16. In a drought, many trees on a plot of land died. The table shows how many oak trees and pine trees survived or died.

Survived/ Died	Survived	Died	Total
Oak	60	20	80
Pine	72	48	120
Total	132	68	200

a. Create a two-way relative frequency table using decimals.

b. As a percent, what was the joint relative frequency of pine trees that died?

_____

c. Compare the conditional relative frequencies, in percent form, that a tree survived given that it was an oak and that it survived given that it was a pine.

_____

Real Numbers, Exponents, and Scientific Notation

Real Numbers

 CA CC 8.NS.1, 8.NS.2, 8.EE.2

Exponents and Scientific Notation

 CA CC 8.EE.1, 8.EE.3, 8.EE.4

MATH IN CAREERS

Astronomer An astronomer is a scientist who studies and tries to interpret the universe beyond Earth. Astronomers use math to calculate distances to celestial objects and to create mathematical models to help them understand the dynamics of systems from stars and planets to black holes. If you are interested in a career as an astronomer, you should study the following mathematical subjects:

- Algebra
- Geometry
- Trigonometry
- Calculus

Research other careers that require creating mathematical models to understand physical phenomena.

ACTIVITY At the end of the unit, check out how **astronomers** use math.

Unit Project Preview

The Large and the Small of It

The Unit Project at the end of this unit will ask you to research amazing facts involving extremely large and extremely small numbers. You will illustrate the facts and write each of them in both standard and scientific notation. To successfully complete the Unit Project you'll need to master these skills:

- Understand integer exponents.
- Write numbers in scientific notation with positive powers of 10.
- Write numbers in scientific notation with negative powers of 10.

1. How is a number like 73,000,000,000,000,000 more challenging to write and comprehend than a number like 73?

_____

_____

2. What does 10^4 mean?

_____

3. How can you use exponents to write 10,000,000?

_____

Tracking Your Learning Progression

This unit addresses important California Common Core Standards in the Critical Area of working with non-rational numbers, radicals, and integer exponents.

Domain 8.NS The Number System

> **Cluster** Know that there are numbers that are not rational, and approximate them by rational numbers.

The unit also supports additional standards.

Domain 8.EE Expressions and Equations

> **Cluster** Work with radicals and integer exponents.

Real Numbers

? **ESSENTIAL QUESTION**

How can you use real numbers to solve real-world problems?

Real-World Video

Living creatures can be classified into groups. The sea otter belongs to the kingdom Animalia and class Mammalia. Numbers can also be classified into groups such as rational numbers and integers.

my.hrw.com

GO DIGITAL

my.hrw.com

 my.hrw.com

Go digital with your write-in student edition, accessible on any device.

 Math On the Spot

Scan with your smart phone to jump directly to the online edition, video tutor, and more.

 Animated Math

Interactively explore key concepts to see how math works.

 Personal Math Trainer

Get immediate feedback and help as you work through practice sets.

Are YOU Ready?

Complete these exercises to review skills you will need for this module.

Find the Square of a Number

EXAMPLE Find the square of $\frac{2}{3}$.

$\frac{2}{3} \times \frac{2}{3} = \frac{2 \times 2}{3 \times 3}$ Multiply the number by itself.

$= \frac{4}{9}$ Simplify.

Find the square of each number.

1. 7 _____   **2.** 21 _____   **3.** −3 _____   **4.** $\frac{4}{5}$ _____

5. 2.7 _____   **6.** $-\frac{1}{4}$ _____   **7.** −5.7 _____   **8.** $1\frac{2}{5}$ _____

Exponents

EXAMPLE $5^3 = 5 \times 5 \times 5$ Use the base, 5, as a factor 3 times.

$= 25 \times 5$ Multiply from left to right.

$= 125$

Simplify each exponential expression.

9. 9^2 _____   **10.** 2^4 _____   **11.** $\left(\frac{1}{3}\right)^2$ _____   **12.** $(-7)^2$ _____

13. 4^3 _____   **14.** $(-1)^5$ _____   **15.** 4.5^2 _____   **16.** 10^5 _____

Write a Mixed Number as an Improper Fraction

EXAMPLE $2\frac{2}{5} = 2 + \frac{2}{5}$ Write the mixed number as a sum of a whole number and a fraction.

$= \frac{10}{5} + \frac{2}{5}$ Write the whole number as an equivalent fraction with the same denominator as the fraction in the mixed number.

$= \frac{12}{5}$ Add the numerators.

Write each mixed number as an improper fraction.

17. $3\frac{1}{3}$ _____   **18.** $1\frac{5}{8}$ _____   **19.** $2\frac{3}{7}$ _____   **20.** $5\frac{5}{6}$ _____

Reading Start-Up

Visualize Vocabulary

Use the ✔ words to complete the graphic. You can put more than one word in each section of the triangle.

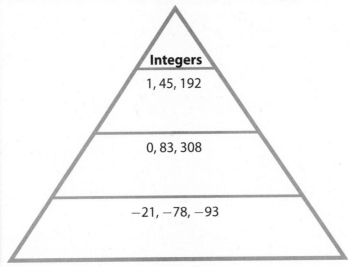

Integers

1, 45, 192

0, 83, 308

−21, −78, −93

Vocabulary

Review Words

  integers *(enteros)*

✔ negative numbers *(números negativos)*

✔ positive numbers *(números positivos)*

✔ whole number *(número entero)*

Preview Words

  cube root *(raíz cúbica)*

  irrational numbers *(número irracional)*

  perfect cube *(cubo perfecto)*

  perfect square *(cuadrado perfecto)*

  principal square root *(raíz cuadrada principal)*

  rational number *(número racional)*

  real numbers *(número real)*

  repeating decimal *(decimal periódico)*

  square root *(raíz cuadrada)*

  terminating decimal *(decimal finito)*

Understand Vocabulary

Complete the sentences using the preview words.

1. One of the two equal factors of a number is a _____.

2. A _____ has integers as its square roots.

3. The _____ is the nonnegative square root of a number.

Active Reading

Layered Book Before beginning the lessons in this module, create a layered book to help you learn the concepts in this module. Label the flaps "Rational Numbers," "Irrational Numbers," "Square Roots," and "Real Numbers." As you study each lesson, write important ideas such as vocabulary, models, and sample problems under the appropriate flap.

GETTING READY FOR
Real Numbers
Understanding the standards and the vocabulary terms in the standards will help you know exactly what you are expected to learn in this module.

 CA CC 8.NS.1

Know that numbers that are not rational are called irrational. Understand informally that every number has a decimal expansion; for rational numbers show that the decimal expansion repeats eventually, and convert a decimal expansion which repeats eventually into a rational number.

Key Vocabulary

rational number *(número racional)*
A number that can be expressed as a ratio of two integers.

irrational number *(número irracional)*
A number that cannot be expressed as a ratio of two integers or as a repeating or terminating decimal.

What It Means to You

You will recognize a number as rational or irrational by looking at its fraction or decimal form.

EXAMPLE 8.NS.1

Classify each number as rational or irrational.

$$0.\overline{3} = \frac{1}{3} \qquad\qquad 0.25 = \frac{1}{4}$$

These numbers are rational because they can be written as ratios of integers or as repeating or terminating decimals.

$$\pi \approx 3.141592654\ldots \qquad \sqrt{5} \approx 2.236067977\ldots$$

These numbers are irrational because they cannot be written as ratios of integers or as repeating or terminating decimals.

 CA CC 8.NS.2

Use rational approximations of irrational numbers to compare the size of irrational numbers, locate them approximately on a number line diagram, and estimate the value of expressions (e.g., π^2).

What It Means to You

You will learn to estimate the values of irrational numbers.

EXAMPLE 8.NS.2

Estimate the value of $\sqrt{8}$.

8 is not a perfect square. Find the two perfect squares closest to 8.

8 is between the perfect squares 4 and 9.
So $\sqrt{8}$ is between $\sqrt{4}$ and $\sqrt{9}$.
   $\sqrt{8}$ is between 2 and 3.

8 is closer to 9, so $\sqrt{8}$ is closer to 3.
$2.8^2 = 7.84 \qquad 2.9^2 = 8.41$
$\sqrt{8}$ is between 2.8 and 2.9
A good estimate for $\sqrt{8}$ is 2.85.

Visit **my.hrw.com** to see all **CA Common Core Standards** explained.

my.hrw.com

Rational and Irrational Numbers

 CA CC 8.NS.1

Know that numbers that are not rational are called irrational. Understand informally that every number has a decimal expansion; for rational numbers show that the decimal expansion repeats eventually, and convert a decimal expansion which repeats eventually into a relation number. *Also 8.NS.2, 8.EE.2*

 ESSENTIAL QUESTION

How do you rewrite rational numbers and decimals, take square roots and cube roots, and approximate irrational numbers?

Expressing Rational Numbers as Decimals

A **rational number** is any number that can be written as a ratio in the form $\frac{a}{b}$, where a and b are integers and b is not 0. Examples of rational numbers are 6 and 0.5.

6 can be written as $\frac{6}{1}$. 　　　 0.5 can be written as $\frac{1}{2}$.

Every rational number can be written as a terminating decimal or a repeating decimal. A **terminating decimal**, such as 0.5, has a finite number of digits. A **repeating decimal** has a block of one or more digits that repeat indefinitely.

Math On the Spot

🔴 my.hrw.com

EXAMPLE 1 　　　　　　　　　　　　 **CA CC** 8.NS.1

Write each fraction as a decimal.

My Notes

A $\frac{1}{4}$

$$
\begin{array}{r}
0.25 \\
4\overline{)1.00} \\
-8 \\
\hline
20 \\
-20 \\
\hline
0
\end{array}
$$

$\frac{1}{4} = 0.25$

Remember that the fraction bar means "divided by." Divide the numerator by the denominator.

Divide until the remainder is zero, adding zeros after the decimal point in the dividend as needed.

$\frac{1}{3} = 0.3333333333333...$

B $\frac{1}{3}$

$$
\begin{array}{r}
0.333 \\
3\overline{)1.000} \\
-9 \\
\hline
10 \\
-9 \\
\hline
10 \\
-9 \\
\hline
1
\end{array}
$$

$\frac{1}{3} = 0.\overline{3}$

Divide until the remainder is zero or until the digits in the quotient begin to repeat.

Add zeros after the decimal point in the dividend as needed.

When a decimal has one or more digits that repeat indefinitely, write the decimal with a bar over the repeating digit(s).

My Notes

Write each fraction as a decimal.

1. $\frac{5}{11}$ _____

2. $\frac{1}{8}$ _____

3. $2\frac{1}{3}$ _____

Expressing Decimals as Rational Numbers

You can express terminating and repeating decimals as rational numbers.

EXAMPLE 2

 CA CC 8.NS.1

Write each decimal as a fraction in simplest form.

A 0.825

The decimal 0.825 means "825 thousandths." Write this as a fraction.

$\frac{825}{1000}$ *To write "825 thousandths", put 825 over 1000.*

Then simplify the fraction.

$\frac{825 \div 25}{1000 \div 25} = \frac{33}{40}$ *Divide both the numerator and the denominator by 25.*

$0.825 = \frac{33}{40}$

B $0.\overline{37}$

Let $x = 0.\overline{37}$. The number $0.\overline{37}$ has 2 repeating digits, so multiply each side of the equation $x = 0.\overline{37}$ by 10^2, or 100.

$x = 0.\overline{37}$

$(100)x = 100(0.\overline{37})$

$100x = 37.\overline{37}$ *100 times $0.\overline{37}$ is $37.\overline{37}$.*

Because $x = 0.\overline{37}$, you can subtract x from one side and $0.\overline{37}$ from the other.

$100x = 37.\overline{37}$

$\underline{-x \qquad -0.\overline{37}}$

$99x = 37$ *$37.\overline{37}$ minus $0.\overline{37}$ is 37.*

Now solve the equation for x. Simplify if necessary.

$\frac{99x}{99} = \frac{37}{99}$ *Divide both sides of the equation by 99.*

$x = \frac{37}{99}$

YOUR TURN

Write each decimal as a fraction in simplest form.

4. 0.12 _____

5. $0.\overline{57}$ _____

6. 1.4 _____

Finding Square Roots and Cube Roots

The **square root** of a positive number p is x if $x^2 = p$. There are two square roots for every positive number. For example, the square roots of 36 are 6 and -6 because $6^2 = 36$ and $(-6)^2 = 36$. The square roots of $\frac{1}{25}$ are $\frac{1}{5}$ and $-\frac{1}{5}$. You can write the square roots of $\frac{1}{25}$ as $\pm\frac{1}{5}$. The symbol $\sqrt{}$ indicates the positive, or **principal square root**.

A number that is a **perfect square** has square roots that are integers. The number 81 is a perfect square because its square roots are 9 and -9.

The **cube root** of a positive number p is x if $x^3 = p$. There is one cube root for every positive number. For example, the cube root of 8 is 2 because $2^3 = 8$. The cube root of $\frac{1}{27}$ is $\frac{1}{3}$ because $\left(\frac{1}{3}\right)^3 = \frac{1}{27}$. The symbol $\sqrt[3]{}$ indicates the cube root.

A number that is a **perfect cube** has a cube root that is an integer. The number 125 is a perfect cube because its cube root is 5.

EXAMPLE 3 CA CC 8.EE.2

Solve each equation for x.

Ⓐ $x^2 = 121$

$x^2 = 121$ *Solve for x by taking the square root of both sides.*

$x = \pm\sqrt{121}$ *Apply the definition of square root.*

$x = \pm 11$ *Think: What numbers squared equal 121?*

The solutions are 11 and -11.

Ⓑ $x^2 = \frac{16}{169}$

$x^2 = \frac{16}{169}$ *Solve for x by taking the square root of both sides.*

$x = \pm\sqrt{\frac{16}{169}}$ *Apply the definition of square root.*

$x = \pm\frac{4}{13}$ *Think: What numbers squared equal $\frac{16}{169}$?*

The solutions are $\frac{4}{13}$ and $-\frac{4}{13}$.

Math Talk
Mathematical Practices

Can you square an integer and get a negative number? What does this indicate about whether negative numbers have square roots?

C $729 = x^3$

$\sqrt[3]{729} = \sqrt[3]{x^3}$ *Solve for x by taking the cube root of both sides.*

$\sqrt[3]{729} = x$ *Apply the definition of cube root.*

$9 = x$ *Think: What number cubed equals 729?*

The solution is 9.

D $x^3 = \frac{8}{125}$

$\sqrt[3]{x^3} = \sqrt[3]{\frac{8}{125}}$ *Solve for x by taking the cube root of both sides.*

$x = \sqrt[3]{\frac{8}{125}}$ *Apply the definition of cube root.*

$x = \frac{2}{5}$ *Think: What number cubed equals $\frac{8}{125}$?*

The solution is $\frac{2}{5}$.

YOUR TURN

Solve each equation for x.

7. $x^2 = 196$ _____

8. $x^2 = \frac{9}{256}$ _____

9. $x^3 = 512$ _____

10. $x^3 = \frac{64}{343}$ _____

EXPLORE ACTIVITY   CA CC 8.NS.2, 8.EE.2

Estimating Irrational Numbers

Irrational numbers are numbers that are not rational. In other words, they cannot be written in the form $\frac{a}{b}$, where a and b are integers and b is not 0. Square roots of perfect squares are rational numbers. Square roots of numbers that are not perfect squares are irrational. Some equations like those in Example 3 involve square roots of numbers that are not perfect squares.

$$x^2 = 2 \qquad x = \pm\sqrt{2} \qquad \text{\textit{$\sqrt{2}$ is irrational.}}$$

Estimate the value of $\sqrt{2}$.

A Find two consecutive perfect squares that 2 is between. Complete the inequality by writing these perfect squares in the boxes.

B Now take the square root of each number.

C Simplify the square roots of perfect squares.

     $\sqrt{2}$ is between _____ and _____.

$\sqrt{\boxed{}} < \sqrt{2} < \sqrt{\boxed{}}$

$\boxed{} < 2 < \boxed{}$

$\boxed{} < \sqrt{2} < \boxed{}$

D Estimate that $\sqrt{2} \approx 1.5$.

$$\sqrt{2} \approx 1.5$$

E To find a better estimate, first choose some numbers between 1 and 2 and square them. For example, choose 1.3, 1.4, and 1.5.

$1.3^2 = $ _____ $1.4^2 = $ _____ $1.5^2 = $ _____

Is $\sqrt{2}$ between 1.3 and 1.4? How do you know?

_____

_____

Is $\sqrt{2}$ between 1.4 and 1.5? How do you know?

_____

_____

2 is closer to _____ than to _____, so $\sqrt{2} \approx$ _____.

F Locate and label this value on the number line.

1.1 1.2 1.3 1.4 1.5

Reflect

11. How could you find an even better estimate of $\sqrt{2}$?

_____

_____

12. Find a better estimate of $\sqrt{2}$.

$1.41^2 = $ _____ $1.42^2 = $ _____ $1.43^2 = $ _____

2 is closer to _____ than to _____, so $\sqrt{2} \approx$ _____.

Draw a number line and locate and label your estimate.

13. Solve $x^2 = 7$. Write your answer as a radical expression. Then estimate to one decimal place.

_____

Write each fraction or mixed number as a decimal. (Example 1)

1. $\frac{2}{5}$ _____

2. $\frac{8}{9}$ _____

3. $3\frac{3}{4}$ _____

4. $\frac{7}{10}$ _____

5. $2\frac{3}{8}$ _____

6. $\frac{5}{6}$ _____

Write each decimal as a fraction or mixed number in simplest form. (Example 2)

7. 0.675 _____

8. 5.6 _____

9. 0.44 _____

10. $0.\overline{4}$

$10x = \boxed{}$

$-x \quad -\boxed{}$

$\boxed{}\,x = \boxed{}$

$x =$ _____

11. $0.\overline{26}$

$100x = \boxed{}$

$-x \quad -\boxed{}$

$\boxed{}\,x = \boxed{}$

$x =$ _____

12. $0.\overline{325}$

$1000x = \boxed{}$

$-x \quad -\boxed{}$

$\boxed{}\,x = \boxed{}$

$x =$ _____

Solve each equation for x. (Example 3 and Explore Activity)

13. $x^2 = 17$

$x = \pm\sqrt{\boxed{}} \approx \pm\boxed{}$

14. $x^2 = \frac{25}{289}$

$x = \pm\sqrt{\dfrac{\boxed{}}{\boxed{}}} = \pm\dfrac{\boxed{}}{\boxed{}}$

15. $x^3 = 216$

$x = \sqrt[3]{\boxed{}} = \boxed{}$

Approximate each irrational number to one decimal place without a calculator.
(Explore Activity)

16. $\sqrt{5} \approx \boxed{}$

17. $\sqrt{3} \approx \boxed{}$

18. $\sqrt{10} \approx \boxed{}$

? ESSENTIAL QUESTION CHECK-IN

19. What is the difference between rational and irrational numbers?

_____

_____

_____

1.1 Independent Practice

CA CC 8.NS.1, 8.NS.2, 8.EE.2

Personal
Math Trainer

Online Practice
and Help

my.hrw.com

20. A $\frac{7}{16}$ -inch-long bolt is used in a machine. What is this length written as a decimal?

_____

21. The weight of an object on the moon is $\frac{1}{6}$ its weight on Earth. Write $\frac{1}{6}$ as a decimal.

_____

22. The distance to the nearest gas station is $2\frac{4}{5}$ kilometers. What is this distance written as a decimal?

_____

23. A baseball pitcher has pitched $98\frac{2}{3}$ innings. What is the number of innings written as a decimal?

_____

24. A heartbeat takes 0.8 second. How many seconds is this written as a fraction?

_____

25. There are 26.2 miles in a marathon. Write the number of miles using a fraction.

_____

26. The average score on a biology test was $72.\overline{1}$. Write the average score using a fraction.

_____

27. The metal in a penny is worth about 0.505 cent. How many cents is this written as a fraction?

_____

28. **Multistep** An artist wants to frame a square painting with an area of 400 square inches. She wants to know the length of the wood trim that is needed to go around the painting.

a. If x is the length of one side of the painting, what equation can you set up to find the length of a side? How many solutions does the equation have?

_____

b. Do all of the solutions that you found make sense in the context of the problem? Explain.

_____

_____

c. What is the length of the wood trim needed to go around the painting?

_____

Solve each equation for x. Write your answers as radical expressions. Then estimate to one decimal place, if necessary.

29. $x^2 = 14$ _____

30. $x^3 = 1331$ _____

31. $x^2 = 144$ _____

32. $x^2 = 29$ _____

33. Analyze Relationships To find $\sqrt{15}$, Beau found $3^2 = 9$ and $4^2 = 16$. He said that since 15 is between 9 and 16, $\sqrt{15}$ must be between 3 and 4. He thinks a good estimate for $\sqrt{15}$ is $\frac{3+4}{2} = 3.5$. Is Beau's estimate high, low, or correct? Explain.

_____

_____

_____

34. Justify Reasoning What is a good estimate for the solution to the equation $x^3 = 95$? How did you come up with your estimate?

_____

_____

_____

35. The volume of a sphere is $36\pi \, \text{ft}^3$. What is the radius of the sphere? Use the formula $V = \frac{4}{3}\pi r^3$ to find your answer.

_____

H.O.T. FOCUS ON HIGHER ORDER THINKING

Work Area

36. Draw Conclusions Can you find the cube root of a negative number? If so, is it positive or negative? Explain your reasoning.

_____

_____

_____

37. Make a Conjecture Evaluate and compare the following expressions.

$$\sqrt{\frac{4}{25}} \text{ and } \frac{\sqrt{4}}{\sqrt{25}} \qquad \sqrt{\frac{16}{81}} \text{ and } \frac{\sqrt{16}}{\sqrt{81}} \qquad \sqrt{\frac{36}{49}} \text{ and } \frac{\sqrt{36}}{\sqrt{49}}$$

Use your results to make a conjecture about a division rule for square roots. Since division is multiplication by the reciprocal, make a conjecture about a multiplication rule for square roots.

_____

_____

38. Persevere in Problem Solving The difference between the solutions to the equation $x^2 = a$ is 30. What is a? Show that your answer is correct.

_____

_____

LESSON 1.2 Sets of Real Numbers

CA CC 8.NS.1

Know that numbers that are not rational are called irrational. Understand informally that every number has a decimal expansion; for rational numbers show that the decimal expansion repeats eventually, and convert a decimal expansion which repeats eventually into a relation number.

ESSENTIAL QUESTION

How can you describe relationships between sets of real numbers?

Classifying Real Numbers

Biologists classify animals based on shared characteristics. A cardinal is an animal, a vertebrate, a bird, and a passerine.

You already know that the set of rational numbers consists of whole numbers, integers, and fractions. The set of **real numbers** consists of the set of rational numbers and the set of irrational numbers.

Animals
Vertebrates
Birds
Passerines

Math On the Spot
⊙ my.hrw.com

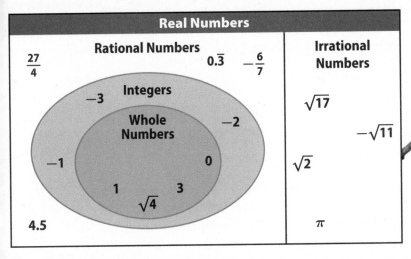

Real Numbers

Rational Numbers
$\frac{27}{4}$ $0.\overline{3}$ $-\frac{6}{7}$

Integers
-3

Whole Numbers
-2

-1 0

1 3
$\sqrt{4}$

4.5

Irrational Numbers

$\sqrt{17}$

$-\sqrt{11}$

$\sqrt{2}$

π

Passerines, such as the cardinal, are also called "perching birds."

EXAMPLE 1

CA CC 8.NS.1

Animated Math
⊙ my.hrw.com

Write all names that apply to each number.

A $\sqrt{5}$ *5 is a whole number that is not a perfect square.*
irrational, real

B -17.84 *-17.84 is a terminating decimal.*
rational, real

C $\frac{\sqrt{81}}{9}$ $\frac{\sqrt{81}}{9} = \frac{9}{9} = 1$
whole, integer, rational, real

Math Talk
Mathematical Practices

What types of numbers are between 3.1 and 3.9 on a number line?

YOUR TURN

Write all names that apply to each number.

1. A baseball pitcher has pitched $12\frac{2}{3}$ innings.

   _____

2. The length of the side of a square that has an

   area of 10 square yards. _____

Understanding Sets and Subsets of Real Numbers

By understanding which sets are subsets of types of numbers, you can verify whether statements about the relationships between sets are true or false.

EXAMPLE 2

Tell whether the given statement is true or false. Explain your choice.

A All irrational numbers are real numbers.

True. Every irrational number is included in the set of real numbers. The irrational numbers are a subset of the real numbers.

B No rational numbers are whole numbers.

False. A whole number can be written as a fraction with a denominator of 1, so every whole number is included in the set of rational numbers. The whole numbers are a subset of the rational numbers.

Math Talk
Mathematical Practices

Give an example of a rational number that is a whole number. Show that the number is both whole and rational.

YOUR TURN

Tell whether the given statement is true or false. Explain your choice.

3. All rational numbers are integers.

   _____

   _____

   _____

4. Some irrational numbers are integers.

   _____

   _____

Identifying Sets for Real-World Situations

Real numbers can be used to represent real-world quantities. Highways have posted speed limit signs that are represented by natural numbers such as 55 mph. Integers appear on thermometers. Rational numbers are used in many daily activities, including cooking. For example, ingredients in a recipe are often given in fractional amounts such as $\frac{2}{3}$ cup flour.

Math On the Spot

⏻ my.hrw.com

EXAMPLE 3   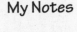 **CA CC** 8.NS.1

Identify the set of numbers that best describes each situation. Explain your choice.

A the number of people wearing glasses in a room

The set of whole numbers best describes the situation. The number of people wearing glasses may be 0 or a counting number.

B the circumference of a flying disk has a diameter of 8, 9, 10, 11, or 14 inches

The set of irrational numbers best describes the situation. Each circumference would be a product of π and the diameter, and any multiple of π is irrational.

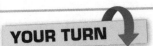

Identify the set of numbers that best describes the situation. Explain your choice.

5. the amount of water in a glass as it evaporates

_____

_____

_____

6. the weight of a person in pounds

_____

_____

_____

Personal Math Trainer

Online Practice and Help

⏻ my.hrw.com

Write all names that apply to each number. (Example 1)

1. $\frac{7}{8}$

_____

2. $\sqrt{36}$

_____

3. $\sqrt{24}$

_____

4. 0.75

_____

5. 0

_____

6. $-\sqrt{100}$

_____

7. $5.\overline{45}$

_____

8. $-\frac{18}{6}$

_____

Tell whether the given statement is true or false. Explain your choice.
(Example 2)

9. All whole numbers are rational numbers.

_____

_____

10. No irrational numbers are whole numbers.

_____

Identify the set of numbers that best describes each situation. Explain your choice. (Example 3)

11. the change in the value of an account when given to the nearest dollar

_____

_____

12. the markings on a standard ruler

_____

$\frac{1}{16}$ inch

IN.   1

? ESSENTIAL QUESTION CHECK-IN

13. What are some ways to describe the relationships between sets of numbers?

_____

_____

1.2 Independent Practice

CA CC 8.NS.1

Write all names that apply to each number. Then place the numbers in the correct location on the Venn diagram.

14. $-\sqrt{9}$ _____

15. 257 _____

16. $\sqrt{50}$ _____

17. $8\frac{1}{2}$ _____

18. 16.6 _____

19. $\sqrt{16}$ _____

```
Real Numbers
```

Rational Numbers

Irrational Numbers

Integers

Whole Numbers

Identify the set of numbers that best describes each situation. Explain your choice.

20. the height of an airplane as it descends to an airport runway

_____

21. the score with respect to par of several golfers: 2, −3, 5, 0, −1

_____

_____

22. **Critique Reasoning** Ronald states that the number $\frac{1}{11}$ is not rational because, when converted into a decimal, it does not terminate. Nathaniel says it is rational because it is a fraction. Which boy is correct? Explain.

_____

_____

23. **Critique Reasoning** The circumference of a circular region is shown. What type of number best describes the diameter of the circle? Explain your answer. _____

π mi

24. **Critical Thinking** A number is not an integer. What type of number can it be?

_____

25. A grocery store has a shelf with half-gallon containers of milk. What type of number best represents the total number of gallons?

_____

H.O.T. FOCUS ON HIGHER ORDER THINKING

Work Area

26. **Explain the Error** Katie said, "Negative numbers are integers." What was her error?

_____

_____

27. **Justify Reasoning** Can you ever use a calculator to determine if a number is rational or irrational? Explain.

_____

_____

_____

_____

_____

_____

_____

28. **Draw Conclusions** The decimal $0.\overline{3}$ represents $\frac{1}{3}$. What type of number best describes $0.\overline{9}$, which is $3 \cdot 0.\overline{3}$? Explain.

_____

29. **Communicate Mathematical Ideas** Irrational numbers can never be precisely represented in decimal form. Why is this?

_____

_____

_____

_____

Ordering Real Numbers

 CA CC 8.NS.2

Use rational approximations of irrational numbers to compare the size of irrational numbers, locate them approximately on a number line diagram, and estimate the value of expressions (e.g., π^2).

ESSENTIAL QUESTION

How do you order a set of real numbers?

Comparing Irrational Numbers

Between any two real numbers is another real number. To compare and order real numbers, you can approximate irrational numbers as decimals.

EXAMPLE 1 CA CC 8.NS.2

Compare $\sqrt{3} + 5$ ⬤ $3 + \sqrt{5}$. **Write** $<$, $>$, **or** $=$.

STEP 1 First approximate $\sqrt{3}$.

$\sqrt{3}$ is between 1 and 2.

Next approximate $\sqrt{5}$.

$\sqrt{5}$ is between 2 and 3.

> Use perfect squares to estimate square roots.
> $1^2 = 1 \quad 2^2 = 4 \quad 3^2 = 9$

STEP 2 Then use your approximations to simplify the expressions.

$\sqrt{3} + 5$ is between 6 and 7.

$3 + \sqrt{5}$ is between 5 and 6.

So, $\sqrt{3} + 5 > 3 + \sqrt{5}$.

Reflect

1. If $7 + \sqrt{5}$ is equal to $\sqrt{5}$ plus a number, what do you know about the number? Why?

_____

2. What are the closest two integers that $\sqrt{300}$ is between?

_____

YOUR TURN

Compare. Write $<$, $>$, **or** $=$.

3. $\sqrt{2} + 4$ ◯ $2 + \sqrt{4}$

4. $\sqrt{12} + 6$ ◯ $12 + \sqrt{6}$

Math On the Spot

my.hrw.com

My Notes

Personal Math Trainer

Online Practice and Help

my.hrw.com

Ordering Real Numbers

You can compare and order real numbers and list them from least to greatest.

EXAMPLE 2

 CA CC 8.NS.2

Order $\sqrt{22}$, $\pi + 1$, and $4\frac{1}{2}$ from least to greatest.

STEP 1 First approximate $\sqrt{22}$.

$\sqrt{22}$ is between 4 and 5. Since you don't know where it falls between 4 and 5, you need to find a better estimate for $\sqrt{22}$ so you can compare it to $4\frac{1}{2}$.

Since 22 is closer to 25 than 16, use squares of numbers between 4.5 and 5 to find a better estimate of $\sqrt{22}$.

$4.5^2 = 20.25$ $4.6^2 = 21.16$ $4.7^2 = 22.09$ $4.8^2 = 23.04$

Since $4.7^2 = 22.09$, an approximate value for $\sqrt{22}$ is 4.7.

An approximate value of π is 3.14. So an approximate value of $\pi + 1$ is 4.14.

STEP 2 Plot $\sqrt{22}$, $\pi + 1$, and $4\frac{1}{2}$ on a number line.

Read the numbers from left to right to place them in order from least to greatest.

From least to greatest, the numbers are $\pi + 1$, $4\frac{1}{2}$, and $\sqrt{22}$.

YOUR TURN

Order the numbers from least to greatest. Then graph them on the number line.

5. $\sqrt{5}$, 2.5, $\sqrt{3}$ _____

6. π^2, 10, $\sqrt{75}$ _____

Math Talk
Mathematical Practices

If real numbers a, b, and c are in order from least to greatest, what is the order of their opposites from least to greatest? Explain.

Ordering Real Numbers in a Real-World Context

Calculations and estimations in the real world may differ. It can be important to know not only which are the most accurate but which give the greatest or least values, depending upon the context.

EXAMPLE 3   **CA CC** 8.NS.2

Four people have found the distance in kilometers across a canyon using different methods. Their results are given in the table. Order the distances from greatest to least.

Distance Across Quarry Canyon (km)			
Juana	Lee Ann	Ryne	Jackson
$\sqrt{28}$	$\frac{23}{4}$	$5.\overline{5}$	$5\frac{1}{2}$

STEP 1 Write each value as a decimal.

$\sqrt{28}$ is between 5.2 and 5.3. Since $5.3^2 = 28.09$, an approximate value for $\sqrt{28}$ is 5.3.

$\frac{23}{4} = 5.75$

$5.\overline{5}$ is 5.555..., so $5.\overline{5}$ to the nearest hundredth is 5.56.

$5\frac{1}{2} = 5.5$

STEP 2 Plot $\sqrt{28}$, $\frac{23}{4}$, $5.\overline{5}$, and $5\frac{1}{2}$ on a number line.

From greatest to least, the distances are:

$\frac{23}{4}$ km, $5.\overline{5}$ km, $5\frac{1}{2}$ km, $\sqrt{28}$ km.

YOUR TURN

7. Four people have found the distance in miles across a crater using different methods. Their results are given below.

Jonathan: $\frac{10}{3}$, Elaine: $3.\overline{45}$, José: $3\frac{1}{2}$, Lashonda: $\sqrt{10}$

Order the distances from greatest to least.

_____

My Notes

Compare. Write <, >, or =. (Example 1)

1. $\sqrt{3} + 2 \bigcirc \sqrt{3} + 3$

2. $\sqrt{8} + 17 \bigcirc \sqrt{11} + 15$

3. $\sqrt{6} + 5 \bigcirc 6 + \sqrt{5}$

4. $\sqrt{9} + 3 \bigcirc 9 + \sqrt{3}$

5. $\sqrt{17} - 3 \bigcirc -2 + \sqrt{5}$

6. $12 - \sqrt{2} \bigcirc 14 - \sqrt{8}$

7. $\sqrt{7} + 2 \bigcirc \sqrt{10} - 1$

8. $\sqrt{17} + 3 \bigcirc 3 + \sqrt{11}$

9. Order $\sqrt{3}$, 2π, and 1.5 from least to greatest. Then graph them on the number line. (Example 2)

   $\sqrt{3}$ is between _____ and _____, so $\sqrt{3} \approx$ _____.

   $\pi \approx 3.14$, so $2\pi \approx$ _____.

   From least to greatest, the numbers are _____, _____,

   _____.

10. Four people have found the perimeter of a forest using different methods. Their results are given in the table. Order their calculations from greatest to least. (Example 3)

Forest Perimeter (km)			
Leon	**Mika**	**Jason**	**Ashley**
$\sqrt{17} - 2$	$1 + \dfrac{\pi}{2}$	$\dfrac{12}{5}$	2.5

    _____

    _____

? ESSENTIAL QUESTION CHECK-IN

11. Explain how to order a set of real numbers.

    _____

    _____

    _____

    _____

    _____

1.3 Independent Practice

 CA CC 8.NS.2

Order the numbers from least to greatest.

12. $\sqrt{7}, 2, \frac{\sqrt{8}}{2}$

_____

13. $\sqrt{10}, \pi, 3.5$

_____

14. $\sqrt{220}, -10, \sqrt{100}, 11.5$

_____

15. $\sqrt{8}, -3.75, 3, \frac{9}{4}$

_____

16. Your sister is considering two different shapes for her garden. One is a square with side lengths of 3.5 meters, and the other is a circle with a diameter of 4 meters.

  a. Find the area of the square. _____

  b. Find the area of the circle. _____

  c. Compare your answers from parts **a** and **b**. Which garden would give your sister the most space to plant?

_____

_____

17. Winnie measured the length of her father's ranch four times and got four different distances. Her measurements are shown in the table.

Distance Across Father's Ranch (km)			
1	2	3	4
$\sqrt{60}$	$\frac{58}{8}$	$7.\overline{3}$	$7\frac{3}{5}$

  a. To estimate the actual length, Winnie first approximated each distance to the nearest hundredth. Then she averaged the four numbers. Using a calculator, find Winnie's estimate.

_____

_____

  b. Winnie's father estimated the distance across his ranch to be $\sqrt{56}$ km. How does this distance compare to Winnie's estimate?

_____

_____

Give an example of each type of number.

18. a real number between $\sqrt{13}$ and $\sqrt{14}$ _____

19. an irrational number between 5 and 7 _____

20. A teacher asks his students to write the numbers shown in order from least to greatest. Paul thinks the numbers are already in order. Sandra thinks the order should be reversed. Who is right?

$\sqrt{115}$, $\frac{115}{11}$, and 10.5624

_____

_____

_____

21. **Math History** There is a famous irrational number called Euler's number, symbolized with an *e*. Like π, its decimal form never ends or repeats. The first few digits of *e* are 2.7182818284.

a. Between which two square roots of integers could you find this number?

_____

b. Between which two square roots of integers can you find π?

_____

H.O.T. **FOCUS ON HIGHER ORDER THINKING**

Work Area

22. **Analyze Relationships** There are several approximations used for π, including 3.14 and $\frac{22}{7}$. π is approximately 3.14159265358979…

a. Label π and the two approximations on the number line.

3.140   3.141   3.142   3.143

b. Which of the two approximations is a better estimate for π? Explain.

_____

c. Find a whole number *x* so that the ratio $\frac{x}{113}$ is a better estimate for π

than the two given approximations. _____

23. **Communicate Mathematical Ideas** What is the fewest number of distinct points that must be graphed on a number line, in order to represent natural numbers, whole numbers, integers, rational numbers, irrational numbers, and real numbers? Explain.

_____

_____

24. **Critique Reasoning** Jill says that $12.\overline{6}$ is less than 12.63. Explain her error.

_____

Ready to Go On?

Personal Math Trainer

Online Practice and Help

⏻ my.hrw.com

1.1 Rational and Irrational Numbers

Write each fraction as a decimal or each decimal as a fraction.

1. $\frac{7}{20}$ _____

2. $1.\overline{27}$ _____

3. $1\frac{7}{8}$ _____

Solve each equation for x.

4. $x^2 = 81$ _____

5. $x^3 = 343$ _____

6. $x^2 = \frac{1}{100}$ _____

7. A square patio has an area of 200 square feet. How long is each side

of the patio to the nearest tenth? _____

1.2 Sets of Real Numbers

Write all names that apply to each number.

8. $\frac{121}{\sqrt{121}}$ _____

9. $\frac{\pi}{2}$ _____

10. Tell whether the statement "All integers are rational numbers" is true or false. Explain your choice.

_____

_____

1.3 Ordering Real Numbers

Compare. Write <, >, or =.

11. $\sqrt{8} + 3$ ◯ $8 + \sqrt{3}$

12. $\sqrt{5} + 11$ ◯ $5 + \sqrt{11}$

Order the numbers from least to greatest.

13. $\sqrt{99}$, π^2, $9.\overline{8}$ _____

14. $\sqrt{\frac{1}{25}}$, $\frac{1}{4}$, $0.\overline{2}$ _____

? ESSENTIAL QUESTION

15. How are real numbers used to describe real-world situations?

_____

_____

MODULE 1
MIXED REVIEW

Assessment Readiness

Personal Math Trainer

Online Practice and Help

my.hrw.com

1. Look at each number. Is the number between 2π and $\sqrt{52}$?

Select Yes or No for expressions A–C.

A. $6\frac{2}{3}$ ○ Yes   ○ No

B. $\frac{5\pi}{2}$ ○ Yes   ○ No

C. $3\sqrt{5}$ ○ Yes   ○ No

2. Consider the number $-\frac{11}{15}$.

Choose True or False for each statement.

A. The number is rational.   ○ True   ○ False

B. The number can be written as a repeating decimal.   ○ True   ○ False

C. The number is less than -0.8.   ○ True   ○ False

3. The volume of a cube is given by $V = x^3$, where x is the length of an edge of the cube. A cube-shaped end table has a volume of $3\frac{3}{8}$ cubic feet. What is the length of an edge of the end table? Explain how you solved this problem.

4. A student says that $\sqrt{83}$ is greater than $\frac{29}{3}$. Is the student correct? Justify your reasoning.

Exponents and Scientific Notation

ESSENTIAL QUESTION

How can you use scientific notation to solve real-world problems?

Real-World Video

The distance from Earth to other planets, moons, and stars is a very great number of kilometers. To make it easier to write very large and very small numbers, we use scientific notation.

my.hrw.com

GO DIGITAL
my.hrw.com

my.hrw.com

Go digital with your write-in student edition, accessible on any device.

Math On the Spot

Scan with your smart phone to jump directly to the online edition, video tutor, and more.

Animated Math

Interactively explore key concepts to see how math works.

Personal Math Trainer

Get immediate feedback and help as you work through practice sets.

Are YOU Ready?

Complete these exercises to review skills you will need for this module.

Exponents

EXAMPLE $10^4 = 10 \times 10 \times 10 \times 10$ Write the exponential expression as a product.
$= 10,000$ Simplify.

Write each exponential expression as a decimal.

1. 10^2 _____

2. 10^3 _____

3. 10^5 _____

4. 10^7 _____

Multiply and Divide by Powers of 10

EXAMPLE $0.0478 \times 10^5 = 0.0478 \times 100,000$ Identify the number of zeros in the power of 10.
$= 4,780$ When multiplying, move the decimal point to the *right* the same number of places as the number of zeros.

$37.9 \div 10^4 = 37.9 \div 10,000$ Identify the number of zeros in the power of 10.
$= 0.00379$ When dividing, move the decimal point to the *left* the same number of places as the number of zeros.

Find each product or quotient.

5. 45.3×10^3

6. $7.08 \div 10^2$

7. 0.00235×10^6

8. $3,600 \div 10^4$

_____   _____   _____   _____

9. 0.5×10^2

10. $67.7 \div 10^5$

11. 0.0057×10^4

12. $195 \div 10^6$

_____   _____   _____   _____

Reading Start-Up

Visualize Vocabulary

Use the ✔ words to complete the Venn diagram. You can put more than one word in each section of the diagram.

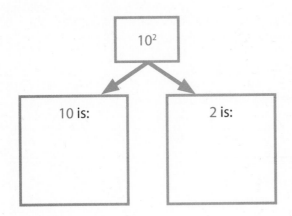

10²

10 is:

2 is:

Understand Vocabulary

Complete the sentences using the preview words.

1. A number produced by raising a base to an exponent

   is a _____.

2. _____ is a method of writing very large or very small numbers by using powers of 10.

3. A _____ is any number that can be expressed as a ratio of two integers.

Vocabulary

Review Words
✔ base *(base)*
✔ exponent *(exponente)*
  integers *(enteros)*
✔ positive number *(número positivo)*
  standard notation *(notación estándar)*

Preview Words
  power *(potencia)*
  rational number *(número racional)*
  real numbers *(número real)*
  scientific notation *(notación científica)*
  whole number *(número entero)*

Active Reading

Two-Panel Flip Chart Create a two-panel flip chart to help you understand the concepts in this module. Label one flap "Positive Powers of 10" and the other flap "Negative Powers of 10." As you study each lesson, write important ideas under the appropriate flap. Include sample problems that will help you remember the concepts later when you look back at your notes.

Exponents and Scientific Notation

Understanding the standards and the vocabulary terms in the standards will help you know exactly what you are expected to learn in this module.

CA CC 8.EE.1

Know and apply the properties of integer exponents to generate equivalent numerical expressions.

Key Vocabulary

integer (entero)
The set of whole numbers and their opposites

exponent (exponente)
The number that indicates how many times the base is used as a factor.

What It Means to You

You will use the properties of integer exponents to find equivalent expressions.

EXAMPLE 8.EE.1

Evaluate two different ways.

$$\frac{8^3}{8^5}$$

$$\frac{8^3}{8^5} = \frac{8 \cdot 8 \cdot 8}{8 \cdot 8 \cdot 8 \cdot 8 \cdot 8} = \frac{1}{8 \cdot 8} = \frac{1}{64}$$

$$\frac{8^3}{8^5} = 8^{(3-5)} = 8^{-2} = \frac{1}{8^2} = \frac{1}{8 \cdot 8} = \frac{1}{64}$$

$$(3^2)^4$$

$$(3^2)^4 = (3^2)(3^2)(3^2)(3^2) = 3^{2+2+2+2} = 3^8 = 6{,}561$$

$$(3^2)^4 = 3^{(2 \cdot 4)} = 3^8 = 6{,}561$$

CA CC 8.EE.3

Use numbers expressed in the form of a single digit times an integer power of 10 to estimate very large or very small quantities, and to express how many times as much one is than the other.

Key Vocabulary

scientific notation (notación científica)
A method of writing very large or very small numbers by using powers of 10.

What It Means to You

You will convert very large numbers to scientific notation.

EXAMPLE 8.EE.3

There are about 55,000,000,000 cells in an average-sized adult. Write this number in scientific notation.

Move the decimal point to the left until you have a number that is greater than or equal to 1 and less than 10.

5.5 0 0 0 0 0 0 0 0 0   *Move the decimal point 10 places to the left.*

5.5   *Remove the extra zeros.*

You would have to multiply 5.5 by 10^{10} to get 55,000,000,000.

$$55{,}000{,}000{,}000 = 5.5 \times 10^{10}$$

Visit **my.hrw.com** to see all **CA Common Core Standards** explained.

my.hrw.com

LESSON

2.1 Integer Exponents

 CA CC 8.EE.1

Know and apply the
properties of integer
exponents to generate
equivalent numerical
expressions.

ESSENTIAL QUESTION How can you develop and use the properties of integer exponents?

EXPLORE ACTIVITY 1 CA CC 8.EE.1

Using Patterns of Integer Exponents

The table below shows powers of 5, 4, and 3.

$5^4 = 625$	$5^3 = 125$	$5^2 = 25$	$5^1 = 5$	$5^0 =$	$5^{-1} =$	$5^{-2} =$
$4^4 = 256$	$4^3 = 64$	$4^2 = 16$	$4^1 = 4$	$4^0 =$	$4^{-1} =$	$4^{-2} =$
$3^4 = 81$	$3^3 = 27$	$3^2 = 9$	$3^1 = 3$	$3^0 =$	$3^{-1} =$	$3^{-2} =$

A What pattern do you see in the powers of 5?

_____

_____

B What pattern do you see in the powers of 4?

_____

_____

C What pattern do you see in the powers of 3?

_____

_____

D Complete the table for the values of $5^0, 5^{-1}, 5^{-2}$.

E Complete the table for the values of $4^0, 4^{-1}, 4^{-2}$.

F Complete the table for the values of $3^0, 3^{-1}, 3^{-2}$.

Reflect

1. **Make a Conjecture** Write a general rule for the value of $a^0, a \neq 0$. _____

2. **Make a Conjecture** Write a general rule for the value of a^{-n}, where _____
   $a \neq 0$ and n is an integer.

Exploring Properties of Integer Exponents

A Complete the following equations:

$3 \cdot 3 \cdot 3 \cdot 3 \cdot 3 = 3^{\boxed{}}$

$(3 \cdot 3 \cdot 3 \cdot 3) \cdot 3 = 3^{\boxed{}} \cdot 3^{\boxed{}} = 3^{\boxed{}}$

$(3 \cdot 3 \cdot 3) \cdot (3 \cdot 3) = 3^{\boxed{}} \cdot 3^{\boxed{}} = 3^{\boxed{}}$

What pattern do you see when multiplying two powers with the same base?

_____

_____

Use your pattern to complete this equation: $5^2 \cdot 5^5 = 5^{\boxed{}}$.

B Complete the following equation:

$\dfrac{4^5}{4^3} = \dfrac{4 \cdot 4 \cdot 4 \cdot 4 \cdot 4}{4 \cdot 4 \cdot 4} = \dfrac{\cancel{4} \cdot \cancel{4} \cdot \cancel{4} \cdot 4 \cdot 4}{\cancel{4}_1 \cdot \cancel{4}_1 \cdot \cancel{4}_1} = 4 \cdot 4 = 4^{\boxed{}}$

What pattern do you see when dividing two powers with the same base?

_____

_____

_____

Use your pattern to complete this equation: $\dfrac{6^8}{6^3} = 6^{\boxed{}}$.

C Complete the following equations:

$(5^3)^2 = (5 \cdot 5 \cdot 5)^{\boxed{}} = (5 \cdot 5 \cdot 5) \cdot (5 \cdot 5 \cdot 5) = 5^{\boxed{}}$

What pattern do you see when raising a power to a power?

_____

_____

Use your pattern to complete this equation: $(7^2)^4 = 7^{\boxed{}}$.

Math Talk
Mathematical Practices

Do the patterns you found in parts A–D apply if the exponents are negative? If so, give an example of each.

D Complete the following equation:

$(3 \cdot 4)^2 = (3 \cdot 4) \cdot (3 \cdot 4) = (3 \cdot 3) \cdot (4 \cdot 4) = 3^{\boxed{}} \cdot 4^{\boxed{}}$

What pattern do you see when raising a product to a power?

_____

Use your pattern to complete this equation: $(5 \cdot 6)^3 = 5^{\boxed{}} 6^{\boxed{}}$.

Reflect

Let *m* and *n* be integers.

3. **Make a Conjecture** Write a general rule for the value of $a^m \cdot a^n$. _____

4. **Make a Conjecture** Write a general rule for the value of $\frac{a^m}{a^n}$, $a \neq 0$. _____

5. **Make a Conjecture** Write a general rule for the value of $(a^m)^n$. _____

6. **Make a Conjecture** Write a general rule for the value of $(a \cdot b)^n$. _____

Simplifying Expressions with Powers

You can use the general rules you found in the Explore Activities to simplify expressions involving powers.

Math On the Spot

my.hrw.com

EXAMPLE 1

CA CC 8.EE.1

Simplify each expression.

A $(10^3)^2 = 10^{3 \cdot 2}$
$= 10^6$
$= 1{,}000{,}000$

B $4^3 \cdot 5^3 = (4 \cdot 5)^3$
$= 20^3$
$= 8000$

C $8^0 \cdot 8^{-3} \cdot 8^5 = 1 \cdot 8^{-3+5}$
$= 1 \cdot 8^2$
$= 8^2$
$= 64$

D $\frac{7^9}{7^{11}} = 7^{9-11}$
$= 7^{-2}$
$= \frac{1}{7^2}$
$= \frac{1}{49}$

YOUR TURN

Simplify each expression.

7. $(2 \cdot 11)^2$ _____

8. $(2^2)^3$ _____

9. $5^3 \cdot 5^{-4} \cdot 5^{-1}$ _____

Personal Math Trainer

Online Practice and Help

my.hrw.com

Applying Properties of Integer Exponents

The general rules you found in the Explore Activities are summarized below. You can use them to simplify more complicated expressions.

Properties of Integer Exponents

Let _m_ and _n_ be integers.

Zero Exponent Property	$a^0 = 1, a \neq 0$	$2^0 = 1$
Negative Exponent Property	$a^{-n} = \dfrac{1}{a^n}, a \neq 0$	$3^{-2} = \dfrac{1}{3^2} = \dfrac{1}{9}$
Product of Powers Property	$a^m \cdot a^n = a^{m+n}$	$2^3 \cdot 2^4 = 2^7 = 128$
Quotient of Powers Property	$\dfrac{a^m}{a^n} = a^{m-n}, a \neq 0$	$\dfrac{2^7}{2^4} = 2^3 = 8$
Power of a Product Property	$(a \cdot b)^n = a^n \cdot b^n$	$(2 \cdot 3)^2 = 2^2 \cdot 3^2 = 36$
Power of a Power Property	$(a^m)^n = a^{mn}$	$(3^2)^3 = 3^6 = 729$

My Notes

EXAMPLE 2

 CA CC 8.EE.1

Simplify each expression.

A $(5 - 2)^5 \cdot 3^{-8} + (5 + 2)^0$

$(3)^5 \cdot 3^{-8} + (7)^0$ Simplify within parentheses.

$3^{5 + (-8)} + 1$ Use properties of exponents.

$3^{-3} + 1$ Simplify.

$\dfrac{1}{27} + 1 = 1\dfrac{1}{27}$ Apply the rule for negative exponents and add.

B $\dfrac{\left[(3 + 1)^2\right]^3}{(7 - 3)^2}$

$\dfrac{(4^2)^3}{4^2}$ Simplify within parentheses.

$\dfrac{4^6}{4^2}$ Use properties of exponents.

4^{6-2} Use properties of exponents.

$4^4 = 256$ Simplify.

YOUR TURN

Simplify each expression.

10. $\dfrac{[(6 - 1)^2]^2}{(3 + 2)^3}$ _____

11. $(2^2)^3 - (10 - 6)^3 \cdot 4^{-5}$ _____

Guided Practice

Find the value of each power. (Explore Activity 1)

1. $8^{-1} =$ _____

2. $6^{-2} =$ _____

3. $256^0 =$ _____

4. $10^2 =$ _____

5. $5^4 =$ _____

6. $2^{-5} =$ _____

7. $4^{-5} =$ _____

8. $89^0 =$ _____

9. $11^{-3} =$ _____

Use properties of exponents to write an equivalent expression. (Explore Activity 2)

10. $4 \cdot 4 \cdot 4 = 4^{\boxed{}}$

11. $(2 \cdot 2) \cdot (2 \cdot 2 \cdot 2) = 2^{\boxed{}} \cdot 2^{\boxed{}} = 2^{\boxed{}}$

12. $\dfrac{6^7}{6^5} = \dfrac{6 \cdot 6 \cdot 6 \cdot 6 \cdot 6 \cdot 6 \cdot 6}{6 \cdot 6 \cdot 6 \cdot 6 \cdot 6} = \boxed{}^{\boxed{}}$

13. $\dfrac{8^{12}}{8^9} = 8^{\boxed{} - \boxed{}} = \boxed{}^{\boxed{}}$

14. $5^{10} \cdot 5 \cdot 5 = 5^{\boxed{}}$

15. $7^8 \cdot 7^5 = \boxed{}^{\boxed{}}$

16. $(6^2)^4 = 6^{\boxed{} \cdot \boxed{}} = 6^{\boxed{}}$

17. $(8 \cdot 12)^3 = 8^{\boxed{}} \cdot 12^{\boxed{}}$

Simplify each expression. (Examples 1 and 2)

18. $6^9 \cdot 6^0 \cdot 6^{-10}$ _____

19. $\dfrac{10^2 \cdot 10^7}{10^5}$ _____

20. $(10 - 6)^3 \cdot 4^2 + (10 + 2)^2$ _____

21. $\dfrac{(12 - 5)^7}{\left[(3 + 4)^2 \right]^2}$ _____

? ESSENTIAL QUESTION CHECK-IN

22. Summarize the rules for multiplying powers with the same base, dividing powers with the same base, raising a product to a power, and raising a power to a power.

_____

_____

_____

_____

_____

2.1 Independent Practice

CA CC 8.EE.1

Personal Math Trainer

Online Practice and Help

my.hrw.com

Simplify each expression.

23. $5^{-7} \cdot 5^{12} \cdot 5^{-2}$

_____

24. $8^{12} \cdot (8^7)^{-2}$

_____

25. $5 \cdot (3 \cdot 5)^2$

_____

26. $\dfrac{9^2}{9^5}$

_____

27. $\dfrac{(6^2)^5}{6^8}$

_____

28. $\dfrac{11^{10}}{11^3 \cdot 11^5}$

_____

29. $(2^2)^3 + 2^0 + 2^7 \cdot 2^{-5}$

_____

30. $3^{-2} \cdot (7-4)^2 + (7+4)^2$

_____

31. $10^4 \cdot [(8+2)^2]^{-3}$

_____

32. $\dfrac{7^5(2+5)^4}{(8-1)^7}$

_____

33. $\dfrac{[(4+2)^3]^5}{(9-3)^{12}}$

_____

34. $\dfrac{(4 \cdot 6)^3}{(5+1)^3}$

_____

35. **Vocabulary** Identify the property that is being applied at each step to simplify the expression.

$$4^{-5} \cdot (4 \cdot 9)^5 \cdot 9^{-3} = 4^{-5} \cdot (4^5 \cdot 9^5) \cdot 9^{-3}$$

$$= (4^{-5} \cdot 4^5) \cdot (9^5 \cdot 9^{-3})$$

$$= 4^0 \cdot 9^2$$

$$= 1 \cdot 9^2$$

$$= 9^2$$

$$= 81$$

36. **Communicate Mathematical Ideas** Camille simplified an expression as shown. Discuss why this method is justified.

$$\frac{6 \cdot 10^5}{3 \cdot 10^2} = \frac{6}{3} \cdot \frac{10^5}{10^2} = 2 \cdot 10^3 = 2000$$

_____

_____

_____

_____

_____

37. Explain why the exponents cannot be added in the product $12^3 \cdot 11^3$.

_____

_____

38. List three ways to express 3^5 as a product of powers.

_____

39. **Astronomy** The distance from Earth to the moon is about 22^4 miles. The distance from Earth to Neptune is about 22^7 miles. Which distance is the greater distance, and about how many times greater is it?

_____

40. **Critique Reasoning** A student claims that $8^3 \cdot 8^{-5}$ is greater than 1. Explain whether the student is correct or not.

_____

_____

_____

Find the missing exponent.

41. $\left(b^2\right)^{\boxed{}} = b^{-6}$

42. $x^{\boxed{}} \cdot x^6 = x^9$

43. $\dfrac{y^{25}}{\boxed{}_{\,y}} = y^6$

44. **Communicate Mathematical Ideas** Why do you subtract exponents when dividing powers with the same base?

_____

_____

_____

_____

45. **Astronomy** The mass of the Sun is about 2×10^{27} metric tons, or 2×10^{30} kilograms. How many kilograms are in one metric ton?

_____

46. **Represent Real-World Problems** In computer technology, a kilobyte is 2^{10} bytes in size. A gigabyte is 2^{30} bytes in size. The size of a terabyte is the product of the size of a kilobyte and the size of a gigabyte. What is the size of a terabyte?

_____

47. Write equivalent expressions for $x^7 \cdot x^{-2}$ and $\frac{x^7}{x^2}$. What do you notice? Explain how your results relate to the properties of integer exponents.

_____

_____

_____

_____

A toy store is creating a large window display of different colored cubes stacked in a triangle shape. The table shows the number of cubes in each row of the triangle, starting with the top row.

Row	1	2	3	4
Number of cubes in each row	3	3^2	3^3	3^4

48. Look for a Pattern Describe any pattern you see in the table.

_____

49. Using exponents, how many cubes will be in Row 6?
How many times as many cubes will be in Row 6 than in Row 3?   _____

50. Justify Reasoning If there are 6 rows in the triangle, what is the total number of cubes in the triangle? Explain how you found your answer.

_____

_____

H.O.T. **FOCUS ON HIGHER ORDER THINKING**

51. Critique Reasoning A student simplified the expression $\frac{6^2}{36^2}$ as $\frac{1}{3}$. Do you agree with this student? Explain why or why not.

_____

52. Draw Conclusions Evaluate $-a^n$ when $a = 3$ and $n = 2, 3, 4,$ and 5. Now evaluate $(-a)^n$ when $a = 3$ and $n = 2, 3, 4,$ and 5. Based on this sample, does it appear that $-a^n = (-a)^n$? If not, state the relationships, if any, between $-a^n$ and $(-a)^n$.

_____

_____

_____

_____

53. Persevere in Problem Solving A number to the 12th power divided by the same number to the 9th power equals 125. What is the number?

_____

Scientific Notation with Positive Powers of 10

CA CC 8.EE.3

Use numbers expressed in the form of a single digit times an integer power of 10 to estimate very large or very small quantities, and to express how many times as much one is than the other.

ESSENTIAL QUESTION

How can you use scientific notation to express very large quantities?

EXPLORE ACTIVITY   **CA CC** 8.EE.3

Using Scientific Notation

Scientific notation is a method of expressing very large and very small numbers as a product of a number greater than or equal to 1 and less than 10, and a power of 10.

The weights of various sea creatures are shown in the table. Write the weight of the blue whale in scientific notation.

Sea Creature	Blue whale	Gray whale	Whale shark
Weight (lb)	250,000	68,000	41,200

A Move the decimal point in 250,000 to the left as many places as necessary to find a number that is greater than or equal to 1 and less than 10.

What number did you find? _____

B Divide 250,000 by your answer to **A**. Write your answer as a power of 10.

_____

C Combine your answers to **A** and **B** to represent 250,000.

$250{,}000 = \boxed{} \times 10^{\boxed{}}$

Repeat steps **A** through **C** to write the weight of the whale shark in scientific notation.

$41{,}200 = \boxed{} \times 10^{\boxed{}}$

Reflect

1. How many places to the left did you move the decimal point to write

41,200 in scientific notation? _____

2. What is the exponent on 10 when you write 41,200 in scientific notation?

_____

Writing a Number in Scientific Notation

To translate between standard notation and scientific notation, you can count the number of places the decimal point moves.

Writing Large Quantities in Scientific Notation		
When the number is greater than or equal to 10, use a positive exponent.	$8\,4,0\,0\,0 = 8.4 \times 10^4$	*The decimal point moves 4 places to the left.*

EXAMPLE 1 Real World

CA CC 8.EE.3

The distance from Earth to the Sun is about 93,000,000 miles. Write this distance in scientific notation.

Math Talk
Mathematical Practices

Is 12×10^7 written in scientific notation? Explain.

STEP 1 Move the decimal point in 93,000,000 to the left until you have a number that is greater than or equal to 1 and less than 10.

$9.3\,0\,0\,0\,0\,0\,0.$ *Move the decimal point 7 places to the left.*

9.3 *Remove extra zeros.*

STEP 2 Divide the original number by the result from Step 1.

$10,000,000$ *Divide 93,000,000 by 9.3.*

10^7 *Write your answer as a power of 10.*

STEP 3 Write the product of the results from Steps 1 and 2.

$93,000,000 = 9.3 \times 10^7$ miles   *Write a product to represent 93,000,000 in scientific notation.*

YOUR TURN

Write each number in scientific notation.

3. 6,400

4. 570,000,000,000

_____

_____

5. A light-year is the distance that light travels in a year and is equivalent to 9,461,000,000,000 km. Write this distance in scientific notation.

_____

Writing a Number in Standard Notation

To translate between scientific notation and standard notation, move the decimal point the number of places indicated by the exponent in the power of 10. When the exponent is positive, move the decimal point to the right and add placeholder zeros as needed.

Math On the Spot
⏻ my.hrw.com

EXAMPLE 2   CA CC 8.EE.3

Write 3.5×10^6 in standard notation.

STEP 1   Use the exponent of the power of 10 to see how many places to move the decimal point.   6 places

STEP 2   Place the decimal point. Since you are going to write a number greater than 3.5, move the decimal point to the *right*. Add placeholder zeros if necessary.   3 500 000.

The number 3.5×10^6 written in standard notation is 3,500,000.

Reflect

6. Explain why the exponent in 3.5×10^6 is 6, while there are only 5 zeros in 3,500,000.

_____

_____

_____

7. What is the exponent on 10 when you write 5.3 in scientific notation?

_____

YOUR TURN

Write each number in standard notation.

8. 7.034×10^9 **9.** 2.36×10^5

_____   _____

10. The mass of one roosting colony of Monarch butterflies in Mexico was estimated at 5×10^6 grams. Write this mass in standard notation.

_____

Personal Math Trainer
Online Practice and Help
⏻ my.hrw.com

Write each number in scientific notation. (Explore Activity and Example 1)

1. 58,927
Hint: Move the decimal left 4 places.

_____

2. 1,304,000,000
Hint: Move the decimal left 9 places.

_____

3. 6,730,000

_____

4. 13,300

_____

5. An ordinary quarter contains about 97,700,000,000,000,000,000,000 atoms.

_____

6. The distance from Earth to the Moon is about 384,000 kilometers.

_____

Write each number in standard notation. (Example 2)

7. 4×10^5
Hint: Move the decimal right 5 places.

_____

8. 1.8499×10^9
Hint: Move the decimal right 9 places.

_____

9. 6.41×10^3

_____

10. 8.456×10^7

_____

11. 8×10^5

_____

12. 9×10^{10}

_____

13. Diana calculated that she spent about 5.4×10^4 seconds doing her math homework during October. Write this time in standard notation. (Example 2)

_____

14. The town recycled 7.6×10^6 cans this year. Write the number of cans in standard notation. (Example 2)

_____

? **ESSENTIAL QUESTION CHECK-IN**

15. Describe how to write 3,482,000,000 in scientific notation.

_____

_____

_____

_____

2.2 Independent Practice

 CA CC 8.EE.3

Personal Math Trainer

Online Practice and Help
my.hrw.com

Paleontology Use the table for problems 16–21. Write the estimated weight of each dinosaur in scientific notation.

Estimated Weight of Dinosaurs	
Name	**Pounds**
Argentinosaurus	220,000
Brachiosaurus	100,000
Apatosaurus	66,000
Diplodocus	50,000
Camarasaurus	40,000
Cetiosauriscus	19,850

16. Apatosaurus _____

17. Argentinosaurus _____

18. Brachiosaurus _____

19. Camarasaurus _____

20. Cetiosauriscus _____

21. Diplodocus _____

22. A single little brown bat can eat up to 1000 mosquitoes in a single hour. Express in scientific notation how many mosquitoes a little brown bat might eat in 10.5 hours.

_____

23. **Multistep** Samuel can type nearly 40 words per minute. Use this information to find the number of hours it would take him to type 2.6×10^5 words.

_____

24. **Entomology** A tropical species of mite named *Archegozetes longisetosus* is the record holder for the strongest insect in the world. It can lift up to 1.182×10^3 times its own weight.

   a. If you were as strong as this insect, explain how you could find how many pounds you could lift.

   _____

   _____

   _____

   b. Complete the calculation to find how much you could lift, in pounds, if you were as strong as an *Archegozetes longisetosus* mite. Express your answer in both scientific notation and standard notation.

   _____

   _____

25. During a discussion in science class, Sharon learns that at birth an elephant weighs around 230 pounds. In four herds of elephants tracked by conservationists, about 20 calves were born during the summer. In scientific notation, express approximately how much the calves weighed all together.

_____

26. **Classifying Numbers** Which of the following numbers are written in scientific notation?

   0.641×10^3 9.999×10^4

   2×10^1 4.38×5^{10}

_____

27. Explain the Error Polly's parents' car weighs about 3500 pounds. Samantha, Esther, and Polly each wrote the weight of the car in scientific notation. Polly wrote 35.0×10^2, Samantha wrote 0.35×10^4, and Esther wrote 3.5×10^4.

a. Which of these girls, if any, is correct?

_____

b. Explain the mistakes of those who got the question wrong.

_____

_____

_____

28. Justify Reasoning If you were a biologist counting very large numbers of cells as part of your research, give several reasons why you might prefer to record your cell counts in scientific notation instead of standard notation.

_____

_____

_____

H.O.T. FOCUS ON HIGHER ORDER THINKING

Work Area

29. Draw Conclusions Which measurement would be least likely to be written in scientific notation: number of stars in a galaxy, number of grains of sand on a beach, speed of a car, or population of a country? Explain your reasoning.

_____

_____

30. Analyze Relationships Compare the two numbers to find which is greater. Explain how you can compare them without writing them in standard notation first.

$$4.5 \times 10^6 \qquad 2.1 \times 10^8$$

_____

_____

31. Communicate Mathematical Ideas To determine whether a number is written in scientific notation, what test can you apply to the first factor, and what test can you apply to the second factor?

_____

_____

LESSON 2.3 Scientific Notation with Negative Powers of 10

CA CC 8.EE.3

Use numbers expressed in the form of a single digit times an integer power of 10 to estimate very large or very small quantities, and to express how many times as much one is than the other.

ESSENTIAL QUESTION

How can you use scientific notation to express very small quantities?

EXPLORE ACTIVITY Real World CA CC 8.EE.3

Animated Math

my.hrw.com

Negative Powers of 10

You can use what you know about writing very large numbers in scientific notation to write very small numbers in scientific notation.

A typical human hair has a diameter of 0.000025 meter. Write this number in scientific notation.

A Notice how the decimal point moves in the list below. Complete the list.

$1.345 \times 10^0 \quad = 1.3\,4\,5$ It moves one place to the right with each increasing power of 10.

$1.345 \times 10^1 \quad = 1\,3.4\,5$

$1.345 \times 10^2 \quad = 1\,3\,4.5$

$1.345 \times 10^{\boxed{}} = 1\,3\,4\,5.$

$1.345 \times 10^0 \quad = \quad\quad 1.3\,4\,5$ It moves one place to the left with each decreasing power of 10.

$1.345 \times 10^{-1} = \quad\quad 0.1\,3\,4\,5$

$1.345 \times 10^{-2} = \quad 0.0\,1\,3\,4\,5$

$1.345 \times 10^{\boxed{}} = 0.0\,0\,1\,3\,4\,5$

B Move the decimal point in 0.000025 to the right as many places as necessary to find a number that is greater than or equal to 1 and less than 10. What number did you find? _____

C Divide 0.000025 by your answer to **B**. _____

Write your answer as a power of 10. _____

D Combine your answers to **B** and **C** to represent 0.000025 in scientific notation. _____

Reflect

1. When you move the decimal point, how can you know whether you are increasing or decreasing the number?

_____

2. Explain how the two steps of moving the decimal and multiplying by a power of 10 leave the value of the original number unchanged.

_____

Writing a Number in Scientific Notation

To write a number less than 1 in scientific notation, move the decimal point right and use a negative exponent.

Writing Small Quantities in Scientific Notation		
When the number is between 0 and 1, use a negative exponent.	$0.0783 = 7.83 \times 10^{-2}$	*The decimal point moves 2 places to the right.*

EXAMPLE 1

CA CC 8.EE.3

The average size of an atom is about 0.00000003 centimeter across. Write the average size of an atom in scientific notation.

Move the decimal point as many places as necessary to find a number that is greater than or equal to 1 and less than 10.

STEP 1 Place the decimal point. 3.0

STEP 1 Count the number of places you moved the decimal point. 8

STEP 3 Multiply 3.0 times a power of 10. 3.0×10^{-8}

> *Since 0.00000003 is less than 1, you moved the decimal point to the right and the exponent on 10 is negative.*

The average size of an atom in scientific notation is 3.0×10^{-8}.

Reflect

3. **Critical Thinking** When you write a number that is less than 1 in scientific notation, how does the power of 10 differ from when you write a number greater than 1 in scientific notation?

_____

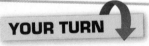

YOUR TURN

Write each number in scientific notation.

4. 0.0000829

5. 0.000000302

_____   _____

6. A typical red blood cell in human blood has a diameter of approximately 0.000007 meter. Write this diameter

in scientific notation. _____

Writing a Number in Standard Notation

To translate between scientific notation and standard notation with very small numbers, you can move the decimal point the number of places indicated by the exponent on the power of 10. When the exponent is negative, move the decimal point to the left.

EXAMPLE 2

 CA CC 8.EE.3

Platelets are one component of human blood. A typical platelet has a diameter of approximately 2.33×10^{-6} meter. Write 2.33×10^{-6} in standard notation.

STEP 1 Use the exponent of the power of 10 to see how many places to move the decimal point.

6 places

STEP 1 Place the decimal point. Since you are going to write a number less than 2.33, move the decimal point to the *left*. Add placeholder zeros if necessary.

0.00000233

The number 2.33×10^{-6} in standard notation is 0.00000233.

> **Math Talk**
> Mathematical Practices
>
> Describe the two factors that multiply together to form a number written in scientific notation.

Reflect

7. **Justify Reasoning** Explain whether 0.9×10^{-5} is written in scientific notation. If not, write the number correctly in scientific notation.

_____

_____

_____

8. Which number is larger, 2×10^{-3} or 3×10^{-2}? Explain.

_____

Write each number in standard notation.

9. 1.045×10^{-6}

10. 9.9×10^{-5}

_____   _____

11. Jeremy measured the length of an ant as 1×10^{-2} meter. Write this length in standard notation.

_____

Personal Math Trainer
Online Practice and Help
my.hrw.com

Write each number in scientific notation. (Explore Activity and Example 1)

1. 0.000487
Hint: Move the decimal right 4 places.

_____

2. 0.000028
Hint: Move the decimal right 5 places.

_____

3. 0.000059

_____

4. 0.0417

_____

5. Picoplankton can be as small as 0.00002 centimeter.

_____

6. The average mass of a grain of sand on a beach is about 0.000015 gram.

_____

Write each number in standard notation. (Example 2)

7. 2×10^{-5}
Hint: Move the decimal left 5 places.

_____

8. 3.582×10^{-6}
Hint: Move the decimal left 6 places.

_____

9. 8.3×10^{-4}

_____

10. 2.97×10^{-2}

_____

11. 9.06×10^{-5}

_____

12. 4×10^{-5}

_____

13. The average length of a dust mite is approximately 0.0001 meter. Write this number in scientific notation. (Example 1)

_____

14. The mass of a proton is about 1.7×10^{-24} gram. Write this number in standard notation. (Example 2)

_____

? **ESSENTIAL QUESTION CHECK-IN**

15. Describe how to write 0.0000672 in scientific notation.

_____

_____

_____

2.3 Independent Practice

 CA CC 8.EE.3

Personal Math Trainer

Online Practice and Help

my.hrw.com

Use the table for problems 16–21. Write the diameter of the fibers in scientific notation.

Average Diameter of Natural Fibers	
Animal	**Fiber Diameter (cm)**
Vicuña	0.0008
Angora rabbit	0.0013
Alpaca	0.00277
Angora goat	0.0045
Llama	0.0035
Orb web spider	0.015

16. Alpaca

_____

17. Angora rabbit

_____

18. Llama

_____

19. Angora goat

_____

20. Orb web spider

_____

21. Vicuña

_____

22. Make a Conjecture Which measurement would be least likely to be written in scientific notation: the thickness of a dog hair, the radius of a period on this page, the ounces in a cup of milk? Explain your reasoning.

_____

_____

23. Multiple Representations Convert the length 7 centimeters to meters. Compare the numerical values when both numbers are written in scientific notation.

_____

_____

_____

_____

24. Draw Conclusions A graphing calculator displays 1.89×10^{12} as 1.89E12. How do you think it would display 1.89×10^{-12}? What does the E stand for?

_____

_____

_____

25. Communicate Mathematical Ideas When a number is written in scientific notation, how can you tell right away whether or not it is greater than or equal to 1?

_____

_____

_____

26. The volume of a drop of a certain liquid is 0.000047 liter. Write the volume of the drop of liquid in scientific notation.

_____

27. Justify Reasoning If you were asked to express the weight in ounces of a ladybug in scientific notation, would the exponent of the 10 be positive or negative? Justify your response.

_____

_____

Physical Science The table shows the length of the radii of several very small or very large items. Complete the table.

	Item	Radius in Meters (Standard Notation)	Radius in Meters (Scientific Notation)
28.	The Moon	1,740,000	
29.	Atom of silver		1.25×10^{-10}
30.	Atlantic wolfish egg	0.0028	
31.	Jupiter		7.149×10^{7}
32.	Atom of aluminum	0.000000000182	
33.	Mars		3.397×10^{6}

34. List the items in the table in order from the smallest to the largest.

_____

_____

 FOCUS ON HIGHER ORDER THINKING

Work Area

35. Analyze Relationships Write the following diameters from least to greatest.

1.5×10^{-2} m 1.2×10^{2} m 5.85×10^{-3} m 2.3×10^{-2} m 9.6×10^{-1} m

_____

_____

36. Critique Reasoning Jerod's friend Al had the following homework problem:

Express 5.6×10^{-7} in standard form.

Al wrote 56,000,000. How can Jerod explain Al's error and how to correct it?

_____

_____

_____

37. Make a Conjecture Two numbers are written in scientific notation. The number with a positive exponent is divided by the number with a negative exponent. Describe the result. Explain your answer.

_____

_____

_____

LESSON 2.4 Operations with Scientific Notation

CA CC 8.EE.4

Perform operations ... in scientific notation. ... choose units of appropriate size for measurements .... Interpret scientific notation ... generated by technology. (For the full text of the standard, see the table at the front of the book beginning on page CA2.) *Also 8.EE.3*

ESSENTIAL QUESTION

How do you add, subtract, multiply, and divide using scientific notation?

Adding and Subtracting with Scientific Notation

Numbers in scientific notation can be added and subtracted, either directly or by rewriting them in standard form.

Math On the Spot

my.hrw.com

EXAMPLE 1

CA CC 8.EE.4

The table below shows the population of the three largest countries in North America in 2011. Find the total population of these countries.

Country	United States	Canada	Mexico
Population	3.1×10^8	3.38×10^7	1.1×10^8

Method 1:

STEP 1 First, write each population with the same power of 10.

United States: 3.1×10^8

Canada: 0.338×10^8

Mexico: 1.1×10^8

STEP 2 Add the multipliers for each population.

$3.1 + 0.338 + 1.1 = 4.538$

STEP 3 Write the final answer in scientific notation: 4.538×10^8.

Method 2:

STEP 1 First, write each number in standard notation.

United States: 310,000,000

Canada: 33,800,000

Mexico: 110,000,000

STEP 2 Find the sum of the numbers in standard notation.

$310{,}000{,}000 + 33{,}800{,}000 + 110{,}000{,}000 = 453{,}800{,}000$

STEP 3 Write the answer in scientific notation: 4.538×10^8.

YOUR TURN

1. Using the population table in the example, how many more people live in Mexico than in Canada? Write your answer in scientific notation.

_____

Multiplying and Dividing with Scientific Notation

Numbers in scientific notation can be multiplied and divided directly by using properties of exponents.

EXAMPLE 2 Problem Solving   **CA CC** 8.EE.3, 8.EE.4

When the Sun makes an orbit around the center of the Milky Way, it travels 2.025×10^{14} kilometers. The orbit takes 225 million years. At what rate does the Sun travel? Write your answer in scientific notation.

 Analyze Information

The answer is the number of kilometers per year that the Sun travels around the Milky Way.

 Formulate a Plan

Set up a division problem using Rate $= \frac{\text{Distance}}{\text{Time}}$ to represent the situation.

 Solve

Math Talk

Mathematical Practices

Could you write 2.025×10^{14} in standard notation to do the division? Would this be a good way to solve the problem?

STEP 1 Substitute the values from the problem into the Rate formula.

Rate $= \frac{2.025 \times 10^{14} \text{ kilometers}}{225,000,000 \text{ years}}$

STEP 2 Write the expression for rate with years in scientific notation.

Rate $= \frac{2.025 \times 10^{14} \text{ kilometers}}{2.25 \times 10^{8} \text{ years}}$ $225 \text{ million} = 2.25 \times 10^{8}$

STEP 3 Find the quotient by dividing the decimals and using the laws of exponents.

$2.025 \div 2.25 = 0.9$ *Divide the multipliers.*

$\frac{10^{14}}{10^{8}} = 10^{14-8} = 10^{6}$ *Divide the powers of 10.*

STEP 4 Combine the answers to write the rate in scientific notation.

Rate $= 0.9 \times 10^{6} = 9.0 \times 10^{5}$ km per year

 Justify and Evaluate

Use estimation to check the reasonableness of your answer.

$\frac{2.025 \times 10^{14}}{225,000,000} \approx \frac{2 \times 10^{14}}{2 \times 10^{8}} = 10^{6}$

9.0×10^{5} is close to 10^{6}, so the answer is reasonable.

YOUR TURN

2. Light travels at a speed of 1.86×10^5 miles per second. It takes light from the Sun about 4.8×10^3 seconds to reach Saturn. Find the approximate distance from the Sun to Saturn. Write your answer

in scientific notation. _____

3. Light travels at the speed of 1.17×10^7 miles per minute. Pluto's average distance from the Sun is 3,670,000,000 miles. On average, how long does it take sunlight to reach Pluto? Write your answer in scientific

notation. _____

Scientific Notation on a Calculator

On many scientific calculators, you can enter numbers in scientific notation by using a function labeled "ee" or "EE". Usually, the letter "E" takes the place of "×10". So, the number 4.1×10^9 would appear as 4.1E9 on the calculator.

Math On the Spot

my.hrw.com

EXAMPLE 3 Real World   CA CC 8.EE.4

The table shows the approximate areas for three continents given in square meters. What is the total area of these three continents? Write the answer in scientific notation using more appropriate units.

Continent	Asia	Africa	Europe
Area (m²)	4.4×10^{13}	3.02×10^{13}	1.04×10^{13}

Find $4.4 \times 10^{13} + 3.02 \times 10^{13} + 1.04 \times 10^{13}$.

Enter 4.4E13 + 3.02E13 + 1.04E13 on your calculator.

Write the results from your calculator: 8.46E13.

Write this number in scientific notation: 8.46×10^{13} m².

Square kilometers is more appropriate: 8.46×10^7 km².

> Because 1 km = 1,000 m, 1 km² = 1,000² m², or 10⁶ m². Divide by 10⁶.

 YOUR TURN

Write each number using calculator notation.

4. 7.5×10^5 5. 3×10^{-7} 6. 2.7×10^{13}

_____   _____   _____

Write each number using scientific notation.

7. 4.5E−1   8. 5.6E12   9. 6.98E−8

_____   _____

Guided Practice

Add or subtract. Write your answer in scientific notation. (Example 1)

1. $4.2 \times 10^6 + 2.25 \times 10^5 + 2.8 \times 10^6$

$4.2 \times 10^6 + \boxed{} \times 10^{\boxed{}} + 2.8 \times 10^6$

$4.2 + \boxed{} + \boxed{}$

$\boxed{} \times 10^{\boxed{}}$

2. $8.5 \times 10^3 - 5.3 \times 10^3 - 1.0 \times 10^2$

$8.5 \times 10^3 - 5.3 \times 10^3 - \boxed{} \times 10^{\boxed{}}$

$\boxed{} - \boxed{} - \boxed{}$

$\boxed{} \times 10^{\boxed{}}$

3. $1.25 \times 10^2 + 0.50 \times 10^2 + 3.25 \times 10^2$

_____

4. $6.2 \times 10^5 - 2.6 \times 10^4 - 1.9 \times 10^2$

_____

Multiply or divide. Write your answer in scientific notation. (Example 2)

5. $\left(1.8 \times 10^9\right)\left(6.7 \times 10^{12}\right)$ _____

6. $\dfrac{3.46 \times 10^{17}}{2 \times 10^9}$ _____

7. $\left(5 \times 10^{12}\right)\left(3.38 \times 10^6\right)$ _____

8. $\dfrac{8.4 \times 10^{21}}{4.2 \times 10^{14}}$ _____

Write each number using calculator notation. (Example 3)

9. 3.6×10^{11}

_____

10. 7.25×10^{-5}

_____

11. 8×10^{-1}

_____

Write each number using scientific notation. (Example 3)

12. 7.6E−4

_____

13. 1.2E16

_____

14. 9E1

_____

? ESSENTIAL QUESTION CHECK-IN

15. How do you add, subtract, multiply, and divide numbers written in scientific notation?

_____

_____

_____

_____

_____

2.4 Independent Practice

CA CC 8.EE.3, 8.EE.4

Personal Math Trainer

Online Practice and Help

my.hrw.com

16. An adult blue whale can eat 4.0×10^7 krill in a day. At that rate, how many krill can an adult blue whale eat in 3.65×10^2 days?

_____

17. A newborn baby has about 26,000,000,000 cells. An adult has about 4.94×10^{13} cells. About how many times as many cells does an adult have than a newborn? Write your estimate in standard notation.

_____

_____

Represent Real-World Problems The table shows the number of tons of waste generated and recovered (recycled) in 2010.

	Paper	Glass	Plastics
Tons generated	7.131×10^7	1.153×10^7	3.104×10^7
Tons recovered	4.457×10^7	0.313×10^7	0.255×10^7

18. What is the total amount of paper, glass, and plastic waste generated?

_____

_____

19. What is the total amount of paper, glass, and plastic waste recovered?

_____

_____

20. What is the total amount of paper, glass, and plastic waste **not** recovered?

_____

21. Which type of waste has the lowest recovery ratio?

_____

Social Studies The table shows the approximate populations of three countries.

Country	China	France	Australia
Population	1.3×10^9	6.48×10^7	2.15×10^7

22. How many more people live in France than in Australia?

_____

23. The area of Australia is 2.95×10^6 square miles. What is the approximate average number of people per square mile in Australia?

_____

_____

24. How many times greater is the population of China than the population of France? Write your answer in standard notation.

_____

_____

25. Mia is 7.01568×10^6 minutes old. Convert her age to more appropriate units. Assume that each year has 6 months that have 30 days and 6 months that have 31 days.

_____

_____

26. Courtney takes 2.4×10^4 steps during her a long-distance run. Each step covers an average of 810 mm. What total distance (in mm) did Courtney cover during her run? Write your answer in scientific notation. Then convert the distance to a more appropriate unit. Write that answer in standard form.

_____

27. Social Studies The U.S. public debt as of October 2010 was $\$9.06 \times 10^{12}$. Estimate the average U.S. public debt per American if the population in 2010 was 3.08×10^8 people.

_____

H.O.T. FOCUS ON HIGHER ORDER THINKING

Work Area

28. Communicate Mathematical Ideas How is multiplying and dividing numbers in scientific notation different from adding and subtracting numbers in scientific notation?

_____

_____

_____

_____

_____

29. Explain the Error A student found the product of 8×10^6 and 5×10^9 to be 4×10^{15}. What is the error? What is the correct product?

_____

_____

30. Communicate Mathematical Ideas Describe a procedure that can be used to simplify $\dfrac{\left(4.87 \times 10^{12}\right) - \left(7 \times 10^{10}\right)}{\left(3 \times 10^7\right) + \left(6.1 \times 10^8\right)}$. Write the expression in scientific notation in simplified form.

_____

_____

_____

_____

_____

_____

_____

Ready to Go On?

2.1 Integer Exponents

Find the value of each power.

1. 3^{-4} _____

2. 35^0 _____

3. 4^4 _____

Use the properties of exponents to write an equivalent expression.

4. $8^3 \cdot 8^7$ _____

5. $\dfrac{12^6}{12^2}$ _____

6. $(10^3)^5$ _____

2.2 Scientific Notation with Positive Powers of 10

Convert each number to scientific notation or standard notation.

7. 2,000 _____

8. 91,007,500 _____

9. 1.0395×10^9 _____

10. 4×10^2 _____

2.3 Scientific Notation with Negative Powers of 10

Convert each number to scientific notation or standard notation.

11. 0.02 _____

12. 0.000701 _____

13. 8.9×10^{-5} _____

14. 4.41×10^{-2} _____

2.4 Operations with Scientific Notation

Perform the operation. Write your answer in scientific notation.

15. $7 \times 10^6 - 5.3 \times 10^6$ _____

16. $3.4 \times 10^4 + 7.1 \times 10^5$ _____

17. $(2 \times 10^4)(5.4 \times 10^6)$ _____

18. $\dfrac{7.86 \times 10^9}{3 \times 10^4}$ _____

19. Neptune's average distance from the Sun is 4.503×10^9 km. Mercury's average distance from the Sun is 5.791×10^7 km. About how many times farther from the Sun is Neptune than Mercury? Write your answer in scientific notation.

_____

 ESSENTIAL QUESTION

20. How is scientific notation used in the real world?

_____

_____

MODULE 2
MIXED REVIEW

CALIFORNIA

Assessment Readiness

Personal Math Trainer

my.hrw.com

Online Practice and Help

1. Consider each expression. Is the expression equivalent to 2^{-4}?

Select Yes or No for expressions A–C.

A. $2^2 - 2^6$ ○ Yes   ○ No

B. $(2^{-2})^2$ ○ Yes   ○ No

C. $\dfrac{2^3}{2^7}$ ○ Yes   ○ No

2. The variable r represents a rational number.

Choose True or False for each statement.

A. r is a real number.   ○ True   ○ False

B. r could be a repeating decimal.   ○ True   ○ False

C. r could be $\sqrt{39}$.   ○ True   ○ False

3. So far this year, a company has sold 8.28×10^5 tablet computers. How many more tablets must the company sell for its tablet sales to reach 1 million this year? Explain how you solved this problem.

4. Brazil has an area of approximately 8.51×10^6 square kilometers and a population of about 1.99×10^8 people. Portugal has an area of approximately 9.21×10^4 square kilometers and a population of about 1.08×10^7 people. On average, which country has a greater number of people per square kilometer? Explain how you know.

Study Guide Review

Key Vocabulary

cube root *(raiz cúbica)*

irrational number *(número irracional)*

perfect cube *(cubo perfecto)*

perfect square *(cuadrado perfecto)*

principal square root *(raíz cuadrada principal)*

rational number *(número racional)*

real number *(número real)*

repeating decimal *(decimal periódico)*

square root *(raíz cuadrada)*

terminating decimal *(decimal finito)*

ESSENTIAL QUESTION

How can you use real numbers to solve real-world problems?

EXAMPLE 1

Write $0.\overline{81}$ as a fraction in simplest form.

$$x = 0.\overline{81}$$

$$(100)x = (100)0.\overline{81}$$

$$100x = 81.\overline{81}$$ 100 times $0.\overline{81}$ is $81.\overline{81}$.

$$\underline{-x = -0.\overline{81}}$$

$$99x = 81$$

$$x = \frac{81}{99}$$ Divide both sides by 99.

$$x = \frac{9}{11}$$ Simplify.

EXAMPLE 2

Solve each equation for x.

A $x^2 = 289$

$$x = \pm\sqrt{289}$$

$$x = \pm 17$$

The solutions are 17 and -17.

B $x^3 = 1000$

$$x = \sqrt[3]{1000}$$

$$x = 10$$

The solution is 10.

EXAMPLE 3

Write all names that apply to each number.

A $5.\overline{4}$
rational, real

     $5.\overline{4}$ is a repeating decimal.

B $\frac{8}{4}$
whole, integer, rational, real

     $\frac{8}{4} = 2$

C $\sqrt{13}$
irrational, real

     13 is a whole number that is not a perfect square.

EXERCISES

Find the two square roots of each number. If the number is not a perfect square, approximate the values to one decimal place. (Lesson 1.1)

1. 16 _____

2. $\frac{4}{25}$ _____

3. 225 _____

4. $\frac{1}{49}$ _____

5. $\sqrt{10}$ _____

6. $\sqrt{18}$ _____

Write each decimal as a fraction in simplest form. (Lesson 1.1)

7. $0.\overline{5}$ _____

8. $0.\overline{63}$ _____

9. $0.2\overline{14}$ _____

Solve each equation for x. (Lesson 1.1)

10. $x^2 = 361$

11. $x^3 = 1728$

12. $x^2 = \frac{49}{121}$

_____

_____

_____

Write all names that apply to each number. (Lesson 1.2)

13. $\frac{2}{3}$

14. $-\sqrt{100}$

_____

_____

15. $\frac{15}{5}$

16. $\sqrt{21}$

_____

_____

Compare. Write $<$, $>$, or $=$. (Lesson 1.3)

17. $\sqrt{7} + 5 \bigcirc 7 + \sqrt{5}$

18. $6 + \sqrt{8} \bigcirc \sqrt{6} + 8$

19. $\sqrt{4} - 2 \bigcirc 4 - \sqrt{2}$

Order the numbers from least to greatest. (Lesson 1.3)

20. $\sqrt{81}, \frac{72}{7}, 8.9$ _____

21. $\sqrt{7}, 2.55, \frac{7}{3}$ _____

Exponents and Scientific Notation

Key Vocabulary
scientific notation
(notación científica)

ESSENTIAL QUESTION

How can you use scientific notation to solve real-world problems?

EXAMPLE 1

Write each measurement in scientific notation.

A The diameter of Earth at the equator is approximately 12,700 kilometers.

Move the decimal point in 12,700 four places to the left: 1.2 7 0 0.

$12{,}700 = 1.27 \times 10^4$

B The diameter of a human hair is approximately 0.00254 centimeters.

Move the decimal point in 0.00254 three places to the right: 0.0 0 2.5 4

$0.00254 = 2.54 \times 10^{-3}$

EXAMPLE 2

Find the quotient: $\dfrac{2.4 \times 10^7}{9.6 \times 10^3}$.

Divide the multipliers: $2.4 \div 9.6 = 0.25$

Divide the powers of ten: $\dfrac{10^7}{10^3} = 10^{7-3} = 10^4$

Combine the answers and write the product in scientific notation.

$0.25 \times 10^4 = 0.25 \times (10 \times 10^3) = (0.25 \times 10) \times 10^3 = 2.5 \times 10^3$

EXERCISES

Write each number in scientific notation. (Lessons 2.2, 2.3)

1. 25,500,000 _____

2. 0.00734 _____

Write each number in standard notation. (Lessons 2.2, 2.3)

3. 5.23×10^4 _____

4. 1.33×10^{-5} _____

Simplify each expression. (Lessons 2.1, 2.4)

5. $(9 - 7)^3 \cdot 5^0 + (8 + 3)^2$ _____

6. $\dfrac{(4 + 2)^2}{[(9 - 3)^3]^2}$ _____

7. $3.2 \times 10^5 + 1.25 \times 10^4 + 2.9 \times 10^5$

8. $(2600)(3.24 \times 10^4)$

_____

_____

Unit Project CA CC 8.EE.1.3

The Large and the Small of It

Did you know that, according to one estimate, there are about 300,000,000,000 birds in the world? Or that the mass of a dust particle is about 0.0000000008 kg?

For this project, find five interesting facts that involve numbers greater than one million. Find five more facts that involve positive numbers less than one-millionth. Then create a presentation that includes the following:

• Each of the ten numbers written in both standard notation and scientific notation
• A description of the fact that each number represents
• The source where you found the information
• An image for each fact

Use the space below to write down any questions you have or important information from your teacher.

MATH IN CAREERS | **ACTIVITY**

Astronomer An astronomer is studying Mercury, which is the closest planet to our Sun. Mercury is 57,910,000,000 meters away from the Sun. Earth is 149,600,000,000 meters away from the Sun. How much longer does it take for light to travel from the Sun to Earth than to Mercury? The speed of light is 3.0×10^8 miles per second.

UNIT 1
MIXED REVIEW

Assessment Readiness

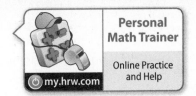

Personal Math Trainer

Online Practice and Help

my.hrw.com

1. Look at each number. Is it between $\sqrt{50}$ and $\frac{5\pi}{2}$?

   Select Yes or No for each number.

   A. $\frac{22}{3}$ ○ Yes   ○ No

   B. $\pi + 4$ ○ Yes   ○ No

   C. $3\sqrt{7}$ ○ Yes   ○ No

2. Mark wrote the following statements in his notebook.

   Choose True or False for each statement.

   A. Integers can be irrational numbers.   ○ True   ○ False

   B. All integers are whole numbers.   ○ True   ○ False

   C. All whole numbers are integers.   ○ True   ○ False

3. The total land area on Earth is about 6×10^7 square miles. The land area of Australia is about 3×10^6 square miles. About how many times larger is the land area on Earth than the land area of Australia? Explain your reasoning.

4. Jonathan says that the simplest form of the expression below is 49.

   $$\frac{[(9-2)^2]^4}{(4+3)^5}$$

   Is he correct? Explain.

Performance Tasks

★**5.** Amanda says the human fingernail has a thickness of about 4.2×10^{-4} meters. Justin says a human fingernail has a thickness of about 0.42 millimeter. Do Amanda's and Justin's estimations agree? Explain.

★★**6.** Cory is making a poster of common geometric shapes. He draws a square with a side of length 4^3 cm, an equilateral triangle with a height of $\sqrt{200}$ cm, a circle with a circumference of 8π cm, a rectangle with a length of $\frac{122}{5}$ cm, and a parallelogram with a base of 3.14 cm.

a. Write the numbers in this problem in order from least to greatest.

b. Explain how you decided on your arrangement.

★★★**7.** The closest star to our Sun, Proxima Centauri, is 39,900,000,000,000,000 meters away from Earth.

a. Write this distance in scientific notation.

b. Light travels at a speed of 3.0×10^8 meters per second. How can you calculate the time in seconds that it takes light from Proxima Centauri to reach Earth? How many seconds does it take? Write your answer in scientific notation and standard notation.

Proportional and Nonproportional Relationships and Functions

 MODULE 3

Proportional Relationships

 CA CC 8.EE.5, 8.EE.6, 8.F.2, 8.F.4

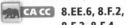 **MODULE 4**

Nonproportional Relationships

CA CC 8.EE.6, 8.F.2, 8.F.3, 8.F.4

 MODULE 5

Writing Linear Equations

CA CC 8.F.4, 8.SP.1, 8.SP.2, 8.SP.3

 MODULE 6

Functions

CA CC 8.EE.5, 8.F.1, 8.F.2, 8.F.3, 8.F.4, 8.F.5

MATH IN CAREERS

Cost Estimator A cost estimator determines the cost of a product or project, which helps businesses decide whether or not to manufacture a product or build a structure. Cost estimators analyze the costs of labor, materials, and use of equipment, among other things. Cost estimators use math when they assemble and analyze data. If you are interested in a career as a cost estimator, you should study these mathematical subjects:

- Algebra
- Trigonometry
- Calculus

Research other careers that require analyzing costs.

ACTIVITY At the end of the unit, check out how **cost estimators** use math.

Mapping San Diego

The Unit Project at the end of this unit involves drawing a map of a section of the city of San Diego on a coordinate grid. Using information you determine from the map, you will find the coordinates of specific locations on the map and the equations of several streets. To successfully complete the Unit Project you'll need to master these skills:

- Write and solve proportions.
- Identify the coordinates of points on a graph.
- Write linear equations from a graph.

1. How is a map like a coordinate grid?

_____

_____

_____

2. How can you use the east-west lines of latitude and north-south lines of longitude on Earth's surface to describe a specific location?

_____

_____

Tracking Your Learning Progression

This unit addresses important California Common Core Standards in the Critical Areas of understanding functions and applying proportional relationships to lines and linear equations.

Domain 8.F Functions

    Cluster Define, evaluate, and compare functions.

The unit also supports additional standards.

Domain 8.F Functions

    Cluster Use functions to model relationships between quantities.

Domain 8.EE Expressions and Equations

    Cluster Understand the connections between proportional relationships, lines, and linear equations.

Proportional Relationships

? **ESSENTIAL QUESTION**

How can you use proportional relationships to solve real-world problems?

Real-World Video

Speedboats can travel at fast rates while sailboats travel more slowly. If you graphed distance versus time for both types of boats, you could tell by the steepness of the graph which boat was faster.

⏻ my.hrw.com

GO DIGITAL

my.hrw.com

my.hrw.com

Go digital with your write-in student edition, accessible on any device.

Math On the Spot

Scan with your smart phone to jump directly to the online edition, video tutor, and more.

Animated Math

Interactively explore key concepts to see how math works.

Personal Math Trainer

Get immediate feedback and help as you work through practice sets.

Are YOU Ready?

Complete these exercises to review skills you will need for this module.

Write Fractions as Decimals

EXAMPLE $\frac{1.7}{2.5} = ?$

Multiply the numerator and the denominator by a power of 10 so that the denominator is a whole number.

$\frac{1.7 \times 10}{2.5 \times 10} = \frac{17}{25}$

Write the fraction as a division problem. Write a decimal point and zeros in the dividend.
Place a decimal point in the quotient.
Divide as with whole numbers.

$$
\begin{array}{r}
0.68 \\
25\overline{)17.00} \\
-15\,0 \\
\hline
2\,00 \\
-2\,00 \\
\hline
0
\end{array}
$$

Write each fraction as a decimal.

1. $\frac{3}{8}$ _____

2. $\frac{0.3}{0.4}$ _____

3. $\frac{0.13}{0.2}$ _____

4. $\frac{0.39}{0.75}$ _____

5. $\frac{4}{5}$ _____

6. $\frac{0.1}{2}$ _____

7. $\frac{3.5}{14}$ _____

8. $\frac{7}{14}$ _____

9. $\frac{0.3}{10}$ _____

Solve Proportions

EXAMPLE $\frac{5}{7} = \frac{x}{14}$

$\frac{5 \times 2}{7 \times 2} = \frac{x}{14}$ $7 \times 2 = 14$, so multiply the numerator and denominator by 2.

$\frac{10}{14} = \frac{x}{14}$ $5 \times 2 = 10$

$x = 10$

Solve each proportion for x.

10. $\frac{20}{18} = \frac{10}{x}$ _____

11. $\frac{x}{12} = \frac{30}{72}$ _____

12. $\frac{x}{4} = \frac{4}{16}$ _____

13. $\frac{11}{x} = \frac{132}{120}$ _____

14. $\frac{36}{48} = \frac{x}{4}$ _____

15. $\frac{x}{9} = \frac{21}{27}$ _____

16. $\frac{24}{16} = \frac{x}{2}$ _____

17. $\frac{30}{15} = \frac{6}{x}$ _____

18. $\frac{3}{x} = \frac{18}{36}$ _____

Reading Start-Up

Visualize Vocabulary

Use the ✔ words to complete the diagram.

Reviewing Proportions

2:6, 3 to 4

$\frac{5}{10}, \frac{25}{50}, \frac{35}{70}$

$\frac{12 \text{ inches}}{1 \text{ foot}}$,
1.25 per ounce

Vocabulary

Review Words
- constant *(constante)*
- ✔ equivalent ratios *(razones equivalentes)*
- proportion *(proporción)*
- rate *(tasa)*
- ✔ ratios *(razón)*
- ✔ unit rates *(tasas unitarias)*

Preview Words
- constant of proportionality *(constante de proporcionalidad)*
- proportional relationship *(relación proporcional)*
- rate of change *(tasa de cambio)*
- slope *(pendiente)*

Understand Vocabulary

Match the term on the left to the definition on the right.

1. unit rate

2. constant of proportionality

3. proportional relationship

A. A constant ratio of two variables related proportionally.

B. A rate in which the second quantity in the comparison is one unit.

C. A relationship between two quantities in which the ratio of one quantity to the other quantity is constant.

Active Reading

Key-Term Fold Before beginning the module, create a key-term fold to help you learn the vocabulary in this module. Write the highlighted vocabulary words on one side of the flap. Write the definition for each word on the other side of the flap. Use the key-term fold to quiz yourself on the definitions used in this module.

Proportional Relationships

CALIFORNIA

CA CC 8.EE.5

Graph proportional relationships, interpreting the unit rate as the slope of the graph. Compare two different proportional relationships represented in different ways.

Key Vocabulary

proportional relationship *(relación proporcional)*
A relationship between two quantities in which the ratio of one quantity to the other quantity is constant.

slope *(pendiente)*
A measure of the steepness of a line on a graph; the rise divided by the run.

unit rate *(tasa unitaria)*
A rate in which the second quantity in the comparison is one unit.

What It Means to You

You will use data from a table and a graph to apply your understanding of rates to analyzing real-world situations.

EXAMPLE 8.EE.5

The table shows the volume of water released by Hoover Dam over a certain period of time. Use the data to make a graph. Find the slope of the line and explain what it shows.

Water Released from Hoover Dam	
Time (s)	**Volume of water (m³)**
5	75,000
10	150,000
15	225,000
20	300,000

Water Released from Hoover Dam

The slope of the line is 15,000. This means that for every second that passed, 15,000 m³ of water was released from Hoover Dam.

Suppose another dam releases water over the same period of time at a rate of 180,000 m³ per minute. How do the two rates compare?

180,000 m³ per minute is equal to 3,000 m³ per second. This rate is one fifth the rate released by the Hoover Dam over the same time period.

Representing Proportional Relationships

 CA CC 8EE.6

Graph proportional relationships, interpreting the unit rate as the slope of the graph. Compare two different proportional relationships represented in different ways.

ESSENTIAL QUESTION

How can you use tables, graphs, and equations to represent proportional situations?

EXPLORE ACTIVITY   **CA CC** Prep for 8.EE.6

Representing Proportional Relationships with Tables

In 1870, the French writer Jules Verne published *20,000 Leagues Under the Sea*, one of the most popular science fiction novels ever written. One definition of a *league* is a unit of measure equaling 3 miles.

A Complete the table.

Distance (leagues)	1	2	6	12	20,000
Distance (miles)	3	6	18	36	60,000

B What relationships do you see among the numbers in the table?

_____

_____

C For each column of the table, find the ratio of the distance in miles to the distance in leagues. Write each ratio in simplest form.

$\frac{3}{1} = \boxed{3}$ $\frac{6}{2} = \boxed{3}$ $\frac{18}{6} = \boxed{3}$ $\frac{36}{12} = \boxed{3}$ $\frac{60,000}{20,000} = \boxed{3}$

D What do you notice about the ratios? _____

Reflect

1. If you know the distance between two points in leagues, how can you find the distance in miles? _multiply_____

2. If you know the distance between two points in miles, how can you find the distance in leagues? _____

Representing Proportional Relationships with Equations

The ratio of the distance in miles to the distance in leagues is constant. This relationship is said to be *proportional*. A **proportional relationship** is a relationship between two quantities in which the ratio of one quantity to the other quantity is constant.

A proportional relationship can be described by an equation of the form $y = kx$, where k is a number called the **constant of proportionality**.

Sometimes it is useful to use another form of the equation, $k = \frac{y}{x}$.

EXAMPLE 1

 CA CC 8.EE.6

Meghan earns $12 an hour at her part-time job. Show that the relationship between the amount she earned and the number of hours she worked is a proportional relationship. Then write an equation for the relationship.

> For every hour Meghan works, she earns $12. So, for 8 hours of work, she earns $8 \times \$12 = \$96$.

STEP 1 Make a table relating amount earned to number of hours.

Number of hours	1	2	4	8
Amount earned ($)	12	24	48	96

STEP 2 For each number of hours, write the relationship of the amount earned and the number of hours as a ratio in simplest form.

$\frac{\text{amount earned}}{\text{number of hours}}$ $\frac{12}{1} = \frac{12}{1}$ $\frac{24}{2} = \frac{12}{1}$ $\frac{48}{4} = \frac{12}{1}$ $\frac{96}{8} = \frac{12}{1}$

Since the ratios for the two quantities are all equal to $\frac{12}{1}$, the relationship is proportional.

STEP 3 Write an equation.

> First tell what the variables represent.

Let x represent the number of hours.
Let y represent the amount earned.

Use the ratio as the constant of proportionality in the equation $y = kx$.

The equation is $y = \frac{12}{1}x$ or $y = 12x$.

Math Talk
Mathematical Practices

Describe two real-world quantities with a proportional relationship that can be described by the equation $y = 25x$.

YOUR TURN

3. Fifteen bicycles are produced each hour at the Speedy Bike Works. Show that the relationship between the number of bikes produced and the number of hours is a proportional relationship. Then write an equation for the relationship.   _____

Representing Proportional Relationships with Graphs

You can represent a proportional relationship with a graph. The graph will be a line that passes through the origin (0, 0). The graph shows the relationship between distance measured in miles to distance measured in leagues.

EXAMPLE 2

CA CC 8.EE.6

The graph shows the relationship between the weight of an object on the Moon and its weight on Earth. Write an equation for this relationship.

STEP 1 Use the points on the graph to make a table.

Earth weight (lb)	6	12	18	30
Moon weight (lb)	1	2	3	5

STEP 2 Find the constant of proportionality.

$\dfrac{\text{Moon weight}}{\text{Earth weight}}$ $\dfrac{1}{6} = \dfrac{1}{6}$ $\dfrac{2}{12} = \dfrac{1}{6}$ $\dfrac{3}{18} = \dfrac{1}{6}$ $\dfrac{5}{30} = \dfrac{1}{6}$

The constant of proportionality is $\dfrac{1}{6}$.

STEP 3 Write an equation.

Let x represent weight on Earth.

Let y represent weight on the Moon.

The equation is $y = \dfrac{1}{6}x$.   *Replace k with $\frac{1}{6}$ in $y = kx$.*

YOUR TURN

The graph shows the relationship between the amount of time that a backpacker hikes and the distance traveled.

4. What does the point (5, 6) represent?

_____

5. What is the equation of the relationship?

_____

Hiking Distance

Personal Math Trainer

Online Practice and Help

my.hrw.com

Lesson 3.1   **75**

1. **Vocabulary** A proportional relationship is a relationship between two quantities in which the ratio of one quantity to the other quantity

   | is / is not | constant.

2. **Vocabulary** When writing an equation of a proportional relationship in the form $y = kx$, k represents the _____.

3. Write an equation that describes the proportional relationship between the number of days and the number of weeks in a given length of time. (Explore Activity and Example 1)

   a. Complete the table.

Time (weeks)	1	2	4		10
Time (days)	7			56	

   b. Let x represent _____.

   Let y represent _____.

   The equation that describes the relationship is _____.

Each table or graph represents a proportional relationship. Write an equation that describes the relationship. (Example 1 and Example 2)

4. **Physical Science** The relationship between the numbers of oxygen atoms and hydrogen atoms in water

Oxygen atoms	2	5		120
Hydrogen atoms	4		34	

   _____

5.

   Map of Iowa

   _____

6. If you know the equation of a proportional relationship, how can you draw the graph of the equation?

   _____

   _____

3.1 Independent Practice

CA CC 8.EE.6, 8.F.4

Personal Math Trainer

Online Practice and Help

my.hrw.com

The table shows the relationship between temperatures measured on the Celsius and Fahrenheit scales.

Celsius temperature	0	10	20	30	40	50
Fahrenheit temperature	32	50	68	86	104	122

7. Is the relationship between the temperature scales proportional? Why or why not?

_____

_____

8. Describe the graph of the Celsius-Fahrenheit relationship.

_____

_____

9. **Analyze Relationships** Ralph opened a savings account with a deposit of $100. Every month after that, he deposited $20 more.

   a. Why is the relationship described not proportional?

   _____

   _____

   b. How could the situation be changed to make the situation proportional?

   _____

   _____

10. **Represent Real-World Problems** Describe a real-world situation that can be modeled by the equation $y = \frac{1}{20}x$. Be sure to describe what each variable represents.

_____

_____

Look for a Pattern **The variables _x_ and _y_ are related proportionally.**

11. When $x = 8$, $y = 20$. Find y when $x = 42$. _____

12. When $x = 12$, $y = 8$. Find x when $y = 12$. _____

13. The graph shows the relationship between the distance that a snail crawls and the time that it crawls.

Snail Crawling

a. Use the points on the graph to make a table.

Time (min)					
Distance (in.)					

b. Write the equation for the relationship and tell what each variable represents.

_____

c. How long does it take the snail to crawl 85 inches? _____

 FOCUS ON HIGHER ORDER THINKING

Work Area

14. Communicate Mathematical Ideas Explain why all of the graphs in this lesson show the first quadrant but omit the other three quadrants.

_____

_____

_____

_____

15. Analyze Relationships Complete the table.

Length of side of square	1	2	3	4	5
Perimeter of square					
Area of square					

a. Are the length of a side of a square and the perimeter of the square related proportionally? Why or why not?

_____

_____

b. Are the length of a side of a square and the area of the square related proportionally? Why or why not?

_____

_____

16. Make a Conjecture A table shows a proportional relationship where k is the constant of proportionality. The rows are then switched. How does the new constant of proportionality relate to the original one?

_____

Rate of Change and Slope

CA CC 8. F.4

Construct a function to model a linear relationship between two quantities. Determine the rate of change and initial value of the function from a description of a relationship or from two (x, y) values, including reading these from a table or from a graph. Interpret the rate of change and initial value of a linear function in terms of the situation it models, and in terms of its graph or a table of values.

ESSENTIAL QUESTION

How do you find a rate of change or a slope?

Investigating Rates of Change

A **rate of change** is a ratio of the amount of change in the dependent variable to the amount of change in the independent variable.

Math On the Spot
⊙ my.hrw.com

EXAMPLE 1

CA CC 8.F.4

Eve keeps a record of the number of lawns she has mowed and the money she has earned. Tell whether the rates of change are constant or variable.

	Day 1	Day 2	Day 3	Day 4
Number of lawns	1	3	6	8
Amount earned ($)	15	45	90	120

STEP 1 Identify the independent and dependent variables.

independent: number of lawns   dependent: amount earned

STEP 2 Find the rates of change.

Day 1 to Day 2: $\dfrac{\text{change in \$}}{\text{change in lawns}} = \dfrac{45 - 15}{3 - 1} = \dfrac{30}{2} = 15$

Day 2 to Day 3: $\dfrac{\text{change in \$}}{\text{change in lawns}} = \dfrac{90 - 45}{6 - 3} = \dfrac{45}{3} = 15$

Day 3 to Day 4: $\dfrac{\text{change in \$}}{\text{change in lawns}} = \dfrac{120 - 90}{8 - 6} = \dfrac{30}{2} = 15$

The rates of change are constant: $15 per lawn.

Math Talk
Mathematical Practices

Would you expect the rates of change of a car's speed during a drive through a city to be constant or variable? Explain.

YOUR TURN

1. The table shows the approximate height of a football after it is kicked. Tell whether the rates of change are constant or variable.

Find the rates of change:

_____

The rates of change are | **constant / variable**.

Time (s)	Height (ft)
0	0
0.5	18
1.5	31
2	26

Personal Math Trainer

Online Practice and Help

⊙ my.hrw.com

Using Graphs to Find Rates of Change

You can also use a graph to find rates of change.

**The graph shows the distance Nathan bicycled over time.
What is Nathan's rate of change?**

A Find the rate of change from 1 hour to 2 hours.

$$\frac{\text{change in distance}}{\text{change in time}} = \frac{30 - \boxed{}}{2 - 1} = \frac{\boxed{}}{1} = \boxed{} \text{ miles per hour}$$

B Find the rate of change from 1 hour to 4 hours.

$$\frac{\text{change in distance}}{\text{change in time}} = \frac{60 - \boxed{}}{4 - \boxed{}} = \frac{\boxed{}}{\boxed{}} = \boxed{} \text{ miles per hour}$$

C Find the rate of change from 2 hours to 4 hours.

$$\frac{\text{change in distance}}{\text{change in time}} = \frac{60 - \boxed{}}{4 - \boxed{}} = \frac{\boxed{}}{\boxed{}} = \boxed{} \text{ miles per hour}$$

D Recall that the graph of a proportional relationship is a line through the origin. Explain whether the relationship between Nathan's time and distance is a proportional relationship.

_____

_____

Reflect

2. **Make a Conjecture** Does a proportional relationship have a constant rate of change?

_____

3. Does it matter what interval you use when you find the rate of change of a proportional relationship? Explain.

_____

_____

Calculating Slope *m*

When the rate of change of a relationship is constant, any segment of its graph has the same steepness. The constant rate of change is called the *slope* of the line.

Math On the Spot
⊙ my.hrw.com

Slope Formula

The **slope** of a line is the ratio of the change in *y*-values (rise) for a segment of the graph to the corresponding change in *x*-values (run).

$$m = \frac{y_2 - y_1}{x_2 - x_1}$$

EXAMPLE 2   CA CC 8.F.4

Find *m* the slope of the line.

My Notes

STEP 1 Choose two points on the line.
$P_1(x_1, y_1)$ $P_2(x_2, y_2)$

STEP 2 Find the change in *y*-values (rise = $y_2 - y_1$) and the change in *x*-values (run = $x_2 - x_1$) as you move from one point to the other.

rise = $y_2 - y_1$	run = $x_2 - x_1$
= 4 − 2	= −6 − (−3)
= 2	= −3

If you move up or right, the change is positive. If you move down or left, the change is negative.

STEP 3 $m = \dfrac{\text{rise}}{\text{run}} = \dfrac{y_2 - y_1}{x_2 - x_1}$

$= \dfrac{2}{-3}$

$= -\dfrac{2}{3}$

YOUR TURN

4. The graph shows the rate at which water is leaking from a tank. The slope of the line gives the leaking rate in gallons per minute. Find the slope of the line.

Leaking tank

Rise = _____   Run = _____

Slope = _____

Personal Math Trainer
Online Practice and Help
⊙ my.hrw.com

Tell whether the rates of change are constant or variable. (Example 1)

1. building measurements _____

Feet	3	12	27	75
Yards	1	4	9	25

2. computers sold _____

Week	2	4	9	20
Number Sold	6	12	25	60

3. distance an object falls _____

Distance (ft)	16	64	144	256
Time (s)	1	2	3	4

4. cost of sweaters _____

Number	2	4	7	9
Cost ($)	38	76	133	171

Erica walks to her friend Philip's house. The graph shows Erica's distance from home over time. (Explore Activity)

Distance from Erica's Home

5. Find the rate of change from 1 minute to 2 minutes.

$$\frac{\text{change in distance}}{\text{change in time}} = \frac{400 - \boxed{}}{2 - \boxed{}} = \frac{\boxed{}}{\boxed{}} = \boxed{} \text{ ft per min}$$

6. Find the rate of change from 1 minute to 4 minutes. _____

Find the slope of each line. (Example 2)

7.

slope = _____

8.

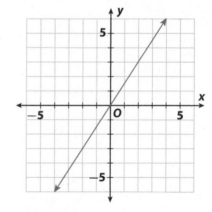

slope = _____

9. If you know two points on a line, how can you find the rate of change of the variables being graphed?

_____

_____

_____

3.2 Independent Practice

CA CC 8.F.4

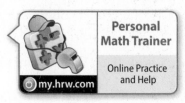

Personal
Math Trainer

Online Practice
and Help

my.hrw.com

10. Rectangle *EFGH* is graphed on a coordinate plane with vertices at
$E(-3, 5)$, $F(6, 2)$, $G(4, -4)$, and $H(-5, -1)$.

    a. Find the slopes of each side.

    _____

    _____

    b. What do you notice about the slopes of opposite sides?

    _____

    c. What do you notice about the slopes of adjacent sides?

    _____

11. A bicyclist started riding at 8:00 A.M. The diagram below shows the
distance the bicyclist had traveled at different times. What was
the bicyclist's average rate of speed in miles per hour?

8:00 A.M. ←— 4.5 miles —→ 8:18 A.M. ←——— 7.5 miles ———→ 8:48 A.M.

_____

12. Multistep A line passes through (6, 3), (8, 4), and $(n, -2)$. Find the value of n.

_____

13. A large container holds 5 gallons of water. It begins leaking at a constant
rate. After 10 minutes, the container has 3 gallons of water left.

    a. At what rate is the water leaking?

    _____

    b. After how many minutes will the container be empty?

    _____

14. Critique Reasoning Billy found the slope of the line through the
points (2, 5) and $(-2, -5)$ using the equation $\frac{2 - (-2)}{5 - (-5)} = \frac{2}{5}$. What mistake
did he make?

_____

_____

15. Multiple Representations Graph parallelogram *ABCD* on a coordinate plane with vertices at *A*(3, 4), *B*(6, 1), *C*(0, −2), and *D*(−3, 1).

   a. Find the slope of each side.

   _____

   _____

   b. What do you notice about the slopes?

   _____

   _____

   c. Draw another parallelogram on the coordinate plane. Do the slopes have the same characteristics?

   _____

FOCUS ON HIGHER ORDER THINKING

Work Area

16. Communicate Mathematical Ideas Ben and Phoebe are finding the slope of a line. Ben chose two points on the line and used them to find the slope. Phoebe used two different points to find the slope. Did they get the same answer? Explain.

_____

_____

_____

17. Analyze Relationships Two lines pass through the origin. The lines have slopes that are opposites. Compare and contrast the lines.

_____

_____

_____

_____

_____

18. Reason Abstractly What is the slope of the *x*-axis? Explain.

_____

_____

_____

Interpreting the Unit Rate as Slope

 CA CC 8.EE.5
Graph proportional relationships, interpreting the unit rate as the slope of the graph. Compare two different proportional relationships represented in different ways. *Also 8.F.2, 8.F.4*

ESSENTIAL QUESTION

How do you interpret the unit rate as slope?

EXPLORE ACTIVITY   CA CC 8.EE.5, 8.F.4

Relating the Unit Rate to Slope

A rate is a comparison of two quantities that have different units, such as miles and hours. A **unit rate** is a rate in which the second quantity in the comparison is one unit.

A storm is raging on Misty Mountain. The graph shows the constant rate of change of the snow level on the mountain.

Misty Mountain Storm

A Find the slope of the graph using the points (1, 2) and (5, 10). Remember that the slope is the constant rate of change.

B Find the unit rate of snowfall in inches per hour. Explain your method.

_____

_____

C Compare the slope of the graph and the unit rate of change in the snow level. What do you notice?

_____

D Which unique point on this graph can represent the slope of the graph and the unit rate of change in the snow level? Explain how you found the point.

_____

_____

_____

_____

Graphing Proportional Relationships

You can use a table or a graph to find the unit rate and slope that describe a real-world proportional relationship. The constant of proportionality for a proportional relationship is the same as the slope and the unit rate.

EXAMPLE 1

 CA CC 8.EE.5

Every 3 seconds, 4 cubic feet of water pass over a dam. Draw a graph of the situation. Find the unit rate of this proportional relationship.

 STEP 1 Make a table.

Time (sec)	3	6	9	12	15
Volume (ft³)	4	8	12	16	20

STEP 2 Draw a graph.

 STEP 3 Find the slope.

$$\text{slope} = \frac{\text{rise}}{\text{run}} = \frac{8}{6}$$

$$= \frac{4}{3}$$

Water Over the Dam

The slope and the unit rate of the graph are equal, therefore $\frac{4}{3}$ cubic feet per second is the unit rate and the slope.

> **Math Talk**
> **Mathematical Practices**
>
> In a proportional relationship, how are the constant of proportionality, the unit rate, and the slope of the graph of the relationship related?

Reflect

1. **What If?** Without referring to the graph, how do you know that the point $\left(1, \frac{4}{3}\right)$ is on the graph?

_____

_____

 YOUR TURN

2. Tomas rides his bike at a steady rate of 4 miles every 6 minutes. Graph the situation. Find the unit rate of this proportional relationship.

_____

_____

_____

Tomas's Ride

Using Slopes to Compare Unit Rates

You can compare proportional relationships presented in different ways.

Math On the Spot
⊙ my.hrw.com

EXAMPLE 2

CA CC 8.EE.5, 8.F.2

The equation $y = 2.75x$ represents the rate, in barrels per hour, that oil is pumped from Well A. The graph represents the rate that oil is pumped from Well B. Which well pumped oil at a faster rate?

Well B Pumping Rate

STEP 1 Use the equation $y = 2.75x$ to make a table for Well A's pumping rate, in barrels per hour.

Time (h)	1	2	3	4
Quantity (barrels)	2.75	5.5	8.25	11

STEP 2 Use the table to find the slope of the graph of Well A.

slope = unit rate = $\frac{5.5 - 2.75}{2 - 1} = \frac{2.75}{1} =$ **2.75** barrels/hour

STEP 3 Use the graph to find the slope of the graph of Well B.

slope = unit rate = $\frac{rise}{run} = \frac{10}{4} =$ **2.5** barrels/hour

STEP 4 Compare the unit rates.

$2.75 > 2.5$, so Well A's rate, 2.75 barrels/hour, is faster.

Reflect

3. Describe the relationships among the slope of the graph of Well A's rate, the equation representing Well A's rate, and the constant of proportionality.

_____

_____

YOUR TURN

4. The equation $y = 375x$ represents the relationship between x, the time that a plane flies in hours, and y, the distance the plane flies in miles for Plane A. The table represents the relationship for Plane B. Find the slope of the graph for each plane and the plane's rate of speed. Determine which plane is flying at a faster rate of speed.

Time (h)	1	2	3	4
Distance (mi)	425	850	1275	1700

Personal Math Trainer

Online Practice and Help

⊙ my.hrw.com

_____

Give the slope of the graph and the unit rate. (Explore Activity and Example 1)

1. Jorge: 5 miles every 6 hours

Jorge

2. Akiko

Time (h)	Distance (mi)
4	5
8	10
12	15
16	20

Akiko

_____

_____

3. The equation $y = 0.5x$ represents the distance Henry hikes in miles per hour. The graph represents the rate that Clark hikes. Determine which hiker is faster. Explain. (Example 2)

Clark

_____

_____

_____

Write an equation relating the variables in each table. (Example 2)

4.

Time (x)	1	2	4	6
Distance (y)	15	30	60	90

5.

Time (x)	16	32	48	64
Distance (y)	6	12	18	24

_____

_____

? ESSENTIAL QUESTION CHECK-IN

6. Describe methods you can use to show a proportional relationship between two variables, x and y. For each method, explain how you can find the unit rate and the slope.

_____

_____

_____

_____

_____

Name _____ Class _____ Date _____

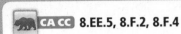

CA CC 8.EE.5, 8.F.2, 8.F.4

Personal
Math Trainer

Online Practice
and Help

my.hrw.com

7. A Canadian goose migrated at a steady rate of 3 miles every 4 minutes.

a. Fill in the table to describe the relationship.

Time (min)	4	8			20
Distance (mi)			9	12	

b. Graph the relationship.

Migration Flight

c. Find the slope of the graph and describe what it means in the context of this problem.

_____

_____

_____

_____

8. Vocabulary A unit rate is a rate in which the

| first quantity / second quantity | in the comparison is one unit.

9. The table and the graph represent the rate at which two machines are bottling milk in gallons per second.

Machine 1

Time (s)	1	2	3	4
Amount (gal)	0.6	1.2	1.8	2.4

Machine 2

a. Determine the slope and unit rate of each machine.

_____

_____

b. Determine which machine is working at a faster rate.

_____

10. Cycling The equation $y = \frac{1}{9}x$ represents the distance y, in kilometers, that Patrick traveled in x minutes while training for the cycling portion of a triathlon. The table shows the distance y Jennifer traveled in x minutes in her training. Who has the faster training rate?

Time (min)	40	64	80	96
Distance (km)	5	8	10	12

_____

_____

_____

Work Area

11. Analyze Relationships There is a proportional relationship between minutes and dollars per minute, shown on a graph of printing expenses. The graph passes through the point (1, 4.75). What is the slope of the graph? What is the unit rate? Explain.

_____

_____

_____

12. Draw Conclusions Two cars start at the same time and travel at different constant rates. A graph for Car A passes through the point (0.5, 27.5), and a graph for Car B passes through (4, 240). Both graphs show distance in miles and time in hours. Which car is traveling faster? Explain.

_____

_____

_____

_____

13. Critical Thinking The table shows the rate at which water is being pumped into a swimming pool.

Time (min)	2	5	7	12
Amount (gal)	36	90	126	216

Use the unit rate and the amount of water pumped after 12 minutes to find how much water will have been pumped into the pool after $13\frac{1}{2}$ minutes. Explain your reasoning.

_____

_____

_____

_____

Ready to Go On?

3.1 Representing Proportional Relationships

1. Find the constant of proportionality for the table of values.

x	2	3	4	5
y	3	4.5	6	7.5

_____

2. Phil is riding his bike. He rides 25 miles in 2 hours, 37.5 miles in 3 hours, and 50 miles in 4 hours. Find the constant of proportionality and write an equation to describe the situation.

_____

3.2 Rate of Change and Slope

Find the slope of each line.

3.

_____

4.

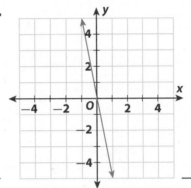

_____

3.3 Interpreting the Unit Rate as Slope

5. The distance Train A travels is represented by $d = 70t$, where d is the distance in kilometers and t is the time in hours. The distance Train B travels at various times is shown in the table. What is the unit rate of each train? Which train is going faster?

Time (hours)	Distance (km)
2	150
4	300
5	375

_____

? ESSENTIAL QUESTION

6. What is the relationship among proportional relationships, lines, rates of change, and slope?

_____

_____

MODULE 3
MIXED REVIEW

Assessment Readiness

Personal Math Trainer

Online Practice and Help

my.hrw.com

1. Consider each table. Are the rates of change within each table constant?

Select Yes or No for tables A–C.

A.

Time (s)	1	2	5	8
Height (m)	14	28	70	112

○ Yes   ○ No

B.

Time (s)	1	2	3	4
Height (m)	60	30	15	7.5

○ Yes   ○ No

C.

Time (s)	2	6	10	12
Height (m)	40	120	200	240

○ Yes   ○ No

2. An influenza virus has a length of 1.3×10^{-7} meter.

Choose True or False if a virus is longer than the influenza virus.

A. a hepatitis virus with a length of 4.5×10^{-8} m   ○ True   ○ False
B. a measles virus with a length of 0.00000022 m   ○ True   ○ False
C. a phage virus with a length of 2×10^{-7} m   ○ True   ○ False

The table shows travel distance and fuel usage for a train. Use the table for items 3 and 4.

Distance (mi), x	20	40	60	80
Amount of fuel (gal), y	120	240	360	480

3. Write an equation for the relationship shown in the table and explain how you determined your answer.

4. The equation $y = 6.5x$ gives the number of gallons of fuel that a second train uses to travel a distance of x miles. Which train uses fuel at a greater rate? Explain how you know.

Nonproportional Relationships

? ESSENTIAL QUESTION

How can you use non-proportional relationships to solve real-world problems?

Real-World Video

The distance a car can travel on a tank of gas or a full battery charge in an electric car depends on factors such as fuel capacity and the car's efficiency. This is described by a nonproportional relationship.

⊙ my.hrw.com

GO DIGITAL

my.hrw.com

 my.hrw.com

Go digital with your write-in student edition, accessible on any device.

 Math On the Spot

Scan with your smart phone to jump directly to the online edition, video tutor, and more.

 Animated Math

Interactively explore key concepts to see how math works.

 Personal Math Trainer

Get immediate feedback and help as you work through practice sets.

Are YOU Ready?

Complete these exercises to review skills you will need for this module.

Personal Math Trainer

Online Practice and Help

my.hrw.com

Integer Operations

EXAMPLE
$-7 - (-4) = -7 + 4$
$\quad\quad\quad |-7| - |4|$
$\quad\quad\quad 7 - 4,\text{ or }3$
$\quad\quad = -3$

To subtract an integer, add its opposite.

The signs are different, so find the difference of the absolute values.

Use the sign of the number with the greater absolute value.

Find each difference.

1. $3 - (-5)$ _____

2. $-4 - 5$ _____

3. $6 - 10$ _____

4. $-5 - (-3)$ _____

5. $8 - (-8)$ _____

6. $9 - 5$ _____

7. $-3 - 9$ _____

8. $0 - (-6)$ _____

9. $12 - (-9)$ _____

10. $-6 - (-4)$ _____

11. $-7 - 10$ _____

12. $5 - 14$ _____

Graph Ordered Pairs (First Quadrant)

EXAMPLE

To graph a point at (6, 2), start at the origin.

Move 6 units right.

Then move 2 units up.

Graph point A(6, 2).

Graph each point on the coordinate grid.

13. $B\,(0, 5)$

14. $C\,(8, 0)$

15. $D\,(5, 7)$

16. $E\,(2, 3)$

Reading Start-Up

Visualize Vocabulary

Use the ✔ words to complete the diagram. You can put more than one word in each box.

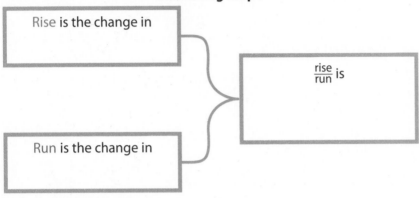

Reviewing Slope

Rise is the change in

Run is the change in

$\dfrac{rise}{run}$ is

Vocabulary

Review Words

　ordered pair *(par ordenado)*

　proportional relationship *(relación proporcional)*

✔ rate of change *(tasa de cambio)*

✔ slope *(pendiente)*

✔ x-coordinate *(coordenada x)*

✔ y-coordinate *(coordenada y)*

Preview Words

　linear equation *(ecuación lineal)*

　slope-intercept form of an equation *(forma de pendiente-intersección)*

　y-intercept *(intersección con el eje y)*

Understand Vocabulary

Complete the sentences using the preview words.

1. The *y*-coordinate of the point where a graph of a line intersects the

   y-axis is the _____.

2. A _____ is an equation whose solutions form

   a straight line on a coordinate plane.

3. A linear equation written in the form $y = mx + b$ is the

   _____.

Active Reading

Booklet Before beginning the module, create a booklet to help you learn the concepts. Write the main idea of each lesson on each page of the booklet. As you study each lesson, write important details that support the main idea, such as vocabulary and formulas. Refer to your finished booklet as you work on assignments and study for tests.

GETTING READY FOR
Nonproportional Relationships

Understanding the standards and the vocabulary terms in the standards will help you know exactly what you are expected to learn in this module.

CA CC 8.F.3

Interpret the equation $y = mx + b$ as defining a linear function, whose graph is a straight line; give examples of functions that are not linear.

Key Vocabulary

slope *(pendiente)*
A measure of the steepness of a line on a graph; the rise divided by the run.

y-intercept *(intersección con el eje y)*
The y-coordinate of the point where the graph of a line crosses the y-axis.

What It Means to You

You will identify the slope and the y-intercept of a line by looking at its equation and use them to graph the line.

EXAMPLE 8.F.3

Graph $y = 3x - 2$ using the slope and the y-intercept.

The slope m is 3, and the y-intercept is -2.

Plot the point $(0, -2)$. Use the slope $3 = \frac{3}{1}$ to find another point by moving *up* 3 and to the *right* 1. Connect the points.

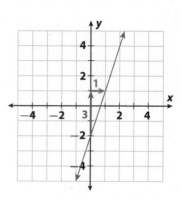

CA CC 8.F.3

Interpret the equation $y = mx + b$ as defining a linear function, whose graph is a straight line; give examples of functions that are not linear.

Key Vocabulary

function *(función)*
An input-output relationship that has exactly one output for each input.

linear function *(función lineal)*
A function whose graph is a straight line.

What It Means to You

You will distinguish linear relationships from nonlinear relationships by looking at graphs.

EXAMPLE 8.F.3

Which relationship is linear and which is nonlinear?

$P = 4s$

$A = s^2$

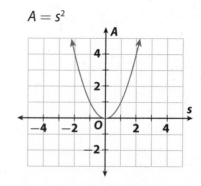

$P = 4s$ is linear because its graph is a line.

$A = s^2$ is not linear because its graph is not a line.

4.1 Representing Linear Nonproportional Relationships

 CA CC 8.F.3

Interpret the equation $y = mx + b$ as defining a linear function, whose graph is a straight line; give examples of functions that are not linear.

 ESSENTIAL QUESTION

How can you use tables, graphs, and equations to represent linear nonproportional situations?

Representing Linear Relationships Using Tables

You can use an equation to describe the relationship between two quantities in a real-world situation. You can use a table to show some values that make the equation true.

Math On the Spot

ⓞ my.hrw.com

EXAMPLE 1 (Real World) **CA CC** Prep for 8.F.3

The equation $y = 3x + 2$ gives the total charge for one person, y, renting a pair of shoes and bowling x games at Baxter Bowling Lanes based on the prices shown. Make a table of values for this situation.

STEP 1 Choose several values for x that make sense in context.

x (number of games)	1	2	3	4
y (total cost in dollars)				

STEP 2 Use the equation $y = 3x + 2$ to find y for each value of x.

x (number of games)	1	2	3	4
y (total cost in dollars)	5	8	11	14

> Substitute 1 for x:
> $y = 3(1) + 2 = 5$.

BAXTER bowling lanes
$3 per game
$2 shoe rental

YOUR TURN

1. Francisco makes $12 per hour doing part-time work on Saturdays. He spends $4 on transportation to and from work. The equation $y = 12x - 4$ gives his earnings y, after transportation costs, for working x hours. Make a table of values for this situation.

x (number of hours)				
y (earnings in dollars)				

Personal Math Trainer

Online Practice and Help

ⓞ my.hrw.com

Examining Linear Relationships

Recall that a proportional relationship is a relationship between two quantities in which the ratio of one quantity to the other quantity is constant. The graph of a proportional relationship is a line through the origin. When ratios between quantities are not constant, a relationship may be linear but not proportional and the graph does not pass through the origin.

The entrance fee for Mountain World theme park is $20. Visitors purchase additional $2 tickets for rides, games, and food. The equation $y = 2x + 20$ gives the total cost, y, to visit the park, including purchasing x tickets.

STEP 1 Complete the table.

x (number of tickets)	0	2	4	6	8
y (total cost in dollars)	20				

STEP 2 Plot ordered pairs from the information in the table. Describe the shape of the graph.

_____

STEP 3 Find the rate of change between each point and the next. Is the rate constant?

_____

STEP 4 Calculate rates of change for the values in the table. Explain why the relationship between number of tickets and total cost is not proportional.

_____

_____

_____

Theme Park Costs

Reflect

2. **Analyze Relationships** Would it be possible to add more points to the graph from $x = 0$ to $x = 10$? Would it make sense to connect the points with a line? Explain.

_____

_____

_____

_____

Representing Linear Relationships Using Graphs

A **linear equation** is an equation whose solutions are ordered pairs that form a line when graphed on a coordinate plane. Linear equations can be written in the form $y = mx + b$. When $b \neq 0$, the relationship between x and y is *nonproportional*.

EXAMPLE 2

 CA CC 8.F.3

The diameter of a Douglas fir tree is currently 10 inches when measured at chest height. Over the next 50 years, the diameter is expected to increase by an average growth rate of $\frac{2}{5}$ inch per year. The equation $y = \frac{2}{5}x + 10$ gives y, the diameter of the tree in inches, after x years. Draw a graph of the equation. Describe the relationship.

STEP 1 Make a table. Choose several values for x that make sense in context. To make calculations easier, choose multiples of 10.

x (years)	0	10	20	30	50
y (diameter in inches)	10	14	18	22	30

STEP 2 Plot ordered pairs from the information in the table. Then draw a line connecting the points to represent all the possible solutions.

STEP 3 The relationship is linear but nonproportional. The graph is a line but it does not go through the origin.

Math Talk
Mathematical Practices

Why can a line be drawn connecting the points in this example, but not in the preceding Explore Activity?

Fir Tree Growth

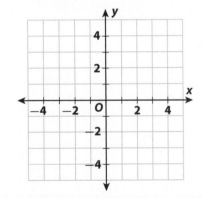

YOUR TURN

3. Make a table and graph the solutions of the equation $y = -2x + 1$.

x	−1	0	1	2
y				

Make a table of values for each equation. (Example 1)

1. $y = 2x + 5$

x	−2	−1	0	1	2
y					

2. $y = \frac{3}{8}x - 5$

x	−8	0	8		
y					

Explain why each relationship is not proportional. (Explore Activity)

3.

x	0	2	4	6	8
y	3	7	11	15	19

First calculate $\frac{y}{x}$ for the values in the table.

_____

_____

_____

_____

_____

4.

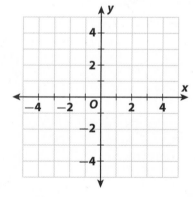

_____

_____

Complete the table for the equation. Then use the table to graph the equation. (Example 2)

5. $y = x - 1$

x	−2	−1	0	1	2
y					

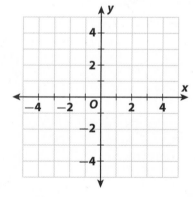

? ESSENTIAL QUESTION CHECK-IN

6. How can you choose values for x when making a table of values representing a real world situation?

_____

_____

_____

4.1 Independent Practice

CA CC 8.F.3

Personal Math Trainer

Online Practice and Help

my.hrw.com

State whether the graph of each linear relationship is a solid line or a set of unconnected points. Explain your reasoning.

7. The relationship between the number of $4 lunches you buy with a $100 school lunch card and the money remaining on the card

_____

_____

_____

_____

8. The relationship between time and the distance remaining on a 3-mile walk for someone walking at a steady rate of 2 miles per hour

_____

_____

_____

_____

9. Analyze Relationships Simone paid $12 for an initial year's subscription to a magazine. The renewal rate is $8 per year. This situation can be represented by the equation $y = 8x + 12$, where x represents the number of years the subscription is renewed and y represents the total cost.

a. Make a table of values for this situation.

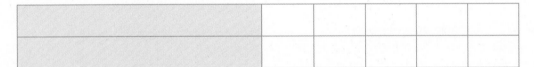

b. Draw a graph to represent the situation. Include a title and axis labels.

c. Explain why this relationship is not proportional.

_____

_____

_____

d. Does it make sense to connect the points on the graph with a solid line? Explain.

_____

_____

_____

10. Analyze Relationships A proportional relationship is a linear relationship because the rate of change is constant (and equal to the constant of proportionality). What is required of a proportional relationship that is *not* required of a general linear relationship?

_____

_____

11. Communicate Mathematical Ideas Explain how you can identify a linear non-proportional relationship from a table, a graph, and an equation.

_____

_____

_____

Work Area

12. Critique Reasoning George observes that for every increase of 1 in the value of x, there is an increase of 60 in the corresponding value of y. He claims that the relationship represented by the table is proportional. Critique George's reasoning.

x	1	2	3	4	5
y	90	150	210	270	330

_____

_____

_____

_____

_____

13. Make a Conjecture Two parallel lines are graphed on a coordinate plane. How many of the lines could represent proportional relationships? Explain.

_____

_____

_____

_____

_____

_____

Determining Slope and *y*-intercept

CA CC 8.EE.6

Use similar triangles to explain why the slope *m* is the same between any two distinct points on a non-vertical line in the coordinate plane; derive the equation $y = mx$ for a line through the origin and the equation $y = mx + b$ for a line intercepting the vertical axis at *b*. Also 8.F.4

ESSENTIAL QUESTION

How can you determine the slope and the *y*-intercept of a line?

EXPLORE ACTIVITY 1 CA CC 8.EE.6

Investigating Slope and *y*-intercept

The graph of every nonvertical line crosses the *y*-axis. The **y-intercept** is the *y*-coordinate of the point where the graph intersects the *y*-axis. The *x*-coordinate of this point is always 0.

The graph represents the linear equation $y = -\frac{2}{3}x + 4$.

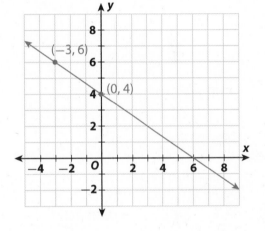

STEP 1 Find the slope of the line using the points (0, 4) and (−3, 6).

$$m = \frac{6 - \Box}{\Box - 0} = \frac{\Box}{\Box} = \Box$$

STEP 2 The line also contains the point (6, 0). What is the slope using (0, 4) and (6, 0)? Using (−3, 6) and (6, 0). What do you notice?

_____

STEP 3 Compare your answers in Steps 1 and 2 with the equation of the graphed line.

_____

_____

STEP 4 Find the value of *y* when $x = 0$ using the equation $y = -\frac{2}{3}x + 4$. Describe the point on the graph that corresponds to this solution.

_____

STEP 5 Compare your answer in Step 4 with the equation of the line.

_____

_____

Determining Rate of Change and Initial Value

The linear equation shown is written in the **slope-intercept form of an equation**. Its graph is a line with **slope *m*** and ***y*-intercept *b***.

$$y = mx + b$$

slope   *y*-intercept

A linear relationship has a constant rate of change. You can find the **rate of change *m*** and the **initial value *b*** for a linear situation from a table of values.

EXAMPLE 1

 CA CC 8.F.4

A phone salesperson is paid a minimum weekly salary and a commission for each phone sold, as shown in the table. Confirm that the relationship is linear and give the constant rate of change and the initial value.

STEP 1   Confirm that the rate of change is constant.

$$\frac{\text{change in income}}{\text{change in phones sold}} = \frac{630 - 480}{20 - 10} = \frac{150}{10} = 15$$

$$\frac{\text{change in income}}{\text{change in phones sold}} = \frac{780 - 630}{30 - 20} = \frac{150}{10} = 15$$

$$\frac{\text{change in income}}{\text{change in phones sold}} = \frac{930 - 780}{40 - 30} = \frac{150}{10} = 15$$

Number of Phones Sold	Weekly Income ($)
10	$480
20	$630
30	$780
40	$930

The rate of change is a constant, **15**.

The salesperson receives a $15 commission for each phone sold.

STEP 2   Find the initial value when the number of phones sold is 0.

−10   −10

Number of phones sold	0	10	20
Weekly income ($)	330	480	630

Work backward from *x* = 10 to *x* = 0 to find the initial value.

−150   −150

The initial value is $330. The salesperson receives a salary of $330 each week before commissions.

Math Talk
Mathematical Practices

How do you use the rate of change to work backward to find the initial value?

YOUR TURN

Find the slope and *y*-intercept of the line represented by each table.

1.

x	2	4	6	8
y	22	32	42	52

2.

x	1	2	3	4
y	8	15	22	29

_____   _____

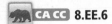

Deriving the Slope-intercept Form of an Equation

In the following Explore Activity, you will derive the slope-intercept form of an equation.

STEP 1 Let L be a line with slope m and y-intercept b. Circle the point that must be on the line. Justify your choice.

$(b, 0)$ $\qquad$ $(0, b)$ $\qquad$ $(0, m)$ $\qquad$ $(m, 0)$

_____

_____

STEP 2 Recall that slope is the ratio of change in y to change in x. Complete the equation for the slope m of the line using the y-intercept $(0, b)$ and another point (x, y) on the line.

$$m = \frac{y - \boxed{}}{\boxed{} - 0}$$

STEP 3 Solve the equation for y.

$$m = \frac{y - b}{x}$$ Simplify the denominator.

$$m \cdot \boxed{} = \frac{y - b}{x} \cdot \boxed{}$$ Multiply both sides of the equation by _____.

$$m\boxed{} = y - b$$

$$mx + \boxed{} = y - b + \boxed{}$$ Add _____ to both sides of the equation.

$$mx + \boxed{} = y$$

$$y = mx + \boxed{}$$ Write the equation with y on the left side.

$y = mx + b$ is the Slope-Intercept form of an equation.

Reflect

3. **Critical Thinking** Write the equation of a line with slope m that passes through the origin. Explain your reasoning.

_____

_____

_____

Find the slope and y-intercept of the line in each graph. (Explore Activity 1)

1.

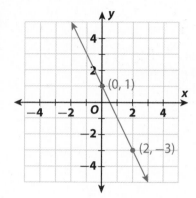

slope m = _____ y-intercept b = _____

2.

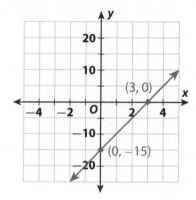

slope m = _____ y-intercept b = _____

3.

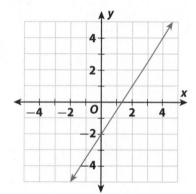

slope m = _____ y-intercept b = _____

4.

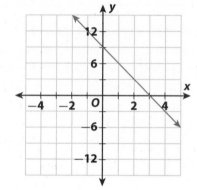

slope m = _____ y-intercept b = _____

Find the slope and y-intercept of the line represented by each table. (Example 1)

5.

x	0	2	4	6	8
y	1	7	13	19	25

slope m = _____ y-intercept b = _____

6.

x	0	5	10	15	20
y	140	120	100	80	60

slope m = _____ y-intercept b = _____

? ESSENTIAL QUESTION CHECK-IN

7. How can you determine the slope and the y-intercept of a line from a graph?

_____

_____

_____

4.2 Independent Practice

CA CC 8.EE.6, 8.F.4

Personal
Math Trainer

Online Practice
and Help

my.hrw.com

8. Some carpet cleaning costs are shown in the table. The relationship is linear. Find and interpret the rate of change and the initial value for this situation.

Rooms cleaned	1	2	3	4
Cost ($)	125	175	225	275

_____

_____

_____

9. **Make Predictions** The total cost to pay for parking at a state park for the day and rent a paddleboat are shown.

a. Find the cost to park for a day and the hourly rate to rent a paddleboat.

_____

b. What will Lin pay if she rents a paddleboat for 3.5 hours and splits the total cost with a friend? Explain.

_____

_____

Number of Hours	Cost ($)
1	$17
2	$29
3	$41
4	$53

10. **Multi-Step** Raymond's parents will pay for him to take sailboard lessons during the summer. He can take half-hour group lessons or half-hour private lessons. The relationship between cost and number of lessons is linear.

Lessons	1	2	3	4
Group ($)	55	85	115	145
Private ($)	75	125	175	225

a. Find the rate of change and the initial value for the group lessons.

_____

_____

b. Find the rate of change and the initial value for the private lessons.

_____

_____

c. Compare and contrast the rates of change and the initial values.

_____

_____

_____

Vocabulary Explain why each relationship is not linear.

11.

x	1	2	3	4
y	4.5	6.5	8.5	11.5

12.

x	3	5	7	9
y	140	126	110	92

_____

_____

13. Communicate Mathematical Ideas Describe the procedure you performed to derive the slope-intercept form of a linear equation.

_____

_____

_____

 FOCUS ON HIGHER ORDER THINKING

Work Area

14. Critique Reasoning Your teacher asked your class to describe a real-world situation in which a *y*-intercept is 100 and the slope is 5. Your partner gave the following description: *My younger brother originally had 100 small building blocks, but he has lost 5 of them every month since.*

a. What mistake did your partner make?

_____

_____

b. Describe a real-world situation that does match the situation.

_____

_____

15. Justify Reasoning John has a job parking cars. He earns a fixed weekly salary of $300 plus a fee of $5 for each car he parks. His potential earnings for a week are shown in the graph. At what point does John begin to earn more from fees than his fixed salary? Justify your answer.

_____

_____

_____

Graphing Linear Nonproportional Relationships Using Slope and *y*-intercept

CA CC 8.F.4

Construct a function to model a linear relationship between two quantities. Determine the rate of change and initial value of the function from a description of a relationship or from two (*x*, *y*) values, including reading these from a table or from a graph. Interpret the rate of change and initial value of a linear function in terms of the situation it models, and in terms of its graph or a table of values. *Also 8.F.3*

ESSENTIAL QUESTION

How can you graph a line using the slope and *y*-intercept?

Using Slope-intercept Form to Graph a Line

Recall that $y = mx + b$ is the slope-intercept form of the equation of a line. In this form, it is easy to see the slope *m* and the *y*-intercept *b*. So you can use this form to quickly graph a line by plotting the point (0, *b*) and using the slope to find a second point.

Math On the Spot
⊙ my.hrw.com

EXAMPLE 1

CA CC 8.F.3

A Graph $y = \frac{2}{3}x - 1$.

STEP 1 The *y*-intercept is $b = -1$. Plot the point that contains the *y*-intercept: (0, −1).

STEP 2 The slope is $m = \frac{2}{3}$. Use the slope to find a second point. From (0, −1), count *up* 2 and *right* 3. The new point is (3, 1).

STEP 3 Draw a line through the points.

Animated Math
⊙ my.hrw.com

Math Talk
Mathematical Practices

Is a line with a positive slope always steeper than a line with a negative slope? Explain.

B Graph $y = -\frac{5}{2}x + 3$.

STEP 1 The *y*-intercept is $b = 3$. Plot the point that contains the *y*-intercept: (0, 3).

STEP 2 The slope is $m = -\frac{5}{2}$. Use the slope to find a second point. From (0, 3), count *down* 5 and *right* 2, or *up* 5 and *left* 2. The new point is (2, −2) or (−2, 8).

STEP 3 Draw a line through the points.

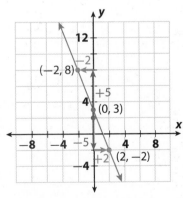

Note that the line passes through all three points: (−2, 8), (0, 3), and (2, −2).

Reflect

1. **Draw Conclusions** How can you use the slope of a line to predict the way the line will be slanted? Explain.

_____

_____

YOUR TURN

Graph each equation.

2. $y = \frac{1}{2}x + 1$

3. $y = -3x + 4$

Analyzing a Graph

Many real-world situations can be represented by linear relationships. You can use graphs of linear relationships to visualize situations and solve problems.

EXAMPLE 2 *Real World*   CA CC 8.F.4

Ken has a weekly goal of burning 2400 calories by taking brisk walks. The equation $y = -300x + 2400$ represents the number of calories y Ken has left to burn after x hours of walking which burns 300 calories per hour.

A Graph the equation $y = -300x + 2400$.

STEP 1 Write the slope as a fraction.

$$m = \frac{-300}{1} = \frac{-600}{2} = \frac{-900}{3}$$

Using the slope as $\frac{-900}{3}$ helps in drawing a more accurate graph.

STEP 2 Plot the point for the y-intercept: $(0, 2400)$.

STEP 3 Use the slope to locate a second point.

From $(0, 2400)$, count *down* 900 and *right* 3.

The new point is $(3, 1500)$.

STEP 4 Draw a line through the two points.

B After how many hours of walking will Ken have 600 calories left to burn? After how many hours will he reach his weekly goal?

STEP 1 Locate 600 calories on the *y*-axis. Read across and down to the *x*-axis.

Ken will have 600 calories left to burn after 6 hours.

STEP 2 Ken will reach his weekly goal when the number of calories left to burn is 0. Because every point on the *x*-axis has a *y*-value of 0, find the point where the line crosses the *x*-axis.

○ Ken will reach his goal after 8 hours of brisk walking.

YOUR TURN

Math Talk
Mathematical Practices

What do the slope and the *y*-intercept of the line represent in this situation?

What If? Ken decides to modify his exercise plans from Example 2 by slowing the speed at which he walks. The equation for the modified plan is $y = -200x + 2400$.

4. Graph the equation.

5. How does the graph of the new equation compare with the graph in Example 2?

_____

_____

_____

6. Will Ken have to exercise more or less to meet his goal? Explain.

_____

_____

_____

7. Suppose that Ken decides that instead of walking, he will jog, and that jogging burns 600 calories per hour. How do you think that this would change the graph?

_____

_____

_____

Personal
Math Trainer

Online Practice
and Help

ⓞ my.hrw.com

Graph each equation using the slope and the *y*-intercept. (Example 1)

1. $y = \frac{1}{2}x - 3$

slope = _____ y-intercept = _____

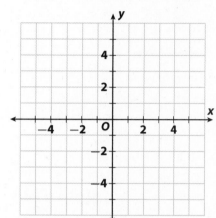

2. $y = -3x + 2$

slope = _____ y-intercept = _____

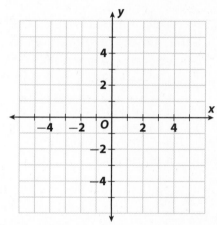

3. A friend gives you two baseball cards for your birthday. Afterward, you begin collecting them. You buy 4 cards each week. The equation $y = 4x + 2$ describes the number of cards, *y*, you have after *x* weeks. (Example 2)

a. Find and interpret the slope and the *y*-intercept of the line that represents this situation. Graph $y = 4x + 2$. Include axis labels.

_____

_____

b. Discuss which points on the line do not make sense in this situation. Then plot three more points on the line that do make sense.

_____

_____

_____

? **ESSENTIAL QUESTION CHECK-IN**

4. Why might someone choose to use the *y*-intercept and the slope to graph a line?

_____

_____

_____

_____

4.3 Independent Practice

CA CC 8.F.3, 8.F.4

Personal
Math Trainer

Online Practice
and Help

my.hrw.com

5. Science A spring stretches in relation to the weight hanging from it according to the equation $y = 0.75x + 0.25$ where x is the weight in pounds and y is the length of the spring in inches.

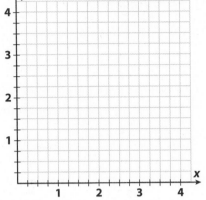

a. Graph the equation. Include axis labels.

b. Interpret the slope and the y-intercept of the line.

_____

_____

_____

_____

_____

c. How long will the spring be if a 2-pound weight is hung on it? Will the length double if you double the weight? Explain

_____

Look for a Pattern Identify the coordinates of four points on the line with each given slope and y-intercept.

6. slope $= 5$, y-intercept $= -1$

_____

7. slope $= -1$, y-intercept $= 8$

_____

8. slope $= 0.2$, y-intercept $= 0.3$

_____

9. slope $= 1.5$, y-intercept $= -3$

_____

10. slope $= -\frac{1}{2}$, y-intercept $= 4$

_____

11. slope $= \frac{2}{3}$, y-intercept $= -5$

_____

12. A music school charges a registration fee in addition to a fee per lesson. Music lessons last 0.5 hour. The equation $y = 40x + 30$ represents the total cost y of x lessons. Find and interpret the slope and y-intercept of the line that represents this situation. Then find four points on the line.

_____

_____

13. A public pool charges a membership fee and a fee for each visit. The equation $y = 3x + 50$ represents the cost y for x visits.

a. After locating the y-intercept on the coordinate plane shown, can you move up three gridlines and right one gridline to find a second point? Explain.

_____

_____

_____

b. Graph the equation $y = 3x + 50$. Include axis labels. Then interpret the slope and y-intercept.

_____

_____

c. How many visits to the pool can a member get for $200?

_____

 FOCUS ON HIGHER ORDER THINKING

Work Area

14. Explain the Error A student says that the slope of the line for the equation $y = 20 - 15x$ is 20 and the y-intercept is 15. Find and correct the error.

_____

_____

_____

15. Critical Thinking Suppose you know the slope of a linear relationship and a point that its graph passes through. Can you graph the line even if the point provided does *not* represent the y-intercept? Explain.

_____

_____

_____

16. Make a Conjecture Graph the lines $y = 3x$, $y = 3x - 3$, and $y = 3x + 3$. What do you notice about the lines? Make a conjecture based on your observation.

_____

_____

_____

Proportional and Nonproportional Situations

 CA CC 8.F.2
Compare properties of two functions each represented in a different way (algebraically, graphically, numerically in tables, or by verbal descriptions). *Also 8.F.3, 8.F.4*

ESSENTIAL QUESTION

How can you distinguish between proportional and nonproportional situations?

Distinguish Between Proportional and Nonproportional Situations Using a Graph

If a relationship is nonlinear, it is nonproportional. If it is linear, it may be either proportional or nonproportional. When the graph of the linear relationship contains the origin, the relationship is proportional.

Math On the Spot
⊙ my.hrw.com

EXAMPLE 1

CA CC 8.F.3

The graph shows the sales tax charged based on the amount spent at a video game store in a particular city. Does the graph show a linear relationship? Is the relationship proportional or nonproportional?

The graph shows a linear proportional relationship because it is a line that contains the origin.

YOUR TURN

Determine if each of the following graphs represents a proportional or nonproportional relationship.

1.

2.

Math Talk
Mathematical Practices

What do the slope and the y-intercept of the graph represent in this situation?

Personal Math Trainer

Online Practice and Help

⊙ my.hrw.com

Distinguish Between Proportional and Nonproportional Situations Using an Equation

If an equation is not a linear equation, it represents a nonproportional relationship. A linear equation of the form $y = mx + b$ may represent either a proportional ($b = 0$) or nonproportional ($b \neq 0$) relationship.

EXAMPLE 2   CA CC 8.F.4

The number of years since Keith graduated from middle school can be represented by the equation $y = a - 14$, where y is the number of years and a is his age. Is the relationship between the number of years since Keith graduated and his age proportional or nonproportional?

$$y = a - 14$$

The equation is in the form $y = mx + b$, with a being used as the variable instead of x. The value of m is 1, and the value of b is -14. Since b is not 0, the relationship between the number of years since Keith graduated and his age is nonproportional.

Reflect

3. **Communicate Mathematical Ideas** In a proportional relationship, the ratio $\frac{y}{x}$ is constant. Show that this ratio is not constant for the equation $y = a - 14$.

_____

_____

4. **What If?** Suppose another equation represents Keith's age in months y given his age in years a. Is this relationship proportional? Explain.

_____

_____

YOUR TURN

Determine if each of the following equations represents a proportional or nonproportional relationship.

5. $d = 65t$

6. $p = 0.1s + 2000$

_____ _____

7. $n = 450 - 3p$

8. $36 = 12d$

_____ _____

Distinguish Between Proportional and Nonproportional Situations Using a Table

Math On the Spot

⏱ my.hrw.com

If there is not a constant rate of change in the data displayed in a table, then the table represents a nonlinear nonproportional relationship.

A linear relationship represented by a table is a proportional relationship when the quotient of each pair of numbers is constant. Otherwise, the linear relationship is nonproportional.

EXAMPLE 3   🐻 **CA CC** 8.F.4

The values in the table represent the numbers of U.S. dollars three tourists traded for Mexican pesos. The relationship is linear. Is the relationship proportional or nonproportional?

U.S. Dollars Traded	Mexican Pesos Received
130	1,690
255	3,315
505	6,565

$$\frac{1,690}{130} = \frac{169}{13} = 13$$

$$\frac{3,315}{255} = \frac{221}{17} = 13$$

Simplify the ratios to compare the pesos received to the dollars traded.

$$\frac{6,565}{505} = \frac{1,313}{101} = 13$$

The ratio of pesos received to dollars traded is constant at 13 Mexican pesos per U.S. dollar. This is a proportional relationship.

Math Talk
Mathematical Practices

How could you confirm that the values in the table have a linear relationship?

YOUR TURN

Determine if the linear relationship represented by each table is a proportional or nonproportional relationship.

9.

x	y
2	30
8	90
14	150

10.

x	y
5	1
40	8
65	13

Personal Math Trainer

Online Practice and Help

⏱ my.hrw.com

Comparing Proportional and Nonproportional Situations

You can use what you have learned about proportional and nonproportional relationships to compare similar real-world situations that are given using different representations.

EXAMPLE 4   **CA CC** 8.F.2

A A laser tag league has the choice of two arenas for a tournament. In both cases, *x* is the number of hours and *y* is the total charge. Compare and contrast these two situations.

Arena A

$y = 225x$

Arena B

- **Arena A's** equation has the form $y = mx + b$, where $b = 0$. So, Arena A's charges are a proportional relationship. The hourly rate, $225, is greater than Arena B's, but there is no additional fee.

- **Arena B's** graph is a line that does not include the origin. So, Arena B's charges are a nonproportional relationship. Arena B has a $50 initial fee but its hourly rate, $200, is lower.

B Jessika is remodeling and has the choice of two painters. In both cases, *x* is the number of hours and *y* is the total charge. Compare and contrast these two situations.

Painter A

$y = \$45x$

Painter B

x	0	1	2	3
y	20	55	90	125

- **Painter A's** equation has the form $y = mx + b$, where $b = 0$. So, Painter A's charges are proportional. The hourly rate, $45, is greater than Painter B's, but there is no additional fee.

- **Painter B's** table is a nonproportional relationship because the ratio of *y* to *x* is not constant. Because the table contains the ordered pair (0, 20), Painter B charges an initial fee of $20, but the hourly rate, $35, is less than Painter A's.

My Notes

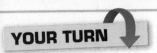
11. Compare and contrast the following two situations.

Test-Prep Center A	Test-Prep Center B
The cost for Test-Prep Center A is given by $c = 20h$, where c is the cost in dollars and h is the number of hours you attend.	Test-Prep Center B charges \$25 per hour to attend, but you have a \$100 coupon that you can use to reduce the cost.

_____

_____

_____

Personal
Math Trainer

Online Practice
and Help

my.hrw.com

Guided Practice

Determine if each relationship is a proportional or nonproportional situation. Explain your reasoning. (Example 1, Example 2, Example 4)

1.

Look at the origin.

_____

_____

2.

_____

_____

3. $q = 2p + \frac{1}{2}$

Compare the equation with $y = mx + b$.

_____

_____

_____

4. $v = \frac{1}{10}u$

_____

_____

_____

The tables represent linear relationships. Determine if each relationship is a proportional or nonproportional situation. (Example 3, Example 4)

5.

x	y
3	12
9	36
21	84

6.

x	y
22	4
46	8
58	10

Find the quotient of y and x.

_____   _____

_____   _____

_____   _____

7. The values in the table represent the numbers of households that watched three TV shows and the ratings of the shows. The relationship is linear. Describe the relationship in other ways. (Example 4)

Number of Households that Watched TV Show	TV Show Rating
15,000,000	12
20,000,000	16
25,000,000	20

_____

_____

_____

_____

_____

? ESSENTIAL QUESTION CHECK-IN

8. How are using graphs, equations, and tables similar when distinguishing between proportional and nonproportional situations?

_____

_____

_____

_____

4.4 Independent Practice

CA CC 8.F.2, 8.F.3, 8.F.4

Personal Math Trainer

Online Practice and Help

my.hrw.com

9. The graph shows the weight of a cross-country team's beverage cooler based on how much sports drink it contains.

Cooler Weight

a. Is the relationship proportional or nonproportional? Explain.

_____

_____

b. Identify and interpret the slope and the *y*-intercept.

_____

_____

In 10–11, tell if the relationship between a rider's height above the first floor and the time since the rider stepped on the elevator or escalator is proportional or nonproportional. Explain your reasoning.

height above floor

height above floor

10. The elevator paused for 10 seconds after you stepped on before beginning to rise at a constant rate of 8 feet per second.

_____

_____

_____

11. Your height in feet above the first floor on the escalator, *h*, is given by $h = 0.75t$, where *t* is the time in seconds.

_____

12. **Analyze Relationships** Compare and contrast the two graphs.

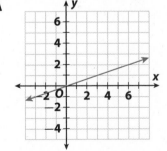

Graph A

$y = \frac{1}{3}x$

Graph B

$y = \sqrt{x}$

_____

_____

13. Represent Real-World Problems Describe a real-world situation where the relationship is linear and nonproportional.

_____

_____

Work Area

14. Mathematical Reasoning Suppose you know the slope of a linear relationship and one of the points that its graph passes through. How can you determine if the relationship is proportional or nonproportional?

_____

_____

_____

15. Multiple Representations An entrant at a science fair has included information about temperature conversion in various forms, as shown. The variables F, C, and K represent temperatures in degrees Fahrenheit, degrees Celsius, and kelvin, respectively.

Equation A $F = \frac{9}{5}C + 32$	Table C	
	Degrees Celsius	kelvin
	8	281.15
Equation B	15	288.15
$K = C + 273.15$	36	309.15

a. Is the relationship between kelvins and degrees Celsius proportional? Justify your answer in two different ways.

_____

_____

_____

_____

b. Is the relationship between degrees Celsius and degrees Fahrenheit proportional? Why or why not?

_____

_____

_____

_____

Ready to Go On?

4.1 Representing Linear Nonproportional Relationships

1. Complete the table using the equation $y = 3x + 2$.

x	−1	0	1	2	3
y					

4.2 Determining Slope and y-intercept

2. Find the slope and y-intercept of the line in the graph.

_____

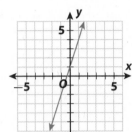

4.3 Graphing Linear Nonproportional Relationships

3. Graph the equation $y = 2x - 3$ using slope and y-intercept.

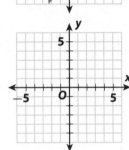

4.4 Proportional and Nonproportional Situations

4. Does the table represent a proportional or a nonproportional linear relationship?

x	1	2	3	4	5
y	4	8	12	16	20

_____

5. Does the graph in Exercise 2 represent a proportional or a nonproportional linear relationship?

_____

6. Does the graph in Exercise 3 represent a proportional or a nonproportional relationship?

_____

? ESSENTIAL QUESTION

7. How can you identify a linear nonproportional relationship from a table, a graph, and an equation?

_____

_____

MODULE 4
MIXED REVIEW

Assessment Readiness

CALIFORNIA

Personal Math Trainer

Online Practice and Help

my.hrw.com

1. Consider each table. Does the table represent a proportional relationship?

   Select Yes or No for tables A–C.

   A.

x	−4	−2	0	2	4
y	−10	−4	2	8	14

   ○ Yes   ○ No

   B.

x	4	8	12	16	20
y	3	6	9	12	15

   ○ Yes   ○ No

   C.

x	−3	−1	1	3	5
y	−12	−4	4	12	20

   ○ Yes   ○ No

2. The graph shows the relationship between the hours Leann works and the money she earns.

   Choose True or False for each statement.

   A. Slope = 8.   ○ True   ○ False
   B. Unit rate = $8/h.   ○ True   ○ False
   C. Equation is $y = \frac{x}{8}$ ○ True   ○ False

3. There is an initial fee to join a gym, plus a monthly charge. The table represents the linear relationship between the total cost of joining the gym and the number of months a person is a member. What is the *y*-intercept of the line, and what does it represent in this situation?

Time (months), *x*	Total Cost ($), *y*
1	125
2	155
3	185

4. The equation $y = 35x - 5$ gives *y* as the cost of *x* tickets to a theme park with a $5 coupon. After the park raises ticket prices by $3, what is the new equation? How are the graphs of the two equations different?

Writing Linear Equations

 ESSENTIAL QUESTION

How can you use linear equations to solve real-world problems?

Real-World Video

Linear equations can be used to describe many situations related to shopping. If a store advertised four books for $32.00, you could write and solve a linear equation to find the price of each book.

 my.hrw.com

GO DIGITAL

my.hrw.com

my.hrw.com

Go digital with your write-in student edition, accessible on any device.

Math On the Spot

Scan with your smart phone to jump directly to the online edition, video tutor, and more.

Animated Math

Interactively explore key concepts to see how math works.

Personal Math Trainer

Get immediate feedback and help as you work through practice sets.

Are YOU Ready?

Complete these exercises to review skills you will need for this module.

Personal Math Trainer

Online Practice and Help

my.hrw.com

Write Fractions as Decimals

EXAMPLE $\frac{0.5}{0.8} = ?$ Multiply the numerator and the denominator by a power of 10 so that the denominator is a whole number.

$\frac{0.5 \times 10}{0.8 \times 10} = \frac{5}{8}$

Write the fraction as a division problem. Write a decimal point and zeros in the dividend. Place a decimal point in the quotient. Divide as with whole numbers.

$$
\begin{array}{r}
0.625 \\
8\overline{)5.000} \\
-48 \\
\hline
20 \\
-16 \\
\hline
40 \\
-40 \\
\hline
0
\end{array}
$$

Write each fraction as a decimal.

1. $\frac{3}{8}$ _____

2. $\frac{0.3}{0.4}$ _____

3. $\frac{0.13}{0.2}$ _____

4. $\frac{0.39}{0.75}$ _____

Inverse Operations

EXAMPLE

$5n = 20$

$\frac{5n}{5} = \frac{20}{5}$

$n = 4$

n is multiplied by 5. To solve the equation, use the inverse operation, division.

$k + 7 = 9$

$k + 7 - 7 = 9 - 7$

$k = 2$

7 is added to k. To solve the equation, use the inverse operation, subtraction.

Solve each equation using the inverse operation.

5. $7p = 28$ _____

6. $h - 13 = 5$ _____

7. $\frac{y}{3} = -6$ _____

8. $b + 9 = 21$ _____

9. $c - 8 = -8$ _____

10. $3n = -12$ _____

11. $-16 = m + 7$ _____

12. $\frac{t}{-5} = -5$ _____

Reading Start-Up

Visualize Vocabulary

Use the ✔ words to complete the diagram. You can put more than one word in each bubble.

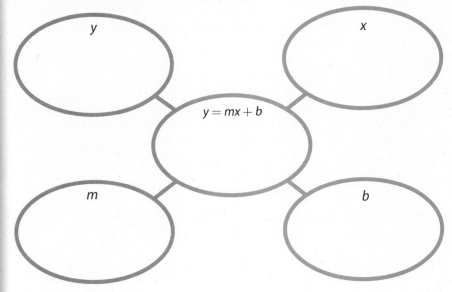

(y)

(x)

($y = mx + b$)

(m)

(b)

Understand Vocabulary

Complete the sentences using the preview words.

1. A set of data that is made up of two paired variables

   is _____.

2. When the rate of change varies from point to point, the relationship

   is a _____.

Active Reading

Tri-Fold Before beginning the module, create a tri-fold to help you learn the concepts and vocabulary in this module. Fold the paper into three sections. Label the columns "What I Know," "What I Need to Know," and "What I Learned." Complete the first two columns before you read. After studying the module, complete the third column.

CALIFORNIA

GETTING READY FOR
Writing Linear Equations
Understanding the standards and the vocabulary terms in the standards will help you know exactly what you are expected to learn in this module.

CA CC 8.F.4

Construct a function to model a linear relationship between two quantities. Determine the rate of change and initial value of the function from a description of a relationship or from two (x, y) values, including reading these from a table or from a graph. Interpret the rate of change and initial value of a linear function in terms of the situation it models, and in terms of its graph or a table of values.

Key Vocabulary

rate of change *(tasa de cambio)*
A ratio that compares the amount of change in a dependent variable to the amount of change in an independent variable.

What It Means to You

You will learn how to write an equation based on a situation that models a linear relationship.

EXAMPLE 8.F.4

In 2006 the fare for a taxicab was an initial charge of $2.50 plus $0.30 per mile. Write an equation in slope-intercept form that can be used to calculate the total fare.

The constant charge is $2.50.
The rate of change is $0.30 per mile.

The input variable, x, is the number of miles driven.
So $0.3x$ is the cost for the miles driven.

The equation for the total fare, y, is as follows:

$$y = 0.3x + 2.5$$

CA CC 8.SP.3

Use the equation of a linear model to solve problems in the context of bivariate measurement data, interpreting the slope and intercept.

Key Vocabulary

bivariate data *(datos bivariados)*
A set of data that is made up of two paired variables.

Visit **my.hrw.com** to see all **CA Common Core Standards** explained.

my.hrw.com

What It Means to You

You will see how to use a linear relationship between sets of data to make predictions.

EXAMPLE 8.SP.3

The graph shows the temperatures in degrees Celsius inside the earth at certain depths in kilometers. Use the graph to write an equation and find the temperature at a depth of 12 km.

The initial temperature is 20°C.
It increases at a rate of 10°C/km.

The equation is $t = 10d + 20$.
At a depth of 12 km, the temperature is 140°C.

Temperature Inside Earth

Writing Linear Equations from Situations and Graphs

 CA CC 8.F.4

Construct a function to model a linear relationship between two quantities. Determine the rate of change and initial value.... Interpret the rate of change and initial value.... (For the full text of the standard, see the table at the front of the book beginning on page CA2.)

ESSENTIAL QUESTION

How do you write an equation to model a linear relationship given a graph or a description?

EXPLORE ACTIVITY   CA CC 8.F.4

Writing an Equation in Slope-Intercept Form

Greta makes clay mugs and bowls as gifts at the Crafty Studio. She pays a membership fee of $15 a month and an equipment fee of $3.00 an hour to use the potter's wheel, table, and kiln. Write an equation in the form $y = mx + b$ that Greta can use to calculate her monthly costs.

A What is the independent variable, x, for this situation?

_____

What is the dependent variable, y, for this situation?

_____

B During April, Greta does not use the equipment at all.

What will be her number of hours (x) for April? _____

What will be her cost (y) for April? _____

What will be the y-intercept, b, in the equation? _____

Math Talk
Mathematical Practices

What change could the studio make that would make a difference to the y-intercept of the equation?

C Greta spends 8 hours in May for a cost of $15 + 8($3) = _____.

In June, she spends 11 hours for a cost of _____.

From May to June, the change in x-values is _____.

From May to June, the change in y-values is _____.

What will be the slope, m, in the equation? _____.

D Use the values for m and b to write an equation for Greta's costs in the form $y = mx + b$: _____

Writing an Equation from a Graph

You can use information presented in a graph to write an equation in slope-intercept form.

EXAMPLE 1

CA CC 8.F.4

A video club charges a one-time membership fee plus a rental fee for each DVD borrowed. Use the graph to write an equation in slope-intercept form to represent the amount spent, y, on x DVD rentals.

Video Club Costs

STEP 1 Choose two points on the graph, (x_1, y_1) and (x_2, y_2), to find the slope.

$m = \dfrac{y_2 - y_1}{x_2 - x_1}$ *Find the change in y-values over the change in x-values.*

$m = \dfrac{18 - 8}{8 - 0}$ *Substitute $(0, 8)$ for (x_1, y_1) and $(8, 18)$ for (x_2, y_2).*

$m = \dfrac{10}{8} = 1.25$ *Simplify.*

STEP 2 Read the y-intercept from the graph.

The y-intercept is 8.

STEP 3 Use your slope and y-intercept values to write an equation in slope-intercept form.

$y = mx + b$ *Slope-intercept form*

$y = 1.25x + 8$ *Substitute 1.25 for m and 8 for y.*

Reflect

1. What does the value of the slope represent in this context?

_____

2. Describe the meaning of the y-intercept.

_____

YOUR TURN

3. The cash register subtracts $2.50 from a $25 Coffee Café gift card for every medium coffee the customer buys. Use the graph to write an equation in slope-intercept form to represent this situation.

_____

Amount on Gift Card

Writing an Equation from a Description

You can use information from a description of a linear relationship to find the slope and y-intercept and to write an equation.

ⓞ my.hrw.com

EXAMPLE 2 Real World 🐻 **CA CC** 8.F.4

The rent charged for space in an office building is a linear relationship related to the size of the space rented. Write an equation in slope-intercept form for the rent at West Main Street Office Rentals.

West Main St. Office Rentals 🏢
Offices for rent at convenient locations.

Monthly Rates:
600 square feet for **$750**
900 square feet for **$1150**

My Notes

STEP 1 Identify the independent and dependent variables.

The independent variable is the square footage of floor space.

The dependent variable is the monthly rent.

STEP 2 Write the information given in the problem as ordered pairs.

The rent for 600 square feet of floor space is $750: (600, 750)

The rent for 900 square feet of floor space is $1150: (900, 1150)

STEP 3 Find the slope.

$$m = \frac{y_2 - y_1}{x_2 - x_1} = \frac{1150 - 750}{900 - 600} = \frac{400}{300} = \frac{4}{3}$$

STEP 4 Find the y-intercept. Use the slope and one of the ordered pairs.

$y = mx + b$ Slope-intercept form

$750 = \frac{4}{3} \cdot 600 + b$ Substitute for y, m, and x.

$750 = 800 + b$ Multiply.

$-50 = b$ Subtract 800 from both sides.

STEP 5 Substitute the slope and y-intercept.

$y = mx + b$ Slope-intercept form

$y = \frac{4}{3}x - 50$ Substitute $\frac{4}{3}$ for m and -50 for b.

Reflect

4. Without graphing, tell whether the graph of this equation rises or falls from left to right. What does the sign of the slope mean in this context?

_____

_____

_____

YOUR TURN

5. Hari's weekly allowance varies depending on the number of chores he does. He received $16 in allowance the week he did 12 chores, and $14 in allowance the week he did 8 chores. Write an equation for his allowance in slope-intercept form. _____

Guided Practice

1. Li is making beaded necklaces. For each necklace, she uses 27 spacer beads, plus 5 glass beads per inch of necklace length. Write an equation to find how many beads Li needs for each necklace. (Explore Activity)

   a. independent variable: _____

   b. dependent variable: _____

   c. equation: _____

2. Kate is planning a trip to the beach. She estimates her average speed to graph her expected progress on the trip. Write an equation in slope-intercept form that represents the situation. (Example 1)

Choose two points on the graph to find the slope.

$m = \dfrac{y_2 - y_1}{x_2 - x_1} =$ _____

Read the y-intercept from the graph: $b =$ _____

Use your slope and y-intercept values to write an equation in slope-intercept form. _____

My Beach Trip

Distance to beach (mi) — 300, 200, 100

Driving time (h) — 1 2 3 4 5 6

3. At 59 °F, crickets chirp at a rate of 76 times per minute, and at 65 °F, they chirp 100 times per minute. Write an equation in slope-intercept form that represents the situation. (Example 2)

Independent variable: _____ Dependent variable: _____

$m = \dfrac{y_2 - y_1}{x_2 - x_1} =$ _____ Use the slope and one of the ordered

pairs in $y = mx + b$ to find b. _____ = _____ · _____ + b; _____ = b

Write an equation in slope-intercept form. _____

? ESSENTIAL QUESTION CHECK-IN

4. Explain what m and b in the equation $y = mx + b$ tell you about the graph of the line with that equation.

_____

5.1 Independent Practice

Personal Math Trainer

Online Practice and Help

my.hrw.com

CA CC 8.F.4

5. A dragonfly can beat its wings 30 times per second. Write an equation in slope-intercept form that shows the relationship between flying time in seconds and the number of times the dragonfly beats its wings.

_____

6. A balloon is released from the top of a platform that is 50 meters tall. The balloon rises at the rate of 4 meters per second. Write an equation in slope-intercept form that tells the height of the balloon above the ground after a given number of seconds.

_____

The graph shows a scuba diver's ascent over time.

7. Use the graph to find the slope of the line. Tell what the slope means in this context.

_____

_____

8. Identify the *y*-intercept. Tell what the *y*-intercept means in this context.

_____

Scuba Diver's Ascent

9. Write an equation in slope-intercept form that represents the diver's depth over time.

_____

10. The formula for converting Celsius temperatures to Fahrenheit temperatures is a linear equation. Water freezes at 0 °C, or 32 °F, and it boils at 100 °C, or 212 °F. Find the slope and *y*-intercept for a graph that gives degrees Celsius on the horizontal axis and degrees Fahrenheit on the vertical axis. Then write an equation in slope-intercept form that converts degrees Celsius into degrees Fahrenheit.

_____

_____

11. The cost of renting a sailboat at a lake is $20 per hour plus $12 for lifejackets. Write an equation in slope-intercept form that can be used to calculate the total amount you would pay for using this sailboat.

_____

The graph shows the activity in a savings account.

Savings Account Activity

12. What was the amount of the initial deposit that started this savings account?

_____

13. Find the slope and *y*-intercept of the graphed line.

_____

14. Write an equation in slope-intercept form for the activity in this savings account.

_____

15. Explain the meaning of the slope in this graph.

_____

_____

 FOCUS ON HIGHER ORDER THINKING

Work Area

16. Communicate Mathematical Ideas Explain how you decide which part of a problem will be represented by the variable *x*, and which part will be represented by the variable *y* in a graph of the situation.

_____

_____

_____

_____

17. Represent Real-World Problems Describe what would be true about the rate of change in a situation that could *not* be represented by a graphed line and an equation in the form $y = mx + b$.

_____

_____

_____

18. Draw Conclusions Must *m*, in the equation $y = mx + b$, always be a positive number? Explain.

_____

_____

_____

Writing Linear Equations from a Table

 CA CC 8.F.4

Construct a function to model a linear relationship between two quantities. Determine the rate of change and initial value of the function from a description of a relationship or from two (x, y) values, including reading these from a table or from a graph. Interpret the rate of change and initial value of a linear function in terms of the situation it models, and in terms of its graph or a table of values.

ESSENTIAL QUESTION

How do you write an equation to model a linear relationship given a table?

Graphing from a Table to Write an Equation

You can use information from a table to draw a graph of a linear relationship and to write an equation for the graphed line.

Math On the Spot
my.hrw.com

EXAMPLE 1   CA CC 8.F.4

The table shows the temperature of a fish tank during an experiment. Graph the data, and find the slope and y-intercept from the graph. Then write the equation for the graph in slope-intercept form.

Time (h)	0	1	2	3	4	5
Temperature (°F)	82	80	78	76	74	72

STEP 1 Graph the ordered pairs from the table (time, temperature).

STEP 2 Draw a line through the points.

STEP 3 Choose two points on the graph to find the slope: for example, choose $(0, 82)$ and $(1, 80)$.

Tank Temperature

$m = \dfrac{y_2 - y_1}{x_2 - x_1}$ Use the slope formula.

$m = \dfrac{80 - 82}{1 - 0}$ Substitute $(0, 82)$ for (x_1, y_1) and $(1, 80)$ for (x_2, y_2).

$m = \dfrac{-2}{1} = -2$ Simplify.

STEP 4 Read the y-intercept from the table or graph.

$b = 82$ The y-intercept is the value when time is 0.

STEP 5 Use these slope and y-intercept values to write an equation in slope-intercept form.

$y = mx + b$
$y = -2x + 82$

Math Talk
Mathematical Practices

Which variable in the equation $y = mx + b$ shows the initial temperature of the fish tank at the beginning of the experiment?

YOUR TURN

1. The table shows the volume of water released by Hoover Dam over a certain period of time. Graph the data, and find the slope and *y*-intercept from the graph. Then write the equation for the graph in slope-intercept form.

Water Released from Hoover Dam

Water Released from Hoover Dam	
Time (s)	Volume of water (m³)
5	75,000
10	150,000
15	225,000
20	300,000

Math Talk

Mathematical Practices

Which variable in the equation $y = mx + b$ tells you the volume of water released every second from Hoover Dam?

Writing an Equation from a Table

The information from a table can also help you to write the equation that represents a given situation without drawing the graph.

EXAMPLE 2 CA CC 8.F.4

Elizabeth's cell phone plan lets her choose how many minutes are included each month. The table shows the plan's monthly cost *y* for a given number of included minutes *x*. Write an equation in slope-intercept form to represent the situation.

Minutes included, x	100	200	300	400	500
Cost of plan ($), y	14	20	26	32	38

STEP 1 Notice that the change in cost is the same for each increase of 100 minutes. So, the relationship is linear. Choose any two ordered pairs from the table to find the slope.

$$m = \frac{\text{change in } y}{\text{change in } x} = \frac{(20 - 14)}{(200 - 100)} = \frac{6}{100} = 0.06$$

STEP 2 Find the *y*-intercept. Use the slope and any point from the table.

$y = mx + b$ Slope-intercept form

$14 = 0.06 \cdot 100 + b$ Substitute for *y*, *m*, and *x*.

$14 = 6 + b$ Multiply.

$8 = b$ Subtract 6 from both sides.

STEP 3 Substitute the slope and *y*-intercept.

$y = mx + b$ Slope-intercept form

$y = 0.06x + 8$ Substitute 0.06 for *m* and 8 for *b*.

Reflect

2. What is the base price for the cell phone plan, regardless of how many minutes are included? What is the cost per minute? Explain.

_____

_____

_____

_____

_____

3. What If? Elizabeth's cell phone company changes the cost of her plan as shown below. Write an equation in slope-intercept form to represent the situation. How did the plan change?

Minutes included, x	100	200	300	400	500
Cost of plan ($), y	30	35	40	45	50

_____

_____

Math Talk
Mathematical Practices

Explain the meaning of the slope and y-intercept of the equation.

YOUR TURN

4. A salesperson receives a weekly salary plus a commission for each computer sold. The table shows the total pay, *p*, and the number of computers sold, *n*. Write an equation in slope-intercept form to represent this situation.

Number of computers sold, n	4	6	8	10	12
Total pay ($), p	550	700	850	1000	1150

_____

5. To rent a van, a moving company charges $40.00 plus $0.50 per mile. The table shows the total cost, *c*, and the number of miles driven, *d*. Write an equation in slope-intercept form to represent this situation.

Number of miles driven, d	10	20	30	40	50
Total cost ($), c	45	50	55	60	65

_____

Personal Math Trainer

Online Practice and Help

my.hrw.com

1. Jaime purchased a $20 bus pass. Each time he rides the bus, a certain amount is deducted from the pass. The table shows the amount, *y*, left on his pass after *x* rides. Graph the data, and find the slope and *y*-intercept from the graph or from the table. Then write the equation for the graph in slope-intercept form. (Example 1)

Number of rides, *x*	0	4	8	12	16
Amount left on pass ($), *y*	20	15	10	5	0

Bus Pass Balance

Amount left on pass ($)

20
16
12
8
4

O 4 8 12 16 20

Number of rides

_____

The table shows the temperature (*y*) at different altitudes (*x*). This is a linear relationship. (Example 2)

Altitude (ft), *x*	0	2,000	4,000	6,000	8,000	10,000	12,000
Temperature (°F), *y*	59	51	43	35	27	19	11

2. Find the slope for this relationship.

_____

3. Find the *y*-intercept by use of the table.

_____

4. Write an equation in slope-intercept form that represents this relationship.

_____

5. Use your equation to determine the temperature at an altitude of 5000 feet.

_____

? ESSENTIAL QUESTION CHECK-IN

6. Describe how you can use the information in a table showing a linear relationship to find the slope and *y*-intercept for the equation.

_____

_____

_____

5.2 Independent Practice

 CA CC 8.F.4

Personal Math Trainer
Online Practice and Help
my.hrw.com

7. The table shows the costs of a large cheese pizza with toppings at a local pizzeria. Graph the data, and find the slope and y-intercept from the graph. Then write the equation for the graph in slope-intercept form.

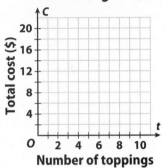

Cost of Large Pizza

Number of toppings, t	0	1	2	3	4	5
Total cost, C	8	10	12	14	16	18

_____

8. The table shows how much an air-conditioning repair company charges for different numbers of hours of work. Graph the data, and find the slope and y-intercept from the graph. Then write the equation for the graph in slope-intercept form.

Number of hours, t	0	1	2	3	4	5
Amount charged, A	50	100	150	200	250	300

_____

9. A friend gave Ms. Morris a gift card for a local car wash. The table shows the linear relationship of how the value left on the card relates to the number of car washes.

Number of car washes, x	0	8	12
Amount left on card ($), y	30	18	12

a. Write an equation that shows the number of dollars left on the card.

_____

b. Explain the meaning of the negative slope in this situation.

_____

_____

c. What is the maximum value of x that makes sense in this context? Explain.

_____

The tables show linear relationships between x and y. Write an equation in slope-intercept form for each relationship.

10.

x	−2	−1	0	2
y	−1	0	1	3

11.

x	−4	1	0	6
y	14	4	6	−6

_____ _____

12. Finance Desiree starts a savings account with $125.00. Every month, she deposits $53.50.

   a. Complete the table to model the situation.

Month, x					
Amount in Savings ($), y					

   b. Write an equation in slope-intercept form that shows how much money Desiree has in her savings account after x months.

      _____

   c. Use the equation to find how much money Desiree will have in savings after 11 months.

      _____

13. Monty documented the amount of rain his farm received on a monthly basis, as shown in the table.

Month, x	1	2	3	4	5
Rainfall (in.), y	5	3	4.5	1	7

   a. Is the relationship linear? Why or why not?

      _____

      _____

   b. Can an equation be written to describe the amount of rain? Explain.

      _____

 FOCUS ON HIGHER ORDER THINKING

Work Area

14. Analyze Relationships If you have a table that shows a linear relationship, when can you read the value for b, in $y = mx + b$, directly from the table without drawing a graph or doing any calculations? Explain.

_____

_____

15. What If? Jaíme graphed linear data given in the form (cost, number). The y-intercept was 0. Jayla graphed the same data given in the form (number, cost). What was the y-intercept of her graph? Explain.

_____

_____

_____

Linear Relationships and Bivariate Data

CA CC 8.SP.1

Construct and interpret scatter plots for bivariate measurement data to investigate patterns of association between two quantities. Describe patterns such as clustering, outliers, positive or negative association, linear association, and nonlinear association. *Also 8.SP.2, 8.SP.3*

ESSENTIAL QUESTION

How can you contrast linear and nonlinear sets of bivariate data?

Math On the Spot
my.hrw.com

Finding the Equation of a Linear Relationship

You can use the points on a graph of a linear relationship to write an equation for the relationship. The equation of a linear relationship is $y = mx + b$, where m is the rate of change, or slope, and b is the value of y when x is 0.

EXAMPLE 1

CA CC 8.SP.2

A handrail runs alongside a stairway. As the horizontal distance from the bottom of the stairway changes, the height of the handrail changes. Show that the relationship is linear, and then find the equation for the relationship.

STEP 1 Show that the relationship is linear.

All of the points (5, 7), (10, 11), (15, 15), (20, 19), and (25, 23) lie on the same line, so the relationship is linear.

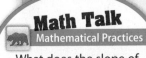

Math Talk
Mathematical Practices

What does the slope of the equation represent in this situation? What does the *y*-intercept represent?

STEP 2 Write the equation of the linear relationship.

Choose two points to find the slope.

(5, 7) and (25, 23)

$$m = \frac{23 - 7}{25 - 5}$$

$$= \frac{16}{20}$$

$$= 0.8$$

Choose a point and use the slope to substitute values for *x*, *y*, and *m*.

$$y = mx + b$$

$$7 = 0.8(5) + b$$

$$7 = 4 + b$$

$$3 = b$$

The equation of the linear relationship is $y = 0.8x + 3$.

YOUR TURN

Find the equation of each linear relationship.

1.

2.

Hours (x)	Number of units (y)
2	480
15	3,600
24	5,760
30	7,200
48	11,520
55	13,200

Making Predictions

You can use an equation of a linear relationship to predict a value between data points that you already know.

EXAMPLE 2 Real World

CA CC 8.SP.3

The graph shows the cost for taxi rides of different distances. Predict the cost of a taxi ride that covers a distance of 6.5 miles.

Taxi Costs

STEP 1 Write the equation of the linear relationship.

(2, 7) and (6, 15) → Select two points.

$m = \dfrac{15 - 7}{6 - 2}$ → Calculate the rate of change.

$= \dfrac{8}{4}$ → Simplify.

$= 2$

$y = mx + b$

$15 = 2(6) + b$ → Fill in values for x, y, and m.

$15 = 12 + b$ → Simplify.

$3 = b$ → Solve for b.

The equation of the linear relationship is $y = 2x + 3$.

You can check your equation using another point on the graph. Try (8, 19). Substituting gives $19 = 2(8) + 3$. The right side simplifies to 19, so $19 = 19$. ✓

STEP 2 Use your equation from Step 1 to predict the cost of a 6.5-mile taxi ride.

$y = 2x + 3$

$y = 2(6.5) + 3$ Substitute $x = 6.5$.

$y = 16$ Solve for y.

A taxi ride that covers a distance of 6.5 miles will cost $16.

Reflect

3. **What If?** Suppose a regulation changes the cost of the taxi ride to $1.80 per mile, plus a fee of $4.30. How does the price of the 6.5 mile ride compare to the original price?

_____

_____

4. How can you use a graph of a linear relationship to predict an unknown value of y for a given value of x within the region of the graph?

_____

_____

_____

5. How can you use a table of linear data to predict a value?

_____

_____

_____

My Notes

YOUR TURN

Paulina's income from a job that pays her a fixed amount per hour is shown in the graph. Use the graph to find the predicted value.

Paulina's Pay

6. Income earned for working 2 hours

_____

7. Income earned for working 3.25 hours

_____

8. Total income earned for working for five 8-hour days all at the standard rate _____

Personal Math Trainer

Online Practice and Help

 my.hrw.com

Contrasting Linear and Nonlinear Data

Bivariate data is a set of data that is made up of two paired variables. If the relationship between the variables is linear, then the rate of change (slope) is constant. If the graph shows a **nonlinear relationship**, then the rate of change varies between pairs of points.

Andrew has two options in which to invest $200. Option A earns simple interest of 5%, while Option B earns interest of 5% compounded annually. The table shows the amount of the investment for both options over 20 years. Graph the data and describe the differences between the two graphs.

	Option A	Option B
Year, x	Total ($)	Total ($)
0	200.00	200.00
5	250.00	255.26
10	300.00	325.78
15	350.00	415.79
20	400.00	530.66

STEP 1 Graph the data from the table for Options A and B on the same coordinate grid.

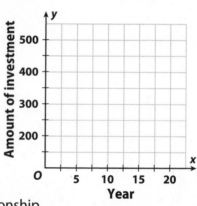

STEP 2 Find the rate of change between pairs of points for Option A and classify the relationship.

Option A	Rate of Change
(0, 200) and (5, 250)	$m = \dfrac{250 - 200}{5 - 0} =$
(5, 250) and (10, 300)	
(10, 300) and (15, 350)	

The rate of change between the data values is _____,

so the graph of Option A shows a _____ relationship.

Find the rate of change between pairs of points for Option B and classify the relationship.

Option B	Rate of Change
(0, 200) and (5, 255.26)	$m = \frac{252.26 - 200}{5 - 0} \approx$
(5, 255.26) and (10, 325.78)	
(10, 325.78) and (15, 415.79)	

The rate of change between the data values is _____,

so the graph of Option B shows a _____ relationship.

Reflect

9. Why are the graphs drawn as lines or curves and not discrete points?

_____

_____

_____

_____

10. Can you determine by viewing the graph if the data have a linear or nonlinear relationship? Explain.

_____

_____

_____

_____

11. **Draw Conclusions** Find the differences in the account balances to the nearest dollar at 5 year intervals for Option B. How does the length of time that money is in an account affect the advantage that compound interest has over simple interest?

_____

_____

_____

Use the following graphs to find the equation of the linear relationship. (Example 1)

1.

_____

2.

_____

3. The graph shows the relationship between the number of hours a kayak is rented and the total cost of the rental. Write an equation of the relationship. Then use the equation to predict the cost of a rental that lasts 5.5 hours. (Example 2)

_____

Does each of the following graphs represent a linear relationship? Why or why not? (Explore Activity)

4.

_____

_____

5.

_____

_____

6. How can you tell if a set of bivariate data shows a linear relationship?

_____

_____

5.3 Independent Practice

 CA CC 8.SP.1, 8.SP.2, 8.SP.3

Personal Math Trainer

Online Practice and Help

my.hrw.com

Does each of the following tables represent a linear relationship? Why or why not?

7.

Number of boxes	Weight (kg)
3	15
9	45
21	105

8.

Day	Height (cm)
5	30
8	76.8
14	235.2

_____

_____

Explain whether or not you think each relationship is linear.

9. the cost of equal-priced DVDs and the number purchased

_____

10. the height of a person and the person's age

_____

11. the area of a square quilt and its side length

_____

_____

12. the number of miles to the next service station and the number of kilometers

_____

_____

13. Multistep The Mars Rover travels 0.75 feet in 6 seconds. Add the point to the graph. Then determine whether the relationship between distance and time is linear, and if so, predict the distance that the Mars Rover would travel in 1 minute.

_____

_____

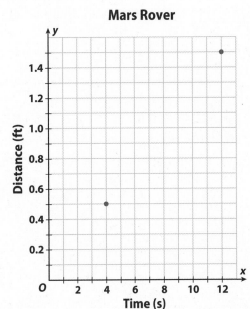

14. Make a Conjecture Zefram analyzed a linear relationship, found that the slope-intercept equation was $y = 3.5x + 16$, and made a prediction for the value of y for a given value of x. He realized that he made an error calculating the y-intercept and that it was actually 12. Can he just subtract 4 from his prediction if he knows that the slope is correct? Explain.

_____

_____

 FOCUS ON HIGHER ORDER THINKING

15. Communicate Mathematical Ideas The table shows a linear relationship. How can you predict the value of y when $x = 6$ without finding the equation of the relationship?

x	y
4	38
8	76
12	114

_____

_____

_____

16. Critique Reasoning Louis says that if the differences between the values of x are constant between all the points on a graph, then the relationship is linear. Do you agree? Explain.

_____

_____

_____

17. Make a Conjecture Suppose you know the slope of a linear relationship and one of the points that its graph passes through. How could you predict another point that falls on the graph of the line?

_____

_____

_____

18. Explain the Error Thomas used (7, 17.5) and (18, 45) from a graph to find the equation of a linear relationship as shown. What was his mistake?

$$m = \frac{45 - 7}{18 - 17.5} = \frac{38}{0.5} = 76$$

$$y = 76x + b$$

$$45 = 76 \cdot 18 + b$$

$$45 = 1368 + b, \text{ so } b = -1323$$

The equation is $y = 76x - 1323$.

_____

Ready to Go On?

Personal Math Trainer

Online Practice and Help

my.hrw.com

5.1 Writing Linear Equations from Situations and Graphs

Write the equation of each line in slope-intercept form.

1.

_____

2.

_____

5.2 Writing Linear Equations from a Table

Write the equation of each linear relationship in slope-intercept form.

3.

x	0	100	200	300
y	1.5	36.5	71.5	106.5

_____

4.

x	25	35	45	55
y	94	88	82	76

_____

5.3 Linear Relationships and Bivariate Data

Write the equation of the line that connects each set of data points.

5.

_____

6.

_____

? ESSENTIAL QUESTION

7. Write a real-world situation that can be represented by a linear relationship.

_____

_____

MODULE 5
MIXED REVIEW

CALIFORNIA

Assessment Readiness

Personal Math Trainer

Online Practice and Help

my.hrw.com

1. Renting a paddle board costs $12 per hour plus a $3 charge for a life jacket.

   Which model(s) below could represent this situation, where *y* is the cost in dollars of renting a paddle board for *x* hours? Select all that apply.

   ○ $y = 3x + 12$

   ○ a line through the points (1, 12) and (3, 15)

   ○ a line with a slope of 12 and a *y*-intercept of 3

   ○
x	0.5	1	1.5
y	9	15	21

2. A ferry leaves a city and travels to an island. The distance the ferry has left to travel is modeled by the linear equation $y = 12 - 0.2x$, where *y* is the distance in miles and *x* is the time in minutes since the ferry left the city.

   Choose True or False for each statement.

   A. The relationship is nonproportional.   ○ True   ○ False

   B. The slope of the line is 0.2.   ○ True   ○ False

   C. The island is 12 miles from the city.   ○ True   ○ False

3. The graph shows the relationship between the time it started raining and the amount of rain that has fallen. Show that the relationship is linear, and then find the equation for the relationship.

4. Alma charges $97 for a job that takes 2 hours and $187 for a job that takes 4 hours. Write an equation in slope-intercept form that gives the charge *y* in dollars for a job that takes *x* hours. Explain how you solved this problem.

Functions

? ESSENTIAL QUESTION

How can you use functions to solve real-world problems?

Real-World Video

Computerized machines can assist doctors in surgeries such as laser vision correction. Each action the surgeon takes results in one end action by the machine. In math, functions also have a one-in-one-out relationship.

my.hrw.com

GO DIGITAL

my.hrw.com

my.hrw.com

Go digital with your write-in student edition, accessible on any device.

Math On the Spot

Scan with your smart phone to jump directly to the online edition, video tutor, and more.

Animated Math

Interactively explore key concepts to see how math works.

Personal Math Trainer

Get immediate feedback and help as you work through practice sets.

Are YOU Ready?

Complete these exercises to review skills you will need for this module.

Evaluate Expressions

Personal
Math Trainer

Online Practice
and Help

my.hrw.com

EXAMPLE   Evaluate $3x - 5$ for $x = -2$.

$3x - 5 = 3(-2) - 5$ *Substitute the given value of x for x.*

$ = -6 - 5$ *Multiply.*

$ = -11$ *Subtract.*

Evaluate each expression for the given value of x.

1. $2x + 3$ for $x = 3$ _____

2. $-4x + 7$ for $x = -1$ _____

3. $1.5x - 2.5$ for $x = 3$ _____

4. $0.4x + 6.1$ for $x = -5$ _____

5. $\frac{2}{3}x - 12$ for $x = 18$ _____

6. $-\frac{5}{8}x + 10$ for $x = -8$ _____

Connect Words and Equations

EXAMPLE   Erik's earnings equal 9 dollars per hour.

e = earnings; h = hours
multiplication

$e = 9 \times h$

Define the variables used in the situation.

Identify the operation involved. "Per" indicates multiplication.

Write the equation.

Define the variables for each situation. Then write an equation.

7. Jana's age plus 5 equals her sister's age.

_____

8. Andrew's class has 3 more students than Lauren's class.

_____

9. The bank is 50 feet shorter than the firehouse.

_____

10. The pencils were divided into 6 groups of 2.

_____

Reading Start-Up

Visualize Vocabulary

Use the ✔ words to complete the diagram. You can put more than one word in each section of the diagram.

(2, 6)	$y = mx + b$
Reviewing Relationships	
m	b

Understand Vocabulary

Complete the sentences using the preview words.

1. A rule that assigns exactly one output to each input

is a _____.

2. The value that is put into a function is the _____.

3. The result after applying the function machine's rule is

the _____.

Vocabulary

Review Words
✔ bivariate data (datos bivariados)
✔ linear equation (ecuación lineal)
   nonlinear relationship (relación no lineal)
✔ ordered pair (par ordenado)
   proporational relationship (relación proporcional)
✔ slope (pendiente)
✔ x-coordinate (coordenada x)
✔ y-coordinate (coordenada y)
✔ y-intercept (intersección con el eje y)

Preview Words
   function (función)
   input (valor de entrada)
   linear function (función lineal)
   output (valor de salida)

Active Reading

Double-Door Fold Create a double-door fold to help you understand the concepts in this module. Label one flap "Proportional Functions" and the other flap "Non-proportional Functions." As you study each lesson, write important ideas under the appropriate flap. Include any sample problems that will help you remember the concepts when you look back at your notes.

Functions

Understanding the standards and the vocabulary terms in the standards will help you know exactly what you are expected to learn in this module.

CA CC 8.F.1

Understand that a function is a rule that assigns to each input exactly one output. The graph of a function is the set of ordered pairs consisting of an input and the corresponding output.

Key Vocabulary

function *(función)*
An input-output relationship that has exactly one output for each input.

What It Means to You

You will identify sets of ordered pairs that are functions. A function is a rule that assigns exactly one output to each input.

EXAMPLE 8.F.1

Does the following table of inputs and outputs represent a function?

Yes, it is a function because each number in the input column is assigned to only one number in the output column.

Input	Output
14	110
20	130
22	120
30	110

CA CC 8.F.2

Compare properties of two functions each represented in a different way (algebraically, graphically, numerically in tables, or by verbal descriptions).

What It Means to You

You will learn to identify and compare functions expressed as equations and tables.

EXAMPLE 8.F.2

A spider descends a 20-foot drainpipe at a rate of 2.5 feet per minute. Another spider descends a drainpipe as shown in the table. Find and compare the rates of change and initial values of the linear functions in terms of the situations they model.

Spider #1: $f(x) = -2.5x + 20$

Spider #2:

Time (min)	0	1	2
Height (ft)	32	29	26

For Spider #1, the rate of change is −2.5, and the initial value is 20. For Spider #2, the rate of change is −3, and the initial value is 32.

Spider #2 started at 32 feet, which is 12 feet higher than Spider #1. Spider #1 is descending at 2.5 feet per minute, which is 0.5 foot per minute slower than Spider #2.

Visit **my.hrw.com** to see all **CA Common Core Standards** explained.

my.hrw.com

Identifying and Representing Functions

CA CC 8.F.1

Understand that a function is a rule that assigns to each input exactly one output. The graph of a function is the set of ordered pairs consisting of an input and the corresponding output.

ESSENTIAL QUESTION

How can you identify and represent functions?

EXPLORE ACTIVITY CA CC 8.F.1

Understanding Relationships

Carlos needs to buy some new pencils from the school supply store at his school. Carlos asks his classmates if they know how much pencils cost. Angela says she bought 2 pencils for $0.50. Paige bought 3 pencils for $0.75, and Spencer bought 4 pencils for $1.00.

Carlos thinks about the rule for the price of a pencil as a machine. When he puts the number of pencils he wants to buy into the machine, the machine applies a rule and tells him the total cost of that number of pencils.

Input   **Output**

	Number of Pencils	Rule	Total Cost
i.	2	?	
ii.	3	?	
iii.	4	?	
iv.	x		
v.	12		

A Use the prices in the problem to fill in total cost in rows **i–iii** of the table.

B Describe any patterns you see. Use your pattern to determine the cost of 1 pencil.

_____

_____

_____

C Use the pattern you identified to write the rule applied by the machine. Write the rule as an algebraic expression and fill in rule column row **iv** of the table.

D Carlos wants to buy 12 pencils. Use your rule to fill in row **v** of the table to show how much Carlos will pay for 12 pencils.

Reflect

1. How did you decide what operation to use in your rule?

_____

_____

2. **What If?** Carlos decides to buy erasers in a package. There are 6 pencil-top erasers in 2 packages of erasers.

    a. Write a rule in words for the number of erasers Carlos gets when he buys x packages. Then write the rule as an algebraic expression.

_____

_____

    b. How many packages does Carlos need to buy to get 18 erasers?

_____

Math On the Spot

my.hrw.com

Identifying Functions from Mapping Diagrams

A **function** assigns exactly one output to each input. The value that is put into a function is the **input**. The result is the **output**.

A mapping diagram can be used to represent a relationship between input values and output values. A mapping diagram represents a function if each input value is paired with only one output value.

EXAMPLE 1

 CA CC 8.F.1

Determine whether each relationship is a function.

A

Input	Output
1	2
3	6
7	8

Since each input value is paired with only one output value, the relationship is a function.

Determine whether each relationship is a function.

B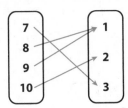

Since 2 is paired with more than one output value (both 4 and 5), the relationship is not a function.

Reflect

3. Is it possible for a function to have more than one input value but only one output value? Provide an illustration to support your answer.

_____

Determine whether each relationship is a function. Explain.

4.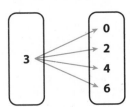

_____

_____

_____

5.

_____

_____

_____

Personal Math Trainer

Online Practice and Help

⏻ my.hrw.com

Math Talk
Mathematical Practices

What is always true about a mapping diagram that represents a function?

Identifying Functions from Tables

Relationships between input values and output values can also be represented using tables. The values in the first column are the input values. The values in the second column are the output values. The relationship represents a function if each input value is paired with only one output value.

Math On the Spot

⏻ my.hrw.com

EXAMPLE 2 CA CC 8.F.1

Determine whether each relationship is a function.

A

Input	Output
5	7
10	6
15	15
20	2
25	15

Since 15 is a repeated output value, one output value is paired with two input values. If this occurs in a relationship, the relationship can still be a function.

Since each input value is paired with only one output value, the relationship is a function.

Determine whether each relationship is a function.

B

Input	Output
1	10
5	8
4	6
1	4
7	2

> Since 1 is a repeated input value, one input value is paired with two output values. Look back at the rule for functions. Is this relationship a function?

Since the input value 1 is paired with more than one output value (both 10 and 4), the relationship is not a function.

Reflect

6. What is always true about the numbers in the first column of a table that represents a function? Why must this be true?

_____

_____

_____

_____

_____

YOUR TURN

Determine whether each relationship is a function. Explain.

7.

Input	Output
53	53
24	24
32	32
17	17
45	45

8.

Input	Output
14	52
8	21
27	16
36	25
8	34

_____   _____

_____   _____

_____   _____

_____   _____

Personal Math Trainer

Online Practice and Help

my.hrw.com

Identifying Functions from Graphs

Graphs can be used to display relationships between two sets of numbers. Each point on a graph represents an ordered pair. The first coordinate in each ordered pair is the input value. The second coordinate is the output value. The graph represents a function if each input value is paired with only one output value.

Math On the Spot

my.hrw.com

EXAMPLE 3 CA CC 8.F.1

The graph shows the relationship between the number of hours students spent studying for an exam and the exam grades. Is the relationship represented by the graph a function?

The input values are the number of hours spent studying by each student. The output values are the exam grades. The points represent the following ordered pairs:

Hours Studied and Exam Grade

(1, 70)	(2, 70)	(2, 85)	(3, 75)	(5, 80)
(6, 82)	(7, 88)	(9, 90)	(9, 95)	(12, 98)

Notice that 2 is paired with both 70 and 85, and 9 is paired with both 90 and 95. Therefore, since these input values are paired with more than one output value, the relationship is not a function.

Reflect

 9. Many real-world relationships are functions. For example, the amount of money made at a car wash is a function of the number of cars washed. Give another example of a real-world function.

_____

_____

YOUR TURN

10. The graph shows the relationship between the heights and weights of the members of a basketball team. Is the relationship represented by the graph a function? Explain.

_____

_____

_____

Heights and Weights of Team Members

Personal Math Trainer

Online Practice and Help

my.hrw.com

Complete each table. In the row with x as the input, write a rule as an algebraic expression for the output. Then complete the last row of the table using the rule. (Explore Activity)

1.

Input	Output
Tickets	Cost ($)
2	40
5	100
7	140
x	
10	

2.

Input	Output
Minutes	Pages
2	1
10	5
20	10
x	
30	

3.

Input	Output
Muffins	Cost ($)
1	2.25
3	6.75
6	13.50
x	
12	

Determine whether each relationship is a function. (Examples 1 and 2)

4.

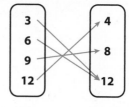

_____

_____

_____

5.

Input	Output
3	20
4	25
5	30
4	35
6	40

_____

_____

_____

6. The graph shows the relationship between the weights of 5 packages and the shipping charge for each package. Is the relationship represented by the graph a function? Explain.

_____

_____

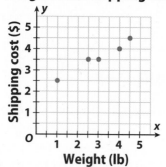

Weights and Shipping Costs

7. What are four different ways of representing functions? How can you tell if a relationship is a function?

_____

_____

6.1 Independent Practice

 CA CC 8.F.1

Personal Math Trainer

Online Practice and Help

my.hrw.com

Determine whether each relationship represented by the ordered pairs is a function. Explain.

8. (2, 2), (3, 1), (5, 7), (8, 0), (9, 1)

_____

_____

_____

9. (0, 4), (5, 1), (2, 8), (6, 3), (5, 9)

_____

_____

_____

10. Draw Conclusions Joaquin receives $0.40 per pound for 1 to 99 pounds of aluminum cans he recycles. He receives $0.50 per pound if he recycles more than 100 pounds. Is the amount of money Joaquin receives a function of the weight of the cans he recycles? Explain your reasoning.

_____

_____

_____

11. A biologist tracked the growth of a strain of bacteria, as shown in the graph.

a. Explain why the relationship represented by the graph is a function.

_____

_____

_____

Bacteria B

b. What If? Suppose there was the same number of bacteria for two consecutive hours. Would the graph still represent a function? Explain.

_____

12. Multiple Representations Give an example of a function in everyday life, and represent it as a graph, a table, and a set of ordered pairs. Describe how you know it is a function.

_____

x				
y				

The graph shows the relationship between the weights of six wedges of cheese and the price of each wedge.

Cost of Cheese

13. Is the relationship represented by the graph a function? Justify your reasoning. Use the words "input" and "output" in your explanation, and connect them to the context represented by the graph.

_____

_____

14. **Analyze Relationships** Suppose the weights and prices of additional wedges of cheese were plotted on the graph. Might that change your answer to question 13? Explain your reasoning.

_____

_____

_____

_____

 FOCUS ON HIGHER ORDER THINKING

Work Area

15. **Justify Reasoning** A mapping diagram represents a relationship that contains three different input values and four different output values. Is the relationship a function? Explain your reasoning.

_____

_____

_____

_____

16. **Communicate Mathematical Ideas** An onion farmer is hiring workers to help harvest the onions. He knows that the number of days it will take to harvest the onions is a function of the number of workers he hires. Explain the use of the word "function" in this context.

_____

_____

_____

_____

_____

_____

LESSON
6.2 Describing Functions

 CA CC 8.F.3
Interpret the equation $y = mx + b$ as defining a linear function, whose graph is a straight line; give examples of functions that are not linear. *Also 8.F.1.1*

ESSENTIAL QUESTION

How can you tell if a function is linear are not?

EXPLORE ACTIVITY **CA CC** 8.F.1

Investigating a Constant Rate of Change

The U.S. Department of Agriculture defines heavy rain as rain that falls at a rate of 1.5 centimeters per hour.

A The table shows the total amount of rain that falls in various amounts of time during a heavy rain. Complete the table.

Time (h)	0	1	2	3	4	5
Total Amount of Rain (cm)	0	1.5				

B Plot the ordered pairs from the table on the coordinate plane at the right.

C How much rain falls in 3.5 hours? _____

D Plot the point corresponding to 3.5 hours of heavy rain.

E What do you notice about all of the points you plotted?

_____

F Is the total amount of rain that falls a function of the number of hours that rain has been falling? Why or why not?

_____

_____

Heavy Rainfall

(Graph: Total Amount of Rain (cm) on y-axis, values 2, 4, 6, 8, 10; Time (h) on x-axis, values 1, 2, 3, 4, 5)

Reflect

1. Suppose you continued to plot points for times between those in the table, such as 1.2 hours or 4.5 hours. What can you say about the locations of these points?

_____

_____

Lesson 6.2 **163**

Graphing Linear Functions

The relationship you investigated in the previous activity can be represented by the equation $y = 1.5x$, where x is the time and y is the total amount of rain. The graph of the relationship is a line, so the equation is a **linear equation**. Since there is exactly one value of y for each value of x, the relationship is a function. It is a **linear function** because its graph is a nonvertical line.

EXAMPLE 1 **CA CC** 8.F.3

The temperature at dawn was 8 °F and increased steadily 2 °F every hour. The equation $y = 2x + 8$ gives the temperature y after x hours. State whether the relationship between the time and the temperature is proportional or nonproportional. Then graph the function.

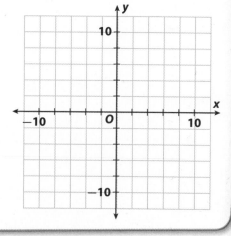

Math Talk
Mathematical Practices

Carrie said that for a function to be a linear function, the relationship it represents must be proportional. Do you agree or disagree? Explain.

STEP 1 Compare the equation with the general linear equation $y = mx + b$. $y = 2x + 8$ is in the form $y = mx + b$, with $m = 2$ and $b = 8$. Therefore, the equation is a linear equation. Since $b \neq 0$, the relationship is nonproportional.

STEP 2 Choose several values for the input x. Substitute these values for x in the equation to find the output y.

x	$2x + 8$	y	(x, y)
0	$2(0) + 8$	8	(0, 8)
2	$2(2) + 8$	12	(2, 12)
4	$2(4) + 8$	16	(4, 16)
6	$2(6) + 8$	20	(6, 20)

STEP 3 Graph the ordered pairs. Then draw a line through the points to represent the solutions of the function.

Temperatures

YOUR TURN

2. State whether the relationship between x and y in $y = 0.5x$ is proportional or nonproportional. Then graph the function.

_____

Personal Math Trainer

Online Practice and Help

ⓞ my.hrw.com

Determining Whether a Function is Linear

The linear equation in Example 1 has the form $y = mx + b$, where m and b are real numbers. Every equation in the form $y = mx + b$ is a linear equation. The linear equations represent linear functions. Equations that cannot be written in this form are not linear equations, and therefore are not linear functions.

Math On the Spot
⊙ my.hrw.com

EXAMPLE 2

A square tile has a side length of x inches. The equation $y = x^2$ gives the area of the tile in square inches. Determine whether the relationship between x and y is linear and, if so, if it is proportional.

STEP 1 Choose several values for the input x. Substitute these values for x in the equation to find the output y.

STEP 2 Graph the ordered pairs.

x	x^2	y	(x, y)
1	1^2	1	(1, 1)
2	2^2	4	(2, 4)
3	3^2	9	(3, 9)
4	4^2	16	(4, 16)

STEP 3 Identify the shape of the graph. The points suggest a curve, not a line. Draw a curve through the points to represent the solutions of the function.

STEP 4 Describe the relationship between x and y.

The graph is not a line so the relationship is not linear.

Only a linear relationship can be proportional, so the relationship is not proportional.

Animated Math
⊙ my.hrw.com

Math Talk
Mathematical Practices

How can you use the numbers in the table to decide whether or not the relationship between x and y is linear?

YOUR TURN

3. A yogurt machine makes $\frac{2}{3}$ gallon of yogurt every minute. The total amount y that the machine makes in x minutes is given by the equation $y = \frac{2}{3}x$. Determine whether the relationship between x and y is linear and, if so, if it is proportional.

Time (min), x	0	3		9
Amount (gal), y			4	

Making Yogurt

Personal Math Trainer
Online Practice and Help
⊙ my.hrw.com

Plot the ordered pairs from the table. Then graph the function represented by the ordered pairs and tell whether the function is linear or nonlinear. (Examples 1 and 2)

1. $y = 5 - 2x$

Input, x	−1	1	3	5
Output, y				

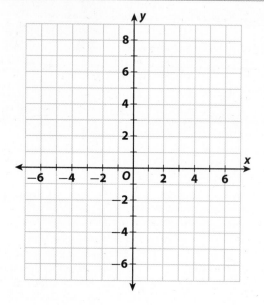

_____

2. $y = 2 - x^2$

Input, x	−2	−1	0	1	2
Output, y					

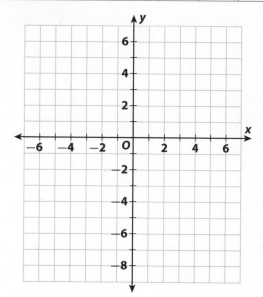

_____

Explain whether each equation is a linear equation. (Example 2)

3. $y = x^2 - 1$

_____

_____

_____

_____

4. $y = 1 - x$

_____

_____

_____

_____

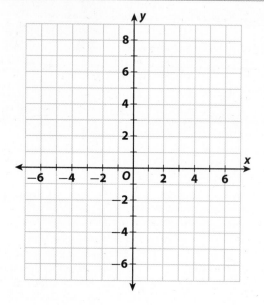 **ESSENTIAL QUESTION CHECK-IN**

5. Explain how you can use a table of values, an equation, and a graph to determine whether a function represents a proportional relationship.

_____

_____

_____

6.2 Independent Practice

Personal Math Trainer

Online Practice and Help

my.hrw.com

CA CC 8.F.1, 8.F.3

6. State whether the relationship between x and y in $y = 4x - 5$ is proportional or nonproportional. Then graph the function.

_____

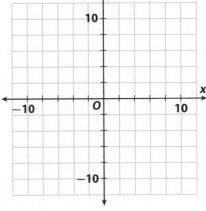

7. The Fortaleza telescope in Brazil is a radio telescope. Its shape can be approximated with the equation $y = 0.013x^2$. Is the relationship between x and y linear? Is it proportional? Explain.

_____

_____

8. Kiley spent $20 on rides and snacks at the state fair. If x is the amount she spent on rides, and y is the amount she spent on snacks, the total amount she spent can be represented by the equation $x + y = 20$. Is the relationship between x and y linear? Is it proportional? Explain.

_____

_____

_____

9. **Represent Real-World Problems** The drill team is buying new uniforms. The table shows y, the total cost in dollars, and x, the number of uniforms purchased.

Number of uniforms, x	1	3	5	9
Total cost ($), y	60	180	300	540

Drill Team Uniforms

a. Use the data to draw a graph. Is the relationship between x and y linear? Explain.

_____

b. Use your graph to predict the cost of purchasing 12 uniforms.

_____

10. Marta, a whale calf in an aquarium, is fed a special milk formula. Her handler uses a graph to track the number of gallons of formula left in the 20-gallon container after each feeding every 4 hours. Is the relationship between x and y linear? Explain.

_____

_____

Marta's Feedings

11. Critique Reasoning A student claims that the equation $y = 7$ is not a linear equation because it does not have the form $y = mx + b$. Do you agree or disagree? Why?

_____

_____

_____

12. Make a Prediction Let x represent the number of hours you read a book and y represent the total number of pages you have read. You have already read 70 pages and can read 30 pages per hour. Write an equation relating x hours and y pages you read. Then predict the total number of pages you will have read after another 3 hours.

_____

H.O.T. FOCUS ON HIGHER ORDER THINKING

Work Area

13. Draw Conclusions Rebecca draws a graph of a real-world relationship that turns out to be a set of unconnected points. Can the relationship be linear? Can it be proportional? Explain your reasoning.

_____

_____

_____

_____

14. Communicate Mathematical Ideas Give two different examples of geometry formulas that represent linear functions and two examples that do not.

_____

_____

15. Justify Reasoning Show that the equation $y + 3 = 3(2x + 1)$ is linear and that it represents a proportional relationship between x and y.

_____

_____

_____

_____

_____

_____

6.3 Comparing Functions

 CA CC 8.F.2

Compare properties of two functions each represented in a different way (algebraically, graphically, numerically in tables, or by verbal descriptions). *Also 8.EE.5, 8.F.4*

ESSENTIAL QUESTION

How can you use tables, graphs, and equations to compare functions?

Comparing a Table and an Equation

To compare a function written as an equation and another function represented by a table, find the equation for the function in the table.

Math On the Spot
my.hrw.com

EXAMPLE 1 Real World

CA CC 8.F.2, 8.F.4

Josh and Maggie buy MP3 files from different music services. The monthly cost, y dollars, for x songs is linear. The cost of Josh's service is $y = 0.50x + 10$. The cost of Maggie's service is shown below.

Monthly Cost of MP3s at Maggie's Music Service					
Songs, x	5	10	15	20	25
Cost (\$), y	4.95	9.90	14.85	19.80	24.75

A Write an equation to represent the monthly cost of Maggie's service.

STEP 1 Choose any two ordered pairs from the table to find the slope.

$$m = \frac{y_2 - y_1}{x_2 - x_1} = \frac{9.90 - 4.95}{10 - 5} = \frac{4.95}{5} = 0.99$$

The points (5, 4.95) and (10, 9.90) were used.

STEP 2 Find the y-intercept. Use the slope and any point.

$y = mx + b$ — Slope-intercept form.

$4.95 = 0.99 \cdot 5 + b$ — Substitute for y, m, and x.

$0 = b$

Math Talk
Mathematical Practices

Describe each service's cost in words using the meanings of the slopes and y-intercepts.

STEP 3 Substitute the slope and y-intercept.

$y = 0.99x + 0$ or $y = 0.99x$ — Substitute 0.99 for m and 0 for y.

B Which service is cheaper when 30 songs are downloaded?

Josh's service:

$y = 0.50 \times 30 + 10$

$y = 25$

Maggie's service:

$y = 0.99 \times 30$

$y = 29.7$

Josh's service is cheaper.

1. Quentin is choosing between buying books at the bookstore or buying online versions of the books for his tablet. The cost, y dollars, of ordering books online for x books is $y = 6.95x + 1.50$. The cost of buying the books at the bookstore is shown in the table. Which method of buying books is more expensive if Quentin wants to buy 6 books?

Cost of Books at the Bookstore					
Books, x	1	2	3	4	5
Cost ($), y	7.50	15.00	22.50	30.00	37.50

_____

EXPLORE ACTIVITY 1 Real World   CA CC 8.F.2, 8.EE.5

Comparing a Table and a Graph

The table and graph show how many words Morgan and Brian typed correctly on a typing test. For both students, the relationship between words typed correctly and time is linear.

Brian's Typing Test

Morgan's Typing Test					
Time (min)	2	4	6	8	10
Words	30	60	90	120	150

A Find Morgan's unit rate.

_____

B Find Brian's unit rate.

_____

C Which student types more correct words per minute?

_____

Reflect

2. Katie types 17 correct words per minute. Explain how a graph of Katie's test results would compare to Morgan's and Brian's.

_____

_____

EXPLORE ACTIVITY 2 (Real World)

Comparing a Graph and a Description

Jamal wants to buy a new game system that costs $200. He does not have enough money to buy it today, so he compares layaway plans at different stores.

The plan at Store A is shown on the graph.

Store B requires an initial payment of $60 and weekly payments of $20 until the balance is paid in full.

Layaway Plan

A Write an equation in slope-intercept form for Store A's layaway plan. Let x represent number of weeks and y represent balance owed.

_____

B Write an equation in slope-intercept form for Store B's layaway plan. Let x represent number of weeks and y represent balance owed.

_____

C Sketch a graph of the plan at Store B on the same grid as Store A.

D How can you use the graphs to tell which plan requires the greater down payment? How can you use the equations?

_____

_____

_____

_____

E How can you use the graphs to tell which plan requires the greater weekly payment? How can you use the equations?

_____

_____

_____

_____

F Which plan allows Jamal to pay for the game system faster? Explain.

_____

_____

Doctors have two methods of calculating maximum heart rate. With the first method, maximum heart rate, y, in beats per minute is $y = 220 - x$, where x is the person's age. Maximum heart rate with the second method is shown in the table. (Example 1)

Age, x	20	30	40	50	60
Heart rate (bpm), y	194	187	180	173	166

1. Which method gives the greater maximum heart rate for a 70-year-old?

_____

_____

2. Are heart rate and age proportional or nonproportional for each method?

_____

Aisha runs a tutoring business. With Plan 1, students may choose to pay $15 per hour. With Plan 2, they may follow the plan shown on the graph. (Explore Activity 1 and 2)

Tutoring Fees

3. Describe the plan shown on the graph.

_____

4. Sketch a graph showing the $15 per hour option.

5. What does the intersection of the two graphs mean?

_____

6. Which plan is cheaper for 10 hours of tutoring?

_____

7. Are cost and time proportional or nonproportional for each plan?

_____

_____

? **ESSENTIAL QUESTION CHECK-IN**

8. When using tables, graphs, and equations to compare functions, why do you find the equations for tables and graphs?

_____

_____

6.3 Independent Practice

CA CC 8.EE.5, 8.F.2, 8.F.4

Personal
Math Trainer

Online Practice
and Help

my.hrw.com

The table and graph show the miles driven and gas used for two scooters.

Scooter A	
Distance (mi), x	Gas used (gal), y
150	2
300	4
450	6
600	8
750	10

Scooter B

9. Which scooter uses fewer gallons of gas when 1350 miles are driven?

_____

10. Are gas used and miles proportional or nonproportional for each scooter?

_____

A cell phone company offers two texting plans to its customers. The monthly cost, y dollars, of one plan is $y = 0.10x + 5$, where x is the number of texts. The cost of the other plan is shown in the table.

Number of texts, x	100	200	300	400	500
Cost ($), y	20	25	30	35	40

11. Which plan is cheaper for under 200 texts? _____

12. The graph of the first plan does not pass through the origin. What does this indicate?

_____

_____

13. Brianna wants to buy a digital camera for a photography class. One store offers the camera for $50 down and a payment plan of $20 per month. The payment plan for a second store is described by $y = 15x + 80$, where y is the total cost in dollars and x is the number of months. Which camera is cheaper when the camera is paid off in 12 months? Explain.

_____

_____

14. The French club and soccer team are washing cars to earn money. The amount earned, y dollars, for washing x cars is a linear function. Which group makes the most money per car? Explain.

French Club

Number of cars, x	Amount earned ($), y
2	10
4	20
6	30
8	40
10	50

Soccer Team

_____

_____

_____

 FOCUS ON HIGHER ORDER THINKING

Work Area

15. Draw Conclusions Gym A charges $60 a month plus $5 per visit. The monthly cost at Gym B is represented by $y = 5x + 40$, where x is the number of visits per month. What conclusion can you draw about the monthly costs of the gyms?

_____

_____

_____

16. Justify Reasoning Why will the value of y for the function $y = 5x + 1$ always be greater than that for the function $y = 4x + 2$ when $x > 1$?

_____

_____

_____

17. Analyze Relationships The equations of two functions are $y = -21x + 9$ and $y = -24x + 8$. Which function is changing more quickly? Explain.

_____

_____

_____

_____

6.4 Analyzing Graphs

 CA CC 8.F.5

Describe qualitatively the functional relationship between two quantities by analyzing a graph. Sketch a graph that exhibits the qualitative features of a function that has been described verbally.

ESSENTIAL QUESTION

How can you describe a relationship given a graph and sketch a graph given a description?

EXPLORE ACTIVITY 1   CA CC 8.F.5

Interpreting Graphs

A roller coaster park is open from May to October each year. The graph shows the number of park visitors over its season.

Park Visitors

A Segment 1 shows that attendance during the opening weeks of the park's season stayed constant. Describe what Segment 2 shows.

_____

B Based on the time frame, give a possible explanation for the change in attendance represented by Segment 2.

_____

C Which segments of the graph show decreasing attendance? Give a possible explanation.

_____

_____

Reflect

1. Explain how the slope of each segment of the graph is related to whether attendance increases or decreases.

_____

_____

Matching Graphs to Situations

Grace, Jet, and Mike are studying 100 words for a spelling bee.

- Grace started by learning how to spell many words each day but then learned fewer and fewer words each day.
- Jet learned how to spell the same number of words each day.
- Mike started by learning how to spell the same number of words each day but then learned a greater number of words each day.

_____   _____   _____

A Describe the progress represented by Graph A.

_____

_____

B Describe the progress represented by Graph B.

_____

_____

_____

_____

Math Talk
Mathematical Practices

Functions are sometimes linear for only some input values. Where is each graph linear or nonlinear?

C Describe the progress represented by Graph C.

_____

_____

_____

D Determine which graph represents each student's study progress and write the students' names under the appropriate graphs.

Reflect

2. What would it mean if Graph C began with a curve but ended with a line?

_____

Sketching a Graph for a Situation

Mrs. Sutton provides free math tutoring to her students every day after school. No one comes to tutoring sessions during the first week of school. Over the next two weeks, use of the tutoring service gradually increases.

A Sketch a graph showing the number of students who use the tutoring service over the first three weeks of school.

B Mrs. Sutton's students are told that they will have a math test at the end of the fifth week of school. How do you think this will affect the number of students who come to tutoring?

_____

_____

C Considering your answer to **B**, sketch a graph showing the number of students who might use the tutoring service over the first six weeks of school.

Reflect

3. If Mrs. Sutton offers bonus credit to students who come to tutoring, how might this affect the number of students?

_____

4. How would your answer to Question 3 affect the graph?

_____

_____

In a lab environment, colonies of bacteria follow a predictable pattern of growth. The graph shows this growth over time. (Explore Activity 1)

Bacterial Growth Curve

1. What is happening to the population during Phase 2?

   _____

   _____

2. What is happening to the population during Phase 4?

   _____

The graphs give the speeds of three people who are riding snowmobiles. Tell which graph corresponds to each situation. (Explore Activity 2)

Graph 1

Graph 2

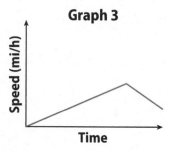

Graph 3

3. Chip begins his ride slowly but then stops to talk with some friends. After a few minutes, he continues his ride, gradually increasing his speed.   _____

4. Linda steadily increases her speed through most of her ride. Then she slows down as she nears some trees.   _____

5. From the top of a ladder, Paulo walked to the end of a diving board. He dove forward into the water. Then he swam straight forward for a time. Finally, he swam forward and upward to the surface of the water. Complete the graph to represent Paulo's elevation at different distances from the edge of the pool. (Explore Activity 3)

6. Tell where the graph is increasing, decreasing, linear, and nonlinear. (Explore Activity 3)

   _____

   _____

Paulo's Elevation

ESSENTIAL QUESTION CHECK-IN

7. What are some questions to ask about a function when sketching its graph?

   _____

   _____

6.4 Independent Practice

 CA CC 8.F.5

Personal Math Trainer

Online Practice and Help

my.hrw.com

Tell which graph corresponds to each situation below.

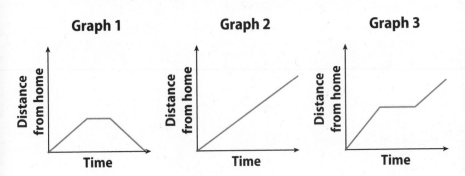

Graph 1

Graph 2

Graph 3

8. Arnold started from home and walked to a friend's house. He stayed with his friend for a while and then walked to another friend's house farther from home.

_____

9. Francisco started from home and walked to the store. After shopping, he walked back home.

_____

10. Celia walks to the library at a steady pace without stopping.

_____

Regina rented a motor scooter. The graph shows how far away she is from the rental site after each half hour of riding.

11. **Represent Real-World Problems** Use the graph to describe Regina's trip. You can start the description like this: "Regina left the rental shop and rode for an hour…"

_____

_____

_____

_____

Distance from Rental Site

12. **Analyze Relationships** Determine during which half hour Regina covered the greatest distance.

_____

The data in the table shows the speed of a ride at an amusement park at different times one afternoon.

Time	3:20	3:21	3:22	3:23	3:24	3:25
Speed (mi/h)	0	14	41	62	8	0

13. Sketch a graph that shows the speed of the ride over time.

14. Between which times is the ride's speed increasing the fastest?

_____

15. Between which times is the ride's speed decreasing the fastest?

_____

H.O.T. FOCUS ON HIGHER ORDER THINKING

A woodland area on an island contains a population of foxes. The graph describes the changes in the population over time.

16. Justify Reasoning What is happening to the fox population before time *t*? Explain your reasoning.

Fox Population

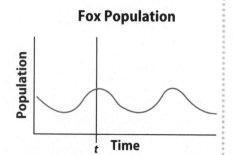

_____

_____

_____

_____

17. What If? Suppose at time *t*, a conservation organization moves a large group of foxes to the island. Sketch a graph to show how this action might affect the population on the island after time *t*.

18. Make a Prediction At some point after time *t*, a forest fire destroys part of the woodland area on the island. Describe how your graph from Exercise 17 might change.

Fox Population

_____

_____

_____

Work Area

Ready to Go On?

Personal
Math Trainer

Online Practice
and Help

⏱ my.hrw.com

6.1 Identifying and Representing Functions

Determine whether each relationship is a function.

1.

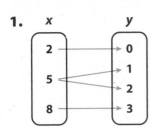

x	y
2	0
5	1
8	2
	3

2.

Input, x	Output, y
−1	6
3	5
6	5

3. (2, 5), (7, 2), (−3, 4), (2, 9), (1, 1)

_____   _____   _____

6.2 Describing Functions

Determine whether each situation is linear or nonlinear, and proportional or nonproportional.

4. Joanna is paid $14 per hour.

5. Alberto calculated the surface area of a cube-shaped box in relation to the length of an edge.

_____   _____

6.3 Comparing Functions

6. Which function is changing more quickly? Explain.

_____

_____

_____

Function 1

Function 2	
Input, x	Output, y
2	11
3	6.5
4	2

6.4 Analyzing Graphs

7. Describe a graph that shows Sam running at a constant rate.

_____

? ESSENTIAL QUESTION

8. How can you use an equation or a graph to decide if a function is linear?

_____

MODULE 6
MIXED REVIEW

Assessment Readiness

Personal Math Trainer

Online Practice and Help

my.hrw.com

1. Look at each table. Is the relationship in the table a function?

Select Yes or No for tables A–C.

A.

Input	−4	8	0	6	13
Output	5	12	−3	5	18

○ Yes   ○ No

B.

Input	26	34	28	30	34
Output	52	62	55	59	60

○ Yes   ○ No

C.

Input	17	20	15	25	19
Output	84	75	72	72	80

○ Yes   ○ No

2. Michelle started with $25 and saves additional money each week to buy a video game system, as shown in the table.

Time (Weeks), x	0	1	2	3
Savings ($), y	25	43	61	79

Choose True or False for each statement.

A. The equation is $y = 25x + 18$.   ○ True   ○ False

B. The y-intercept is 25.   ○ True   ○ False

C. The slope is 18.   ○ True   ○ False

3. The equation $y = 20 - \frac{x}{4}$ gives the number of pounds of dog food y remaining in a bag x days after it is opened. Determine whether the relationship between x and y is linear. Explain your reasoning.

4. The cost y in dollars of getting cable TV from Soto Cable for x months is given by $y = 42.50x + 30$. The cost of getting cable TV from Lang Cable is shown in the table. Mr. Oliver needs cable TV for 6 months. Which service is cheaper for Mr. Oliver? Explain how you solved this problem.

Lang Cable	
Time (months)	Total Cost ($)
1	45.90
2	91.80
3	137.70

Proportional Relationships

Key Vocabulary
constant of proportionality *(constante de proporcionalidad)*
proportional relationship *(relación proporcional)*
slope *(pendiente)*

? ESSENTIAL QUESTION

How can you use proportional relationships to solve real-world problems?

EXAMPLE 1

Write an equation that represents the proportional relationship shown in the graph.

Use the points on the graph to make a table.

Bracelets sold	3	4	5	6
Profit ($)	9	12	15	18

Let x represent the number of bracelets sold.

Let y represent the profit.

The equation is $y = 3x$.

EXAMPLE 2

Find the slope of the line.

$$\text{slope} = \frac{\text{rise}}{\text{run}}$$

$$= \frac{3}{-4}$$

$$= -\frac{3}{4}$$

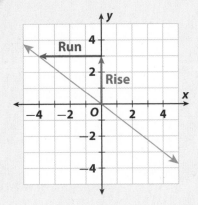

EXERCISES

1. The table represents a proportional relationship. Write an equation that describes the relationship. Then graph the relationship represented by the data. *(Lessons 3.1, 3.3, 3.4)*

Time (*x*)	6	8	10	12
Distance (*y*)	3	4	5	6

_____

Find the slope and the unit rate represented on each graph. *(Lesson 3.2)*

2.

3.
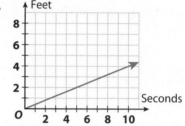

_____   _____

Nonproportional Relationships

Key Vocabulary
linear equation
(ecuación lineal)
slope-intercept form of an equation *(forma de pendiente-intersección)*
y-intercept
(intersección con el eje y)

 ESSENTIAL QUESTION

How can you use nonproportional relationships to solve real-world problems?

EXAMPLE 1

Jai is saving to buy his mother a birthday gift. Each week, he saves $5. He started with $25. The equation *y* = 5*x* + 25 gives the total Jai has saved, *y*, after *x* weeks. Draw a graph of the equation. Then describe the relationship.

Use the equation to make a table. Then, graph the ordered pairs from the table, and draw a line through the points.

x (weeks)	0	1	2	3	4
y (savings in dollars)	25	30	35	40	45

The relationship is linear but nonproportional.

EXAMPLE 2

Graph $y = -\frac{1}{2}x - 2$.

The slope is $\frac{-1}{2}$, or $-\frac{1}{2}$.

The y-intercept is -2.

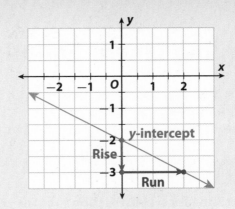

EXERCISES

Complete each table. Explain whether the relationship between *x* and *y* is proportional or nonproportional and whether it is linear. (Lesson 4.1)

1. $y = 10x - 4$

x	0	2		6
y	−4		36	

2. $y = -\frac{3}{2}x$

x	0		2	
y		−1.5		−4.5

_____

_____

3. Find the slope and *y*-intercept for the linear relationship shown in the table. Graph the line. Is the relationship proportional or nonproportional? (Lessons 4.2, 4.4)

x	−4	−1	0	1
y	−4	2	4	6

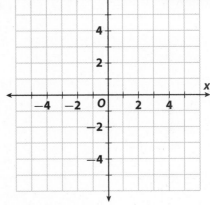

slope _____

y-intercept _____

The relationship is _____.

4. Tom's Taxis charges a fixed rate of $4 per ride plus $0.50 per mile. Carla's Cabs does not charge a fixed rate but charges $1.00 per mile. (Lessons 4.3)

a. Write an equation that represents the cost of Tom's Taxis. _____

b. Write an equation that represents the cost of Carla's cabs. _____

c. Steve calculated that for the distance he needs to travel, Tom's Taxis will charge the same amount as Carla's Cabs. Graph both equations. How far is Steve going to travel and how much will he pay?

_____

_____

Writing Linear Equations

? ESSENTIAL QUESTION

How can you use linear equations to solve real-world problems?

EXAMPLE 1

Jose is renting a backhoe for a construction job. The rental charge for a month is based on the number of days in the month and a set charge per month. In September, which has 30 days, Jose paid $700. In August, which has 31 days, he paid $715. Write an equation in slope-intercept form that represents this situation.

$(x_1, y_1), (x_2, y_2) \rightarrow (30, 700), (31, 715)$ Write the information given as ordered pairs.

$m = \dfrac{y_2 - y_1}{x_2 - x_1} = \dfrac{715 - 700}{31 - 30} = 15$ Find the slope.

$y = mx + b$ Slope-intercept form

$715 = 15(31) + b$ Substitute for y, m, and x to find b.

$250 = b$ Solve for b.

$y = 15x + 250$ Write the equation.

EXAMPLE 2

Determine if the graph shown represents a linear or nonlinear relationship.

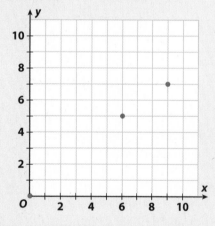

Points	Rate of Change
(0, 0) and (6, 5)	$m = \dfrac{5 - 0}{6 - 0} = \dfrac{5}{6}$
(6, 5) and (9, 7)	$m = \dfrac{7 - 5}{9 - 6} = \dfrac{2}{3}$
(0, 0) and (9, 7)	$m = \dfrac{7 - 0}{9 - 0} = \dfrac{7}{9}$

The rates of change are not constant. The graph represents a nonlinear relationship.

EXERCISES

1. Ms. Thompson is grading math tests. She is giving everyone that took the test a 10-point bonus. Each correct answer is worth 5 points. Write an equation in slope-intercept form that represents the scores on the tests. (Lesson 5.1) _____

The table shows a pay scale based on years of experience. (Lessons 5.1, 5.2)

Experience (years), x	0	2	4	6	8
Hourly pay ($), y	9	14	19	24	29

2. Find the slope for this relationship. _____

3. Find the y-intercept. _____

4. Write an equation in slope-intercept form that represents this relationship. _____

5. Graph the equation, and use it to predict the hourly pay of someone with 10 years of experience.

_____

_____

_____

_____

Does each of the following graphs represent a linear relationship? Why or why not? (Lesson 5.3)

6.

_____

_____

_____

7.

_____

_____

_____

MODULE 6 Functions

? ESSENTIAL QUESTION

How can you use functions to solve real-world problems?

EXAMPLE 1

Determine whether each relationship is a function.

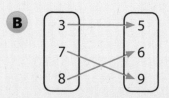

A

Input	Output
3	10
4	4
5	2
4	0
6	5

The relationship is not a function, because an input, 4, is paired with 2 different outputs, 4 and 0.

B

3 → 5
7 → 6
8 → 9

Since each input value is paired with only one output value, the relationship is a function.

EXAMPLE 2

Sally and Louis are on a long-distance bike ride. Sally bikes at a steady rate of 18 miles per hour. The distance y that Sally covers in x hours is given by the equation $y = 18x$. Louis's speed can be found by using the numbers in the table. Who will travel farther in 4 hours and by how much?

Louis's Biking Speed			
Time (h), x	3	5	7
Distance (mi), y	60	100	140

Each distance in the table is 20 times each number of hours. Louis's speed is 20 miles per hour, and his distance covered is represented by $y = 20x$.

Sally's ride:

$y = 18x$

$y = 18(4)$

$y = 72$

Louis's ride:

$y = 20x$

$y = 20(4)$

$y = 80$

Sally will ride 72 miles in 4 hours. Louis will ride 80 miles in 4 hours. Louis will go 8 miles farther.

EXERCISES

Determine whether each relationship is a function. (Lesson 6.1)

1.

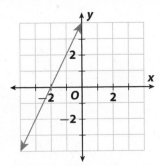

2.

Input	Output
−1	8
0	4
1	8
2	16

_____

_____

Tell whether the function is linear or nonlinear. (Lesson 6.2)

3. $y = 5x + \dfrac{1}{2}$ _____

4. $y = x^2 + 3$ _____

5. Elaine has a choice of two health club memberships. The first membership option is to pay $500 now and then pay $150 per month. The second option is shown in the table. Elaine plans to go to the club for 12 months. Which option is cheaper? Explain. (Lesson 6.3)

Months, x	1	2	3
Total paid ($), y	215	430	645

_____

_____

_____

6. Jenny rode her bike around her neighborhood. Use the graph to describe Jenny's bike ride. (Lesson 6.4)

_____

_____

_____

_____

_____

Jenny's Ride

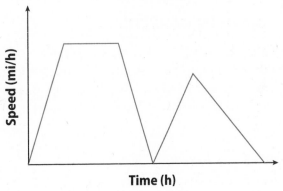

_____

_____

_____

Mapping San Diego

For this project, locate and draw a map of a small section of San Diego on a coordinate grid. Make Commercial Street your x-axis. Make 28th Street your y-axis. Mark the point (−4, 0) at the intersection of Commercial Street and 26th Street. Mark the point (4, 0) at the intersection of Commercial Street and 30th Street. Use the scale determined by those points to determine the scale on the y-axis.

You may make your map as detailed as you wish, but to complete the project you should find each of the following:

- The equation of 27th Street
- The equation of L Street
- The equation of Franklin Avenue
- In each quadrant, the coordinates of at least two specific locations, such as a business, school, park or other landmark

Use the space below to write down any questions you have or important information from your teacher.

MATH IN CAREERS | **ACTIVITY**

Cost Estimator A company plans on selling MP3 players for $120. To make the MP3 players, a cost estimator determined it costs the company $1500 per week for overhead and $45 for each MP3 player made. How much profit would the company make if it sold 100 players in one week? Explain.

UNIT 2
MIXED REVIEW

Assessment Readiness

Personal Math Trainer

Online Practice and Help

⏻ my.hrw.com

1. Does the equation represent a proportional relationship?

Select Yes or No for each equation.

A. $c = 0.6n$ ○ Yes   ○ No

B. $s = 28 - 8t$ ○ Yes   ○ No

C. $p = 6m + 9m$ ○ Yes   ○ No

2. The graph shows the relationship between the number of bicycles a factory has made and the number of hours the factory has been open today.

Choose True or False for each statement.

A. The relationship is a function.   ○ True   ○ False

B. The slope of the line is 400.   ○ True   ○ False

C. If the pattern continues, the factory will make 3200 bicycles in 6 hours.   ○ True   ○ False

3. A baseball team is ordering caps. The table shows how the cost of a cap depends on the number of colors used in the team logo placed on a cap. Write an equation in slope-intercept form for the cost of a cap. Explain how you determined your answer.

Number of Colors, x	Cost of Cap ($), y
1	19.95
2	22.85
3	25.75
4	28.65

4. A garden has a width of x feet and a length of $(x + 1)$ feet. The function $y = x(x + 1)$ gives the area of the garden in square feet. Is the function linear or nonlinear? Explain how you know.

Performance Tasks

★**5.** The linear equation $y = \frac{1}{4}x + 4$ models the height y in inches of Abby's tomato plant x days after she bought it. Explain how you can use the slope and y-intercept to graph the equation. Then complete the graph.

★★**6.** The table shows the amount y remaining on Barry's bus fare card after he has ridden the bus x times.

a. Graph the relationship in the table.

b. Write an equation for the relationship.

c. Interpret the meaning of the slope and y-intercept in this situation.

d. Predict the total number of times Barry will be able to ride the bus using his card. Justify your reasoning.

Bus Rides, x	Amount on Card ($), y
1	13.50
2	12.00
3	10.50
4	9.00

★★★**7.** Hobbs Mules charges $80 for a 2-hour mule ride and $144 for a 4-hour mule ride. The table shows how much McGee Mules charges for a mule ride. The relationship between the time in hours and the cost in dollars is linear for both companies.

a. If a group wants to take a 3-hour mule ride, which company should it choose? Justify your answer.

b. If the group decides to take a 5-hour mule ride instead, would this change your answer to part **a**? Explain your reasoning.

McGee Mules	
Time (h)	Cost ($)
0.5	25
1.0	42
1.5	59
2.0	76

Solving Equations and Systems of Equations

MODULE 7
Solving Linear Equations
CA CC 8.EE.7, 8.EE.7a, 8.EE.7b

MODULE 8
Solving Systems of Linear Equations
CA CC 8.EE.8, 8.EE.8a, 8.EE.8b, 8.EE.8c

MATH IN CAREERS

Hydraulic Engineer A hydraulic engineer specializes in the behavior of fluids, mainly water. A hydraulic engineer applies the mathematics of fluid dynamics to the collection, transport, measurement, and regulation of water and other fluids.

If you are interested in a career in hydraulic engineering, you should study the following mathematical subjects:
- Algebra
- Geometry
- Trigonometry
- Probability and Statistics
- Calculus

Research other careers that require the understanding of the mathematics of fluid dynamics.

ACTIVITY At the end of the unit, check out how **hydraulic engineers** use math.

Which Car Costs Less?

The Unit Project at the end of this unit focuses on comparing the costs of two cars when only their original prices and their fuel efficiencies are considered. To successfully complete the Unit Project you'll need to master these skills:

- Write a system of linear equations.
- Graph a system of linear equations.
- Interpret the point of intersection of two lines

1. What is the average fuel efficiency of a car?

_____

_____

_____

2. Is it possible for the total cost of an expensive car after a few years to be less than the total cost of an inexpensive car? Explain.

_____

_____

_____

_____

_____

_____

Tracking Your Learning Progression

This unit addresses important California Common Core Standards in the Critical Area of understanding linear equations and simultaneous linear equations.

Domain 8.EE Expressions and Equations

    Cluster Analyze and solve linear equations and pairs of simultaneous linear equations.

Solving Linear Equations

? ESSENTIAL QUESTION

How can you use equations with the variable on both sides to solve real-world problems?

Real-World Video

Some employees earn commission plus their salary when they make a sale. There may be options about their pay structure. They can find the best option by solving an equation with the variable on both sides.

my.hrw.com

GO DIGITAL

my.hrw.com

my.hrw.com

Go digital with your write-in student edition, accessible on any device.

Math On the Spot

Scan with your smart phone to jump directly to the online edition, video tutor, and more.

Animated Math

Interactively explore key concepts to see how math works.

Personal Math Trainer

Get immediate feedback and help as you work through practice sets.

Are YOU Ready?

Complete these exercises to review skills you will need for this module.

Find Common Denominators

> **EXAMPLE** Find the LCD of 3, 5, and 10.
>
> 3: 3, 6, 9, 12, 15, 18, 21, 24, 27, 30,...   *List the multiples of each number.*
> 5: 5, 10, 15, 20, 25, 30, 35,...   *Choose the least multiple the*
> 10: 10, 20, 30, 40, 50,...   *lists have in common.*
>   *LCD(3, 5, 10) = 30*

Find the LCD.

1. 8, 12 _____   **2.** 9, 12 _____   **3.** 15, 20 _____   **4.** 8, 10 _____

Multiply Decimals by Powers of 10

> **EXAMPLE** 3.719×100 *Count the zeros in 100: 2 zeros*
> $3.719 \times 100 = 371.9$ *Move the decimal point 2 places to the right.*

Find the product.

5. 0.683×100 **6.** $9.15 \times 1{,}000$ **7.** 0.005×100 **8.** $1{,}000 \times 1{,}000$

_____   _____   _____   _____

Connect Words and Equations

> **EXAMPLE** Two times a number decreased by 5 is −6.
>
> Two times x decreased by 5 is −6.   *Represent the unknown with*
> $2x - 5$ is −6   *a variable.*
> $2x - 5 = -6$ *Times means multiplication.*
>   *Decreased by means subtraction.*
>   *Place the equal sign.*

Write an algebraic equation for the sentence.

9. The difference between three times a number and 7 is 14. _____

10. The quotient of five times a number and 7 is no more than 10. _____

11. 14 less than 3 times a number is 5 more than half of the number. _____

Reading Start-Up

Vocabulary

Review Words
- ✔ algebraic expression
  (expresión algebraica)
- coefficient *(coeficiente)*
- common denominator
  (denominador común)
- ✔ constant *(constante)*
- ✔ equation *(ecuación)*
- integers *(entero)*
- least common multiple
  (mínimo común múltiplo)
- operations *(operaciones)*
- solution *(solución)*
- ✔ variable *(variable)*

Visualize Vocabulary

Use the ✔ words to complete the bubble map. You may put more than one word in each oval.

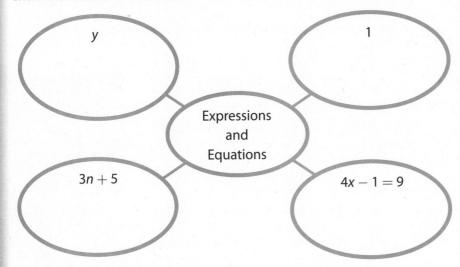

y

1

Expressions
and
Equations

$3n + 5$

$4x - 1 = 9$

Understand Vocabulary

Complete the sentences using the review words.

1. A value of the variable that makes an equation true is a _____.

2. The set of all whole numbers and their opposites are _____.

3. An _____ is an expression that contains at least one variable.

Active Reading

Layered Book Before beginning the module, create a layered book to help you learn the concepts in this module. At the top of the first flap, write the title of the book, "Solving Linear Equations." Then label each flap with one of the lesson titles in this module. As you study each lesson, write important ideas, such as vocabulary and formulas, under the appropriate flap.

GETTING READY FOR
Solving Linear Equations

Understanding the standards and the vocabulary terms in the standards will help you know exactly what you are expected to learn in this module.

CA CC 8.EE.7a

Give examples of linear equations in one variable with one solution, infinitely many solutions, or no solutions. Show which of these possibilities is the case by successively transforming the given equation into simpler forms, until an equivalent equation of the form $x = a$, $a = a$, or $a = b$ results (where a and b are different numbers).

Key Vocabulary

linear equation in one variable
(ecuación lineal en una variable)
An equation that can be written in the form $ax = b$ where a and b are constants and $a \neq 0$.

What It Means to You

You will identify the number of solutions an equation has.

EXAMPLE 8.EE.7a

Your gym charges $50 per month. Find the number of months for which your costs will equal the cost of membership at each gym shown.

A: $40 per month plus $100 one-time fee
$50x = 40x + 100 \rightarrow x = 10$
Equal in 10 months $\rightarrow$ one solution

B: $50 per month plus $25 one-time fee
$50x = 50x + 25 \rightarrow 0 = 25$
Never equal $\rightarrow$ no solution

C: $40 per month plus $10 monthly garage fee
$50x = 40x + 10x \rightarrow x = x$
Equal for any number of months $\rightarrow$ infinitely many solutions

CA CC 8.EE.7b

Solve linear equations with rational number coefficients, including equations whose solutions require expanding expressions using the distributive property and collecting like terms.

Key Vocabulary

solution *(solución)*
In an equation, the value for the variable that makes the equation true.

What It Means to You

You can write and solve an equation that has a variable on both sides of the equal sign.

EXAMPLE 8.EE.7b

Yellow Taxi has no pickup fee but charges $0.25 per mile. AAA Taxi charges $3 for pickup and $0.15 per mile. Find the number of miles for which the cost of the two taxis is the same.

$$0.25x = 3 + 0.15x$$
$$100(0.25x) = 100(3) + 100(0.15x)$$
$$25x = 300 + 15x$$
$$10x = 300$$
$$x = 30$$

The cost is the same for 30 miles.

Visit **my.hrw.com** to see all **CA Common Core Standards** explained.

my.hrw.com

Equations with the Variable on Both Sides

 CA CC 8.EE.7

Solve linear equations in one variable. *Also 8.EE.7b*

ESSENTIAL QUESTION

How can you represent and solve equations with the variable on both sides?

EXPLORE ACTIVITY **CA CC** 8.EE.7, 8.EE.7b

Modeling an Equation with a Variable on Both Sides

Algebra tiles can model equations with a variable on both sides.

KEY

$\boxed{+} = 1$

$\boxed{-} = -1$

$\boxed{+} = x$

$\boxed{+} + \boxed{-} = 0$

Use algebra tiles to model and solve $x + 5 = 3x - 1$.

Model $x + 5$ on the left side of the mat and $3x - 1$ on the right side.
Remember that $3x - 1$ is the same as

$3x +$ _____ .

Remove one x-tile from both sides. This

represents subtracting _____ .
from both sides of the equation.

> **Math Talk**
> **Mathematical Practices**
> Why is a positive unit tile added to both sides in the third step?

Place one $+1$-tile on both sides. This

represents adding _____ to both sides of the equation. Remove zero pairs.

Separate each side into 2 equal groups.

One x-tile is equivalent to _____ $+1$-tiles.

The solution is _____ = _____ .

Reflect

1. How can you check the solution to $x + 5 = 3x - 1$ using algebra tiles?

_____

_____

Solving an Equation with the Variable on Both Sides

Equations with the variable on both sides can be used to compare costs of real-world situations. To solve these equations, use inverse operations to get the variable terms on one side of the equation.

EXAMPLE 1   **CA CC** 8.EE.7, 8.EE.7b

Andy's Rental Car charges an initial fee of $20 plus an additional $30 per day to rent a car. Buddy's Rental Car charges an initial fee of $36 plus an additional $28 per day. For what number of days is the total cost charged by the companies the same?

STEP 1 Write an expression representing the total cost of renting a car from Andy's Rental Car.

$$\text{Initial fee} + \text{Cost for } x \text{ days}$$
$$20 + 30x$$

STEP 2 Write an expression representing the total cost of renting a car from Buddy's Rental Car.

$$\text{Initial fee} + \text{Cost for } x \text{ days}$$
$$36 + 28x$$

STEP 3 Write an equation that can be solved to find the number of days for which the total cost charged by the companies would be the same.

$$\text{Total cost at Andy's} = \text{Total cost at Buddy's}$$
$$20 + 30x = 36 + 28x$$

STEP 4 Solve the equation for x.

$20 + 30x =$	$36 + 28x$	Write the equation.
$-28x$	$-28x$	Subtract $28x$ from both sides.
$20 + 2x =$	36	
-20	-20	Subtract 20 from both sides.
$2x =$	16	
$\dfrac{2x}{2} =$	$\dfrac{16}{2}$	Divide both sides by 2.
$x =$	8	

The total cost is the same if the rental is for 8 days.

Math Talk
Mathematical Practices

When is it more economical to rent from Andy's Rental Car? When is it more economical to rent from Buddy's?

2. A water tank holds 256 gallons but is leaking at a rate of 3 gallons per week. A second water tank holds 384 gallons but is leaking at a rate of 5 gallons per week. After how many weeks will the amount of water in the two tanks be the same?

_____

Writing a Real-World Situation from an Equation

As shown in Example 1, an equation with the variable on both sides can be used to represent a real-world situation. You can reverse this process by writing a real-world situation for a given equation.

EXAMPLE 2   CA CC 8.EE.7

My Notes

Write a real-world situation that could be modeled by the equation $150 + 25x = 55x$.

STEP 1 The left side of the equation consists of a constant plus a variable term. It could represent the total cost for doing a job where there is an initial fee plus an hourly charge.

STEP 2 The right side of the equation consists of a variable term. It could represent the cost for doing the same job based on an hourly charge only.

STEP 3 The equation $150 + 25x = 55x$ could be represented by this situation: A handyman charges $150 plus $25 per hour for house painting. A painter charges $55 per hour. How many hours would a job have to take for the handyman's fee and the painter's fee to be the same?

3. Write a real-world situation that could be modeled by the equation $30x = 48 + 22x$.

_____

_____

_____

_____

Guided Practice

Use algebra tiles to model and solve each equation. (Explore Activity)

1. $x + 4 = -x - 4$ _____

2. $2 - 3x = -x - 8$ _____

Solve each equation. (Example 1)

3. $b + 4 = 2b - 5$ _____

4. $10h + 12 = 8h + 4$ _____

5. $-6x - 29 = 5x - 7$ _____

6. $7a - 17 = 4a + 1$ _____

7. $-n + 5 = n - 11$ _____

8. $5p + 8 = 7p + 2$ _____

9. At Silver Gym, membership is $25 per month, and personal training sessions are $30 each. At Fit Factor, membership is $65 per month, and personal training sessions are $20 each. In one month, how many personal training sessions would Sarah have to buy to make the total cost at the two gyms equal? (Example 1)

_____

10. A moving company charges $840 plus $17 per hour. Another moving company charges $760 plus $22 per hour. How long is a job that costs the same no matter which company is used? (Example 1)

_____

11. Write a real-world situation that could be modeled by the equation $100 - 6x = 160 - 10x$. (Example 2)

_____

_____

_____

_____

? **ESSENTIAL QUESTION CHECK-IN**

12. How can you solve an equation with the variable on both sides?

_____

_____

_____

_____

_____

7.1 Independent Practice

CA CC 8.EE.7, 8.EE.7b

Personal
Math Trainer

Online Practice
and Help

my.hrw.com

13. Derrick's Dog Sitting and Darlene's Dog Sitting are competing for new business. The companies ran the ads shown.

a. Write and solve an equation to find the number of hours for which the total cost will be the same for the two services.

_____

b. **Analyze Relationships** Which dog sitting service is more economical to use if you need 5 hours of service? Explain.

_____

_____

Derrick's
Dog Sitting

$12 plus
$5 per hour

Darlene's
Dog Sitting

$18 plus
$3 per hour

14. Country Carpets charges $22 per square yard for carpeting, and an additional installation fee of $100. City Carpets charges $25 per square yard for the same carpeting, and an additional installation fee of $70.

a. Write and solve an equation to find the number of square yards of carpeting for which the total cost charged by the two companies will be the same.

_____

b. **Justify Reasoning** Mr. Shu wants to hire one of the two carpet companies to install carpeting in his basement. Is he more likely to hire Country Carpets or City Carpets? Explain your reasoning.

_____

_____

_____

_____

Write an equation to represent each relationship. Then solve the equation.

15. Two less than 3 times a number is the same as the number plus 10.

_____

16. A number increased by 4 is the same as 19 minus 2 times the number.

_____

17. Twenty less than 8 times a number is the same as 15 more than the number.

_____

18. The charges for an international call made using the calling card for two phone companies are shown in the table.

Phone Company	Charges
Company A	35¢ plus 3¢ per minute
Company B	45¢ plus 2¢ per minute

a. What is the length of a phone call that would cost the same no matter which company is used?

_____

b. **Analyze Relationships** When is it better to use the card from Company B?

_____

_____

 FOCUS ON HIGHER ORDER THINKING

19. Draw Conclusions Liam is setting up folding chairs for a meeting. If he arranges the chairs in 9 rows of the same length, he has 3 chairs left over. If he arranges the chairs in 7 rows of that same length, he has 19 left over. How many chairs does Liam have?

_____

20. Explain the Error Rent-A-Tent rents party tents for a flat fee of $365 plus $125 a day. Capital Rentals rents party tents for a flat fee of $250 plus $175 a day. Delia wrote the following equation to find the number of days for which the total cost charged by the two companies would be the same:

$$365x + 125 = 250x + 175$$

Find and explain the error in Delia's work. Then write the correct equation.

_____

_____

_____

21. Persevere in Problem Solving Lilliana is training for a marathon. She runs the same distance every day for a week. On Monday, Wednesday, and Friday, she runs 3 laps on a running trail and then runs 6 more miles. On Tuesday and Sunday, she runs 5 laps on the trail and then runs 2 more miles. On Saturday, she just runs laps. How many laps does Lilliana run on Saturday?

_____

Work Area

Equations with Rational Numbers

CA CC 8.EE.7b

Solve linear equations with rational number coefficients, including equations whose solutions require expanding expressions using the distributive property and collecting like terms. *Also 8.EE.7*

ESSENTIAL QUESTION

How can you solve equations with rational number coefficients and constants?

Solving an Equation that Involves Fractions

To solve an equation with the variable on both sides that involves fractions, start by using the least common multiple (LCM) to eliminate the fractions from the equation.

Math On the Spot

my.hrw.com

EXAMPLE 1

CA CC 8.EE.7b, 8.EE.7

Solve $\frac{7}{10}n + \frac{3}{2} = \frac{3}{5}n + 2$.

$$10 = 10 \times 1$$
$$= 2 \times 5$$
$$= 5 \times 2$$

STEP 1 Determine the least common multiple of the denominators: LCM($10, 2, 5$) = 10

STEP 2 Multiply both sides of the equation by the LCM.

$$10\left(\frac{7}{10}n + \frac{3}{2}\right) = 10\left(\frac{3}{5}n + 2\right)$$

$${}^{1}\cancel{10}\left(\frac{7}{\cancel{10}_{1}}n\right) + {}^{5}\cancel{10}\left(\frac{3}{\cancel{2}_{1}}\right) = {}^{2}\cancel{10}\left(\frac{3}{\cancel{5}_{1}}n\right) + 10(2)$$

$$7n + 15 = 6n + 20$$

STEP 3 Use inverse operations to solve the equation.

$$\begin{array}{rcl} 7n + 15 & = & 6n + 20 \\ -15 & & -15 \end{array}$$ Subtract 15 from both sides.

$$\begin{array}{rcl} 7n & = & 6n + 5 \\ -6n & & -6n \end{array}$$ Subtract 6n from both sides.

$$n = 5$$

Math Talk
Mathematical Practices

The constant on the right side, 2, is not a fraction. Why do you still need to multiply it by the LCM, 10?

Reflect

1. What is the advantage of multiplying both sides of the equation by the least common multiple of the denominators in the first step?

_____

2. **What If?** What happens in the first step if you multiply both sides by a common multiple of the denominators that is not the LCM?

_____

_____

YOUR TURN

Solve.

3. $\frac{1}{7}k - 6 = \frac{3}{7}k + 4$ _____

4. $\frac{5}{6}y + 1 = -\frac{1}{2}y + \frac{1}{4}$ _____

Solving an Equation that Involves Decimals

Solving an equation with the variable on both sides that involves decimals is similar to solving an equation with fractions. But instead of first multiplying both sides by the LCM, multiply by a power of 10 to eliminate the decimals.

EXAMPLE 2 **Real World**

 CA CC 8.EE.7, 8.EE.7b

Javier walks from his house to the zoo at a constant rate. After walking 0.75 mile, he meets his brother, Raul, and they continue walking at the same constant rate. When they arrive at the zoo, Javier has walked for 0.5 hour and Raul has walked for 0.2 hour. What is the rate in miles per hour at which the brothers walked to the zoo?

My Notes

STEP 1 Write an equation for the distance from the brothers' house to the zoo, using the fact that distance equals rate times time. Let $r =$ the brothers' walking rate.

$$\underbrace{\text{distance to zoo}}_{0.2r + 0.75} = \underbrace{\text{distance to zoo}}_{0.5r}$$

STEP 2 Multiply both sides of the equation by $10^2 = 100$.

$$100(0.2r) + 100(0.75) = 100(0.5r)$$
$$20r + 75 = 50r$$

> Multiplying by 100 clears the equation of decimals. Multiplying by 10 does not: $10 \times 0.75 = 7.5$.

STEP 3 Use inverse operations to solve the equation.

$$\begin{array}{rcl} 20r + 75 &=& 50r \\ -20r & & -20r \\ \hline 75 &=& 30r \end{array}$$

Write the equation.
Subtract 20r from both sides.

$$\frac{75}{30} = \frac{30r}{30}$$

Divide both sides by 30.

$$2.5 = r$$

So, the brothers' constant rate of speed was 2.5 miles per hour.

YOUR TURN

5. Logan has two aquariums. One aquarium contains 1.3 cubic feet of water and the other contains 1.9 cubic feet of water. The water in the larger aquarium weighs 37.44 pounds more than the water in the smaller aquarium. Write an equation with a variable on both sides to represent the situation. Then find the weight of 1 cubic foot of water.

_____

Personal Math Trainer

Online Practice and Help

⏻ my.hrw.com

Writing a Real-World Situation from an Equation

Real-world situations can often be represented by equations involving fractions and decimals. Fractions and decimals can represent quantities such as weight, volume, capacity, time, and temperature. Decimals can also be used to represent dollars and cents.

Math On the Spot

⏻ my.hrw.com

EXAMPLE 3   CA CC 8.EE.7

Write a real-world situation that can be modeled by the equation 0.95x = 0.55x + 60.

STEP 1 The left side of the equation consists of a variable term. It could represent the total cost for x items.

STEP 2 The right side of the equation consists of a variable term plus a constant. It could represent the total cost for x items plus a flat fee.

STEP 3 The equation 0.95x = 0.55x + 60 could be represented by this situation: Toony Tunes charges \$0.95 for each song you download. Up With Downloads charges \$0.55 for each song but also charges an annual membership fee of \$60. How many songs must a customer download in a year so that the cost will be the same at both websites?

YOUR TURN

6. Write a real-world problem that can be modeled by the equation

$\frac{1}{3}x + 10 = \frac{3}{5}x$.

_____

_____

_____

Personal Math Trainer

Online Practice and Help

⏻ my.hrw.com

1. Sandy is upgrading her Internet service. Fast Internet charges $60 for installation and $50.45 per month. Quick Internet has free installation but charges $57.95 per month. (Example 2)

   a. Write an equation that can be used to find the number of months for which the Internet service would cost the same.

   _____

   b. Solve the equation.

   _____

Solve. (Examples 1 and 2)

2. $\frac{3}{4}n - 18 = \frac{1}{4}n - 4$

   _____

3. $6 + \frac{4}{5}b = \frac{9}{10}b$

   _____

4. $\frac{2}{11}m + 16 = 4 + \frac{6}{11}m$

   _____

5. $2.25t + 5 = 13.5t + 14$

   _____

6. $3.6w = 1.6w + 24$

   _____

7. $-0.75p - 2 = 0.25p$

   _____

8. Write a real-world problem that can be modeled by the equation $1.25x = 0.75x + 50$. (Example 3)

   _____

   _____

   _____

   _____

   _____

9. How does the method for solving equations with fractional or decimal coefficients and constants compare with the method for solving equations with integer coefficients and constants?

   _____

   _____

   _____

   _____

   _____

7.2 Independent Practice

Personal
Math Trainer

Online Practice
and Help

my.hrw.com

CA CC 8.EE.7, 8.EE.7b

10. Members of the Wide Waters Club pay $105 per summer season, plus $9.50 each time they rent a boat. Nonmembers must pay $14.75 each time they rent a boat. How many times would a member and a non-member have to rent a boat in order to pay the same amount?

_____

11. Margo can purchase tile at a store for $0.79 per tile and rent a tile saw for $24. At another store she can borrow the tile saw for free if she buys tiles there for $1.19 per tile. How many tiles must she buy for the cost to be the same at both stores?

_____

12. The charges for two shuttle services are shown in the table. Find the number of miles for which the cost of both shuttles is the same.

	Pickup Charge ($)	Charge per Mile ($)
Easy Ride	10	0.10
Best	0	0.35

_____

13. Multistep Rapid Rental Car charges a $40 rental fee, $15 for gas, and $0.25 per mile driven. For the same car, Capital Cars charges $45 for rental and gas and $0.35 per mile.

   a. For how many miles is the rental cost at both companies the same?

   _____

   b. What is that cost?

   _____

14. Write an equation with the solution $x = 20$. The equation should have the variable on both sides, a fractional coefficient on the left side, and a fraction anywhere on the right side.

_____

15. Write an equation with the solution $x = 25$. The equation should have the variable on both sides, a decimal coefficient on the left side, and a decimal anywhere on the right side. One of the decimals should be written in tenths, the other in hundredths.

_____

16. Geometry The perimeters of the rectangles shown are equal. What is the perimeter of each rectangle?

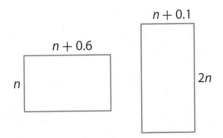

17. Analyze Relationships The formula $F = 1.8C + 32$ gives the temperature in degrees Fahrenheit (F) for a given temperature in degrees Celsius (C). There is one temperature for which the number of degrees Fahrenheit is equal to the number of degrees Celsius. Write an equation you can solve to find that temperature and then use it to find the temperature.

_____

18. Explain the Error Agustin solved an equation as shown. What error did Agustin make? What is the correct answer?

$$\frac{1}{3}x - 4 = \frac{3}{4}x + 1$$

$$12\left(\frac{1}{3}x\right) - 4 = 12\left(\frac{3}{4}x\right) + 1$$

$$4x - 4 = 9x + 1$$

$$-5 = 5x$$

$$x = -1$$

_____

_____

_____

_____

H.O.T. FOCUS ON HIGHER ORDER THINKING

Work Area

19. Write a real-world situation that could be modeled by the equation $20 + 1.25x = 15 + 2.5x$.

_____

_____

_____

_____

_____

20. Look for a Pattern Describe the pattern in the equation. Then solve the equation.

$$0.3x + 0.03x + 0.003x + 0.0003x + \ldots = 3$$

_____

_____

_____

_____

21. Critique Reasoning Jared wanted to find three consecutive even integers whose sum was 4 times the first of those integers. He let k represent the first integer, then wrote and solved this equation: $k + (k + 1) + (k + 2) = 4k$. Did he get the correct answer? Explain.

_____

_____

_____

_____

_____

_____

Equations with the Distributive Property

CA CC 8.EE.7b

Solve linear equations with rational number coefficients, including equations whose solutions require expanding expressions using the distributive property and collecting like terms.

ESSENTIAL QUESTION

How do you use the Distributive Property to solve equations?

Using the Distributive Property

The Distributive Property can be useful in solving equations.

Math On the Spot
my.hrw.com

EXAMPLE 1

CA CC 8.EE.7b

A Solve: $3(x - 5) + 1 = 2 + x$

STEP 1 Use the Distributive Property.

$3x - 15 + 1 = 2 + x$ Distribute 3 to the terms within the parentheses.

$3x - 14 = 2 + x$ Simplify.

STEP 2 Use inverse operations to solve the equation.

$$3x - 14 = 2 + x$$
$$\underline{-x \qquad\qquad -x}$$ Subtract x from both sides.
$$2x - 14 = 2$$
$$\underline{+14 \quad +14}$$ Add 14 to both sides.
$$2x = 16$$ Divide both sides by 2.
$$x = 8$$

B Solve: $5 - 7k = -4(k + 1) - 3$

STEP 1 Use the Distributive Property.

$5 - 7k = -4k - 4 - 3$ Distribute -4 to the terms within the parentheses.

$5 - 7k = -4k - 7$ Simplify.

STEP 2 Use inverse operations to solve the equation.

$$5 - 7k = -4k - 7$$
$$\underline{+4k \quad +4k}$$ Add 4k to both sides.
$$5 - 3k = -7$$
$$\underline{-5 \qquad -5}$$ Subtract 5 from both sides.
$$-3k = -12$$ Divide both sides by -3.
$$k = 4$$

Math Talk
Mathematical Practices

How can you rewrite $7 - (2a + 3) = 12$ without parentheses? Explain your answer.

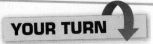
YOUR TURN

Solve each equation.

1. $y - 5 = 3 - 9(y + 2)$ _____

2. $2(x - 7) - 10 = 12 - 4x$ _____

Using the Distributive Property on Both Sides

Some equations require the use of the Distributive Property on both sides.

EXAMPLE 2 CA CC 8.EE.7b

Solve: $\frac{3}{4}(x - 13) = -2(9 + x)$

STEP 1 Eliminate the fraction.

$$\frac{3}{4}(x - 13) = -2(9 + x)$$

$$4 \times \frac{3}{4}(x - 13) = 4 \times [-2(9 + x)] \quad \text{Multiply both sides by 4.}$$

$$3(x - 13) = -8(9 + x)$$

Math Talk
Mathematical Practices

How can you eliminate fractions if there is a fraction being distributed on both sides of an equation?

STEP 2 Use the Distributive Property.

$$3x - 39 = -72 - 8x \qquad \text{Distribute 3 and } -8 \text{ to the terms within the parentheses.}$$

STEP 3 Use inverse operations to solve the equation.

$$\begin{array}{r} 3x - 39 = -72 - 8x \\ \underline{+8x \qquad\qquad +8x} \\ 11x - 39 = -72 \end{array}$$ Add $8x$ to both sides.

$$\begin{array}{r} \underline{+39 \quad +39} \\ 11x = -33 \end{array}$$ Add 39 to both sides.

$$\frac{11x}{11} = \frac{-33}{11}$$ Divide both sides by 11.

$$x = -3$$

YOUR TURN

Solve each equation.

3. $-4(-5 - b) = \frac{1}{3}(b + 16)$ _____

4. $\frac{3}{5}(t + 18) = -3(2 - t)$ _____

Solving a Real-World Problem Using the Distributive Property

Solving a real-world problem may involve using the Distributive Property.

Math On the Spot

⏱ my.hrw.com

EXAMPLE 3 Problem Solving

 CA CC 8.EE.7b

The Coleman family had their bill at a restaurant reduced by $7.50 because of a special discount. They left a tip of $8.90, which was 20% of the reduced amount. How much was their bill before the discount?

Analyze Information

The answer is the amount before the discount.

Formulate a Plan

Use an equation to find the amount before the discount.

Solve

STEP 1 Write the equation $0.2(x - 7.5) = 8.9$, where x is the amount of the Coleman family's bill before the discount.

STEP 2 Use the Distributive Property: $0.2x - 1.5 = 8.9$

STEP 3 Use inverse operations to solve the equation.

$$0.2x - 1.5 = 8.9$$
$$\underline{+ 1.5 \quad + 1.5} \qquad \text{Add 1.5 to both sides.}$$
$$0.2x = 10.4$$

$$\frac{0.2x}{0.2} = \frac{10.4}{0.2} \qquad \text{Divide both sides by 0.2.}$$

$$x = 52$$

The Coleman family's bill before the discount was $52.00.

> **Math Talk**
> Mathematical Practices
>
> Why do you use 0.2 in Step 1?

Justify and Evaluate

$52.00 - $7.50 = $44.50 and 0.2($44.50) = $8.90. This is the amount of the tip the Colemans left. The answer is reasonable.

YOUR TURN

5. The Smiths spend 8% of their budget on entertainment. Their total budget this year is $2,000 more than last year, and this year they plan to spend $3,840 on entertainment. What was their total budget last year? _____

Personal Math Trainer

Online Practice and Help

⏱ my.hrw.com

Solve each equation.

1. $4(x + 8) - 4 = 34 - 2x$ (Ex. 1)

$\boxed{}x + \boxed{} - 4 = 34 - 2x$

$\boxed{}x + \boxed{} = 34 - 2x$

$\boxed{}x + \boxed{} = 34$

$\boxed{}x = \boxed{}$

$\dfrac{\boxed{}x}{\boxed{}} = \dfrac{\boxed{}}{\boxed{}}$

$x = \boxed{}$

2. $\frac{2}{3}(9 + x) = -5(4 - x)$ (Ex. 2)

$\boxed{} \times \frac{2}{3}(9 + x) = \boxed{} \times [-5(4 - x)]$

$\boxed{}(9 + x) = \boxed{}(4 - x)$

$\boxed{} + \boxed{}x = \boxed{} \bigcirc \boxed{}x$

$\boxed{}x = \boxed{}$

$\dfrac{\boxed{}x}{\boxed{}} = \dfrac{\boxed{}}{\boxed{}}$

$x = \boxed{}$

3. $-3(x + 4) + 15 = 6 - 4x$ (Ex. 1)

_____

4. $10 + 4x = 5(x - 6) + 33$ (Ex. 1)

_____

5. $x - 9 = 8(2x + 3) - 18$ (Ex. 1)

_____

6. $-6(x - 1) - 7 = -7x + 2$ (Ex. 1)

_____

7. $\frac{1}{10}(x + 11) = -2(8 - x)$ (Ex. 2)

_____

8. $-(4 - x) = \frac{3}{4}(x - 6)$ (Ex. 2)

_____

9. $-8(8 - x) = \frac{4}{5}(x + 10)$ (Ex. 2)

_____

10. $\frac{1}{2}(16 - x) = -12(x + 7)$ (Ex. 2)

_____

11. Sandra saves 12% of her salary for retirement. This year her salary was $3,000 more than in the previous year, and she saved $4,200. What was her salary in the previous year? (Example 3)

Write an equation. _____

Sandra's salary in the previous year was _____.

12. When solving an equation using the Distributive Property, if the numbers being distributed are fractions, what is your first step? Why?

_____

7.3 Independent Practice

 CA CC 8.EE.7b

13. Multistep Martina is currently 14 years older than her cousin Joey. In 5 years she will be 3 times as old as Joey. Use this information to answer the following questions.

   a. If you let x represent Joey's current age, what expression can you use to represent Martina's current age?

   _____

   b. Based on your answer to part a, what expression represents Joey's age in 5 years? What expression represents Martina's age in 5 years?

   _____

   _____

   c. What equation can you write based on the information given?

   _____

   d. What is Joey's current age? What is Martina's current age?

   _____

14. As part of a school contest, Sarah and Luis are playing a math game. Sarah must pick a number between 1 and 50 and give Luis clues so he can write an equation to find her number. Sarah says, "If I subtract 5 from my number, multiply that quantity by 4, and then add 7 to the result, I get 35." What equation can Luis write based on Sarah's clues and what is Sarah's number?

_____

15. Critical Thinking When solving an equation using the Distributive Property that involves distributing fractions, usually the first step is to multiply by the LCD to eliminate the fractions in order to simplify computation. Is it necessary to do this to solve $\frac{1}{2}(4x + 6) = \frac{1}{3}(9x - 24)$? Why or why not?

_____

_____

16. Solve the equation given in Exercise 15 with and without using the LCD of the fractions. Are your answers the same? Explain.

_____

17. Represent Real-World Problems A chemist mixed x milliliters of 25% acid solution with some 15% acid solution to produce 100 milliliters of a 19% acid solution. Use this information to complete the table.

	ml of Solution	Percent Acid as a Decimal	ml of Acid
25% Solution	x		
15% Solution			
Mixture (19% Solution)	100		

a. What is the relationship between the milliliters of acid in the 25% solution, the milliliters of acid in the 15% solution, and the milliliters of acid in the mixture?

_____

_____

b. What equation can you use to solve for x based on your answer to part a?

_____

c. How many milliliters of the 25% solution and the 15% solution did the chemist use in the mixture?

_____

_____

 FOCUS ON HIGHER ORDER THINKING

Work Area

18. Explain the Error Anne solved $5(2x) - 3 = 20x + 15$ for x by first distributing 5 on the left side of the equation. She got the answer $x = -3$. When she substituted -3 into the original equation her answer was incorrect. Explain Anne's error, and find the correct answer.

_____

_____

_____

19. Communicate Mathematical Ideas Explain how to solve $5[3(x + 4) - 2(1 - x)] - x - 15 = 14x + 45$. Then solve the equation.

_____

_____

_____

_____

Equations with Many Solutions or No Solution

 CA CC 8.EE.7a

Give examples of linear equations in one variable with one solution, infinitely many solutions, or no solutions. Show which of these possibilities is the case by successively transforming the given equation into simpler forms, until an equivalent equation of the form $x = a$, $a = a$, or $a = b$ results (where a and b are different numbers).

ESSENTIAL QUESTION

How can you give examples of equations with a given number of solutions?

Determining the Number of Solutions

So far, when you solved a linear equation in one variable, you found one value of x that makes the equation a true statement. When you simplify some equations, you may find that they do not have one solution.

Math On the Spot

my.hrw.com

Possible Solutions of a Linear Equation

Result	What does this mean?	How many solutions?
$x = a$	When the value of x is a, the equation is a true statement.	1
$a = a$	Any value of x makes the equation a true statement.	Infinitely many
$a = b$, where $a \neq b$	There is no value of x that makes the equation a true statement.	0

EXAMPLE 1　　　　　　　　　　　　 CA CC 8.EE.7a

My Notes

Use the properties of equality to simplify each equation. Tell whether the equation has one, zero, or infinitely many solutions.

A $4x - 3 = 2x + 13$

$4x - 3 = 2x + 13$

$\underline{\quad +3 = \quad +3 \quad}$　　Add 3 to both sides.

$4x = 2x + 16$

$\underline{-2x \quad -2x \quad}$　　Subtract 2x from both sides.

$2x = 16$

$\dfrac{2x}{2} = \dfrac{16}{2}$　　Divide both sides by 2.

$x = 8$

The statement is true. There is one solution.

B $4x - 5 = 2(2x - 1) - 3$

$4x - 5 = 2(2x - 1) - 3$

$4x - 5 = 4x - 2 - 3$ Distributive Property

$4x - 5 = 4x - 5$ Simplify.

$\underline{-4x -4x}$ Subtract 4x from both sides.

$-5 = -5$

The statement is true. There are infinitely many solutions.

C $4x + 2 = 4x - 5$

$4x + 2 = 4x - 5$

$\underline{-2 -2}$ Subtract 2 from both sides.

$4x = 4x - 7$

$\underline{-4x -4x}$ Subtract 4x from both sides.

$0 = -7$

The statement is false. There is no solution.

Reflect

Math Talk
Mathematical Practices

Why do you substitute values for *x* into the *original* equation?

1. What happens when you substitute any value for *x* in the original equation in part B? In the original equation in part C?

_____

_____

_____

YOUR TURN

Use the properties of equality to simplify each equation. Tell whether the equation has one, zero, or infinitely many solutions.

2. $2x + 1 = 5x - 8$

_____

3. $3(4x + 3) - 2 = 12x + 7$

_____

4. $3x - 9 = 5 + 3x$

Personal Math Trainer

Online Practice and Help

⏻ my.hrw.com

Writing Equations with a Given Number of Solutions

You can use the results of linear equations to write an equation that has a given number of solutions.

Math On the Spot

⊙ my.hrw.com

EXAMPLE 2

 CA CC 8.EE.7a

Write a linear equation in one variable that has no solution.

You can use the strategy of working backward:

STEP 1 Start with a false statement such as $3 = 5$. Add the same variable term to both sides.

$3 + x = 5 + x$ *Add x to both sides.*

STEP 2 Next, add the same constant to both sides and combine like terms on each side of the equation.

$10 + x = 12 + x$ *Add 7 to both sides.*

STEP 3 Verify that your equation has no solutions by using properties of equality to simplify your equation.

$$10 + x = 12 + x$$
$$\underline{-x = \quad -x}$$
$$10 = 12$$

Math Talk
Mathematical Practices

What type of statement do you start with to write an equation with infinitely many solutions? Give an example.

Reflect

5. Explain why the result of the process above is an equation with no solution.

_____

_____

_____

_____

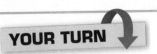

Complete each equation so that it has the indicated number of solutions.

6. No solution: $3x + 1 = 3x +$ _____

7. Infinitely many: $2x - 4 = 2x -$ _____

Personal Math Trainer

Online Practice and Help

⊙ my.hrw.com

Use the properties of equality to simplify each equation. Tell whether the final equation is a true statement. (Example 1)

1. $3x - 2 = 25 - 6x$ _____

   The statement is $\boxed{}$.

2. $2x - 4 = 2(x - 1) + 3$ _____

   The statement is $\boxed{}$.

3. How many solutions are there to the equation in Exercise 2? (Example 1)

   _____

4. After simplifying an equation, Juana gets $6 = 6$. Explain what this means. (Example 1)

   _____

   _____

Tell whether each equation has one, zero, or infinitely many solutions. (Example 1)

5. $6 + 3x = x - 8$ _____

6. $8x + 4 = 4(2x + 1)$ _____

Write a linear equation in one variable that has infinitely many solutions. (Example 2)

7. Start with a _____ statement.

   $10 = \boxed{}$

   Add the _____ to both sides.

   $10 + x = \boxed{}$

   Add the _____ to both sides.

   $10 + x + 5 = \boxed{}$

   Combine _____ terms.

   $\boxed{} = \boxed{}$

Create an equation with the indicated number of solutions. (Example 2)

8. Infinitely many solutions:

   $2(x - 1) + 6x = 4\left(\boxed{} - 1\right) + 2$

9. No solution:

   $3\left(x - \dfrac{4}{3}\right) = 3x + \boxed{}$

? ESSENTIAL QUESTION CHECK-IN

10. Give an example of an equation with an infinite number of solutions. Then make one change to the equation so that it has no solution.

    _____

    _____

Name _____ Class _____ Date _____

Personal Math Trainer

my.hrw.com   Online Practice and Help

Tell whether each equation has one, zero, or infinitely many solutions.

11. $-(2x + 2) - 1 = -x - (x + 3)$

_____

12. $-2(z + 3) - z = -z - 4(z + 2)$

_____

13. $3(2m - 1) + 5 = 6(m + 1)$

_____

14. $y + 7 + 2y = -14 + 3y + 21$

_____

Create an equation with the indicated number of solutions.

15. One solution of $x = -1$:

$5x - (x - 2) = 2x - \boxed{}$

16. Infinitely many solutions:

$-(x - 8) + 4x = 2\boxed{} + x$

17. Persevere in Problem Solving The Dig It Project is designing two gardens that have the same perimeter. One garden is a trapezoid whose nonparallel sides are equal. The other is a quadrilateral. Two possible designs are shown at the right.

$2x - 2$

$x + 1$ $x + 1$

x

a. Based on these designs, is there more than one value for x? Explain how you know this.

_____
_____
_____
_____
_____

$2x - 9$

x $x + 1$

$x + 8$

b. Why does your answer to part a make sense in this context?

_____
_____
_____

c. Suppose the Dig It Project wants the perimeter of each garden to be 60 meters. What is the value of x in this case? How did you find this?

_____
_____

18. Critique Reasoning Lisa says that the indicated angles cannot have the same measure. Marita disagrees and says she can prove that they can have the same measure. Who do you agree with? Justify your answer.

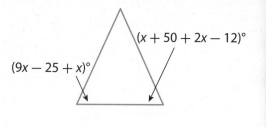

$(9x - 25 + x)°$

$(x + 50 + 2x - 12)°$

_____

_____

_____

_____

_____

19. Represent Real-World Problems Adele opens an account with $100 and deposits $35 a month. Kent opens an account with $50 and also deposits $35 a month. Will they have the same amount in their accounts at any point? If so, in how many months and how much will be in each account? Explain.

_____

_____

_____

 FOCUS ON HIGHER ORDER THINKING

Work Area

20. Communicate Mathematical Ideas Frank solved an equation and got the result $x = x$. Sarah solved the same equation and got $12 = 12$. Frank says that one of them is incorrect because you cannot get different results for the same equation. What would you say to Frank? If both results are indeed correct, explain how this happened.

_____

_____

_____

_____

21. Critique Reasoning Matt said $2x - 7 = 2(x - 7)$ has infinitely many solutions. Is he correct? Justify Matt's answer or show how he is incorrect.

_____

_____

_____

_____

Ready to Go On?

Personal Math Trainer

Online Practice and Help

⏻ my.hrw.com

7.1 Equations with the Variable on Both Sides

Solve each equation.

1. $4a - 4 = 8 + a$ _____

2. $4x + 5 = x + 8$ _____

3. Hue is arranging chairs. She can form 6 rows of a given length with 3 chairs left over, or 8 rows of that same length if she gets 11 more chairs. Write and solve an equation to find how many chairs are in that row length.

_____

7.2 Equations with Rational Numbers

Solve each equation.

4. $\frac{2}{3}n - \frac{2}{3} = \frac{n}{6} + \frac{4}{3}$ _____

5. $1.5d + 3.25 = 1 + 2.25d$ _____

6. Happy Paws charges $19.00 plus $1.50 per hour to keep a dog during the day. Woof Watchers charges $14.00 plus $2.75 per hour. Write and solve an equation to find for how many hours the total cost of the services is equal.

_____

7.3 Equations with the Distributive Property

Solve each equation.

7. $\frac{1}{4}(x - 7) = 1 + 3x$ _____

8. $3(x + 5) = 2(3x + 12)$ _____

7.4 Equations with Many Solutions or No Solution

Tell whether each equation has one, zero, or infinitely many solutions.

9. $5(x - 3) + 6 = 5x - 9$ _____

10. $5(x - 3) + 6 = 5x - 10$ _____

? ESSENTIAL QUESTION

11. How can you use equations with the variable on both sides to solve real-world problems?

_____

MODULE 7
MIXED REVIEW

CALIFORNIA

Assessment Readiness

Personal Math Trainer

Online Practice and Help

my.hrw.com

1. Consider each equation. Does the equation have at least one solution?

   Select Yes or No for equations A—C.

   A. $3(x + 2) = 2x + x + 6$ ○ Yes   ○ No
   B. $2x - 7 = 2(x + 4) + 3x$ ○ Yes   ○ No
   C. $8 + 5x = 5(x + 2) - 1$ ○ Yes   ○ No

2. Vince left home to go on a walk. The graph shows his distance from home over time.

   Choose True or False for each statement.

   A. Vince walked faster during segment 3 than during segment 1.

      ○ True   ○ False

   B. In segment 2, Vince's distance from home increased at a constant rate.   ○ True   ○ False

   C. In segment 4, Vince returned home.   ○ True   ○ False

3. Shawn's Rental's charges $27.50 per hour to rent a surfboard and a wetsuit. Darla's Surf Shop charges $23.25 per hour to rent a surfboard plus $17 extra for a wetsuit. Write and solve an equation to determine the rental period in hours for which the charges for Shawn's Rentals will be the same as the charges for Darla's Surf Shop. Explain the steps of your solution.

4. Beach towels are on sale for $1.50 off the regular price. Ms. Ortiz buys 4 beach towels on sale for a total of $33.96. Write and solve an equation to determine the regular price of a beach towel. Explain how you can check whether your answer is reasonable.

Solving Systems of Linear Equations

MODULE **8**

CALIFORNIA

? **ESSENTIAL QUESTION**

How can you use systems of equations to solve real-world problems?

Real-World Video

The distance contestants in a race travel over time can be modeled by a system of equations. Solving such a system can tell you when one contestant will overtake another who has a head start, as in a boating race or marathon.

 my.hrw.com

GO DIGITAL

my.hrw.com

my.hrw.com

Go digital with your write-in student edition, accessible on any device.

Math On the Spot

Scan with your smart phone to jump directly to the online edition, video tutor, and more.

Animated Math

Interactively explore key concepts to see how math works.

Personal Math Trainer

Get immediate feedback and help as you work through practice sets.

225

Are YOU Ready?

Complete these exercises to review skills you will need for this module.

Simplify Algebraic Expressions

EXAMPLE Simplify $5 - 4y + 2x - 6 + y$.

$-4y + y + 2x - 6 + 5$ Group like terms.

$-3y + 2x - 1$ Combine like terms.

Simplify.

1. $14x - 4x + 21$

_____

2. $-y - 4x + 4y$

_____

3. $5.5a - 1 + 21b + 3a$

_____

4. $2y - 3x + 6x - y$

_____

Graph Linear Equations

EXAMPLE Graph $y = -\frac{1}{3}x + 2$.

Step 1: Make a table of values.

x	$y = -\frac{1}{3}x + 2$	(x, y)
0	$y = -\frac{1}{3}(0) + 2 = 2$	$(0, 2)$
3	$y = -\frac{1}{3}(3) + 2 = 1$	$(3, 1)$

Step 2: Plot the points.
Step 3: Connect the points with a line.

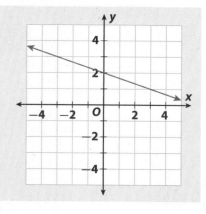

Graph each equation.

5. $y = 4x - 1$

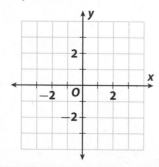

6. $y = \frac{1}{2}x + 1$

7. $y = -x$

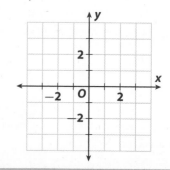

Reading Start-Up

Visualize Vocabulary

Use the ✔ words to complete the graphic.

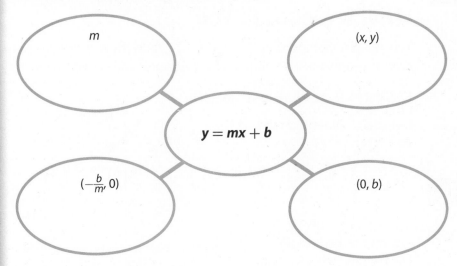

m

(x, y)

$y = mx + b$

$(-\frac{b}{m}, 0)$

$(0, b)$

Understand Vocabulary

Complete the sentences using the preview words.

1. A _____ is any ordered pair

   that satisfies all the equations in a system.

2. A set of two or more equations that contain two or more variables is

   called a _____.

Active Reading

Four-Corner Fold Before beginning the module, create a four-corner fold to help you organize what you learn about solving systems of equations. Use the categories "Solving by Graphing," "Solving by Substitution," "Solving by Elimination," and "Solving by Multiplication." As you study this module, note similarities and differences among the four methods. You can use your four-corner fold later to study for tests and complete assignments.

GETTING READY FOR

Solving Systems of Linear Equations

Understanding the standards and the vocabulary terms in the standards will help you know exactly what you are expected to learn in this module.

CA CC 8.EE.8a

Understand that solutions to a system of two linear equations in two variables correspond to points of intersection of their graphs, because points of intersection satisfy both equations simultaneously.

CA CC 8.EE.8b

Solve systems of two linear equations in two variables algebraically, and estimate solutions by graphing the equations. Solve simple cases by inspection.

Key Vocabulary

solution of a system of equations *(solución de un sistema de ecuaciones)* A set of values that make all equations in a system true.

system of equations *(sistema de ecuaciones)* A set of two or more equations that contain two or more variables.

Visit **my.hrw.com** to see all **CA Common Core Standards** explained.

What It Means to You

You will understand that the points of intersection of two or more graphs represent the solution to a system of linear equations.

EXAMPLE 8.EE.8a, 8.EE.8b

Use the elimination method.

A.
$$-x = -1 + y$$
$$\underline{x + y = 4}$$
$$y = y + 3$$

This is never true, so the system has no solution. The graphs never intersect.

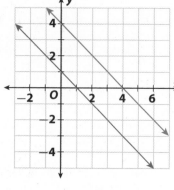

Use the substitution method.

B.
$$2y + x = 1$$
$$y - 2 = x$$

$$2y + (y - 2) = 1$$
$$3y - 2 = 1$$
$$y = 1$$

$$x = y - 2$$
$$x = 1 - 2$$
$$x = -1$$

Only one solution: $x = -1$, $y = 1$.
The graphs intersect at the point $(-1, 1)$.

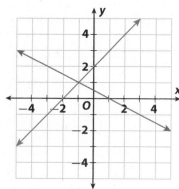

Use the multiplication method.

C.
$$3y - 6x = 3$$
$$y - 2x = 1$$

$$3y - 6x = 3$$
$$\underline{3y - 6x = 3}$$
$$0 = 0$$

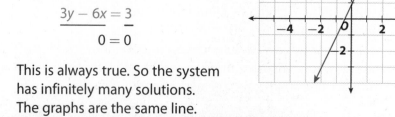

This is always true. So the system has infinitely many solutions. The graphs are the same line.

Solving Systems of Linear Equations by Graphing

🐻 **CA CC** 8.EE.8a

Understand that solutions to a system of two linear equations in two variables correspond to points of intersection of their graphs, because points of intersection satisfy both equations simultaneously. *Also 8.EE.8, 8.EE.8c*

ESSENTIAL QUESTION

How can you solve a system of equations by graphing?

EXPLORE ACTIVITY 🐻 **CA CC** 8.EE.8a

> Slope-intercept form is $y = mx + b$, where m is the slope and b is the y-intercept.

Investigating Systems of Equations

You have learned several ways to graph a linear equation in slope-intercept form. For example, you can use the slope and y-intercept or you can find two points that satisfy the equation and connect them with a line.

A Graph the pair of equations together: $\begin{cases} y = 3x - 2 \\ y = -2x + 3 \end{cases}$

B Explain how to tell whether $(2, -1)$ is a solution of the equation $y = 3x - 2$ without using the graph.

_____

_____

C Explain how to tell whether $(2, -1)$ is a solution of the equation $y = -2x + 3$ without using the graph.

_____

_____

D Use the graph to explain whether $(2, -1)$ is a solution of each equation.

_____

_____

E Determine if the point of intersection is a solution of both equations.

Point of intersection: ([ ] , [ ])

$$y = 3x - 2 \qquad\qquad y = -2x + 3$$

$$[\ ] = 3[\ ] - 2 \qquad\qquad [\ ] = -2[\ ] + 3$$

$$1 = [\ ] \qquad\qquad\qquad 1 = [\ ]$$

The point of intersection ⟨ **is / is not** ⟩ the solution of both equations.

Solving Systems Graphically

An ordered pair (x, y) is a solution of an equation in two variables if substituting the x- and y-values into the equation results in a true statement. A **system of equations** is a set of equations that have the same variables. An ordered pair is a **solution of a system of equations** if it is a solution of every equation in the set.

Since the graph of an equation represents all ordered pairs that are solutions of the equation, if a point lies on the graphs of two equations, the point is a solution of both equations and is, therefore, a solution of the system.

EXAMPLE 1

CA CC   8.EE.8

Solve each system by graphing.

A $\begin{cases} y = -x + 4 \\ y = 3x \end{cases}$

STEP 1 Start by graphing each equation.

STEP 2 Find the point of intersection of the two lines. It appears to be (1, 3). Substitute to check if it is a solution of both equations.

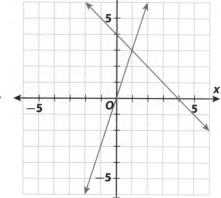

$$y = -x + 4 \qquad y = 3x$$

$$3 \overset{?}{=} -(1) + 4 \qquad 3 \overset{?}{=} 3(1)$$

$$3 = 3 \checkmark \qquad 3 = 3 \checkmark$$

The solution of the system is (1, 3).

B $\begin{cases} y = 3x - 3 \\ y = x - 3 \end{cases}$

STEP 1 Start by graphing each equation.

STEP 2 Find the point of intersection of the two lines. It appears to be (0, −3). Substitute to check if it is a solution of both equations.

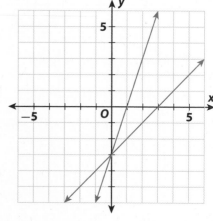

$$y = 3x - 3 \qquad y = x - 3$$

$$-3 \overset{?}{=} 3(0) - 3 \qquad -3 \overset{?}{=} 0 - 3$$

$$-3 = -3 \checkmark \qquad -3 = -3 \checkmark$$

The solution of the system is (0, −3).

Reflect

1. **What If?** If you want to include another linear equation in the system of equations in part A of Example 1 without changing the solution, what must be true about the graph of the equation?

_____

2. **Analyze Relationships** Suppose you include the equation $y = -2x - 3$ in the system of equations in part B of Example 1. What effect will this have on the solution of the system? Explain your reasoning.

_____

_____

_____

YOUR TURN

Solve each system by graphing. Check by substitution.

3. $\begin{cases} y = -x + 2 \\ y = -4x - 1 \end{cases}$ _____

Check:

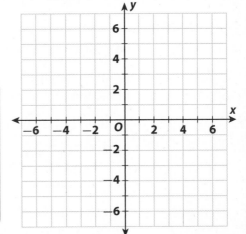

4. $\begin{cases} y = -2x + 5 \\ y = 3x \end{cases}$ _____

Check:

Personal
Math Trainer

Online Practice
and Help

⏻ my.hrw.com

Solving Problems Using Systems of Equations

When using graphs to solve a system of equations, it is best to rewrite both equations in slope-intercept form for ease of graphing.

To write an equation in slope-intercept form starting from $ax + by = c$:

$$ax + by = c$$

$by = c - ax$ Subtract ax from both sides.

$y = \dfrac{c}{b} - \dfrac{ax}{b}$ Divide both sides by b.

$y = -\dfrac{a}{b}x + \dfrac{c}{b}$ Rearrange the equation.

EXAMPLE 2   **CA CC**   8.EE.8c, 8.EE.8

Keisha and her friends visit the concession stand at a football game. The stand charges $2 for a sandwich and $1 for a lemonade. The friends buy a total of 8 items for $11. Tell how many sandwiches and how many lemonades they bought.

STEP 1   Let x represent the number of sandwiches they bought and let y represent the number of lemonades they bought.

Write an equation representing the **number of items they purchased.**

Number of sandwiches + Number of lemonades = Total items

         x + y =   8

Write an equation representing the **money spent on the items.**

Cost of 1 sandwich times number of sandwiches		Cost of 1 lemonade times number of lemonades		Total cost
$2x$	+	$1y$	=	11

STEP 2   Write the equations in slope-intercept form. Then graph.

$x + y = 8$

     $y = 8 - x$

     $y = -x + 8$

$2x + 1y = 11$

       $1y = 11 - 2x$

        $y = -2x + 11$

Graph the equations $y = -x + 8$ and $y = -2x + 11$.

STEP 3 Use the graph to identify the solution of the system of equations. Check your answer by substituting the ordered pair into both equations.

Apparent solution: (3, 5)
Check:

$$x + y = 8 \qquad 2x + y = 11$$
$$3 + 5 \overset{?}{=} 8 \qquad 2(3) + 5 \overset{?}{=} 11$$
$$8 = 8 \checkmark \qquad 11 = 11 \checkmark$$

The point (3, 5) is a solution of both equations.

STEP 4 Interpret the solution in the original context.

Keisha and her friends bought 3 sandwiches and 5 lemonades.

Animated Math

my.hrw.com

Reflect

5. Conjecture Why do you think the graph is limited to the first quadrant?

_____

_____

YOUR TURN

6. During school vacation, Marquis wants to go bowling and to play laser tag. He wants to play 6 total games but needs to figure out how many of each he can play if he spends exactly $20. Each game of bowling is $2 and each game of laser tag is $4.

a. Let x represent the number of games Marquis bowls and let y represent the number of games of laser tag Marquis plays. Write a system of equations that describes the situation. Then write the equations in slope-intercept form.

_____

_____

b. Graph the solutions of both equations.

c. How many games of bowling and how many games of laser tag will Marquis play?

_____

_____

_____

Personal Math Trainer

Online Practice and Help

my.hrw.com

Solve each system by graphing. (Examples 1 and 2)

1. $\begin{cases} y = 3x - 4 \\ y = x + 2 \end{cases}$ _____

2. $\begin{cases} 2x + y = 4 \\ -3x + 9y = -6 \end{cases}$ _____

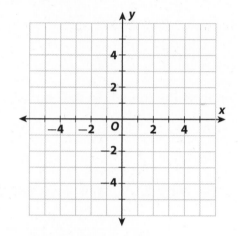

3. **Mrs. Morales wrote a test with 15 questions covering spelling and vocabulary. Spelling questions (x) are worth 5 points and vocabulary questions (y) are worth 10 points. The maximum number of points possible on the test is 100.** (Example 2)

   a. Write an equation in slope-intercept form to represent the number of questions on the test.

   _____

   b. Write an equation in slope-intercept form to represent the total number of points on the test.

   _____

   c. Graph the solutions of both equations.

   d. Use your graph to tell how many of each question type are on the test.

   _____

? ESSENTIAL QUESTION CHECK-IN

4. When you graph a system of linear equations, why does the intersection of the two lines represent the solution of the system?

   _____

   _____

   _____

8.1 Independent Practice

 CA CC 8.EE.8, 8.EE.8a, 8.EE.8c

Personal Math Trainer

Online Practice and Help

my.hrw.com

5. Vocabulary A is a set of equations that have the same variables.

6. Eight friends started a business. They will wear either a baseball cap or a shirt imprinted with their logo while working. They want to spend exactly $36 on the shirts and caps. Shirts cost $6 each and caps cost $3 each.

a. Write a system of equations to describe the situation. Let x represent the number of shirts and let y represent the number of caps.

_____

_____

b. Graph the system. What is the solution and what does it represent?

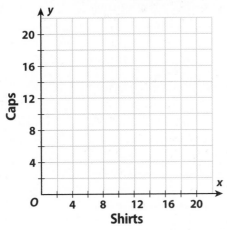

Business Logo Wear

_____

_____

_____

7. Multistep The table shows the cost for bowling at two bowling alleys.

	Shoe Rental Fee	Cost per Game
Bowl-o-Rama	$2.00	$2.50
Bowling Pinz	$4.00	$2.00

a. Write a system of equations, with one equation describing the cost to bowl at Bowl-o-Rama and the other describing the cost to bowl at Bowling Pinz. For each equation, let x represent the number of games played and let y represent the total cost.

_____

_____

b. Graph the system. What is the solution and what does it represent?

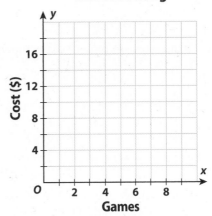

Cost of Bowling

_____

_____

_____

_____

8. Multi-Step Jeremy runs 7 miles per week and increases his distance by 1 mile each week. Tony runs 3 miles per week and increases his distance by 2 miles each week. In how many weeks will Jeremy and Tony be running the same distance? What will that distance be?

_____

9. Critical Thinking Write a real-world situation that could be represented by the system of equations shown below.

$$\begin{cases} y = 4x + 10 \\ y = 3x + 15 \end{cases}$$

_____

_____

_____

 FOCUS ON HIGHER ORDER THINKING

10. Multistep The table shows two options provided by a high-speed Internet provider.

	Setup Fee ($)	Cost per Month ($)
Option 1	50	30
Option 2	No setup fee	$40

a. In how many months will the total cost of both options be the same? What will that cost be?

_____

b. If you plan to cancel your Internet service after 9 months, which is the cheaper option? Explain.

_____

_____

_____

11. Draw Conclusions How many solutions does the system formed by $x - y = 3$ and $ay - ax + 3a = 0$ have for a nonzero number a? Explain.

_____

_____

_____

_____

Solving Systems by Substitution

CA CC 8.EE.8b

Solve systems of two linear equations in two variables algebraically, and estimate solutions by graphing the equations. Solve simple cases by inspection. *Also 8.EE.8c*

ESSENTIAL QUESTION

How do you use substitution to solve a system of linear equations?

Solving a Linear System by Substitution

The **substitution method** is used to solve systems of linear equations by solving an equation for one variable and then substituting the resulting expression for that variable into the other equation. The steps for this method are as follows:

1. Solve one of the equations for one of its variables.

2. Substitute the expression from step 1 into the other equation and solve for the other variable.

3. Substitute the value from step 2 into either original equation and solve to find the value of the variable in step 1.

Math On the Spot

⏱ my.hrw.com

EXAMPLE 1

CA CC 8.EE.8b

My Notes

Solve the system of linear equations by substitution. Check your answer.

$$\begin{cases} -3x + y = 1 \\ 4x + y = 8 \end{cases}$$

STEP 1   Solve an equation for one variable.

$$-3x + y = 1 \qquad \text{\textit{Select one of the equations.}}$$

$$y = 3x + 1 \qquad \text{\textit{Solve for the variable y. Isolate y on one side.}}$$

STEP 2   Substitute the expression for *y* in the other equation and solve.

$$4x + (3x + 1) = 8 \qquad \text{\textit{Substitute the expression for the variable y.}}$$

$$7x + 1 = 8 \qquad \text{\textit{Combine like terms.}}$$

$$7x = 7 \qquad \text{\textit{Subtract 1 from each side.}}$$

$$x = 1 \qquad \text{\textit{Divide each side by 7.}}$$

STEP 3   Substitute the value of *x* you found into one of the equations and solve for the other variable, *y*.

$$-3(1) + y = 1 \qquad \text{\textit{Substitute the value of x into the first equation.}}$$

$$-3 + y = 1 \qquad \text{\textit{Simplify.}}$$

$$y = 4 \qquad \text{\textit{Add 3 to each side.}}$$

So, (1, 4) is the solution of the system.

STEP 4 Check the solution by graphing.

$$-3x + y = 1 \qquad\qquad 4x + y = 8$$

x-intercept: $-\frac{1}{3}$ x-intercept: 2

y-intercept: 1   y-intercept: 8

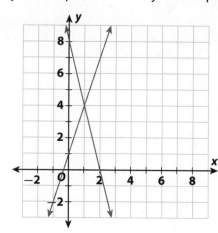

The point of intersection is (1, 4).

Reflect

1. **Justify Reasoning** Is it more efficient to solve $-3x + y = 1$ for x? Why or why not?

_____

_____

2. Is there another way to solve the system?

_____

_____

3. What is another way to check your solution?

_____

_____

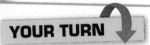

YOUR TURN

Solve each system of linear equations by substitution.

4. $\begin{cases} 3x + y = 11 \\ -2x + y = 1 \end{cases}$

5. $\begin{cases} 2x - 3y = -24 \\ x + 6y = 18 \end{cases}$

6. $\begin{cases} x - 2y = 5 \\ 3x - 5y = 8 \end{cases}$

_____   _____   _____

Personal
Math Trainer

Online Practice
and Help

my.hrw.com

Using a Graph to Estimate the Solution of a System

You can use a graph to estimate the solution of a system of equations before solving the system algebraically.

EXAMPLE 2   🐻 CA CC 8.EE.8b

Solve the system $\begin{cases} x - 4y = 4 \\ 2x - 3y = -3 \end{cases}$.

STEP 1   Sketch a graph of each equation by substituting values for x and generating values of y.

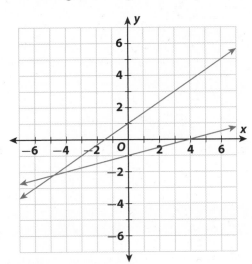

Math Talk
🐻 Mathematical Practices

In Step 2, how can you tell that $(-5, -2)$ is not the solution?

STEP 2   Find the intersection of the lines. The lines appear to intersect near $(-5, -2)$.

STEP 3   Solve the system algebraically.

Solve $x - 4y = 4$ for x.   Substitute to find y.   Substitute to find x.

$x - 4y = 4$

$\quad x = 4 + 4y$

$2(4 + 4y) - 3y = -3$

$8 + 8y - 3y = -3$

$8 + 5y = -3$

$5y = -11$

$y = -\dfrac{11}{5}$

$x = 4 + 4y$

$\quad = 4 + 4\left(-\dfrac{11}{5}\right)$

$\quad = \dfrac{20 - 44}{5}$

$\quad = -\dfrac{24}{5}$

The solution is $\left(-\dfrac{24}{5}, -\dfrac{11}{5}\right)$.

STEP 4   Use the estimate you made using the graph to judge the reasonableness of your solution.

$-\dfrac{24}{5}$ is close to the estimate of -5, and $-\dfrac{11}{5}$ is close to the estimate of -2, so the solution seems reasonable.

YOUR TURN

7. Estimate the solution of the system $\begin{cases} x + y = 4 \\ 2x - y = 6 \end{cases}$ by sketching a graph of each linear function. Then solve the system algebraically. Use your estimate to judge the reasonableness of your solution.

The estimated solution is _____.

The algebraic solution is _____.

The solution ⟨ **is/is not** ⟩ reasonable because

_____

_____

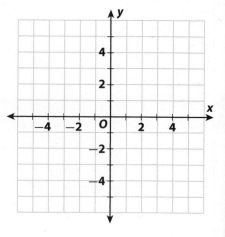

Solving Problems with Systems of Equations

EXAMPLE 3 (Real World)

CA CC 8.EE.8c

As part of Class Day, the eighth grade is doing a treasure hunt. Each team is given the following riddle and map. At what point is the treasure located?

There's pirate treasure to be found. So search on the island, all around. Draw a line through *A* and *B*. Then another through *C* and *D*. Dance a jig, "X" marks the spot. Where the lines intersect, that's the treasure's plot!

STEP 1 Give the coordinates of each point and find the slope of the line through each pair of points.

A: $(-2, -1)$	C: $(-1, 4)$
B: $(2, 5)$	D: $(1, -4)$
Slope:	Slope:

$$\frac{5 - (-1)}{2 - (-2)} = \frac{6}{4} \qquad \frac{-4 - 4}{1 - (-1)} = \frac{-8}{2}$$

$$= \frac{3}{2} \qquad\qquad\qquad = -4$$

STEP 2 Write equations in slope-intercept form describing the line through points A and B and the line through points C and D.

Line through A and B:

Use the slope and a point to find b.

$$5 = \left(\frac{3}{2}\right)2 + b$$
$$b = 2$$

The equation is $y = \frac{3}{2}x + 2$.

Line through C and D:

Use the slope and a point to find b.

$$4 = -4(-1) + b$$
$$b = 0$$

The equation is $y = -4x$.

STEP 3 Solve the system algebraically.

Substitute $\frac{3}{2}x + 2$ for y in $y = -4x$ to find x.

$$\frac{3}{2}x + 2 = -4x$$
$$\frac{11}{2}x = -2$$
$$x = -\frac{4}{11}$$

Substitute to find x.
$$y = -4\left(-\frac{4}{11}\right) = \frac{16}{11}$$

The solution is $\left(-\frac{4}{11}, \frac{16}{11}\right)$.

YOUR TURN

8. Ace Car Rental rents cars for x dollars per day plus y dollars for each mile driven. Carlos rented a car for 4 days, drove it 160 miles, and spent $120. Vanessa rented a car for 1 day, drove it 240 miles, and spent $80. Write equations to represent Carlos's expenses and Vanessa's expenses. Then solve the system and tell what each number represents.

_____

_____

_____

_____

_____

Personal Math Trainer

Online Practice and Help

⊙ my.hrw.com

Solve each system of linear equations by substitution. (Example 1)

1. $\begin{cases} 3x - 2y = 9 \\ y = 2x - 7 \end{cases}$ _____

2. $\begin{cases} y = x - 4 \\ 2x + y = 5 \end{cases}$ _____

3. $\begin{cases} x + 4y = 6 \\ y = -x + 3 \end{cases}$ _____

4. $\begin{cases} x + 2y = 6 \\ x - y = 3 \end{cases}$ _____

Solve each system. Estimate the solution first. (Example 2)

5. $\begin{cases} 6x + y = 4 \\ x - 4y = 19 \end{cases}$

   Estimate _____

   Solution _____

6. $\begin{cases} x + 2y = 8 \\ 3x + 2y = 6 \end{cases}$

   Estimate _____

   Solution _____

7. $\begin{cases} 3x + y = 4 \\ 5x - y = 22 \end{cases}$

   Estimate _____

   Solution _____

8. $\begin{cases} 2x + 7y = 2 \\ x + y = -1 \end{cases}$

   Estimate _____

   Solution _____

9. Adult tickets to Space City amusement park cost x dollars.
   Children's tickets cost y dollars. The Henson family bought
   3 adult and 1 child tickets for $163. The Garcia family bought
   2 adult and 3 child tickets for $174. (Example 3)

   a. Write equations to represent the Hensons' cost and the Garcias' cost.

      Hensons' cost: _____   Garcias' cost: _____

   b. Solve the system.

      adult ticket price: _____   child ticket price: _____

? ESSENTIAL QUESTION CHECK-IN

10. How can you decide which variable to solve for first when you are solving
    a linear system by substitution?

    _____

    _____

    _____

    _____

8.2 Independent Practice

 8.EE.8b, 8.EE.8c

Personal
Math Trainer

Online Practice
and Help

my.hrw.com

11. Check for Reasonableness Zach solves the system $\begin{cases} x+y=-3 \\ x-y=1 \end{cases}$
and finds the solution $(1, -2)$. Use a graph to explain whether
Zach's solution is reasonable.

_____

_____

_____

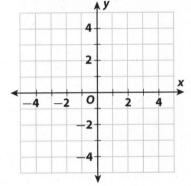

12. Represent Real-World Problems Angelo bought apples and
bananas at the fruit stand. He bought 20 pieces of fruit and spent
$11.50. Apples cost $0.50 and bananas cost $0.75 each.

  a. Write a system of equations to model the problem. (Hint: One
     equation will represent the number of pieces of fruit. A second
     equation will represent the money spent on the fruit.)

     _____

  b. Solve the system algebraically. Tell how many apples and
     bananas Angelo bought.

     _____

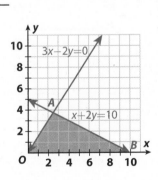

Apples $0.50
Bananas $0.75

13. Represent Real-World Problems A jar contains n nickels and
d dimes. There is a total of 200 coins in the jar. The value of the coins
is $14.00. How many nickels and how many dimes are in the jar?

_____

14. Multistep The graph shows a triangle formed by the x-axis, the
line $3x - 2y = 0$, and the line $x + 2y = 10$. Follow these steps to
find the area of the triangle.

  a. Find the coordinates of point A by solving the system $\begin{cases} 3x - 2y = 0 \\ x + 2y = 10 \end{cases}$.

     Point A: _____

  b. Use the coordinates of point A to find the height of the triangle.

     height: _____

  c. What is the length of the base of the triangle?

     base: _____

  d. What is the area of the triangle? _____

15. Jed is graphing the design for a kite on a coordinate grid. The four vertices of the kite are at $A\left(-\frac{4}{3}, \frac{2}{3}\right)$, $B\left(\frac{14}{3}, -\frac{4}{3}\right)$, $C\left(\frac{14}{3}, -\frac{16}{3}\right)$, and $D\left(\frac{2}{3}, -\frac{16}{3}\right)$. One kite strut will connect points A and C. The other will connect points B and D. Find the point where the struts cross.

_____

 FOCUS ON HIGHER ORDER THINKING

Work Area

16. Analyze Relationships Consider the system $\begin{cases} 6x - 3y = 15 \\ x + 3y = -8 \end{cases}$. Describe three different substitution methods that can be used to solve this system. Then solve the system.

_____

_____

_____

_____

_____

_____

17. Communicate Mathematical Ideas Explain the advantages, if any, that solving a system of linear equations by substitution has over solving the same system by graphing.

_____

_____

_____

18. Persevere in Problem Solving Create a system of equations of the form $\begin{cases} Ax + By = C \\ Dx + Ey = F \end{cases}$ that has $(7, -2)$ as its solution. Explain how you found the system.

_____

_____

_____

_____

Solving Systems by Elimination

CA CC 8.EE.8b

Solve systems of two linear equations in two variables algebraically, and estimate solutions by graphing the equations. Solve simple cases by inspection. Also 8.EE.8c

ESSENTIAL QUESTION

How do you solve a system of linear equations by adding or subtracting?

Solving a Linear System by Adding

The **elimination method** is another method used to solve a system of linear equations. In this method, one variable is *eliminated* by adding or subtracting the two equations of the system to obtain a single equation in one variable. The steps for this method are as follows:

1. Add or subtract the equations to eliminate one variable.

2. Solve the resulting equation for the other variable.

3. Substitute the value into either original equation to find the value of the eliminated variable.

Math On the Spot
my.hrw.com

EXAMPLE 1

CA CC 8.EE.8b

Solve the system of equations by adding. Check your answer.

$$\begin{cases} 2x - 3y = 12 \\ x + 3y = 6 \end{cases}$$

My Notes

STEP 1 Add the equations.

$$\begin{array}{r} 2x - 3y = 12 \\ + (x + 3y = 6) \\ \hline 3x + 0 = 18 \end{array}$$

Write the equations so that like terms are aligned.

Notice that the terms $-3y$ and $3y$ are opposites.

Add to eliminate the variable y.

$3x = 18$ Simplify and solve for x.

$\dfrac{3x}{3} = \dfrac{18}{3}$ Divide each side by 3.

$x = 6$ Simplify.

STEP 2 Substitute the solution into one of the original equations and solve for y.

$x + 3y = 6$ Use the second equation.

$6 + 3y = 6$ Substitute 6 for the variable x.

$3y = 0$ Subtract 6 from each side.

$y = 0$ Divide each side by 3 and simplify.

STEP 3 Write the solution as an ordered pair: (6, 0)

STEP 4 Check the solution by graphing.

$$2x - 3y = 12 \qquad x + 3y = 6$$

x-intercept: 6   *x*-intercept: 6

y-intercept: −4   *y*-intercept: 2

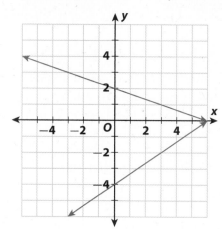

The point of intersection is (6, 0).

Reflect

1. Can this linear system be solved by subtracting one of the original equations from the other? Why or why not?

   _____

   _____

   _____

2. What is another way to check your solution?

   _____

   _____

   _____

YOUR TURN

Solve each system of equations by adding. Check your answers.

3. $\begin{cases} x + y = -1 \\ x - y = 7 \end{cases}$

4. $\begin{cases} 2x + 2y = -2 \\ 3x - 2y = 12 \end{cases}$

5. $\begin{cases} 6x + 5y = 4 \\ -6x + 7y = 20 \end{cases}$

   _____   _____   _____

Personal Math Trainer

Online Practice and Help

⏻ my.hrw.com

Solving a Linear System by Subtracting

If both equations contain the same x- or y-term, you can solve by subtracting.

Math On the Spot
my.hrw.com

EXAMPLE 2

CA CC 8.EE.8b

Solve the system of equations by subtracting. Check your answer.

$$\begin{cases} 3x + 3y = 6 \\ 3x - y = -6 \end{cases}$$

My Notes

STEP 1   Subtract the equations.

$\quad\quad 3x + 3y = 6$ *Write the equations so that like terms are aligned.*

$\quad\quad \underline{-(3x - y = -6)}$ *Notice that both equations contain the term 3x.*

$\quad\quad\quad 0 + 4y = 12$ *Subtract to eliminate the variable x.*

$\quad\quad\quad\quad 4y = 12$ *Simplify and solve for y.*

$\quad\quad\quad\quad\quad y = 3$ *Divide each side by 4 and simplify.*

STEP 2   Substitute the solution into one of the original equations and solve for x.

$\quad\quad 3x - y = -6$ *Use the second equation.*

$\quad\quad 3x - 3 = -6$ *Substitute 3 for the variable y.*

$\quad\quad\quad 3x = -3$ *Add 3 to each side.*

$\quad\quad\quad\quad x = -1$ *Divide each side by 3 and simplify.*

STEP 3   Write the solution as an ordered pair: $(-1, 3)$

STEP 4   Check the solution by graphing.

$3x + 3y = 6$ $3x - y = -6$

x-intercept: 2 x-intercept: -2

y-intercept: 2 y-intercept: 6

The point of intersection is $(-1, 3)$.

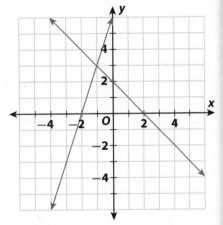

Reflect

6. What If? What would happen if you added the original equations?

_____

_____

7. How can you decide whether to add or subtract to eliminate a variable in a linear system? Explain your reasoning.

_____

_____

_____

_____

_____

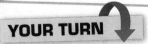

YOUR TURN

Solve each system of equations by subtracting. Check your answers.

8. $\begin{cases} 6x - 3y = 6 \\ 6x + 8y = -16 \end{cases}$

9. $\begin{cases} 4x + 3y = 19 \\ 6x + 3y = 33 \end{cases}$

10. $\begin{cases} 2x + 6y = 17 \\ 2x - 10y = 9 \end{cases}$

_____   _____   _____

Solving Problems with Systems of Equations

Many real-world situations can be modeled and solved with a system of equations.

EXAMPLE 3   CA CC 8.EE.8c

The Polar Bear Club wants to buy snowshoes and camp stoves. The club will spend $554.50 to buy them at Top Sports and $602.00 to buy them at Outdoor Explorer, before taxes, but Top Sports is farther away. How many of each item does the club intend to buy?

	Snowshoes	Camp Stoves
Top Sports	$79.50 per pair	$39.25
Outdoor Explorer	$89.00 per pair	$39.25

STEP 1 Choose variables and write a system of equations.
Let x represent the number of pairs of snowshoes.
Let y represent the number of camp stoves.

Top Sports cost: $79.50x + 39.25y = 554.50$
Outdoor Explorer cost: $89.00x + 39.25y = 602.00$

STEP 2 Subtract the equations.

$$79.50x + 39.25y = 554.50$$
$$-(89.00x + 39.25y = 602.00)$$
$$\overline{-9.50x + 0 = -47.50}$$

Both equations contain the term $39.25y$.

Subtract to eliminate the variable y.

$$-9.50x = -47.50$$

Simplify and solve for x.

$$\frac{-9.50x}{-9.50} = \frac{-47.50}{-9.50}$$

Divide each side by -9.50.

$$x = 5$$

Simplify.

STEP 3 Substitute the solution into one of the original equations and solve for y.

$$79.50x + 39.25y = 554.50$$

Use the first equation.

$$79.50(5) + 39.25y = 554.50$$

Substitute 5 for the variable x.

$$397.50 + 39.25y = 554.50$$

Multiply.

$$39.25y = 157.00$$

Subtract 397.50 from each side.

$$\frac{39.25y}{39.25} = \frac{157.00}{39.25}$$

Divide each side by 39.25.

$$y = 4$$

Simplify.

STEP 4 Write the solution as an ordered pair: (5, 4)

The club intends to buy 5 pairs of snowshoes and 4 camp stoves.

YOUR TURN

11. At the county fair, the Baxter family bought 6 bags of roasted almonds and 4 juice drinks for $16.70. The Farley family bought 3 bags of roasted almonds and 4 juice drinks for $10.85. Find the price of a bag of roasted almonds and the price of a juice drink.

_____

_____

Personal Math Trainer

Online Practice and Help

my.hrw.com

1. Solve the system $\begin{cases} 4x + 3y = 1 \\ x - 3y = -11 \end{cases}$ by adding. (Example 1)

STEP 1 Add the equations.

$$4x + 3y = 1$$ Write the equations so that like terms are aligned.

$$+ \quad x - 3y = -11$$

$$5x + \boxed{} = \boxed{}$$ Add to eliminate the variable $\boxed{}$.

$$5x = \boxed{}$$ Simplify and solve for x.

$$x = \boxed{}$$ Divide both sides by $\boxed{}$ and simplify.

STEP 2 Substitute into one of the original equations and solve for y.

$$y = \boxed{} \qquad \text{So, } \boxed{} \text{ is the solution of the system.}$$

Solve each system of equations by adding or subtracting. (Examples 1, 2)

2. $\begin{cases} x + 2y = -2 \\ -3x + 2y = -10 \end{cases}$

3. $\begin{cases} 3x + y = 23 \\ 3x - 2y = 8 \end{cases}$

4. $\begin{cases} -4x - 5y = 7 \\ 3x + 5y = -14 \end{cases}$

_____

_____

_____

5. $\begin{cases} x - 2y = -19 \\ 5x + 2y = 1 \end{cases}$

6. $\begin{cases} 3x + 4y = 18 \\ -2x + 4y = 8 \end{cases}$

7. $\begin{cases} -5x + 7y = 11 \\ -5x + 3y = 19 \end{cases}$

_____

_____

_____

8. The Green River Freeway has a minimum and a maximum speed limit. Tony drove for 2 hours at the minimum speed limit and 3.5 hours at the maximum limit, a distance of 355 miles. Rae drove 2 hours at the minimum speed limit and 3 hours at the maximum limit, a distance of 320 miles. What are the two speed limits? (Example 3)

a. Write equations to represent Tony's distance and Rae's distance.

Tony: _____   Rae: _____

b. Solve the system.

minimum speed limit: _____   maximum speed limit: _____

? ESSENTIAL QUESTION CHECK-IN

9. Can you use addition or subtraction to solve any system? Explain.

_____

_____

_____

8.3 Independent Practice

CA CC **8.EE.8b, 8.EE.8c**

Personal Math Trainer

Online Practice and Help

my.hrw.com

10. **Represent Real-World Problems** Marta bought new fish for her home aquarium. She bought 3 guppies and 2 platies for a total of $13.95. Hank also bought guppies and platies for his aquarium. He bought 3 guppies and 4 platies for a total of $18.33. Find the price of a guppy and the price of a platy.

_____

11. **Represent Real-World Problems** The rule for the number of fish in a home aquarium is 1 gallon of water for each inch of fish length. Marta's aquarium holds 13 gallons and Hank's aquarium holds 17 gallons. Based on the number of fish they bought in Exercise 10, how long is a guppy and how long is a platy?

_____

12. Line *m* passes through the points (6, 1) and (2, −3). Line *n* passes through the points (2, 3) and (5, −6). Find the point of intersection of these lines.

_____

13. **Represent Real-World Problems** Two cars got an oil change at the same auto shop. The shop charges customers for each quart of oil plus a flat fee for labor. The oil change for one car required 5 quarts of oil and cost $22.45. The oil change for the other car required 7 quarts of oil and cost $25.45. How much is the labor fee and how much is each quart of oil?

_____

14. **Represent Real-World Problems** A sales manager noticed that the number of units sold for two T-shirt styles, style A and style B, was the same during June and July. In June, total sales were $2779 for the two styles, with A selling for $15.95 per shirt and B selling for $22.95 per shirt. In July, total sales for the two styles were $2385.10, with A selling at the same price and B selling at a discount of 22% off the June price. How many T-shirts of each style were sold in June and July combined?

_____

_____

15. **Represent Real-World Problems** Adult tickets to a basketball game cost $5. Student tickets cost $1. A total of $2,874 was collected on the sale of 1,246 tickets. How many of each type of ticket were sold?

_____

16. Communicate Mathematical Ideas Is it possible to solve the system $\begin{cases} 3x - 2y = 10 \\ x + 2y = 6 \end{cases}$ by using substitution? If so, explain how. Which method, substitution or elimination, is more efficient? Why?

_____

_____

_____

_____

_____

_____

_____

17. Jenny used substitution to solve the system $\begin{cases} 2x + y = 8 \\ x - y = 1 \end{cases}$. Her solution is shown below.

Step 1 $y = -2x + 8$ Solve the first equation for y.

Step 2 $2x + (-2x + 8) = 8$ Substitute the value of y in an original equation.

Step 3 $2x - 2x + 8 = 8$ Use the Distributive Property.

Step 4 $8 = 8$ Simplify.

a. Explain the Error Explain the error Jenny made. Describe how to correct it.

_____

_____

_____

_____

b. Communicate Mathematical Ideas Would adding the equations have been a better method for solving the system? If so, explain why.

_____

_____

_____

_____

CA CC 8.EE.8b

Solve systems of two linear equations in two variables algebraically, and estimate solutions by graphing the equations. Solve simple cases by inspection. *Also 8.EE.8c*

Math On the Spot
⏻ my.hrw.com

⬤ **ESSENTIAL QUESTION**

How do you solve a system of linear equations by multiplying?

Solving a System by Multiplying and Adding

In some linear systems, neither variable can be eliminated by adding or subtracting the equations directly. In systems like these, you need to multiply one of the equations by a constant so that adding or subtracting the equations will eliminate one variable. The steps for this method are as follows:

1. Decide which variable to eliminate.

2. Multiply one equation by a constant so that adding or subtracting will eliminate that variable.

3. Solve the system using the elimination method.

EXAMPLE 1 **CA CC** 8.EE.8b

Solve the system of equations by multiplying and adding.

$$\begin{cases} 2x + 10y = 2 \\ 3x - 5y = -17 \end{cases}$$

My Notes

 The coefficient of y in the first equation, 10, is 2 times the coefficient of y, 5, in the second equation. Also, the y-term in the first equation is being added, while the y-term in the second equation is being subtracted. To eliminate the y-terms, multiply the second equation by 2 and add this new equation to the first equation.

$$2(3x - 5y = -17)$$ *Multiply each term in the second equation by 2 to get opposite coefficients for the y-terms.*

$$6x - 10y = -34$$ *Simplify.*

$$\begin{array}{r} 6x - 10y = -34 \\ + 2x + 10y = 2 \\ \hline 8x + 0y = -32 \end{array}$$

Add the first equation to the new equation.

Add to eliminate the variable y.

$$8x = -32$$ *Simplify and solve for x.*

$$\frac{8x}{8} = \frac{-32}{8}$$ *Divide each side by 8.*

$$x = -4$$ *Simplify.*

STEP 2 Substitute the solution into one of the original equations and solve for y.

$$2x + 10y = 2 \qquad \textit{Use the first equation.}$$

$$2(-4) + 10y = 2 \qquad \textit{Substitute −4 for the variable x.}$$

$$-8 + 10y = 2 \qquad \textit{Simplify.}$$

$$10y = 10 \qquad \textit{Add 8 to each side.}$$

$$y = 1 \qquad \textit{Divide each side by 10 and simplify.}$$

STEP 3 Write the solution as an ordered pair: $(-4, 1)$

STEP 4 Check your answer algebraically.

Substitute −4 for x and 1 for y in the original system.

$$\begin{cases} 2x + 10y = 2 \rightarrow 2(-4) + 10(1) = -8 + 10 = 2 \; \checkmark \\ 3x - 5y = -17 \rightarrow 3(-4) - 5(1) = -12 - 5 = -17 \; \checkmark \end{cases}$$

The solution is correct.

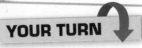

Math Talk

Mathematical Practices

When you check your answer algebraically, why do you substitute your values for x and y into the original system? Explain.

Reflect

1. How can you solve this linear system by subtracting? Which is more efficient, adding or subtracting? Explain your reasoning.

_____

_____

_____

2. Can this linear system be solved by adding or subtracting without multiplying? Why or why not?

_____

_____

3. What would you need to multiply the second equation by to eliminate x by adding? Why might you choose to eliminate y instead of x?

_____

_____

YOUR TURN

Solve each system of equations by multiplying and adding.

4. $\begin{cases} 5x + 2y = -10 \\ 3x + 6y = 66 \end{cases}$

5. $\begin{cases} 4x + 2y = 6 \\ 3x - y = -8 \end{cases}$

6. $\begin{cases} -6x + 9y = -12 \\ 2x + y = 0 \end{cases}$

_____ _____ _____

Personal Math Trainer

Online Practice and Help

⊙ my.hrw.com

Solving a System by Multiplying and Subtracting

You can solve some systems of equations by multiplying one equation by a constant and then subtracting.

Math On the Spot
my.hrw.com

EXAMPLE 2

 CA CC 8.EE.8b

Solve the system of equations by multiplying and subtracting.

$$\begin{cases} 6x + 5y = 7 \\ 2x - 4y = -26 \end{cases}$$

My Notes

STEP 1 Multiply the second equation by 3 and subtract this new equation from the first equation.

$$3(2x - 4y = -26)$$
Multiply each term in the second equation by 3 to get the same coefficients for the x-terms.

$$6x - 12y = -78$$ *Simplify.*

$$\begin{array}{r} 6x + 5y = 7 \\ -(6x - 12y = -78) \\ \hline \end{array}$$
Subtract the new equation from the first equation.

$$0x + 17y = 85$$ *Subtract to eliminate the variable x.*

$$17y = 85$$ *Simplify and solve for y.*

$$\frac{17y}{17} = \frac{85}{17}$$ *Divide each side by 17.*

$$y = 5$$ *Simplify.*

STEP 2 Substitute the solution into one of the original equations and solve for x.

$$6x + 5y = 7$$ *Use the first equation.*

$$6x + 5(5) = 7$$ *Substitute 5 for the variable y.*

$$6x + 25 = 7$$ *Simplify.*

$$6x = -18$$ *Subtract 25 from each side.*

$$x = -3$$ *Divide each side by 6 and simplify.*

STEP 3 Write the solution as an ordered pair: $(-3, 5)$

STEP 4 Check your answer algebraically.
Substitute -3 for x and 5 for y in the original system.

$$\begin{cases} 6x + 5y = 7 \rightarrow 6(-3) + 5(5) = -18 + 25 = 7 \ \checkmark \\ 2x - 4y = -26 \rightarrow 2(-3) - 4(5) = -6 - 20 = -26 \ \checkmark \end{cases}$$

The solution is correct.

YOUR TURN

Solve each system of equations by multiplying and subtracting.

7. $\begin{cases} 3x - 7y = 2 \\ 6x - 9y = 9 \end{cases}$

8. $\begin{cases} -3x + y = 11 \\ 2x + 3y = -11 \end{cases}$

9. $\begin{cases} 9x + y = 9 \\ 3x - 2y = -11 \end{cases}$

_____   _____   _____

Solving Problems with Systems of Equations

Many real-world situations can be modeled with a system of equations.

 EXAMPLE 3 Problem Solving
CA CC 8.EE.8c

The Simon family attended a concert and visited an art museum. Concert tickets were $24.75 for adults and $16.00 for children, for a total cost of $138.25. Museum tickets were $8.25 for adults and $4.50 for children, for a total cost of $42.75. How many adults and how many children are in the Simon family?

 Analyze Information

The answer is the number of adults and children.

 Formulate a Plan

Solve a system to find the number of adults and children.

 Solve

STEP 1 Choose variables and write a system of equations. Let x represent the number of adults. Let y represent the number of children.

Concert cost: $24.75x + 16.00y = 138.25$
Museum cost: $8.25x + 4.50y = 42.75$

STEP 2 Multiply both equations by 100 to eliminate the decimals.

$100(24.75x + 16.00y = 138.25) \rightarrow 2{,}475x + 1{,}600y = 13{,}825$

$100(8.25x + 4.50y = 42.75) \rightarrow 825x + 450y = 4{,}275$

STEP 3 Multiply the second equation by 3 and subtract this new equation from the first equation.

$$3(825x + 450y = 4,275)$$

Multiply each term in the second equation by 3 to get the same coefficients for the x-terms.

$$2,475x + 1,350y = 12,825$$ Simplify.

$$\begin{array}{r} 2,475x + 1,600y = 13,825 \\ -(2,475x + 1,350y = 12,825) \\ \hline \end{array}$$

Subtract the new equation from the first equation.

$$0x + 250y = 1,000$$

Subtract to eliminate the variable x.

$$250y = 1,000$$

Simplify and solve for y.

$$\frac{250y}{250} = \frac{1,000}{250}$$ Divide each side by 250.

$$y = 4$$ Simplify.

STEP 4 Substitute the solution into one of the original equations and solve for x.

$$8.25x + 4.50y = 42.75$$ Use the second equation.

$$8.25x + 4.50(4) = 42.75$$ Substitute 4 for the variable y.

$$8.25x + 18 = 42.75$$ Simplify.

$$8.25x = 24.75$$ Subtract 18 from each side.

$$x = 3$$ Divide each side by 8.25 and simplify.

STEP 5 Write the solution as an ordered pair: (3, 4).
There are 3 adults and 4 children in the family.

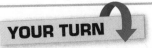 **Justify and Evaluate**

Substituting $x = 3$ and $y = 4$ into the original equations results in true statements. The answer is correct.

YOUR TURN

10. Contestants in the Run-and-Bike-a-thon run for a specified length of time, then bike for a specified length of time. Jason ran at an average speed of 5.2 mi/h and biked at an average speed of 20.6 mi/h, going a total of 14.2 miles. Seth ran at an average speed of 10.4 mi/h and biked at an average speed of 18.4 mi/h, going a total of 17 miles. For how long do contestants run and for how long do they bike?

_____

_____

Personal Math Trainer

Online Practice and Help

my.hrw.com

My Notes

1. Solve the system $\begin{cases} 3x - y = 8 \\ -2x + 4y = -12 \end{cases}$ by multiplying and adding. (Example 1)

STEP 1 Multiply the first equation by 4. Add to the second equation.

$4(3x - y = 8)$ — Multiply each term in the first equation by 4 to get opposite coefficients for the y-terms.

$\boxed{}x - \boxed{}y = \boxed{}$ — Simplify.

$+ \ (-2x) + \ 4y \ = -12$ — Add the second equation to the new equation.

$10x = \boxed{}$ — Add to eliminate the variable $\boxed{}$.

$x = \boxed{}$ — Divide both sides by $\boxed{}$ and simplify.

STEP 2 Substitute into one of the original equations and solve for y.

$y = \boxed{}$ So, $\boxed{}$ is the solution of the system.

Solve each system of equations by multiplying first. (Examples 1, 2)

2. $\begin{cases} x + 4y = 2 \\ 2x + 5y = 7 \end{cases}$ _____

3. $\begin{cases} 3x + y = -1 \\ 2x + 3y = 18 \end{cases}$ _____

4. $\begin{cases} 2x + 8y = 21 \\ 6x - 4y = 14 \end{cases}$ _____

5. $\begin{cases} 2x + y = 3 \\ -x + 3y = -12 \end{cases}$ _____

6. $\begin{cases} 6x + 5y = 19 \\ 2x + 3y = 5 \end{cases}$ _____

7. $\begin{cases} 2x + 5y = 16 \\ -4x + 3y = 20 \end{cases}$ _____

8. Bryce spent \$5.26 on some apples priced at \$0.64 each and some pears priced at \$0.45 each. At another store he could have bought the same number of apples at \$0.32 each and the same number of pears at \$0.39 each, for a total cost of \$3.62. How many apples and how many pears did Bryce buy? (Example 3)

   a. Write equations to represent Bryce's expenditures at each store.

   First store: _____ Second store: _____

   b. Solve the system.

   Number of apples: _____ Number of pears: _____

? ESSENTIAL QUESTION CHECK-IN

9. When solving a system by multiplying and then adding or subtracting, how do you decide whether to add or subtract?

_____

_____

_____

8.4 Independent Practice

CA CC 8.EE.8b, 8.EE.8c

Personal
Math Trainer

Online Practice
and Help

my.hrw.com

10. Explain the Error Gwen used elimination with multiplication to solve the system $\begin{cases} 2x + 6y = 3 \\ x - 3y = -1 \end{cases}$. Her work to find x is shown. Explain her error. Then solve the system.

$$2(x - 3y) = -1$$
$$2x - 6y = -1$$
$$+2x + 6y = 3$$
$$\overline{4x + 0y = 2}$$
$$x = \frac{1}{2}$$

_____

_____

11. Represent Real-World Problems At Raging River Sports, polyester-fill sleeping bags sell for $79. Down-fill sleeping bags sell for $149. In one week the store sold 14 sleeping bags for $1456.

Sleeping Bags

Nylon
Down-filled, 35°
$149

Flannel-lined
Polyester-filled, 40°
$79

a. Let x represent the number of polyester-fill bags sold and let y represent the number of down-fill bags sold. Write a system of equations you can solve to find the number of each type sold.

_____

b. Explain how you can solve the system for y by multiplying and subtracting.

_____

_____

c. Explain how you can solve the system for y using substitution.

_____

_____

d. How many of each type of bag were sold?

_____

12. Twice a number plus twice a second number is 310. The difference between the numbers is 55. Find the numbers by writing and solving a system of equations. Explain how you solved the system.

_____

_____

_____

13. **Represent Real-World Problems** A farm stand sells apple pies and jars of applesauce. The table shows the number of apples needed to make a pie and a jar of applesauce. Yesterday, the farm picked 169 Granny Smith apples and 95 Golden Delicious apples. How many pies and jars of applesauce can the farm make if every apple is used?

Type of apple	Granny Smith	Golden Delicious
Needed for a pie	5	3
Needed for a jar of applesauce	4	2

_____

H.O.T. FOCUS ON HIGHER ORDER THINKING

Work Area

14. **Make a Conjecture** Lena tried to solve a system of linear equations algebraically and in the process found the equation $5 = 9$. Lena thought something was wrong, so she graphed the equations and found that they were parallel lines. Explain what Lena's graph and equation could mean.

_____

_____

_____

_____

_____

15. Consider the system $\begin{cases} 2x + 3y = 6 \\ 3x + 7y = -1 \end{cases}$.

a. **Communicate Mathematical Ideas** Describe how to solve the system by multiplying the first equation by a constant and subtracting. Why would this method be less than ideal?

_____

_____

_____

b. **Draw Conclusions** Is it possible to solve the system by multiplying both equations by integer constants? If so, explain how.

_____

_____

_____

c. Use your answer from part b to solve the system.

_____

CA CC 8.EE.8b

Solve systems of two linear equations in two variables algebraically, and estimate solutions by graphing the equations. Solve simple cases by inspection. *Also 8.EE.8c*

LESSON 8.5 Solving Special Systems

ESSENTIAL QUESTION

How do you solve systems with no solution or infinitely many solutions?

EXPLORE ACTIVITY **CA CC** 8.EE.8b

Solving Special Systems by Graphing

As with linear equations in one variable, some systems may have no solution or infinitely many solutions. One way to tell how many solutions a system has is by inspecting its graph.

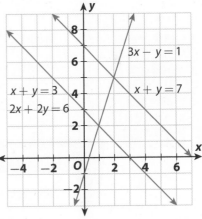

Use the graph to solve each system of linear equations.

A $\begin{cases} x + y = 7 \\ 2x + 2y = 6 \end{cases}$

Is there a point of intersection? Explain.

_____

_____

Does this linear system have a solution? Use the graph to explain.

_____

_____

B $\begin{cases} 2x + 2y = 6 \\ x + y = 3 \end{cases}$

Is there a point of intersection? Explain.

_____

Does this linear system have a solution? Use the graph to explain.

_____

_____

Reflect

1. **Justify Reasoning** Use the graph to identify two lines that represent a linear system with exactly one solution. What are the equations of the lines? Explain your reasoning.

_____

2. A system of linear equations has infinitely many solutions. Does that mean any ordered pair in the coordinate plane is a solution?

_____

_____

3. Identify the three possible numbers of solutions for a system of linear equations. Explain when each type of solution occurs.

_____

_____

_____

Math On the Spot

my.hrw.com

Solving Special Systems Algebraically

As with equations, if you solve a system of equations with no solution, you get a false statement, and if you solve a system with infinitely many solutions, you get a true statement.

EXAMPLE 1

 CA CC 8.EE.8b

A Solve the system of linear equations by substitution.

$$\begin{cases} x - y = -2 \\ -x + y = 4 \end{cases}$$

> **Math Talk**
> **Mathematical Practices**
>
> The system can be written using $-x + y = 2$ and $-x + y = 4$. How does this show you there is no solution just by looking at it?

STEP 1 Solve $x - y = -2$ for x:
$$x = y - 2$$

STEP 2 Substitute the resulting expression into the other equation and solve.

$$-(y - 2) + y = 4 \qquad \text{Substitute the expression for the variable } x.$$

$$2 = 4 \qquad \text{Simplify.}$$

STEP 3 Interpret the solution. The result is the false statement $2 = 4$, which means there is no solution.

STEP 4 Graph the equations to check your answer. The graphs do not intersect, so there is no solution.

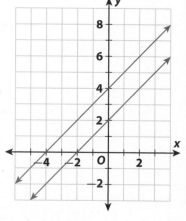

B Solve the system of linear equations by elimination.

$$\begin{cases} 2x + y = -2 \\ 4x + 2y = -4 \end{cases}$$

Math Talk
Mathematical Practices

What solution do you get when you solve the system in part B by substitution? Does this result change the number of solutions? Explain.

STEP 1 Multiply the first equation by -2.

$$-2(2x + y = -2) \rightarrow -4x + (-2y) = 4$$

STEP 2 Add the new equation from Step 1 to the original second equation.

$$\begin{array}{r} -4x + (-2y) = 4 \\ + 4x + 2y = -4 \\ \hline 0x + 0y = 0 \\ 0 = 0 \end{array}$$

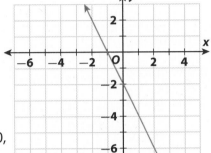

STEP 3 Interpret the solution. The result is the statement $0 = 0$, which is always true. This means that the system has infinitely many solutions.

STEP 4 Graph the equations to check your answer. The graphs are the same line, so there are infinitely many solutions.

Reflect

4. If x represents a variable and a and b represent constants so that $a \neq b$, interpret what each result means when solving a system of equations.

$x = a$ _____

$a = b$ _____

$a = a$ _____

5. **Draw Conclusions** In part B, can you tell without solving that the system has infinitely many solutions? If so, how?

_____

_____

_____

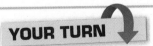
YOUR TURN

Solve each system. Tell how many solutions each system has.

6. $\begin{cases} 4x - 6y = 9 \\ -2x + 3y = 4 \end{cases}$ 7. $\begin{cases} x + 2y = 6 \\ 2x - 3y = 26 \end{cases}$ 8. $\begin{cases} 12x - 8y = -4 \\ -3x + 2y = 1 \end{cases}$

_____   _____   _____

_____   _____   _____

Personal Math Trainer

Online Practice and Help

⊙ my.hrw.com

1. Use the graph to find the number of solutions of each system of linear equations. (Explore Activity)

   A. $\begin{cases} 4x - 2y = -6 \\ 2x - y = 4 \end{cases}$ **B.** $\begin{cases} 4x - 2y = -6 \\ x + y = 6 \end{cases}$ **C.** $\begin{cases} 2x - y = 4 \\ 6x - 3y = 12 \end{cases}$

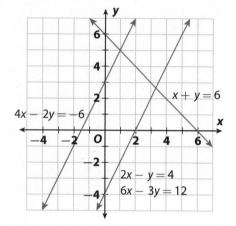

   STEP 1 Decide if the graphs of the equations in each system intersect, are parallel, or are the same line.

   System A: The graphs _____ .

   System B: The graphs _____ .

   System C: The graphs _____ .

   STEP 2 Use the results of Step 1 to decide how many points the graphs have in common.

   System A has _____ point(s) in common.

   System B has _____ point(s) in common.

   System C has _____ point(s) in common.

Solve each system. Tell how many solutions each system has. (Example 1)

2. $\begin{cases} x - 3y = 4 \\ -5x + 15y = -20 \end{cases}$ 3. $\begin{cases} 6x + 2y = -4 \\ 3x + y = 4 \end{cases}$ 4. $\begin{cases} 6x - 2y = -10 \\ 3x + 4y = -25 \end{cases}$

_____   _____   _____

Find the number of solutions of each system without solving algebraically or graphing. Explain your reasoning. (Example 1)

5. $\begin{cases} -6x + 2y = -8 \\ 3x - y = 4 \end{cases}$ 6. $\begin{cases} 8 = 7x + 2y \\ 7x + 2y = 4 \end{cases}$

_____   _____

_____   _____

? ESSENTIAL QUESTION CHECK-IN

7. When you solve a system of equations algebraically, how can you tell whether the system has zero, one, or an infinite number of solutions?

_____

_____

_____

8.5 Independent Practice

CA CC 8.EE.8b, 8.EE.8c

Personal Math Trainer

Online Practice and Help

my.hrw.com

Solve each system by graphing. Check your answer algebraically.

8. $\begin{cases} -2x + 6y = 12 \\ x - 3y = 3 \end{cases}$

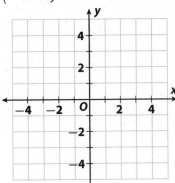

Solution: _____

9. $\begin{cases} 15x + 5y = 5 \\ 3x + y = 1 \end{cases}$

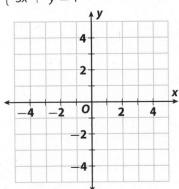

Solution: _____

For Exs. 10–16, state the number of solutions for each system of linear equations.

10. a system whose graphs have the same slope but different y-intercepts

_____

11. a system whose graphs have the same y-intercepts but different slopes

_____

12. a system whose graphs have the same y-intercepts and the same slopes

_____

13. a system whose graphs have different y-intercepts and different slopes

_____

14. the system $\begin{cases} y = 2 \\ y = -3 \end{cases}$ _____

15. the system $\begin{cases} x = 2 \\ y = -3 \end{cases}$ _____

16. the system whose graphs were drawn using these tables of values:

Equation 1

x	0	1	2	3
y	1	3	5	7

Equation 2

x	0	1	2	3
y	3	5	7	9

_____

17. **Draw Conclusions** The graph of a linear system appears in a textbook. You can see that the lines do not intersect on the graph, but also they do not appear to be parallel. Can you conclude that the system has no solution? Explain.

_____

_____

_____

18. Represent Real-World Problems Two school groups go to a roller skating rink. One group pays $243 for 36 admissions and 21 skate rentals. The other group pays $81 for 12 admissions and 7 skate rentals. Let x represent the cost of admission and let y represent the cost of a skate rental. Is there enough information to find values for x and y? Explain.

_____

19. Represent Real-World Problems Juan and Tory are practicing for a track meet. They start their practice runs at the same point, but Tory starts 1 minute after Juan. Both run at a speed of 704 feet per minute. Does Tory catch up to Juan? Explain.

_____

_____

_____

H.O.T. **FOCUS ON HIGHER ORDER THINKING**

Work Area

20. Justify Reasoning A linear system with no solution consists of the equation $y = 4x - 3$ and a second equation of the form $y = mx + b$. What can you say about the values of m and b? Explain your reasoning.

_____

_____

_____

_____

_____

21. Justify Reasoning A linear system with infinitely many solutions consists of the equation $3x + 5 = 8$ and a second equation of the form $Ax + By = C$. What can you say about the values of A, B, and C? Explain your reasoning.

_____

_____

_____

_____

22. Draw Conclusions Both the points $(2, -2)$ and $(4, -4)$ are solutions of a system of linear equations. What conclusions can you make about the equations and their graphs?

_____

_____

Ready to Go On?

Personal Math Trainer

Online Practice and Help

⏻ my.hrw.com

8.1 Solving Systems of Linear Equations by Graphing

Solve each system by graphing.

1. $\begin{cases} y = x - 1 \\ y = 2x - 3 \end{cases}$

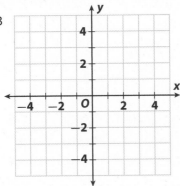

_____

2. $\begin{cases} x + 2y = 1 \\ -x + y = 2 \end{cases}$

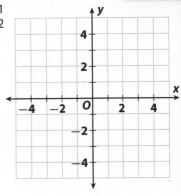

_____

8.2 Solving Systems by Substitution

Solve each system of equations by substitution.

3. $\begin{cases} y = 2x \\ x + y = -9 \end{cases}$ _____

4. $\begin{cases} 3x - 2y = 11 \\ x + 2y = 9 \end{cases}$ _____

8.3 Solving Systems by Elimination

Solve each system of equations by adding or subtracting.

5. $\begin{cases} 3x + y = 9 \\ 2x + y = 5 \end{cases}$ _____

6. $\begin{cases} -x - 2y = 4 \\ 3x + 2y = 4 \end{cases}$ _____

8.4 Solving Systems by Elimination with Multiplication

Solve each system of equations by multiplying first.

7. $\begin{cases} x + 3y = -2 \\ 3x + 4y = -1 \end{cases}$ _____

8. $\begin{cases} 2x + 8y = 22 \\ 3x - 2y = 5 \end{cases}$ _____

8.5 Solving Special Systems

Solve each system. Tell how many solutions each system has.

9. $\begin{cases} -2x + 8y = 5 \\ x - 4y = -3 \end{cases}$ _____

10. $\begin{cases} 6x + 18y = -12 \\ x + 3y = -2 \end{cases}$ _____

? ESSENTIAL QUESTION

11. What are the possible solutions to a system of linear equations, and what do they represent graphically?

_____

_____

MODULE 8
MIXED REVIEW

Assessment Readiness

Personal Math Trainer

Online Practice and Help

my.hrw.com

1. Consider each system of equations. Does the system have at least one solution? Select Yes or No for systems A–C.

   A. $\begin{cases} 3x - 2y = 4 \\ -6x + 4y = -8 \end{cases}$ ○ Yes   ○ No

   B. $\begin{cases} -4x + y = 1 \\ 12x - 3y = 3 \end{cases}$ ○ Yes   ○ No

   C. $\begin{cases} 2x + y = 0 \\ 4x - y = -6 \end{cases}$ ○ Yes   ○ No

2. Ruby ran 5 laps on the inside lane around a track. Dana ran 3 laps around the same lane on the same track, and then she ran 0.5 mile to her house. Both girls ran the same number of miles in all. The equation $5d = 3d + 0.5$ models this situation.

   Choose True or False for each statement.

   A. The variable d represents the distance around the track in miles.   ○ True   ○ False

   B. The expression $5d$ represents the time it took Ruby to run 5 laps.   ○ True   ○ False

   C. The expression $3d + 0.5$ represents the distance in miles Dana ran.   ○ True   ○ False

3. Daisies cost $0.99 each and tulips cost $1.15 each. Maria bought a bouquet of daisies and tulips. It contained 12 flowers and cost $12.52. Solve the system $\begin{cases} x + y = 12 \\ 0.99x + 1.15y = 12.52 \end{cases}$ to find the number of daisies x and the number of tulips y in Maria's bouquet. State the method you used to solve the system and why you chose that method.

4. Kylie bought 4 daily bus passes and 2 weekly bus passes for $29.00. Luis bought 7 daily bus passes and 2 weekly bus passes for $36.50. Write and solve a system of equations to find the cost of a daily pass and the cost of a weekly pass. Explain how you can check your answer.

MODULE 7 Solving Linear Equations

? ESSENTIAL QUESTION

How can you use equations with the variable on both sides to solve real-world problems?

EXAMPLE 1

Solve $-2.4(3x + 5) = 0.8(x + 3.5)$.

$-2.4(3x + 5) = 0.8(x + 3.5)$	
$10(-2.4)(3x + 5) = 10(0.8)(x + 3.5)$	Multiply each side by 10 to clear some decimals.
$-24(3x + 5) = 8(x + 3.5)$	
$-24(3x) - 24(5) = 8(x) + 8(3.5)$	Apply the Distributive Property.
$-72x - 120 = 8x + 28$	
$\underline{-8x -8x}$	Subtract 8x from both sides of the equation.
$-80x - 120 = 28$	
$\underline{+ 120 + 120}$	Add 120 to both sides of the equation.
$-80x = 148$	
$\dfrac{-80x}{-80} = \dfrac{148}{-80}$	Divide both sides of the equation by -80.
$x = -1.85$	

EXAMPLE 2

Solve $4(3x - 6) = 2(6x - 5)$. Tell whether the equation has one, zero, or infinitely many solutions.

$4(3x - 6) = 2(6x - 5)$	
$12x - 24 = 12x - 10$	Apply the Distributive Property.
$\underline{-12x -12x}$	Subtract 8x from both sides of the equation.
$-24 = -10$	The statement is false.

There is no value of *x* that makes a true statement. Therefore, this equation has no solution.

EXERCISES

Solve. (Lessons 7.1, 7.2, 7.3, 7.4)

1. $13.02 - 6y = 8y$ _____

2. $\frac{1}{5}x + 5 = 19 - \frac{1}{2}x$ _____

3. $7.3t + 22 = 2.1t - 22.2$ _____

4. $-7(3 + t) = 4(2t + 6)$ _____

5. $\frac{3}{4}(x + 8) = \frac{1}{3}(x + 27)$ _____

6. $3(4x - 8) = \frac{1}{5}(35x + 30)$ _____

7. $-1.6(2y + 15) = -1.2(2y - 10)$

_____

8. $9(4a - 2) = 12(3a + 8)$

_____

9. $6(x - \frac{1}{3}) = -2(x + 23)$

_____

10. $8(p - 0.25) = 4(2p - 0.5)$

_____

MODULE **8** ## Solving Systems of Linear Equations

Key Vocabulary

solution of a system of equations *(solución de un sistema de ecuaciones)*

system of equations *(sistema de ecuaciones)*

? ESSENTIAL QUESTION

How can you use systems of equations to solve real-world problems?

EXAMPLE 1

Solve the system of equations by substitution.

$$\begin{cases} 3x + y = 7 \\ x + y = 3 \end{cases}$$

Step 1 Solve an equation for one variable.

$3x + y = 7$

$y = -3x + 7$

Step 2 Substitute the expression for y in the other equation and solve.

$x + y = 3$

$x + (-3x + 7) = 3$

$-2x + 7 = 3$

$-2x = -4$

$x = 2$

Step 3 Substitute the value of x into one of the equations and solve for the other variable, y.

$x + y = 3$

$2 + y = 3$

$y = 1$

$(2, 1)$ is the solution of the system.

EXAMPLE 2

Solve the system of equations by elimination.

$$\begin{cases} x + y = 8 \\ 2x - 3y = 1 \end{cases}$$

Step 1 Multiply the first equation by 3 and add this new equation to the second equation.

$3(x + y = 8) = 3x + 3y = 24$

$3x + 3y = 24$

$\underline{2x - 3y = 1}$

$5x + 0y = 25$

$5x \quad\; = 25$

$x \quad\; = 5$

Step 2 Substitute the solution into one of the original equations and solve for y.

$x + y = 8$

$5 + y = 8$

$\quad\; y = 3$

(5, 3) is the solution of the system.

EXERCISES

Solve each system of linear equations. (Lessons 8.1, 8.2, 8.3, 8.4, and 8.5)

11. $\begin{cases} x + y = -2 \\ 2x - y = 5 \end{cases}$

12. $\begin{cases} y = 2x + 1 \\ x + 2y = 17 \end{cases}$

13. $\begin{cases} y = -2x - 3 \\ 2x + y = 9 \end{cases}$

_____

_____

_____

14. $\begin{cases} y = 5 - x \\ 2x + 2y = 10 \end{cases}$

15. $\begin{cases} 2x - y = 26 \\ 3x - 2y = 42 \end{cases}$

16. $\begin{cases} 2x + 3y = 11 \\ 5x - 2y = 18 \end{cases}$

_____

_____

_____

17. Last week Andrew bought 3 pounds of zucchini and 2 pounds of tomatoes for $7.05 at a farm stand. This week he bought 4 pounds of zucchini and 3 pounds of tomatoes, at the same prices, for $9.83. What is the cost of 1 pound of zucchini and 1 pound of tomatoes at the farm stand?

_____

Unit Project

CA CC 8.EE.8, 8.EE.8a, 8.EE.8b, 8.EE.8c

Which Car Costs Less?

A new Zephyr hybrid car costs $42,000 and gets an average of 45 miles per gallon of gas. A Zephyr sedan costs $30,000 and gets an average of 30 miles per gallon. Both cars are driven 13,500 miles per year. Create a presentation to show which car is cheaper over a period of years when both its original cost and the annual cost of gas are considered. Use the following directions as guidelines:

- Find the number of gallons of gas used annually by both cars.
- Find the annual gas cost. (You'll need to estimate the average price of a gallon of gas in your town.)
- For each car, write an equation for y, the total cost of operating the vehicle for x years. Your equation will have the form
  $y =$ price of car $+$ (annual gas cost)x.
- Graph the two equations.
- Estimate the point of intersection of the graphs, and explain what it means.

Use the space below to write down any questions you have or important information from your teacher.

MATH IN CAREERS | **ACTIVITY**

Hydraulic Engineer A hydraulic engineer is studying the pressure in a particular fluid. The pressure is equal to the atmospheric pressure 101 kN/m² plus 8 kN/m² for every meter below the surface, where kN/m² is kilonewtons per square meter, a unit of pressure. Using an equation, find the depth at which the pressure is 200 kN/m². Show your work.

UNIT 3
MIXED REVIEW

Assessment Readiness

Personal Math Trainer

Online Practice and Help

⏻ my.hrw.com

1. Consider each operation. Would the operation eliminate all of the fractions from the equation $\frac{3}{4}x + \frac{1}{2} = \frac{1}{3}x + 3$?

Select Yes or No.

A. Multiply both sides by 6. ○ Yes ○ No

B. Multiply both sides by 12. ○ Yes ○ No

C. Multiply both sides by 24. ○ Yes ○ No

2. Consider the system of equations $\begin{cases} y = 2x + 4 \\ 3x - y = -4 \end{cases}$.

Choose True or False for each statement.

A. A graph of the system has a single point of intersection. ○ True ○ False

B. The system has infinitely many solutions. ○ True ○ False

C. The equations in the system have the same y-intercept. ○ True ○ False

3. A box containing 10 physics textbooks and 3 physics workbooks weighs 50.1 pounds. A box containing 8 physics textbooks and 12 physics workbooks weighs 51.9 pounds. The weight of each box when empty is 1.5 pounds. How much does each textbook and each workbook weigh? Explain how you solved this problem.

4. Adrian and Rory started comic book collections at the same time. Adrian started with 12 comic books and buys 4 more each month. Rory started with 8 comic books and buys 4 more each month. Will they ever have the same number of comic books? If so, after how many months? Use an equation to justify your answer.

Performance Tasks

★**5.** A school is constructing new tennis courts. Each rectangular court will be enclosed by a 600 ft fence. The length of the rectangular region will be 60 feet longer than the width. What are the dimensions of the new courts? Use an equation or a system of equations to explain how you determined your answer.

★★**6.** A worker is installing blue and white square tiles in a kitchen. Blue tiles have different lengths than white tiles. A row of 8 blue tiles and 16 white tiles has a length of 39 inches. A row of 40 blue tiles and 8 white tiles has a length of 42 inches.

   a. Write a system of equations that represents in inches the relationship between the length x of a blue tile and the length y of a white tile.

   b. Graph the system, and estimate the solution.

   c. Explain why it is difficult to determine the exact solution from the graph in this case.

   d. Determine the exact lengths of the blue and white tiles. Explain how you determined your answer and how you know your answer is reasonable.

★★★**7.** Barbara is deciding between Banquet Chefs and CeCe's Catering to cater an awards banquet. Barbara needs to choose the company that costs less, but she does not yet know how many guests will be attending.

How can Barbara decide once she does know the number of guests? Give the range of guests for which Barbara should choose Banquet Chefs and the range of guests for which she should choose CeCe's Catering. Use mathematics to justify your reasoning.

BANQUET CHEFS

$28 per guest
plus
$590 service

CECE'S CATERING

$31 per guest
plus
$425 service fee

UNIT 4
Transformational Geometry

MODULE 9
Transformations and Congruence

🐻 **CA CC** 8.G.1, 8.G.2, 8.G.3

MODULE 10
Transformations and Similarity

🐻 **CA CC** 8.G.3, 8.G.4

MATH IN CAREERS

Contractor A contractor is engaged in the construction, repair, and dismantling of structures such as buildings, bridges, and roads. Contractors use math when researching and implementing building codes, making measurements and scaling models, and in financial management.

If you are interested in a career as a contractor, you should study the following mathematical subjects:
- Business Math
- Geometry
- Algebra
- Trigonometry

Research other careers that require the use of business math and scaling.

ACTIVITY At the end of the unit, check out how **contractors** use math.

Transforming the World

The Unit Project at the end of this unit will ask you to extend your understanding of a mathematical concept to everyday life. In the project, you will look for real-world examples of translations, rotations, and reflections. To successfully complete the Unit Project you'll need to master these skills:

- Understand and identify translations.
- Understand and identify rotations.
- Understand and identify reflections.

1. Describe the pattern that you see in the kaleidoscope image.

_____

_____

_____

_____

_____

2. What is the "reflection" of a figure?

_____

_____

_____

_____

Tracking Your Learning Progression

This unit addresses important California Common Core Standards in the Critical Area of understanding and applying congruence and similarity.

Domain 8.G Geometry

> **Cluster** Understand congruence and similarity using physical models, transparencies, or geometry software.

Transformations and Congruence

 ESSENTIAL QUESTION

How can you use transformations and congruence to solve real-world problems?

Real-World Video

When a marching band lines up and marches across the field, they are modeling a translation. As they march, they maintain size and orientation. A translation is one type of transformation.

⏻ my.hrw.com

GO DIGITAL
my.hrw.com

my.hrw.com

Go digital with your write-in student edition, accessible on any device.

Math On the Spot

Scan with your smart phone to jump directly to the online edition, video tutor, and more.

Animated Math

Interactively explore key concepts to see how math works.

Personal Math Trainer

Get immediate feedback and help as you work through practice sets.

Are YOU Ready?

Complete these exercises to review skills you will need for this module.

Integer Operations

EXAMPLE

$$-3 - (-6) = -3 + 6$$
$$= |-3| - |6|$$
$$= 3$$

To subtract an integer, add its opposite. The signs are different, so find the difference of the absolute values: $6 - 3 = 3$. Use the sign of the number with the greater absolute value.

Find each difference.

1. $5 - (-9)$ _____

2. $-6 - 8$ _____

3. $2 - 9$ _____

4. $-10 - (-6)$ _____

5. $3 - (-11)$ _____

6. $12 - 7$ _____

7. $-4 - 11$ _____

8. $0 - (-12)$ _____

Measure Angles

EXAMPLE

$m\angle JKL = 70°$

Place the center point of the protractor on the angle's vertex.

Align one ray with the base of the protractor.

Read the angle measure where the other ray intersects the semicircle.

Use a protractor to measure each angle.

9.

_____

10.

_____

11.

_____

Reading Start-Up

Visualize Vocabulary

Use the ✔ words to complete the graphic organizer. You will put one word in each oval.

Types of Quadrilaterals

A quadrilateral in which all sides are congruent and opposite sides are parallel.

A quadrilateral in which opposite sides are parallel and congruent.

A quadrilateral with exactly one pair of parallel sides.

Vocabulary

Review Words

coordinate plane *(plano cartesiano)*

✔ parallelogram *(paralelogramo)*

quadrilateral *(cuadrilátero)*

✔ rhombus *(rombo)*

✔ trapezoid *(trapecio)*

Preview Words

center of rotation *(centro de rotación)*

congruent *(congruente)*

image *(imagen)*

line of reflection *(línea de reflexión)*

preimage *(imagen original)*

reflection *(reflexión)*

rotation *(rotación)*

transformation *(transformación)*

translation *(traslación)*

Understand Vocabulary

Match the term on the left to the correct expression on the right.

1. transformation

A. A function that describes a change in the position, size, or shape of a figure.

2. reflection

B. A function that slides a figure along a straight line.

3. translation

C. A transformation that flips a figure across a line.

Active Reading

Booklet Before beginning the module, create a booklet to help you learn the concepts in this module. Write the main idea of each lesson on each page of the booklet. As you study each lesson, write important details that support the main idea, such as vocabulary and formulas. Refer to your finished booklet as you work on assignments and study for tests.

GETTING READY FOR
Transformations and Congruence
Understanding the standards and the vocabulary terms in the standards
will help you know exactly what you are expected to learn in this module.

CALIFORNIA

CA CC 8.G.2

Understand that a two-dimensional figure is congruent to another if the second can be obtained from the first by a sequence of rotations, reflections, and translations; given two congruent figures, describe a sequence that exhibits the congruence between them.

What It Means to You

You will identify a rotation, a reflection, a translation, and a sequence of transformations, and understand that the image has the same shape and size as the preimage.

EXAMPLE 8.G.2

The figure shows triangle *ABC* and its image after three different transformations. Identify and describe the translation, the reflection, and the rotation of triangle *ABC*.

Figure 1 is a translation 4 units down. Figure 2 is a reflection across the *y*-axis. Figure 3 is a rotation of 180°.

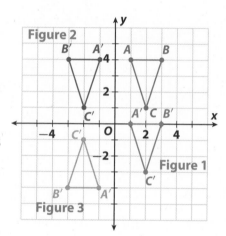

CA CC 8.G.3

Describe the effect of dilations, translations, rotations, and reflections on two-dimensional figures using coordinates.

What It Means to You

You can use an algebraic representation to translate, reflect, or rotate a two-dimensional figure.

EXAMPLE 8.G.3

Rectangle *RSTU* with vertices (−4, 1), (−1, 1), (−1, −3), and (−4, −3) is reflected across the *y*-axis. Find the coordinates of the image.

The rule to reflect across the *y*-axis is to change the sign of the *x*-coordinate.

Coordinates	Reflect across the y-axis (−x, y)	Coordinates of image
(−4, 1), (−1, 1), (−1, −3), (−4, −3)	(−(−4), 1), (−(−1), 1), (−(−1), −3), (−(−4), −3)	(4, 1), (1, 1), (1, −3), (4, −3)

The coordinates of the image are (4, 1), (1, 1), (1, −3), and (4, −3).

CA CC 8.G.1a

Verify experimentally the properties of rotations, reflections, and translations: Lines are taken to lines, and line segments to line segments of the same length. *Also 8.G.1b, 8.G.1c, 8.G.3*

💬 **ESSENTIAL QUESTION**

How do you describe the properties of translation and their effect on the congruence and orientation of figures?

EXPLORE ACTIVITY 1 🐻 CA CC 8.G.1a

Exploring Translations

You learned that a function is a rule that assigns exactly one output to each input. A **transformation** is a function that describes a change in the position, size, or shape of a figure. The input of a transformation is the **preimage**, and the output of a transformation is the **image**.

A **translation** is a transformation that slides a figure along a straight line.

The triangle shown on the grid is the preimage (input). The arrow shows the motion of a translation and how point A is translated to point A'.

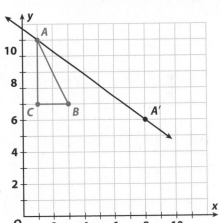

A Trace triangle *ABC* and line *AA'* onto a piece of paper.

B Slide your triangle along the line to model the translation that maps point *A* to point *A'*.

C The image of the translation is the triangle produced by the translation. Sketch the image of the translation.

D The vertices of the image are labeled using prime notation. For example, the image of *A* is *A'*. Label the images of points *B* and *C*.

E Describe the motion modeled by the translation.

Move _____ units right and _____ units down.

F Check that the motion you described in part **E** is the same motion that maps point *A* onto *A'*, point *B* onto *B'*, and point *C* onto *C'*.

Reflect

1. How is the orientation of the triangle affected by the translation?

_____

Properties of Translations

Use trapezoid *TRAP* to investigate the properties
of translations.

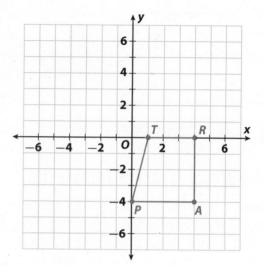

A Trace the trapezoid onto a piece of paper.
Cut out your traced trapezoid.

B Place your trapezoid on top of the
trapezoid in the figure. Then translate your
trapezoid 5 units to the left and 3 units
up. Sketch the image of the translation by
tracing your trapezoid in this new location.
Label the vertices of the image *T′, R′, A′,*
and *P′*.

C Use a ruler to measure the sides of trapezoid
TRAP in centimeters.

TR = _____   RA = _____   AP = _____   TP = _____

D Use a ruler to measure the sides of trapezoid *T′R′A′P′* in centimeters.

T′R′ = _____   R′A′ = _____   A′P′ = _____   T′P′ = _____

E What do you notice about the lengths of corresponding sides of
the two figures?

_____

F Use a protractor to measure the angles of trapezoid *TRAP*.

m∠T = _____   m∠R = _____   m∠A = _____   m∠P = _____

G Use a protractor to measure the angles of trapezoid *T′R′A′P′*.

m∠T′ = _____   m∠R′ = _____   m∠A′ = _____   m∠P′ = _____

H What do you notice about the measures of corresponding angles of
the two figures?

_____

I Which sides of trapezoid *TRAP* are parallel? How do you know?

_____

Which sides of trapezoid *T′R′A′P′* are parallel? _____

What do you notice? _____

_____

Reflect

2. Make a Conjecture Use your results from parts **E**, **H**, and **I** to make a conjecture about translations.

_____

_____

3. Two figures that have the same size and shape are called *congruent*. What can you say about translations and congruence?

_____

Graphing Translations

To translate a figure in the coordinate plane, translate each of its vertices. Then connect the vertices to form the image.

Math On the Spot
my.hrw.com

EXAMPLE 1

CA CC 8.G.3

The figure shows triangle *XYZ*. Graph the image of the triangle after a translation of 4 units to the right and 1 unit up.

STEP 1 Translate point *X*.

Count right 4 units and up 1 unit and plot point *X'*.

STEP 2 Translate point *Y*.

Count right 4 units and up 1 unit and plot point *Y'*.

STEP 3 Translate point *Z*.

Count right 4 units and up 1 unit and plot point *Z'*.

STEP 4 Connect *X'*, *Y'*, and *Z'* to form triangle *X'Y'Z'*.

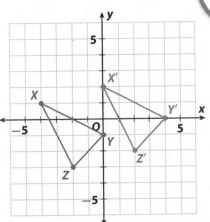

Each vertex is moved 4 units right and 1 unit up.

Math Talk
Mathematical Practices

Is the image congruent to the preimage? How do you know?

YOUR TURN

4. The figure shows parallelogram *ABCD*. Graph the image of the parallelogram after a translation of 5 units to the left and 2 units down.

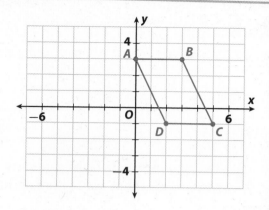

Guided Practice

1. Vocabulary A _____ is a change in the position, size, or shape of a figure.

2. Vocabulary When you perform a transformation of a figure on the coordinate plane, the input of the transformation is called

the _____, and the output of the transformation is

called the _____.

3. Joni translates a right triangle 2 units down and 4 units to the right. How does the orientation of the image of the triangle compare with the orientation of the preimage? (Explore Activity 1)

_____

4. Rashid drew rectangle *PQRS* on a coordinate plane. He then translated the rectangle 3 units up and 3 units to the left and labeled the image *P'Q'R'S'*. How do rectangle *PQRS* and rectangle *P'Q'R'S'* compare? (Explore Activity 2)

_____

5. The figure shows trapezoid *WXYZ*. Graph the image of the trapezoid after a translation of 4 units up and 2 units to the left. (Example 1)

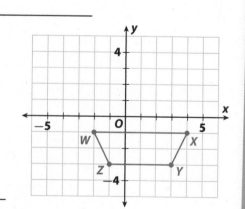

? **ESSENTIAL QUESTION CHECK-IN**

6. What are the properties of translations?

_____

_____

9.1 Independent Practice

CA CC 8.G.1a, 8.G.1b, 8.G.1c, 8.G.3

Personal Math Trainer

Online Practice and Help

my.hrw.com

7. The figure shows triangle *DEF*.

  a. Graph the image of the triangle after the translation that maps point *D* to point *D'*.

  b. How would you describe the translation?

  _____

  _____

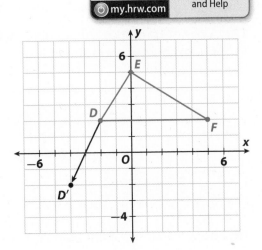

  c. How does the image of triangle *DEF* compare with the preimage?

  _____

8. a. Graph quadrilateral *KLMN* with vertices *K*(−3, 2), *L*(2, 2), *M*(0, −3), and *N*(−4, 0) on the coordinate grid.

  b. On the same coordinate grid, graph the image of quadrilateral *KLMN* after a translation of 3 units to the right and 4 units up.

  c. Which side of the image is congruent to side $\overline{LM}$?

  _____

  Name three other pairs of congruent sides.

  _____

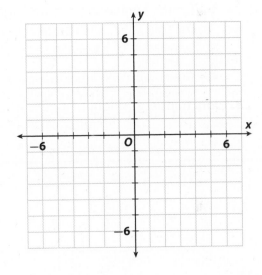

Draw the image of the figure after each translation.

9. 4 units left and 2 units down

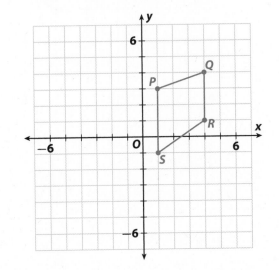

10. 5 units right and 3 units up

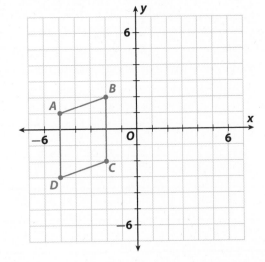

11. The figure shows the ascent of a hot air balloon. How would you describe the translation?

_____

_____

12. **Critical Thinking** Is it possible that the orientation of a figure could change after it is translated? Explain.

_____

_____

_____

FOCUS ON HIGHER ORDER THINKING

13. a. **Multistep** Graph triangle XYZ with vertices $X(-2, -5)$, $Y(2, -2)$, and $Z(4, -4)$ on the coordinate grid.

b. On the same coordinate grid, graph and label triangle $X'Y'Z'$, the image of triangle XYZ after a translation of 3 units to the left and 6 units up.

c. Now graph and label triangle $X''Y''Z''$, the image of triangle $X'Y'Z'$ after a translation of 1 unit to the left and 2 units down.

d. **Analyze Relationships** How would you describe the translation that maps triangle XYZ onto triangle $X''Y''Z''$?

_____

_____

14. **Critical Thinking** The figure shows rectangle $P'Q'R'S'$, the image of rectangle $PQRS$ after a translation of 5 units to the right and 7 units up. Graph and label the preimage $PQRS$.

15. **Communicate Mathematical Ideas** Explain why the image of a figure after a translation is congruent to its preimage.

_____

_____

_____

_____

_____

Properties of Reflections

CA CC 8.G.1b

Verify experimentally the properties of rotations, reflections, and translations: Angles are taken to angles of the same measure. *Also 8.G.1a, 8.G.1c, 8.G.3*

ESSENTIAL QUESTION

How do you describe the properties of reflection and their effect on the congruence and orientation of figures?

EXPLORE ACTIVITY 1   CA CC 8.G.1b

Exploring Reflections

A **reflection** is a transformation that flips a figure across a line. The line is called the **line of reflection**. Each point and its image are the same distance from the line of reflection.

The triangle shown on the grid is the preimage. You will explore reflections across the *x*- and *y*-axes.

A Trace triangle *ABC* and the *x*- and *y*-axes onto a piece of paper.

B Fold your paper along the *x*-axis and trace the image of the triangle on the opposite side of the *x*-axis. Unfold your paper and label the vertices of the image *A'*, *B'*, and *C'*.

C What is the line of reflection for this transformation?

_____

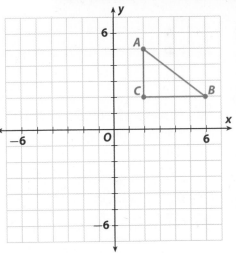

D Find the perpendicular distance from each point to the line of reflection.

Point *A* _____   Point *B* _____   Point *C* _____

E Find the perpendicular distance from each point to the line of reflection.

Point *A'* _____   Point *B'* _____   Point *C'* _____

F What do you notice about the distances you found in **D** and **E**?

_____

Reflect

1. Fold your paper from **A** along the *y*-axis and trace the image of triangle *ABC* on the opposite side. Label the vertices of the image *A''*, *B''*, and *C''*. What is the line of reflection for this transformation? _____

2. How does each image in your drawings compare with its preimage?

_____

Properties of Reflections

Use trapezoid *TRAP* to investigate the properties
of reflections.

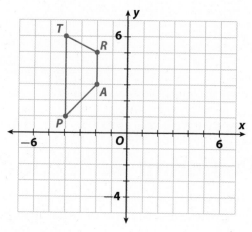

A Trace the trapezoid onto a piece of paper. Cut out
your traced trapezoid.

B Place your trapezoid on top of the trapezoid in the
figure. Then reflect your trapezoid across the *y*-axis.
Sketch the image of the reflection by tracing your
trapezoid in this new location. Label the vertices of
the image *T′*, *R′*, *A′*, and *P′*.

C Use a ruler to measure the sides of trapezoid *TRAP* in centimeters.

TR = _____   *RA* = _____   *AP* = _____   *TP* = _____

D Use a ruler to measure the sides of trapezoid *T′R′A′P′* in centimeters.

T′R′ = _____   *R′A′* = _____   *A′P′* = _____   *T′P′* = _____

E What do you notice about the lengths of corresponding sides of
the two figures?

_____

_____

F Use a protractor to measure the angles of trapezoid *TRAP*.

m∠T = _____   *m∠R* = _____   *m∠A* = _____   *m∠P* = _____

G Use a protractor to measure the angles of trapezoid *T′R′A′P′*.

m∠T′ = _____   *m∠R′* = _____   *m∠A′* = _____   *m∠P′* = _____

H What do you notice about the measures of corresponding angles of the
two figures?

_____

_____

I Which sides of trapezoid *TRAP* are parallel? _____

Which sides of trapezoid *T′R′A′P′* are parallel? _____
What do you notice?

_____

_____

Reflect

3. **Make a Conjecture** Use your results from Ⓔ, Ⓗ, and Ⓘ to make a conjecture about reflections.

_____

_____

_____

Math Talk
Mathematical Practices

What can you say about reflections and congruence?

Graphing Reflections

To reflect a figure across a line of reflection, reflect each of its vertices. Then connect the vertices to form the image. Remember that each point and its image are the same distance from the line of reflection.

Math On the Spot
ⓜ my.hrw.com

EXAMPLE 1

 CA CC 8.G.3

The figure shows triangle _XYZ_. Graph the image of the triangle after a reflection across the _x_-axis.

STEP 1 Reflect point _X_.

Point _X_ is 3 units below the _x_-axis. Count 3 units above the _x_-axis and plot point _X′_.

STEP 2 Reflect point _Y_.

Point _Y_ is 1 unit below the _x_-axis. Count 1 unit above the _x_-axis and plot point _Y′_.

STEP 3 Reflect point _Z_.

Point _Z_ is 5 units below the _x_-axis. Count 5 units above the _x_-axis and plot point _Z′_.

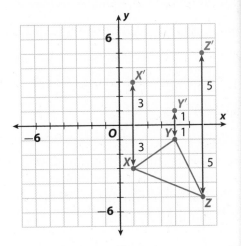

STEP 4 Connect _X′_, _Y′_, and _Z′_ to form triangle _X′Y′Z′_.

Each vertex of the image is the same distance from the _x_-axis as the corresponding vertex in the original figure.

My Notes

YOUR TURN

4. The figure shows pentagon *ABCDE*. Graph the image of the pentagon after a reflection across the *y*-axis.

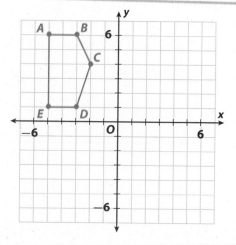

Guided Practice

1. **Vocabulary** A reflection is a transformation that flips a figure across

   a line called the _____.

2. The figure shows trapezoid *ABCD*. (Explore Activities 1 and 2 and Example 1)

   a. Graph the image of the trapezoid after a reflection across the *x*-axis. Label the vertices of the image.

   b. How do trapezoid *ABCD* and trapezoid *A'B'C'D'* compare?

   _____

   c. **What If?** Suppose you reflected trapezoid *ABCD* across the *y*-axis. How would the orientation of the image of the trapezoid compare with the orientation of the preimage?

   _____

   _____

   _____

   _____

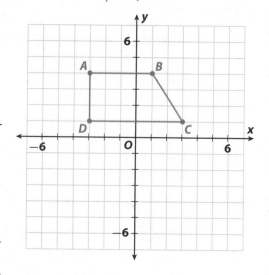

❓ ESSENTIAL QUESTION CHECK-IN

3. What are the properties of reflections?

   _____

   _____

9.2 Independent Practice

CA CC 8.G.1a, 8.G.1b, 8.G.1c, 8.G.3

Personal
Math Trainer

Online Practice
and Help

my.hrw.com

The graph shows four right triangles. Use the graph for Exercises 4–7.

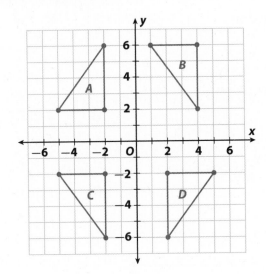

4. Which two triangles are reflections of each other across the *x*-axis?

_____

5. For which two triangles is the line of reflection the *y*-axis?

_____

6. Which triangle is a translation of triangle *C*? How would you describe the translation?

_____

_____

7. Which triangles are congruent? How do you know?

_____

_____

_____

_____

8. a. Graph quadrilateral *WXYZ* with vertices *W*(−2, −2), *X*(3, 1), *Y*(5, −1), and *Z*(4, −6) on the coordinate grid.

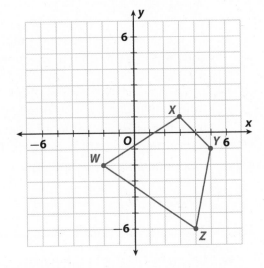

b. On the same coordinate grid, graph quadrilateral *W′X′Y′Z′*, the image of quadrilateral *WXYZ* after a reflection across the *x*-axis.

c. Which side of the image is congruent to side $\overline{YZ}$?

_____

Name three other pairs of congruent sides.

_____

_____

d. Which angle of the image is congruent to $\angle X$?

_____

Name three other pairs of congruent angles.

_____

_____

9. Critical Thinking Is it possible that the image of a point after a reflection could be the same point as the preimage? Explain.

_____

_____

 FOCUS ON HIGHER ORDER THINKING

10. a. Graph the image of the figure shown after a reflection across the *y*-axis.

   b. On the same coordinate grid, graph the image of the figure you drew in part **a** after a reflection across the *x*-axis.

   c. **Make a Conjecture** What other sequence of transformations would produce the same final image from the original preimage? Check your answer by performing the transformations. Then make a conjecture that generalizes your findings.

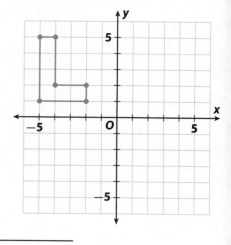

_____

_____

_____

_____

_____

11. a. Graph triangle *DEF* with vertices *D*(2, 6), *E*(5, 6), and *F*(5, 1) on the coordinate grid.

   b. Next graph triangle *D′E′F′*, the image of triangle *DEF* after a reflection across the *y*-axis.

   c. On the same coordinate grid, graph triangle *D″E″F″*, the image of triangle *D′E′F′* after a translation of 7 units down and 2 units to the right.

   d. **Analyze Relationships** Find a different sequence of transformations that will transform triangle *DEF* to triangle *D″E″F″*.

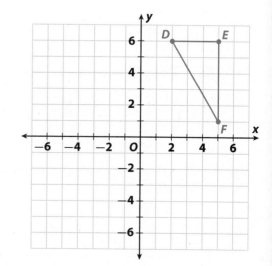

_____

_____

_____

_____

LESSON 9.3 Properties of Rotations

CA CC 8.G.1c

Verify experimentally the properties of rotations, reflections, and translations: Parallel lines are taken to parallel lines. *Also 8.G.1a, 8.G.1b, 8.G.3*

ESSENTIAL QUESTION

How do you describe the properties of rotation and their effect on the congruence and orientation of figures?

EXPLORE ACTIVITY 1   CA CC 8.G.1c

Exploring Rotations

A **rotation** is a transformation that turns a figure around a given point called the **center of rotation**. The image has the same size and shape as the preimage.

The triangle shown on the grid is the preimage. You will use the origin as the center of rotation.

A Trace triangle *ABC* onto a piece of paper. Cut out your traced triangle.

B Rotate your triangle 90° counterclockwise about the origin. The side of the triangle that lies along the *x*-axis should now lie along the *y*-axis.

C Sketch the image of the rotation. Label the images of points *A*, *B*, and *C* as *A'*, *B'*, and *C'*.

D Describe the motion modeled by the rotation.

Rotate _____ degrees _____ about the origin.

E Check that the motion you described in **D** is the same motion that maps point *A* onto *A'*, point *B* onto *B'*, and point *C* onto *C'*.

Reflect

1. **Communicate Mathematical Ideas** How are the size and the orientation of the triangle affected by the rotation?

_____

_____

_____

2. Rotate triangle *ABC* 90° clockwise about the origin. Sketch the result on the coordinate grid above. Label the image vertices *A"*, *B"*, and *C"*.

CA CC 8.G.1c

Properties of Rotations

Use trapezoid *TRAP* to investigate the properties of rotations.

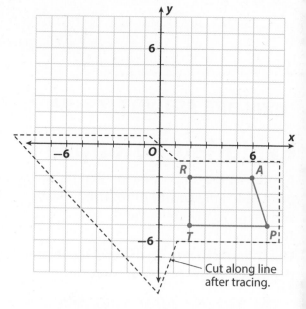

A Trace the trapezoid onto a piece of paper. Include the portion of the *x*- and *y*-axes bordering the third quadrant. Cut out your tracing.

B Place your trapezoid and axes on top of those in the figure. Then use the axes to help rotate your trapezoid 180° counterclockwise about the origin. Sketch the image of the rotation of your trapezoid in this new location. Label the vertices of the image *T'*, *R'*, *A'*, and *P'*.

C Use a ruler to measure the sides of trapezoid *TRAP* in centimeters.

$TR =$ _____ $RA =$ _____

$AP =$ _____ $TP =$ _____

D Use a ruler to measure the sides of trapezoid *T'R'A'P'* in centimeters.

$T'R' =$ _____ $R'A' =$ _____

$A'P' =$ _____ $T'P' =$ _____

E What do you notice about the lengths of corresponding sides of the two figures?

_____

F Use a protractor to measure the angles of trapezoid *TRAP*.

$m\angle T =$ _____ $m\angle R =$ _____ $m\angle A =$ _____ $m\angle P =$ _____

G Use a protractor to measure the angles of trapezoid *T'R'A'P'*.

$m\angle T' =$ _____ $m\angle R' =$ _____ $m\angle A' =$ _____ $m\angle P' =$ _____

H What do you notice about the measures of corresponding angles of the two figures?

_____

I Which sides of trapezoid *TRAP* are parallel? _____

Which sides of trapezoid *T'R'A'P'* are parallel? _____

What do you notice? _____

_____

Reflect

3. **Make a Conjecture** Use your results from **E**, **H**, and **I** to make a conjecture about rotations.

_____

_____

4. Place your tracing back in its original position. Then perform a 180° _clockwise_ rotation about the origin. Compare the result with the result in **B**.

_____

_____

Graphing Rotations

To rotate a figure in the coordinate plane, rotate each of its vertices. Then connect the vertices to form the image.

Math On the Spot

my.hrw.com

EXAMPLE 1

CA CC 8.G.3

The figure shows triangle *ABC*. Graph the image of triangle *ABC* after a rotation of 90° clockwise.

STEP 1 Rotate the figure clockwise from the *y*-axis to the *x*-axis. Point *A* will still be at (0, 0).

Point *B* is 2 units to the left of the *y*-axis, so point *B'* is 2 units above the *x*-axis.

Point *C* is 2 units to the right of the *y*-axis, so point *C'* is 2 units below the *x*-axis.

STEP 2 Connect *A'*, *B'*, and *C'* to form the image triangle *A'B'C'*.

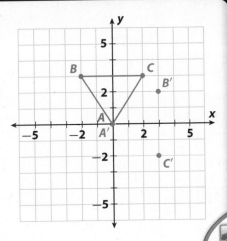

Math Talk

Mathematical Practices

How is the orientation of the triangle affected by the rotation?

Reflect

5. Is the image congruent to the preimage? How do you know?

_____

_____

_____

_____

Personal Math Trainer

Online Practice and Help

⏻ my.hrw.com

YOUR TURN

Graph the image of quadrilateral *ABCD* after each rotation.

6. 180°

7. 270° clockwise

8. Find the coordinates of Point *C* after a 90° counterclockwise rotation followed by a 180° rotation.

_____

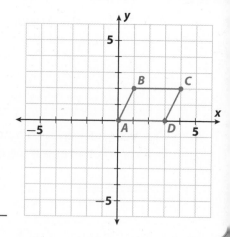

Guided Practice

1. Vocabulary A rotation is a transformation that turns a figure around a

given _____ called the center of rotation.

Siobhan rotates a right triangle 90° counterclockwise about the origin.

2. How does the orientation of the image of the triangle compare with the orientation of the preimage? (Explore Activity 1)

_____

3. Is the image of the triangle congruent to the preimage? (Explore Activity 2)

_____

Draw the image of the figure after the given rotation about the origin. (Example 1)

4. 90° counterclockwise

5. 180°

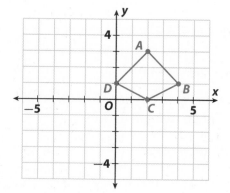

? **ESSENTIAL QUESTION CHECK-IN**

6. What are the properties of rotations?

_____

9.3 Independent Practice

CA CC 8.G.1a, 8.G.1b, 8.G.1c, 8.G.3

Personal Math Trainer

Online Practice and Help

my.hrw.com

7. The figure shows triangle *ABC* and a rotation of the triangle about the origin.

  a. How would you describe the rotation?

  _____

  _____

  b. What are the coordinates of the image?

  _____,_____,_____

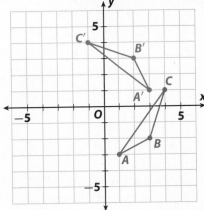

8. The graph shows a figure and its image after a transformation.

  a. How would you describe this as a rotation?

  _____

  _____

  b. Can you describe this as a transformation other than a rotation? Explain.

  _____

  _____

9. What type of rotation will preserve the orientation of the H-shaped figure in the grid?

_____

10. A point with coordinates $(-2, -3)$ is rotated 90° clockwise about the origin. What are the coordinates of its image?

_____

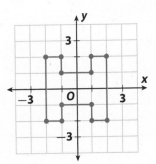

Complete the table with rotations of 180° or 90°. Include the direction of rotation for rotations of 90°.

	Shape in quadrant	Image in quadrant	Rotation
11.	I	IV	
12.	III	I	
13.	IV	III	

Draw the image of the figure after the given rotation about the origin.

14. 180°

15. 270° counterclockwise

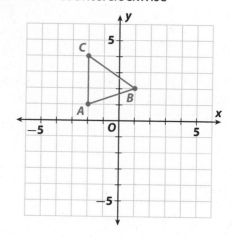

16. Is there a rotation for which the orientation of the image is always the same as that of the preimage? If so, what?

_____

 FOCUS ON HIGHER ORDER THINKING

Work Area

17. Problem Solving Lucas is playing a game where he has to rotate a figure for it to fit in an open space. Every time he clicks a button, the figure rotates 90 degrees clockwise. How many times does he need to click the button so that each figure returns to its original orientation?

Figure A _____

Figure B _____

Figure C _____

18. Make a Conjecture Triangle *ABC* is reflected across the y-axis to form the image *A'B'C'*. Triangle *A'B'C'* is then reflected across the x-axis to form the image *A"B"C"*. What type of rotation can be used to describe the relationship between triangle *A"B"C"* and triangle *ABC*?

_____

19. Communicate Mathematical Ideas Point *A* is on the y-axis. Describe all possible locations of image *A'* for rotations of 90°, 180°, and 270°. Include the origin as a possible location for *A*.

_____

_____

_____

_____

Algebraic Representations of Transformations

CA CC 8.G.3
Describe the effect of dilations, translations, rotations, and reflections on two-dimensional figures using coordinates.

ESSENTIAL QUESTION

How can you describe the effect of a translation, rotation, or reflection on coordinates using an algebraic representation?

Algebraic Representations of Translations

The rules shown in the table describe how coordinates change when a figure is translated up, down, right, and left on the coordinate plane.

Math On the Spot
my.hrw.com

Translations	
Right a units	Add a to the x-coordinate: $(x, y) \rightarrow (x + a, y)$
Left a units	Subtract a from the x-coordinate: $(x, y) \rightarrow (x - a, y)$
Up b units	Add b to the y-coordinate: $(x, y) \rightarrow (x, y + b)$
Down b units	Subtract b from the y-coordinate: $(x, y) \rightarrow (x, y - b)$

EXAMPLE 1

CA CC 8.G.3

Triangle *XYZ* has vertices *X*(0, 0), *Y*(2, 3), and *Z*(4, −1). Find the vertices of triangle *X′Y′Z′* after a translation of 3 units to the right and 1 unit down. Then graph the triangle and its image.

> Add 3 to the *x*-coordinate of each vertex and subtract 1 from the *y*-coordinate of each vertex.

STEP 1 Apply the rule to find the vertices of the image.

Vertices of △*XYZ*	Rule: $(x + 3, y - 1)$	Vertices of △*X′ Y′ Z′*
X(0, 0)	(0 + 3, 0 − 1)	*X′*(3, −1)
Y(2, 3)	(2 + 3, 3 − 1)	*Y′*(5, 2)
Z(4, −1)	(4 + 3, −1 − 1)	*Z′*(7, −2)

STEP 2 Graph triangle *XYZ* and its image.

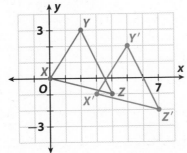

Math Talk
Mathematical Practices

When you translate a figure to the left or right, which coordinate do you change?

YOUR TURN

1. A rectangle has vertices at $(0, -2)$, $(0, 3)$, $(3, -2)$, and $(3, 3)$. What are the coordinates of the vertices of the image after the translation $(x, y) \rightarrow (x - 6, y - 3)$? Describe the translation.

_____

_____

Algebraic Representations of Reflections

The signs of the coordinates of a figure change when the figure is reflected across the *x*-axis and *y*-axis. The table shows the rules for changing the signs of the coordinates after a reflection.

Reflections	
Across the *x*-axis	Multiply each *y*-coordinate by -1: $(x, y) \rightarrow (x, -y)$
Across the *y*-axis	Multiply each *x*-coordinate by -1: $(x, y) \rightarrow (-x, y)$

EXAMPLE 2

CA CC 8.G.3

Rectangle *RSTU* has vertices $R(-4, -1)$, $S(-1, -1)$, $T(-1, -3)$, and $U(-4, -3)$. Find the vertices of rectangle $R'S'T'U'$ after a reflection across the *y*-axis. Then graph the rectangle and its image.

> Multiply the x-coordinate of each vertex by –

My Notes

STEP 1 Apply the rule to find the vertices of the image.

Vertices of *RSTU*	Rule: $(-1 \cdot x, y)$	Vertices of $R'S'T'U'$
$R(-4, -1)$	$(-1 \cdot (-4), -1)$	$R'(4, -1)$
$S(-1, -1)$	$(-1 \cdot (-1), -1)$	$S'(1, -1)$
$T(-1, -3)$	$(-1 \cdot (-1), -3)$	$T'(1, -3)$
$U(-4, -3)$	$(-1 \cdot (-4), -3)$	$U'(4, -3)$

STEP 2 Graph rectangle *RSTU* and its image.

YOUR TURN

2. Triangle *ABC* has vertices *A*(−2, 6), *B*(0, 5), and *C*(3, −1). Find the vertices of triangle *A′B′C′* after a reflection across the *x*-axis.

Algebraic Representations of Rotations

When points are rotated about the origin, the coordinates of the image can be found using the rules shown in the table.

Rotations	
90° clockwise	Multiply each *x*-coordinate by −1; then switch the *x*- and *y*-coordinates: $(x, y) \rightarrow (y, -x)$
90° counterclockwise	Multiply each *y*-coordinate by −1; then switch the *x*- and *y*-coordinates: $(x, y) \rightarrow (-y, x)$
180°	Multiply both coordinates by −1: $(x, y) \rightarrow (-x, -y)$

EXAMPLE 3

CA CC 8.G.3

Quadrilateral *ABCD* has vertices at *A*(−4, 2), *B*(−3, 4), *C*(2, 3), and *D*(0, 0). Find the vertices of quadrilateral *A′B′C′D′* after a 90° clockwise rotation. Then graph the quadrilateral and its image.

> Multiply the x-coordinate of each vertex by −1, and then switch the x- and y-coordinates.

STEP 1 Apply the rule to find the vertices of the image.

Vertices of *ABCD*	Rule: $(y, -x)$	Vertices of *A′B′C′D′*
A(−4, 2)	$(2, -1 \cdot (-4))$	*A′*(2, 4)
B(−3, 4)	$(4, -1 \cdot (-3))$	*B′*(4, 3)
C(2, 3)	$(3, -1 \cdot 2)$	*C′*(3, −2)
D(0, 0)	$(0, -1 \cdot 0)$	*D′*(0, 0)

STEP 2 Graph the quadrilateral and its image.

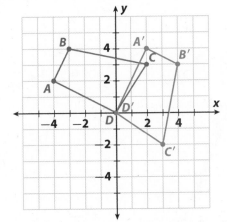

Reflect

3. Communicate Mathematical Ideas How would you find the vertices of an image if a figure were rotated 270° clockwise? Explain.

_____

_____

_____

YOUR TURN

4. A triangle has vertices at $J(-2, -4)$, $K(1, 5)$, and $L(2, 2)$. What are the coordinates of the vertices of the image after the triangle is rotated 90° counterclockwise?

_____

Guided Practice

1. Triangle XYZ has vertices $X(-3, -2)$, $Y(-1, 0)$, and $Z(1, -6)$. Find the vertices of triangle $X'Y'Z'$ after a translation of 6 units to the right. Then graph the triangle and its image. (Example 1)

_____

2. Describe what happens to the x- and y-coordinates after a point is reflected across the x-axis. (Example 2)

_____

_____

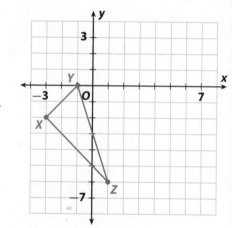

3. Use the rule $(x, y) \rightarrow (y, -x)$ to graph the image of the triangle at right. Then describe the transformation. (Example 3)

_____

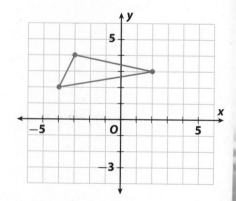

? ESSENTIAL QUESTION CHECK-IN

4. How do the x- and y-coordinates change when a figure is translated right a units and down b units?

_____

_____

9.4 Independent Practice

CA CC 8.G.3

Personal Math Trainer

Online Practice and Help

my.hrw.com

Write an algebraic rule to describe each transformation.
Then describe the transformation.

5.

_____

_____

6.

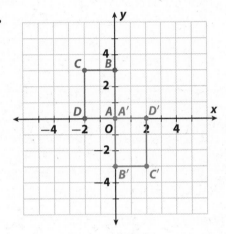

_____

_____

7. Triangle *XYZ* has vertices *X*(6, −2.3), *Y*(7.5, 5), and *Z*(8, 4). When translated, *X′* has coordinates (2.8, −1.3). Write a rule to describe this transformation. Then find the coordinates of *Y′* and *Z′*.

_____

_____

8. Point *L* has coordinates (3, −5). The coordinates of point *L′* after a reflection are (−3, −5). Without graphing, tell which axis point *L* was reflected across. Explain your answer.

_____

_____

_____

9. Use the rule $(x, y) \rightarrow (x − 2, y − 4)$ to graph the image of the rectangle. Then describe the transformation.

_____

_____

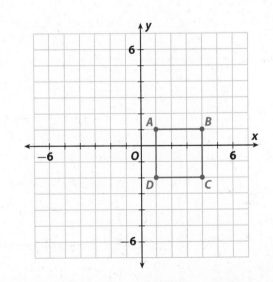

10. Parallelogram *ABCD* has vertices $A(-2, -5\frac{1}{2})$, $B(-4, -5\frac{1}{2})$, $C(-3, -2)$, and $D(-1, -2)$. Find the vertices of parallelogram *A′B′C′D′* after a translation of $2\frac{1}{2}$ units down.

_____

_____

11. Alexandra drew the logo shown on half-inch graph paper. Write a rule that describes the translation Alexandra used to create the shadow on the letter A.

_____

12. Kite *KLMN* has vertices at *K*(1, 3), *L*(2, 4), *M*(3, 3), and *N*(2, 0). After the kite is rotated, *K'* has coordinates (−3, 1). Describe the rotation, and include a rule in your description. Then find the coordinates of *L'*, *M'*, and *N'*.

_____

_____

 FOCUS ON HIGHER ORDER THINKING

13. Make a Conjecture Graph the triangle with vertices (−3, 4), (3, 4), and (−5, −5). Use the transformation (*y*, *x*) to graph its image.

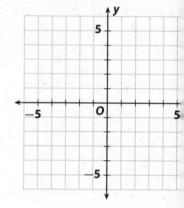

a. Which vertex of the image has the same coordinates as a vertex of the original figure? Explain why this is true.

_____

_____

b. What is the equation of a line through the origin and this point?

_____

c. Describe the transformation of the triangle.

_____

14. Critical Thinking Mitchell says the point (0, 0) does not change when reflected across the *x*- or *y*-axis or when rotated about the origin. Do you agree with Mitchell? Explain why or why not.

_____

_____

_____

Work Area

15. Analyze Relationships Triangle *ABC* with vertices *A*(−2, −2), *B*(−3, 1), and *C*(1, 1) is translated by $(x, y) \rightarrow (x - 1, y + 3)$. Then the image, triangle *A'B'C'*, is translated by $(x, y) \rightarrow (x + 4, y - 1)$, resulting in *A"B"C"*.

a. Find the coordinates for the vertices of triangle *A"B"C"*.

_____

b. Write a rule for one translation that maps triangle *ABC* to triangle *A"B"C"*.

_____

CA CC 8.G.2

Understand that a two-dimensional figure is congruent to another if the second can be obtained from the first by a sequence of rotations, reflections, and translations; given two congruent figures, describe a sequence that exhibits the congruence between them.

ESSENTIAL QUESTION

How can transformations be used to verify that two figures have the same shape and size?

EXPLORE ACTIVITY   CA CC 8.G.2

Combining Transformations

Apply the indicated series of transformations to the triangle. Each transformation is applied to the image of the previous transformation, not the original figure. Label each image with the letter of the transformation applied.

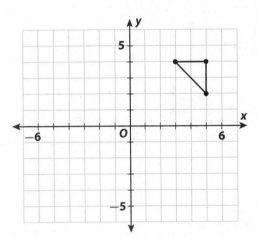

A Reflection across the *x*-axis

B $(x, y) \rightarrow (x - 3, y)$

C Reflection across the *y*-axis

D $(x, y) \rightarrow (x, y + 4)$

E Rotation 90° clockwise around the origin

F Compare the size and shape of the final image to that of the original figure.

_____

_____

Reflect

1. Which transformation(s) change the orientation of figures? Which do not?

_____

2. **Make a Conjecture** After a series of transformations, two figures have the same size and shape, but different orientations. What does this indicate about the transformations?

_____

_____

_____

Congruent Figures

Recall that segments and their images have the same length and angles and their images have the same measure under a translation, reflection, or rotation. Two figures are said to be **congruent** if one can be obtained from the other by a sequence of translations, reflections, and rotations. Congruent figures have the same size and shape.

When you are told that two figures are congruent, there must be a sequence of translations, reflections, and/or rotations that transforms one into the other.

EXAMPLE 1

 CA CC 8.G.2

A Identify a sequence of transformations that will transform figure A into figure B.

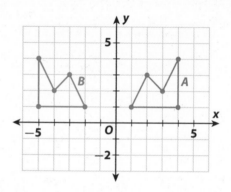

To transform figure A into figure B, you need to reflect it over the y-axis and translate one unit to the left. A sequence of transformations that will accomplish this is $(x, y) \rightarrow (-x, y)$ and $(x, y) \rightarrow (x - 1, y)$.

B Identify a sequence of transformations that will transform figure B into figure C.

Math Talk
Mathematical Practices

How do you know that the sequence of transformations in Parts B and C must include a rotation?

Any sequence of transformations that changes figure B into figure C will need to include a rotation. A 90° counterclockwise rotation around the origin would properly orient figure B, but not locate it in the same position as figure C. The rotated figure would be 2 units below and 1 unit to the left of where figure C is. You would need to translate the rotated figure up 2 units and right 1 unit.

A sequence of transformations is a 90° counterclockwise rotation about the origin, $(x, y) \rightarrow (-y, x)$, followed by $(x, y) \rightarrow (x + 1, y + 2)$.

C Identify a sequence of transformations that will transform figure *D* into figure *E*.

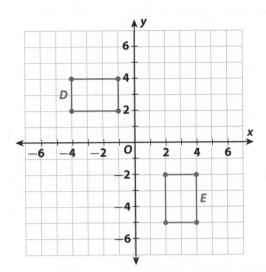

A sequence of transformations that changes figure *D* to figure *E* will need to include a rotation. A 90° clockwise rotation around the origin would result in the figure being oriented as figure *E*.

However, the rotated figure would be 6 units above where figure *E* is. You would need to translate the rotated figure down 6 units.

A sequence of transformations is a 90° clockwise rotation about the origin, $(x, y) \rightarrow (y, -x)$, followed by $(x, y) \rightarrow (x, y - 6)$.

YOUR TURN

3. Identify a sequence of transformations that will transform figure *A* into figure *B*.

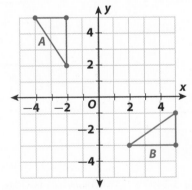

_____

_____

_____

Personal Math Trainer

Online Practice and Help

⏻ my.hrw.com

1. Apply the indicated series of transformations to the rectangle. Each transformation is applied to the image of the previous transformation, not the original figure. Label each image with the letter of the transformation applied. (Explore Activity)

   A. Reflection across the y-axis

   B. Rotation 90° clockwise around the origin

   C. $(x, y) \rightarrow (x - 2, y)$

   D. Rotation 90° counterclockwise around the origin

   E. $(x, y) \rightarrow (x - 7, y - 2)$

Identify a sequence of transformations that will transform figure A into figure C. (Example 1)

2. What transformation is used to transform figure A into figure B?

   _____

   _____

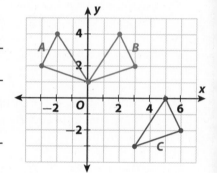

3. What transformation is used to transform figure B into figure C?

   _____

   _____

4. What sequence of transformations is used to transform figure A into figure C? Express the transformations algebraically.

   _____

   _____

5. **Vocabulary** What does it mean for two figures to be congruent?

   _____

   _____

? **ESSENTIAL QUESTION CHECK-IN**

6. After a sequence of translations, reflections, and rotations, what is true about the first figure and the final figure?

   _____

   _____

9.5 Independent Practice

 CA CC 8.G.2

Personal Math Trainer

Online Practice and Help

my.hrw.com

For each given figure A, graph figures B and C using the given sequence of transformations. State whether figures A and C have the same or different orientation.

7.

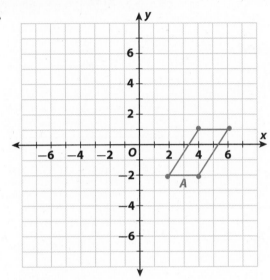

Figure *B*: a translation of 1 unit to the right and 3 units up

Figure *C*: a 90° clockwise rotation around the origin

8.

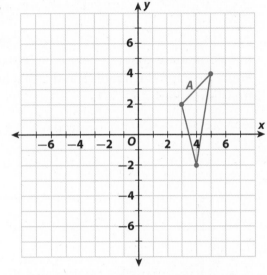

Figure *B*: a reflection across the *y*-axis

Figure *C*: a 180° rotation around the origin

9.

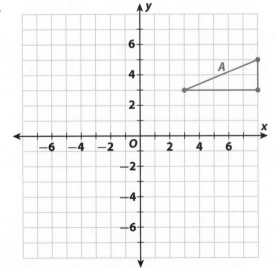

Figure *B*: a reflection across the *y*-axis

Figure *C*: a translation 2 units down

10.

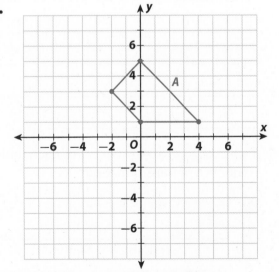

Figure *B*: a translation 2 units up

Figure *C*: a rotation of 180° around the origin

11. Represent Real-World Problems A city planner wanted to place the new town library at site *A*. The mayor thought that it would be better at site *B*. What transformations were applied to the building at site *A* to relocate the building to site *B*? Did the mayor change the size or orientation of the library?

_____

_____

_____

12. Persevere in Problem Solving Find a sequence of three transformations that can be used to obtain figure *D* from figure *A*. Graph the figures *B* and *C* that are created by the transformations.

_____

_____

_____

_____

 FOCUS ON HIGHER ORDER THINKING

Work Area

13. Counterexamples The Commutative Properties for Addition and Multiplication state that the order of two numbers being added or multiplied does not change the sum or product. Are translations and rotations commutative? If not, give a counterexample.

_____

_____

_____

_____

_____

14. Multiple Representations For each representation, describe a possible sequence of transformations.

a. $(x, y) \rightarrow (-x - 2, y + 1)$

_____

_____

b. $(x, y) \rightarrow (y, -x - 3)$

_____

Ready to Go On?

9.1–9.3 Properties of Translations, Reflections, and Rotations

1. Graph the image of triangle *ABC* after a translation of 6 units to the right and 4 units down. Label the vertices of the image *A′*, *B′*, and *C′*.

2. On the same coordinate grid, graph the image of triangle *ABC* after a reflection across the *x*-axis. Label the vertices of the image *A″*, *B″*, and *C″*.

3. Graph the image of *HIJK* after it is rotated 180° about the origin. Label the vertices of the image *H′I′J′K′*.

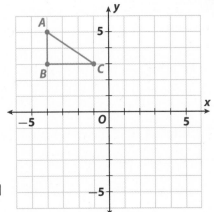

9.4 Algebraic Representations of Transformations

4. A triangle has vertices at (2, 3), (−2, 2), and (−3, 5). What are the coordinates of the vertices of the image after the translation $(x, y) \rightarrow (x + 4, y - 3)$?

_____

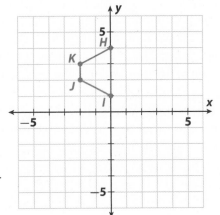

9.5 Congruent Figures

5. **Vocabulary** Translations, reflections, and rotations produce a figure

that is _____ to the original figure.

6. Use the coordinate grid for Exercise 3. Reflect *H′I′J′K′* over the *y*-axis, then rotate it 180° about the origin. Label the new figure *H″I″J″K″*.

❓ ESSENTIAL QUESTION

7. What properties allow transformations to be used as problem solving tools?

_____

_____

MODULE 9
MIXED REVIEW

Assessment Readiness

Personal Math Trainer

Online Practice and Help

my.hrw.com

1. Consider each rational number. Is the number greater than $-2\frac{1}{3}$ but less than $-\frac{4}{5}$?

   Select Yes or No for A–C.

   A. -0.4 ○ Yes   ○ No
   B. $-\frac{9}{7}$ ○ Yes   ○ No
   C. -0.9 ○ Yes   ○ No

2. Triangle *DEF* is rotated 90° clockwise about the origin.

   Choose True or False for each statement.

   A. $E'F' = 3$ ○ True   ○ False
   B. $m\angle F' = 90°$ ○ True   ○ False
   C. $\overline{D'F'}$ is vertical.   ○ True   ○ False

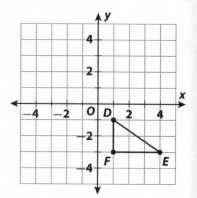

3. A graphic artist is working on a logo for a car company. The artist draws parallelogram *LMNP* with vertices *L*(1, 0), *M*(2, 2), *N*(5, 3), and *P*(4, 1). The artist then reflects the parallelogram across the *x*-axis. Find the coordinates of the vertices of parallelogram *L'M'N'P'*, and describe the algebraic rule you used to find the coordinates.

4. The map shows two of a farmer's fields. Is field *A* congruent to field *B*? Use a sequence of transformations to explain your reasoning.

Transformations and Similarity

? **ESSENTIAL QUESTION**

How can you use dilations and similarity to solve real-world problems?

Real-World Video

To plan a mural, the artist first makes a smaller drawing showing what the mural will look like. Then the image is enlarged by a scale factor on the mural canvas. This enlargement is called a dilation.

my.hrw.com

GO DIGITAL

my.hrw.com

my.hrw.com

Go digital with your write-in student edition, accessible on any device.

Math On the Spot

Scan with your smart phone to jump directly to the online edition, video tutor, and more.

Animated Math

Interactively explore key concepts to see how math works.

Personal Math Trainer

Get immediate feedback and help as you work through practice sets.

Are YOU Ready?

Complete these exercises to review skills you will need for this module.

Personal Math Trainer

Online Practice and Help

my.hrw.com

Simplify Ratios

EXAMPLE
$$\frac{35}{21} = \frac{35 \div 7}{21 \div 7}$$
$$= \frac{5}{3}$$

To write a ratio in simplest form, find the greatest common factor of the numerator and denominator. Divide the numerator and denominator by the GCF.

Write each ratio in simplest form.

1. $\frac{6}{15}$ _____

2. $\frac{8}{20}$ _____

3. $\frac{30}{18}$ _____

4. $\frac{36}{30}$ _____

Multiply with Fractions and Decimals

EXAMPLE
$$2\frac{3}{5} \times 20$$
$$= \frac{13 \times 20}{5 \times 1}$$
$$= \frac{13 \times \overset{4}{\cancel{20}}}{\underset{1}{\cancel{5}} \times 1}$$
$$= 52$$

Write numbers as fractions and multiply.

Simplify.

$$\begin{array}{r} 68 \\ \times 4.5 \\ \hline 340 \\ +272 \\ \hline 306.0 \end{array}$$

Multiply as you would with whole numbers.

Place the decimal point in the answer based on the total number of decimal places in the two factors.

Multiply.

5. $60 \times \frac{25}{100}$

6. 3.5×40

7. 4.4×44

8. $24 \times \frac{8}{9}$

_____ _____ _____ _____

Graph Ordered Pairs (First Quadrant)

EXAMPLE

Graph the point A(4, 3.5).
Start at the origin.
Move 4 units right.
Then move 3.5 units up.
Graph point A(4, 3.5).

Graph each point on the coordinate grid above.

9. B (9, 0)

10. C (2, 7)

11. D (0, 4.5)

12. E (6, 2.5)

Reading Start-Up

Visualize Vocabulary

Use the ✔ words to complete the graphic organizer.
You will put one word in each rectangle.

The four regions on a coordinate plane.	The point where the axes intersect to form the coordinate plane.

Reviewing the Coordinate Plane

The horizontal axis of a coordinate plane.	The vertical axis of a coordinate plane.

Understand Vocabulary

Complete the sentences using the preview words.

1. A figure larger than the original, produced through dilation, is

   an _____.

2. A figure smaller than the original, produced through dilation, is

   a _____.

Vocabulary

Review Words

   coordinate plane (plano cartesiano)

   image (imagen)

✔ origin (origen)

   preimage (imagen original)

✔ quadrants (cuadrante)

   ratio (razón)

   scale (escala)

✔ x-axis (eje x)

✔ y-axis (eje y)

Preview Words

   center of dilation (centro de dilatación)

   dilation (dilatación)

   enlargement (agrandamiento)

   reduction (reducción)

   scale factor (factor de escala)

   similar (similar)

Active Reading

Key-Term Fold Before beginning the module, create a key-term fold to help you learn the vocabulary in this module. Write the highlighted vocabulary words on one side of the flap. Write the definition for each word on the other side of the flap. Use the key-term fold to quiz yourself on the definitions used in this module.

Transformations and Similarity

Understanding the standards and the vocabulary terms in the standards will help you know exactly what you are expected to learn in this module.

CA CC 8.G.3

Describe the effect of dilations, translations, rotations, and reflections on two-dimensional figures using coordinates.

What It Means to You

You will use an algebraic representation to describe a dilation.

EXAMPLE 8.G.3

The blue square *ABCD* is the preimage. Write two algebraic representations, one for the dilation to the green square and one for the dilation to the purple square.

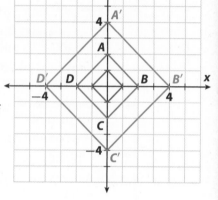

The coordinates of the vertices of the original image are multiplied by 2 for the green square.

Green square: $(x, y) \rightarrow (2x, 2y)$

The coordinates of the vertices of the original image are multiplied by $\frac{1}{2}$ for the purple square.

Purple square: $(x, y) \rightarrow \left(\frac{1}{2}x, \frac{1}{2}y\right)$

CA CC 8.G.4

Understand that a two-dimensional figure is similar to another if the second can be obtained from the first by a sequence of rotations, reflections, translations, and dilations; given two similar two-dimensional figures, describe a sequence that exhibits the similarity between them.

What It Means to You

You will describe a sequence of transformations between two similar figures.

EXAMPLE 8.G.4

Identify a sequence of two transformations that will transform figure *A* into figure *B*.

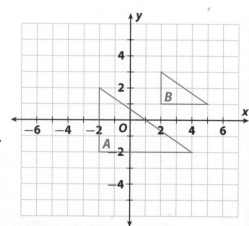

Dilate with center at the origin by a scale factor of $\frac{1}{2}$.

Then translate right 3 units and up 2 units.

Visit **my.hrw.com** to see all **CA Common Core Standards** explained.

my.hrw.com

Properties of Dilations

 CA CC 8.G.4

Understand that a two-dimensional figure is similar to another if the second can be obtained from the first by a sequence of rotations, reflections, translations, and dilations; given two similar two-dimensional figures, describe a sequence that exhibits the similarity between them. *Also 8.G.3*

ESSENTIAL QUESTION

How do you describe the properties of dilations?

EXPLORE ACTIVITY 1 *Real World* CA CC 8.G.4

Exploring Dilations

The missions that placed 12 astronauts on the moon were controlled at the Johnson Space Center in Houston. The toy models at the right are scaled-down replicas of the Saturn V rocket that powered the moon flights. Each replica is a transformation called a **dilation**. Unlike the other transformations you have studied—translations, rotations, and reflections—dilations change the size (but not the shape) of a figure.

Every dilation has a fixed point called the **center of dilation** located where the lines connecting corresponding parts of figures intersect.

Triangle *R'S'T'* is a dilation of triangle *RST*. Point *C* is the center of dilation.

A Use a ruler to measure segments $\overline{CR}$, $\overline{CR'}$, $\overline{CS}$, $\overline{CS'}$, $\overline{CT}$, and $\overline{CT'}$ to the nearest millimeter. Record the measurements and ratios in the table.

CR'	CR	$\frac{CR'}{CR}$	CS'	CS	$\frac{CS'}{CS}$	CT'	CT	$\frac{CT'}{CT}$

B Write a conjecture based on the ratios in the table.

_____

C Measure and record the corresponding side lengths of the triangles.

R'S'	RS	$\frac{R'S'}{RS}$	S'T'	ST	$\frac{S'T'}{ST}$	R'T'	RT	$\frac{R'T'}{RT}$

D Write a conjecture based on the ratios in the table.

_____

E Measure the corresponding angles and describe your results.

_____

Reflect

1. Two figures that have the same shape but different sizes are called *similar*. Are triangles *RST* and *R'S'T'* similar? Why or why not?

_____

_____

2. Compare the orientation of a figure with the orientation of its dilation.

_____

EXPLORE ACTIVITY 2 CA CC 8.G.3

Exploring Dilations on a Coordinate Plane

In this activity you will explore how the coordinates of a figure on a coordinate plane are affected by a dilation.

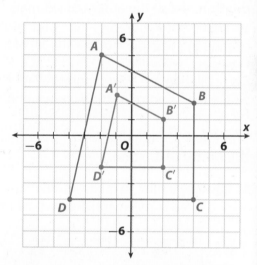

A Complete the table. Record the *x*- and *y*-coordinates of the points in the two figures and the ratios of the *x*-coordinates and the *y*-coordinates.

Vertex	x	y	Vertex	x	y	Ratio of x-coordinates (A'B'C'D' ÷ ABCD)	Ratio of y-coordinates (A'B'C'D' ÷ ABCD)
A'			A				
B'			B				
C'			C				
D'			D				

B Write a conjecture about the ratios of the coordinates of a dilation image to the coordinates of the original figure.

_____

_____

Reflect

3. In Explore Activity 1, triangle *R'S'T'* was larger than triangle *RST*. How is the relationship between quadrilateral *A'B'C'D'* and quadrilateral *ABCD* different?

_____

Math Talk
Mathematical Practices

How are dilations different from the other transformations you have learned about?

Finding a Scale Factor

As you have seen in the two activities, a dilation can produce a larger figure (an **enlargement**) or a smaller figure (a **reduction**). The **scale factor** describes how much the figure is enlarged or reduced. The scale factor is the ratio of a length of the image to the corresponding length on the original figure.

In Explore Activity 1, the side lengths of triangle *R'S'T'* were twice the length of those of triangle *RST*, so the scale factor was 2. In Explore Activity 2, the side lengths of quadrilateral *A'B'C'D'* were half those of quadrilateral *ABCD*, so the scale factor was 0.5.

Math On the Spot

⊙ my.hrw.com

EXAMPLE 1 🐻 CA CC 8.G.4

An art supply store sells several sizes of drawing triangles. All are dilations of a single basic triangle. The basic triangle and one of its dilations are shown on the grid. Find the scale factor of the dilation.

STEP 1 Use the coordinates to find the lengths of the sides of each triangle.

Triangle *ABC*: $AC = 2$ $CB = 3$

Triangle *A'B'C'*: $A'C' = 4$ $C'B' = 6$

Since the scale factor is the same for all corresponding sides, you can record just two pairs of side lengths. Use one pair as a check on the other.

STEP 2 Find the ratios of the corresponding sides.

$\dfrac{A'C'}{AC} = \dfrac{4}{2} = 2$ $\dfrac{C'B'}{CB} = \dfrac{6}{3} = 2$

The scale factor of the dilation is 2.

Animated Math

⊙ my.hrw.com

Reflect

4. Is the dilation an enlargement or a reduction? How can you tell?

_____

_____

5. Find the scale factor of the dilation.

_____

_____

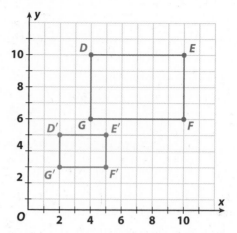

Math Talk

Mathematical Practices

Which scale factors lead to enlargements? Which scale factors lead to reductions?

Guided Practice

Use triangles ABC and A'B'C' for 1–5. (Explore Activities 1 and 2, Example 1)

1. For each pair of corresponding vertices, find the ratio of the x-coordinates and the ratio of the y-coordinates.

   ratio of x-coordinates = _____

   ratio of y-coordinates = _____

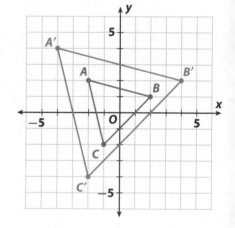

2. I know that triangle A'B'C' is a dilation of triangle ABC because the ratios of the corresponding

   x-coordinates are _____ and the ratios of the

   corresponding y-coordinates are _____.

3. The ratio of the lengths of the corresponding sides of triangle A'B'C' and

   triangle ABC equals _____.

4. The corresponding angles of triangle ABC and triangle A'B'C'

   are _____.

5. The scale factor of the dilation is _____.

? ESSENTIAL QUESTION CHECK-IN

6. How can you find the scale factor of a dilation?

   _____

   _____

10.1 Independent Practice

Personal Math Trainer

Online Practice and Help

my.hrw.com

For 7–11, tell whether one figure is a dilation of the other or not. Explain your reasoning.

7. Quadrilateral *MNPQ* has side lengths of 15 mm, 24 mm, 21 mm, and 18 mm. Quadrilateral *M'N'P'Q'* has side lengths of 5 mm, 8 mm, 7 mm, and 4 mm.

_____

_____

8. Triangle *RST* has angles measuring 38° and 75°. Triangle *R'S'T'* has angles measuring 67° and 38°. The sides are proportional.

_____

_____

_____

9. Two triangles, Triangle 1 and Triangle 2, are similar.

_____

10. Quadrilateral *MNPQ* is the same shape but a different size than quadrilateral *M'N'P'Q*.

_____

_____

_____

_____

_____

_____

11. On a coordinate plane, triangle *UVW* has coordinates *U*(20, −12), *V*(8, 6), and *W*(−24, −4). Triangle *U'V'W'* has coordinates *U'*(15, −9), *V'*(6, 4.5), and *W'*(−18, −3).

_____

_____

_____

_____

_____

_____

_____

Complete the table by writing "same" or "changed" to compare the image with the original figure in the given transformation.

Image Compared to Original Figure			
	Orientation	**Size**	**Shape**
12. **Translation**			
13. **Reflection**			
14. **Rotation**			
15. **Dilation**			

16. Describe the image of a dilation with a scale factor of 1.

_____

_____

Identify the scale factor used in each dilation.

17.

_____

18.

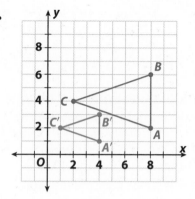

_____

H.O.T. FOCUS ON HIGHER ORDER THINKING

Work Area

19. Critical Thinking Explain how you can find the center of dilation of a triangle and its dilation.

_____

_____

_____

20. Make a Conjecture

a. A square on the coordinate plane has vertices at $(-2, 2)$, $(2, 2)$, $(2, -2)$, and $(-2, -2)$. A dilation of the square has vertices at $(-4, 4)$, $(4, 4)$, $(4, -4)$, and $(-4, -4)$. Find the scale factor and the perimeter of each square.

_____

_____

b. A square on the coordinate plane has vertices at $(-3, 3)$, $(3, 3)$, $(3, -3)$, and $(-3, -3)$. A dilation of the square has vertices at $(-6, 6)$, $(6, 6)$, $(6, -6)$, and $(-6, -6)$. Find the scale factor and the perimeter of each square.

_____

_____

c. Make a conjecture about the relationship of the scale factor to the perimeter of a square and its image.

_____

_____

LESSON

10.2 Algebraic Representations of Dilations

CA CC 8.G.3

Describe the effect of dilations, translations, rotations, and reflections on two-dimensional figures using coordinates.

ESSENTIAL QUESTION

How can you describe the effect of a dilation on coordinates using an algebraic representation?

EXPLORE ACTIVITY 1 CA CC 8.G.3

Graphing Enlargements

When a dilation in the coordinate plane has the origin as the center of dilation, you can find points on the dilated image by multiplying the x- and y-coordinates of the original figure by the scale factor. For scale factor k, the algebraic representation of the dilation is $(x, y) \rightarrow (kx, ky)$. For enlargements, $k > 1$.

The figure shown on the grid is the preimage. The center of dilation is the origin.

A List the coordinates of the vertices of the preimage in the first column of the table.

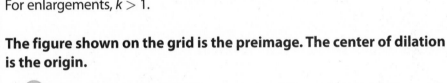

Preimage (x, y)	Image $(3x, 3y)$
(2, 2)	(6, 6)

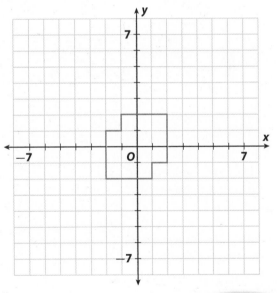

B What is the scale factor for the dilation? _____

C Apply the dilation to the preimage and write the coordinates of the vertices of the image in the second column of the table.

D Sketch the image after the dilation on the coordinate grid.

Math Talk
Mathematical Practices

What effect would the dilation $(x, y) \rightarrow (4x, 4y)$ have on the radius of a circle?

Reflect

1. How does the dilation affect the length of line segments?

_____

_____

2. How does the dilation affect angle measures?

_____

EXPLORE ACTIVITY 2 CA CC 8.G.3

Graphing Reductions

For scale factors between 0 and 1, the image is smaller than the preimage. This is called a reduction.

The arrow shown is the preimage. The center of dilation is the origin.

A List the coordinates of the vertices of the preimage in the first column of the table.

B What is the scale factor for the dilation? _____

C Apply the dilation to the preimage and write the coordinates of the vertices of the image in the second column of the table.

Preimage (x, y)	Image $\left(\frac{1}{2}x, \frac{1}{2}y\right)$

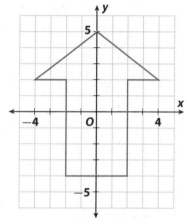

D Sketch the image after the dilation on the coordinate grid.

Reflect

3. How does the dilation affect the length of line segments?

_____

4. How would a dilation with scale factor 1 affect the preimage?

_____

Center of Dilation Outside the Image

The center of dilation can be inside *or* outside the original image and the dilated image. The center of dilation can be anywhere on the coordinate plane as long as the lines that connect each pair of corresponding vertices between the original and dilated image intersect at the center of dilation.

EXAMPLE 1

CA CC 8.G.3

Graph the image of △ABC after a dilation with the origin as its center and a scale factor of 3. What are the vertices of the image?

STEP 1 Multiply each coordinate of the vertices of △ABC by 3 to find the vertices of the dilated image.

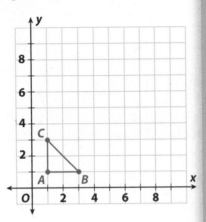

$△ABC \ (x, y) \rightarrow (3x, 3y) \ △A'B'C'$

$A(1, 1) \rightarrow A'(1 \cdot 3, 1 \cdot 3) \rightarrow A'(3, 3)$

$B(3, 1) \rightarrow B'(3 \cdot 3, 1 \cdot 3) \rightarrow B'(9, 3)$

$C(1, 3) \rightarrow C'(1 \cdot 3, 3 \cdot 3) \rightarrow C'(3, 9)$

The vertices of the dilated image are $A'(3, 3)$, $B'(9, 3)$, and $C'(3, 9)$.

STEP 2 Graph the dilated image.

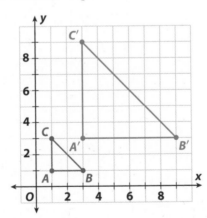

Math Talk
Mathematical Practices

Describe how you can check graphically that you have drawn the image triangle correctly.

YOUR TURN

5. Graph the image of △XYZ after a dilation with a scale factor of $\frac{1}{3}$ and the origin as its center. Then write an algebraic rule to describe the dilation.

_____

1. The grid shows a diamond-shaped preimage. Write the coordinates of the vertices of the preimage in the first column of the table. Then apply the dilation $(x, y) \rightarrow \left(\frac{3}{2}x, \frac{3}{2}y\right)$ and write the coordinates of the vertices of the image in the second column. Sketch the image of the figure after the dilation. (Explore Activities 1 and 2)

Preimage	Image
(2, 0)	(3, 0)

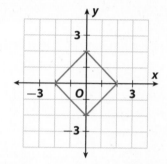

Graph the image of each figure after a dilation with the origin as its center and the given scale factor. Then write an algebraic rule to describe the dilation. (Example 1)

2. scale factor of 1.5

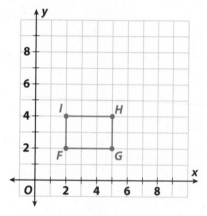

_____

3. scale factor of $\frac{1}{3}$

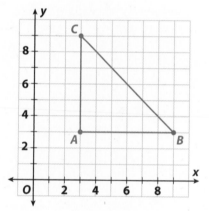

_____

? ESSENTIAL QUESTION CHECK-IN

4. A dilation of $(x, y) \rightarrow (kx, ky)$ when $0 < k < 1$ has what effect on the figure? What is the effect on the figure when $k > 1$?

_____

_____

_____

_____

10.2 Independent Practice

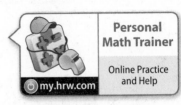

5. The blue square is the preimage. Write two algebraic representations, one for the dilation to the green square and one for the dilation to the purple square.

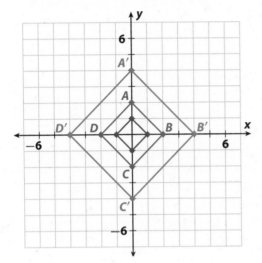

_____

_____

6. Critical Thinking A triangle has vertices $A(-5, -4)$, $B(2, 6)$, and $C(4, -3)$. The center of dilation is the origin and $(x, y)\rightarrow(3x, 3y)$. What are the vertices of the dilated image?

_____

_____

7. Critical Thinking $M'N'O'P'$ has vertices at $M'(3, 4)$, $N'(6, 4)$, $O'(6, 7)$, and $P'(3, 7)$. The center of dilation is the origin. $MNOP$ has vertices at $M(4.5, 6)$, $N(9, 6)$, $O'(9, 10.5)$, and $P'(4.5, 10.5)$. What is the algebraic representation of this dilation?

_____

8. Critical Thinking A dilation with center $(0,0)$ and scale factor k is applied to a polygon. What dilation can you apply to the image to return it to the original preimage?

_____

9. Represent Real-World Problems The blueprints for a new house are scaled so that $\frac{1}{4}$ inch equals 1 foot. The blueprint is the preimage and the house is the dilated image. The blueprints are plotted on a coordinate plane.

a. What is the scale factor in terms of inches to inches?

_____

b. One inch on the blueprint represents how many inches in the actual house? How many feet?

_____

c. Write the algebraic representation of the dilation from the blueprint to the house.

_____

d. A rectangular room has coordinates $Q(2, 2)$, $R(7, 2)$, $S(7, 5)$, and $T(2, 5)$ on the blueprint. The homeowner wants this room to be 25% larger. What are the coordinates of the new room?

_____

_____

_____

e. What are the dimensions of the new room, in inches, on the blueprint? What will the dimensions of the new room be, in feet, in the new house?

_____

_____

_____

_____

10. Write the algebraic representation of the dilation shown.

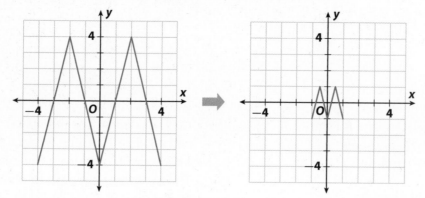

Work Area

11. Critique Reasoning The set for a school play needs a replica of a historic building painted on a backdrop that is 20 feet long and 16 feet high. The actual building measures 400 feet long and 320 feet high. A stage crewmember writes $(x, y) \rightarrow \left(\frac{1}{12}x, \frac{1}{12}y\right)$ to represent the dilation. Is the crewmember's calculation correct if the painted replica is to cover the entire backdrop? Explain.

_____

_____

12. Communicate Mathematical Ideas Explain what each of these algebraic transformations does to a figure.

a. $(x, y) \rightarrow (y, -x)$ _____

b. $(x, y) \rightarrow (-x, -y)$ _____

c. $(x, y) \rightarrow (x, 2y)$ _____

_____

d. $(x, y) \rightarrow \left(\frac{2}{3}x, y\right)$ _____

_____

e. $(x, y) \rightarrow (0.5x, 1.5y)$ _____

_____

13. Communicate Mathematical Ideas Triangle ABC has coordinates $A(1, 5)$, $B(-2, 1)$, and $C(-2, 4)$. Sketch triangle ABC and $A'B'C'$ for the dilation $(x, y) \rightarrow (-2x, -2y)$. What is the effect of a negative scale factor?

_____

_____

LESSON
10.3 Similar Figures

CA CC 8.G.4

Understand that a two-dimensional figure is similar to another if the second can be obtained from the first by a sequence of rotations, reflections, translations, and dilations; given two similar two-dimensional figures, describe a sequence that exhibits the similarity between them.

ESSENTIAL QUESTION

What is the connection between transformations and the orientations of similar figures?

EXPLORE ACTIVITY   CA CC 8.G.4

Combining Transformations with Dilations

When creating an animation, figures need to be translated, reflected, rotated, and sometimes dilated. As an example of this, apply the indicated sequence of transformations to the rectangle. Each transformation is applied to the image of the previous transformation, not to the original figure. Label each image with the letter of the transformation applied.

A $(x, y) \rightarrow (x + 7, y - 2)$

B $(x, y) \rightarrow (x, -y)$

C rotation 90° clockwise around the origin

D $(x, y) \rightarrow (x + 5, y + 3)$

E $(x, y) \rightarrow (3x, 3y)$

F List the coordinates of the vertices of rectangle *E*.

_____

G Compare the following attributes of rectangle *E* to those of the original figure.

Shape	
Size	
Angle Measures	

Reflect

1. Which transformation represents the dilation? How can you tell?

   _____

   _____

2. A sequence of transformations containing a single dilation is applied to a figure. Are the original figure and its final image congruent? Explain.

   _____

   _____

Math On the Spot

⏻ my.hrw.com

Similar Figures

Two figures are **similar** if one can be obtained from the other by a sequence of translations, reflections, rotations, and dilations. Similar figures have the same shape but may be different sizes.

When you are told that two figures are similar, there must be a sequence of translations, reflections, rotations, and/or dilations that can transform one to the other.

EXAMPLE 1

 CA CC 8.G.4

A Identify a sequence of transformations that will transform figure *A* into figure *B*. Tell whether the figures are congruent. Tell whether they are similar.

My Notes

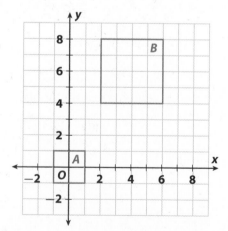

Both figures are squares whose orientations are the same, so no reflection or rotation is needed. Figure *B* has sides twice as long as figure *A*, so a dilation with a scale factor of 2 is needed. Figure *B* is moved to the right and above figure *A*, so a translation is needed. A sequence of transformations that will accomplish this is a dilation by a scale factor of 2 centered at the origin followed by the translation $(x, y) \rightarrow (x + 4, y + 6)$. The figures are not congruent, but they are similar.

B Identify a sequence of transformations that will transform figure *C* into figure *D*. Include a reflection. Tell whether the figures are congruent. Tell whether they are similar.

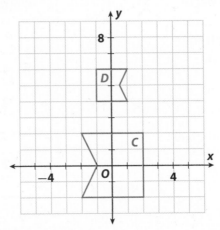

The orientation of figure *D* is reversed from that of figure *C*, so a reflection over the *y*-axis is needed. Figure *D* has sides that are half as long as figure *C*, so a dilation with a scale factor of $\frac{1}{2}$ is needed. Figure *D* is moved above figure *C*, so a translation is needed. A sequence of transformations that will accomplish this is a dilation by a scale factor of $\frac{1}{2}$ centered at the origin, followed by the reflection $(x, y) \rightarrow (-x, y)$, followed by the translation $(x, y) \rightarrow (x, y + 5)$. The figures are not congruent, but they are similar.

Math Talk
Mathematical Practices

A figure and its image have different sizes and orientations. What do you know about the sequence of transformations that generated the image?

C Identify a sequence of transformations that will transform figure *C* into figure *D*. Include a rotation.

The orientation of figure *D* is reversed from that of figure *C*, so a rotation of 180° is needed. Figure *D* has sides that are half as long as figure *C*, so a dilation with a scale factor of $\frac{1}{2}$ is needed. Figure *D* is moved above figure *C*, so a translation is needed. A sequence of transformations that will accomplish this is a rotation of 180° about the origin, followed by a dilation by a scale factor of $\frac{1}{2}$ centered at the origin, followed by the translation $(x, y) \rightarrow (x, y + 5)$.

YOUR TURN

3. Look again at the Explore Activity. Start with the original figure. Create a new sequence of transformations that will yield figure *E*, the final image. Your transformations do not need to produce the images in the same order in which they originally appeared.

_____

_____

_____

Personal Math Trainer

Online Practice and Help

my.hrw.com

1. Apply the indicated sequence of transformations to the square. Apply each transformation to the image of the previous transformation. Label each image with the letter of the transformation applied.
(Explore Activity)

A $(x, y) \rightarrow (-x, y)$

B Rotate the square 180° around the origin.

C $(x, y) \rightarrow (x - 5, y - 6)$

D $(x, y) \rightarrow \left(\frac{1}{2}x, \frac{1}{2}y\right)$

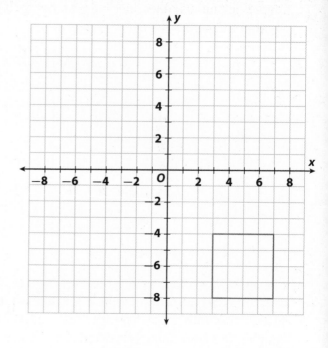

Identify a sequence of two transformations that will transform figure A into the given figure. *(Example 1)*

2. figure B

_____

_____

3. figure C

_____

_____

4. figure D

_____

_____

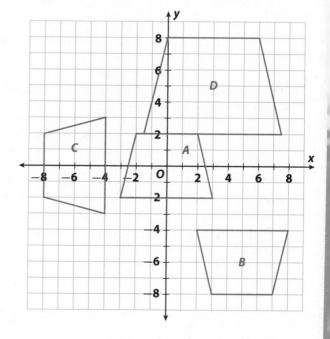

? ESSENTIAL QUESTION CHECK-IN

5. If two figures are similar but not congruent, what do you know about the sequence of transformations used to create one from the other?

_____

_____

10.3 Independent Practice

Personal Math Trainer

Online Practice and Help

my.hrw.com

CA CC 8.G.4

6. A designer creates a drawing of a triangular sign on centimeter grid paper for a new business. The drawing has sides measuring 6 cm, 8 cm, and 10 cm, and angles measuring 37°, 53°, and 90°. To create the actual sign shown, the drawing must be dilated using a scale factor of 40.

Jan's Café

   a. Find the lengths of the sides of the actual sign.

   _____

   b. Find the angle measures of the actual sign.

   _____

   c. The drawing has the hypotenuse on the bottom. The business owner would like it on the top. Describe two transformations that will do this.

   _____

   _____

   d. The shorter leg of the drawing is currently on the left. The business owner wants it to remain on the left after the hypotenuse goes to the top. Which transformation in part c will accomplish this?

   _____

In Exercises 7–10, the transformation of a figure into its image is described. Describe the transformations that will transform the image back into the original figure. Then write them algebraically.

7. The figure is reflected across the *x*-axis and dilated by a scale factor of 3.

   _____

   _____

8. The figure is dilated by a scale factor of 0.5 and translated 6 units left and 3 units up.

   _____

   _____

9. The figure is dilated by a scale factor of 5 and rotated 90° clockwise.

   _____

   _____

10. The figure is reflected across the *y*-axis and dilated by a scale factor of 4.

_____

_____

_____

Work Area

11. Draw Conclusions A figure undergoes a sequence of transformations that include dilations. The figure and its final image are congruent. Explain how this can happen.

_____

_____

_____

_____

_____

12. Multistep A graphic artist is using transformations to sketch ideas for a logo design. Start with the image provided and label each transformation with the letter of the sequence that is applied. Apply each sequence of transformations to the previous image.

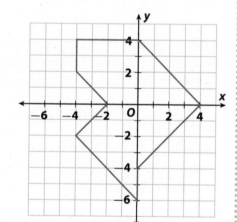

A. $(x, y) \rightarrow (\frac{1}{2}x, \frac{1}{2}y)$ with the center at the origin, $(x, y) \rightarrow (x, y - 1)$.

B. $(x, y) \rightarrow (x - 4, y + 1)$,
$(x, y) \rightarrow (x, -y)$.

13. Justify Reasoning In Exercise 12A, the sketch was dilated by a scale factor of $\frac{1}{2}$ and translated down 1 unit. Is this the same as translating the sketch down 1 unit and then dilating by a scale factor of $\frac{1}{2}$? Explain how the two results are related.

_____

_____

_____

_____

_____

_____

Ready to Go On?

Personal
Math Trainer

Online Practice
and Help

my.hrw.com

10.1 Properties of Dilations

Determine whether one figure is a dilation of the other. Justify your answer.

1. Triangle *XYZ* has angles measuring 54° and 29°. Triangle *X'Y'Z'* has angles measuring 29° and 92°.

_____

2. Quadrilateral *DEFG* has sides measuring 16 m, 28 m, 24 m, and 20 m. Quadrilateral *D'E'F'G'* has sides measuring 20 m, 35 m, 30 m, and 25 m.

_____

_____

10.2 Algebraic Representations of Dilations

Dilate each figure with the origin as the center of dilation.

3. $(x, y) \rightarrow (0.8x, 0.8y)$

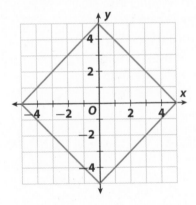

4. $(x, y) \rightarrow (2.5x, 2.5y)$

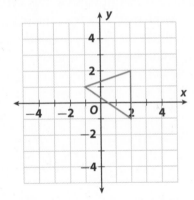

10.3 Similar Figures

5. Describe what happens to a figure when the given sequence of transformations is applied to it: $(x, y) \rightarrow (-x, y)$; $(x, y) \rightarrow (0.5x, 0.5y)$; $(x, y) \rightarrow (x - 2, y + 2)$

_____

_____

? ESSENTIAL QUESTION

6. How can you use dilations to solve real-world problems?

_____

MODULE 10
MIXED REVIEW

Assessment Readiness

Personal
Math Trainer

my.hrw.com

Online Practice
and Help

1. Triangle *ABC* is dilated by a scale factor of 2 with the origin as its center and then reflected across the *y*-axis. Look at each ordered pair. Is the ordered pair a vertex of the image?

Select Yes or No for ordered pairs A–C.

A. (−4, 10) ○ Yes ○ No
B. (−2, 4) ○ Yes ○ No
C. (10, −6) ○ Yes ○ No

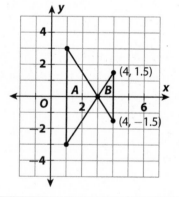

2. Choose True or False for each statement.

A. No integers are irrational numbers. ○ True ○ False
B. No real numbers are rational numbers. ○ True ○ False
C. All integers are whole numbers. ○ True ○ False
D. All whole numbers are integers. ○ True ○ False

3. In a video game, a rectangular map has vertices *M*(10, 10), *N*(10, 20), *P*(40, 20), and *Q*(40, 10). When a player clicks the map, it is enlarged by a scale factor of 4.5 with the origin as the center of dilation. What are the coordinates of the vertices of the enlarged map? Describe the algebraic rule you used to find the coordinates.

4. An engineer is working on the design of a bridge. He draws the two triangles shown. Is triangle *A* similar to triangle *B*? Use a sequence of transformations to explain how you know.

Study Guide Review

Transformations and Congruence

Key Vocabulary

center of rotation *(centro de rotación)*

congruent *(congruente)*

image *(imagen)*

line of reflection *(línea de reflexión)*

preimage *(imagen original)*

reflection *(reflexión)*

rotation *(rotación)*

transformation *(transformación)*

translation *(traslación)*

? ESSENTIAL QUESTION

How can you use transformations and congruence to solve real-world problems?

EXAMPLE

Translate triangle *XYZ* left 4 units and down 2 units. Graph the image and label the vertices.

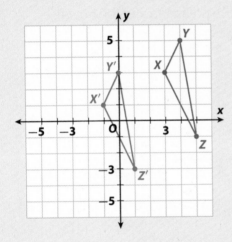

Translate the vertices by subtracting 4 from each *x*-coordinate and 2 from each *y*-coordinate. The new vertices are $X'(-1, 1)$, $Y'(0, 3)$, and $Z'(1, -3)$.

Connect the vertices to draw triangle $X'Y'Z'$.

EXERCISES

Perform the transformation shown. (Lessons 9.1, 9.2, 9.3)

1. Reflection over the *x*-axis

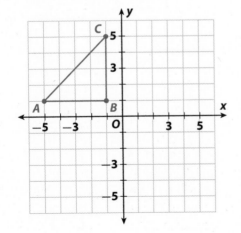

2. Translation 5 units right

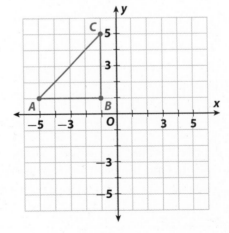

3. Rotation 90° counterclockwise about the origin

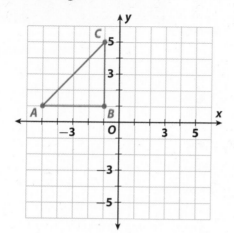

4. Translation 4 units right and 4 units down

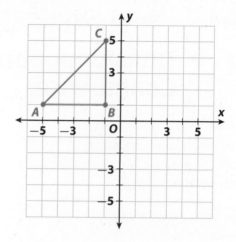

5. Quadrilateral *ABCD* with vertices *A*(4, 4), *B*(5, 1), *C*(5, −1) and *D*(4, −2) is translated left 2 units and down 3 units. Graph the preimage and the image. (Lesson 9.4)

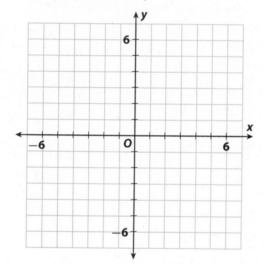

6. Triangle *ABC* with vertices *A*(1, 2), *B*(1, 4), and *C*(3, 3) is translated by $(x, y) \rightarrow (x - 4, y)$, and the result is reflected by $(x, y) \rightarrow (x, -y)$. Graph the preimage and the image. (Lesson 9.5)

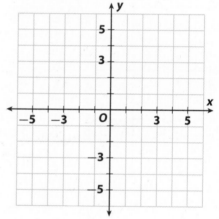

7. Triangle *RST* has vertices at (−8, 2), (−4, 0), and (−12, 8). Find the vertices after the triangle has been reflected over the *y*-axis. (Lesson 9.4)

_____

8. Triangle *XYZ* has vertices at (3, 7), (9, 14), and (12, −1). Find the vertices after the triangle has been rotated 180° about the origin. (Lesson 9.4)

_____

9. Triangle *MNP* has its vertices located at (−1, −4), (−2, −5), and (−3, −3). Find the vertices after the triangle has been reflected by $(x, y) \rightarrow (x, -y)$ and translated by $(x, y) \rightarrow (x + 6, y)$. (Lesson 9.5)

_____

Transformations and Similarity

? ESSENTIAL QUESTION

How can you use dilations, similarity, and proportionality to solve real-world problems?

EXAMPLE

Dilate triangle *ABC* with the origin as the center of dilation and scale factor $\frac{1}{2}$. Graph the dilated image.

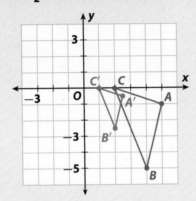

Multiply each coordinate of the vertices of *ABC* by $\frac{1}{2}$ to find the vertices of the dilated image.

$$A(5, -1) \rightarrow A'\left(5 \cdot \frac{1}{2}, -1 \cdot \frac{1}{2}\right) \rightarrow A'\left(2\frac{1}{2}, -\frac{1}{2}\right)$$

$$B(4, -5) \rightarrow B'\left(4 \cdot \frac{1}{2}, -5 \cdot \frac{1}{2}\right) \rightarrow B'\left(2, -2\frac{1}{2}\right)$$

$$C(2, 0) \rightarrow C'\left(2 \cdot \frac{1}{2}, 0 \cdot \frac{1}{2}\right) \rightarrow C'(1, 0)$$

EXERCISES

Dilate each figure with the origin as the center of the dilation. List the vertices of the dilated figure then graph the figure. (Lesson 10.2)

1. $(x, y) \rightarrow \left(\frac{1}{4}x, \frac{1}{4}y\right)$

2. $(x, y) \rightarrow (2x, 2y)$

_____

_____

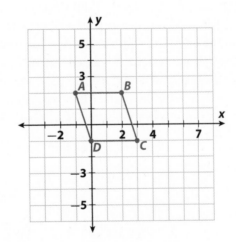

3. Rectangle *WXYZ* has vertices at $(-2, -1)$, $(-2, 1)$, $(2, -1)$, and $(2, 1)$. It is first dilated by $(x, y) \rightarrow (2x, 2y)$, and then translated by $(x, y) \rightarrow (x, y + 3)$. (Lesson 10.3)

What are the vertices of the image? _____

Unit Project

 CA CC 8.G.1, 8.G.3

Transforming the World

For this project, create a presentation that shows real-world examples of transformations. Include three rotations, three translations, and three reflections. Your project can show photographs or drawings that you have found during your research. Your examples do not have to illustrate exact transformations. For example, you can include a photo of a flower with a shape that closely resembles, but does not precisely match, a rotational pattern.

In your project, identify the object, the transformation displayed, and the source where you found the object. Use the space below to write down any questions you have or important information from your teacher.

MATH IN CAREERS   ACTIVITY

Contractor Fernando is expanding his dog's play yard. The original yard has a fence represented by rectangle *LMNO* on the coordinate plane. Fernando hires a contractor to construct a new fence that should enclose 6 times as much area as the current fence. The shape of the yard must remain the same. The contractor constructs the fence shown by rectangle *L'M'N'O'*. Determine if the contractor met Fernando's requirements for the new fence. Explain your answer.

UNIT 4
MIXED REVIEW

Assessment Readiness

Personal
Math Trainer

my.hrw.com

Online Practice
and Help

1. Triangle *DEF* has sides measuring 18 inches, 24 inches, and 36 inches. Look at each set of side lengths below. Could they be the side lengths of a dilation of triangle *DEF*?

   Select Yes or No.

   A. 9 inches, 18 inches, and 27 inches   ○ Yes   ○ No

   B. 12 inches, 16 inches, and 24 inches   ○ Yes   ○ No

   C. 27 inches, 36 inches, and 54 inches   ○ Yes   ○ No

2. Which transformation could be used to transform triangle *A* into triangle *B*?

   Select Yes or No.

   A. translation 4 units right   ○ Yes   ○ No

   B. reflection across the *x*-axis   ○ Yes   ○ No

   C. 180° rotation about the origin   ○ Yes   ○ No

   D. reflection across the *y*-axis   ○ Yes   ○ No

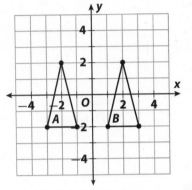

3. A prop assistant needs to rent a telescope to use for a scene in a movie. One company charges $58 per day plus a flat fee of $32 to rent a telescope. Another company charges $62 per day with no flat fee. For how many days would the total cost of renting a telescope be the same at both companies? Justify your answer by writing and solving an equation.

4. An artist is working on the design for a deck. She starts by drawing quadrilateral *JKLM*. She then translates the quadrilateral 3 units right and 2 units down. What are the coordinates of the vertices of the image of the translation? Describe the algebraic rule you used to find the coordinates.

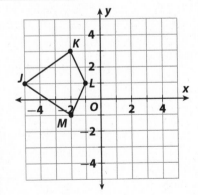

Performance Tasks

★ **5.** The location of a shelter in a park is shown by trapezoid *S* on the map. Another shelter with the same size and shape as the first needs to be shown on the map as trapezoid *T* with vertices at (3, 1), (1, 1), and (0, 3). Draw trapezoid *T*, and explain how you determined the coordinates of its fourth vertex.

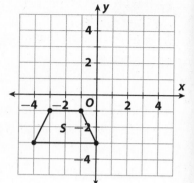

★★ **6.** A rancher has a pen shown on the grid, where 1 unit represents 1 meter. The rancher needs a larger pen to be a dilation of the smaller pen by a scale factor of 3.5 with the origin as the center of dilation.

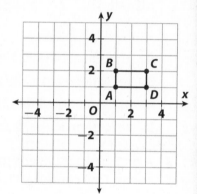

a. Graph the larger pen on a separate coordinate plane, and list the coordinates of its vertices.

b. How can you check that it is a dilation?

c. How many times the perimeter of the smaller pen is the perimeter of the larger pen? Explain how you know.

d. How many times the area of the smaller pen is the area of the larger pen? Explain how you know.

★★★ **7.** A T-shirt designer is working on the design for a new shirt.

a. Describe how the designer can create the design shown by using transformations on triangle *A* to produce the other triangles.

b. Which of the triangles in the design are congruent, and which are similar? Explain how you know.

UNIT 5

Measurement Geometry

MATH IN CAREERS

Hydrologist A hydrologist is a scientist who studies and solves water-related issues. A hydrologist might work to prevent or clean up polluted water sources, locate water supplies for urban or rural needs, or control flooding and erosion. A hydrologist uses math to assess water resources and mathematical models to understand water systems, as well as statistics to analyze phenomena such as rainfall patterns. If you are interested in a career as a hydrologist, you should study the following mathematical subjects:

- Algebra
- Trigonometry
- Calculus
- Statistics

Research other careers that require creating and using mathematical models to understand physical phenomena.

ACTIVITY At the end of the unit, check out how **hydrologists** use math.

Unit Project Preview

The Wheel of Theodorus

The Unit Project at the end of this unit involves an aspiral-shaped figure called a Wheel of Theodorus. First drawn more than two thousand years ago, the wheel is constructed by drawing increasingly larger right triangles. To successfully complete the Unit Project you'll need to master these skills:

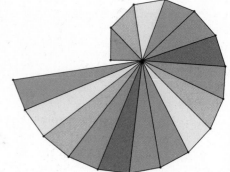

- Construct right triangles.
- Apply the Pythagorean Theorem.

1. List some of the properties of a right triangle.

_____

_____

_____

_____

2. Study the above figure. How would you describe the design of a Wheel of Theodorus?

_____

_____

_____

Tracking Your Learning Progression

This unit addresses important California Common Core Standards in the Critical Areas of understanding the Pythagorean Theorem and solving problems involving solid figures.

Domain 8.G Geometry

    Cluster Understand and apply the Pythagorean Theorem.

The unit also supports additional standards.

Domain 8.G Geometry

    Cluster Solve real-world and mathematical problems involving volume of cylinders, cones, and spheres.

Angle Relationships in Parallel Lines and Triangles

ESSENTIAL QUESTION

How can you use angle relationships in parallel lines and triangles to solve real-world problems?

Real-World Video

Many cities are designed on a grid with parallel streets. If another street runs across the parallel lines, it is a transversal. Special relationships exist between parallel lines and transversals.

my.hrw.com

GO DIGITAL
my.hrw.com

my.hrw.com

Go digital with your write-in student edition, accessible on any device.

Math On the Spot

Scan with your smart phone to jump directly to the online edition, video tutor, and more.

Animated Math

Interactively explore key concepts to see how math works.

Personal Math Trainer

Get immediate feedback and help as you work through practice sets.

Are YOU Ready?

Complete these exercises to review skills you will need for this module.

Solve Two-Step Equations

EXAMPLE		
	$7x + 9 = 30$	Write the equation.
	$7x + 9 - 9 = 30 - 9$	Subtract 9 from both sides.
	$7x = 21$	Simplify.
	$\frac{7x}{7} = \frac{21}{7}$	Divide both sides by 7.
	$x = 3$	Simplify.

Solve for x.

1. $6x + 10 = 46$ 2. $7x - 6 = 36$ 3. $3x + 26 = 59$ 4. $2x + 5 = -25$

_____   _____   _____   _____

5. $6x - 7 = 41$ 6. $\frac{1}{2}x + 9 = 30$ 7. $\frac{1}{3}x - 7 = 15$ 8. $0.5x - 0.6 = 8.4$

_____   _____   _____   _____

Name Angles

EXAMPLE	
	Use three points of an angle, including the vertex, to name the angle. Write the vertex between the other two points: $\angle JKL$ or $\angle LKJ$. You can also use just the vertex letter to name the angle if there is no danger of confusing the angle with another. This is also $\angle K$.

Give two names for the angle formed by the dashed rays.

9. _____   10. _____   11. _____

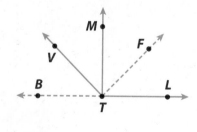

Reading Start-Up

Visualize Vocabulary

Use the ✔ words to complete the graphic. You can put more than one word in each section of the triangle.

Reviewing Angles

B in
∠*ABC*

measures > 0°
and < 90°

measures >90° and < 180°

Understand Vocabulary

Complete the sentences using preview words.

1. A line that intersects two or more lines is a _____.

2. Figures with the same shape but not necessarily the same size are _____.

3. An _____ is an angle formed by one side of the triangle and the extension of an adjacent side.

Vocabulary

Review Words
- ✔ acute angle *(ángulo agudo)*
- ✔ angle *(ángulo)*
- congruent *(congruente)*
- ✔ obtuse angle *(ángulo obtuso)*
- parallel lines *(líneas paralelas)*
- ✔ vertex *(vértice)*

Preview Words
- alternate exterior angles *(ángulos alternos externos)*
- alternate interior angles *(ángulos alternos internos)*
- corresponding angles *(ángulos correspondientes (para líneas))*
- exterior angle *(ángulo externo de un polígono)*
- interior angle *(ángulos internos)*
- remote interior angle *(ángulo interno remoto)*
- same-side interior angles *(ángulos internos del mismo lado)*
- similar *(semejantes)*
- transversal *(transversal)*

Active Reading

Pyramid Before beginning the module, create a pyramid to help you organize what you learn. Label each side with one of the lesson titles from this module. As you study each lesson, write important ideas like vocabulary, properties, and formulas on the appropriate side.

Angle Relationships in Parallel Lines and Triangles

Understanding the standards and the vocabulary terms in the standards will help you know exactly what you are expected to learn in this module.

CA CC 8.G.5

Use informal arguments to establish facts about the angle sum and exterior angle of triangles, about the angles created when parallel lines are cut by a transversal, and the angle-angle criterion for similarity of triangles.

Key Vocabulary

transversal *(transversal)*
A line that intersects two or more lines.

What It Means to You

You will learn about the special angle relationships formed when parallel lines are intersected by a third line called a transversal.

EXAMPLE 8.G.5

Which angles formed by the transversal and the parallel lines seem to be congruent?

It appears that the angles below are congruent.

$\angle 1 \cong \angle 4 \cong \angle 5 \cong \angle 8$

$\angle 2 \cong \angle 3 \cong \angle 6 \cong \angle 7$

CA CC 8.G.5

Use informal arguments to establish facts about the angle sum and exterior angle of triangles, about the angles created when parallel lines are cut by a transversal, and the angle-angle criterion for similarity of triangles.

What It Means to You

You will use the angle-angle criterion to determine similarity of two triangles.

EXAMPLE 8.G.5

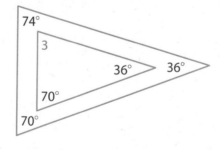

Explain whether the triangles are similar.

Two angles in the large triangle are congruent to two angles in the smaller triangle, so the third pair of angles must also be congruent, which makes the triangles similar.

$70° + 36° + m\angle 3 = 180°$

$m\angle 3 = 74°$

Visit **my.hrw.com** to see all **CA Common Core Standards** unpacked.

Parallel Lines Cut by a Transversal

CA CC 8.G.5

Use informal arguments to establish facts about the angle sum and exterior angle of triangles, about the angles created when parallel lines are cut by a transversal, and the angle-angle criterion for similarity of triangles. *Also 8.EE.7b*

ESSENTIAL QUESTION

What can you conclude about the angles formed by parallel lines that are cut by a transversal?

EXPLORE ACTIVITY 1 CA CC 8.G.5

Parallel Lines and Transversals

A **transversal** is a line that intersects two lines in the same plane at two different points. Transversal *t* and lines *a* and *b* form eight angles.

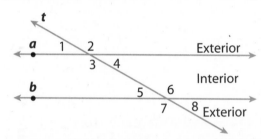

Angle Pairs Formed by a Transversal	
Term	**Example**
Corresponding angles lie on the same side of the transversal *t*, on the same side of lines *a* and *b*.	∠1 and ∠5
Alternate interior angles are nonadjacent angles that lie on opposite sides of the transversal *t*, between lines *a* and *b*.	∠3 and ∠6
Alternate exterior angles lie on opposite sides of the transversal *t*, outside lines *a* and *b*.	∠1 and ∠8
Same-side interior angles lie on the same side of the transversal *t*, between lines *a* and *b*.	∠3 and ∠5

Use geometry software to explore the angles formed when a transversal intersects parallel lines.

A Construct a line and label two points on the line A and B.

B Create point C not on $\overleftrightarrow{AB}$. Then construct a line parallel to $\overleftrightarrow{AB}$ through point C. Create another point on this line and label it D.

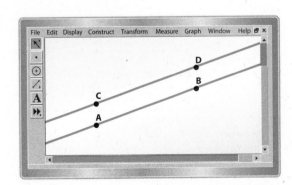

C Create two points outside the two parallel lines and label them *E* and *F*. Construct transversal *EF*. Label the points of intersection *G* and *H*.

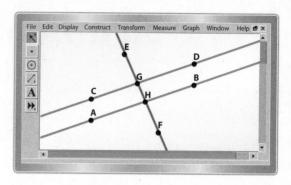

D Measure the angles formed by the parallel lines and the transversal. Write the angle measures in the table below.

E Drag point *E* or point *F* to a different position. Record the new angle measures in the table.

Angle	∠CGE	∠DGE	∠CGH	∠DGH	∠AHG	∠BHG	∠AHF	∠BHF
Measure								
Measure								

Reflect

Make a Conjecture **Identify the pairs of angles in the diagram. Then make a conjecture about their angle measures. Drag a point in the diagram to confirm your conjecture.**

1. corresponding angles

_____

_____

_____

2. alternate interior angles

_____

_____

3. alternate exterior angles

_____

_____

4. same-side interior angles

_____

_____

_____

Justifying Angle Relationships

You can use tracing paper to informally justify your conclusions from the first Explore Activity.

Lines *a* and *b* are parallel. (The black arrows on the diagram indicate parallel lines.)

> Recall that vertical angles are the opposite angles formed by two intersecting lines. ∠1 and ∠4 are vertical angles.

A Trace the diagram onto tracing paper.

B Position the tracing paper over the original diagram so that ∠1 on the tracing is over ∠5 on the original diagram. Compare the two angles. Do they appear to be congruent?

_____

_____

C Use the tracing paper to compare all eight angles in the diagram to each other. List all of the congruent angle pairs.

_____

_____

_____

> **Math Talk**
> Mathematical Practices
>
> How does a decrease in the measure of ∠1 affect the other angle measures?

Finding Unknown Angle Measures

You can find any unknown angle measure when two parallel lines are cut by a transversal if you are given at least one other angle measure.

Math On the Spot
my.hrw.com

EXAMPLE 1 CA CC 8.EE.7b

A Find m∠2 when m∠7 = 125°.

∠2 is congruent to ∠7 because they are alternate exterior angles.

Therefore, m∠2 = 125°.

B Find m∠*VWZ*.

∠*VWZ* is supplementary to ∠*YVW* because they are same-side interior angles.
m∠*VWZ* + m∠*YVW* = 180°

Animated Math
my.hrw.com

From the previous page, $m\angle VWZ + m\angle YVW = 180°$, $m\angle VWZ = 3x°$, and $m\angle YVW = 6x°$.

$$m\angle VWZ + m\angle YVW = 180°$$

$$3x° + 6x° = 180°$$ Replace $m\angle VWZ$ with $3x°$ and $m\angle YVW$ with $6x°$.

$$9x = 180$$ Combine like terms.

$$\frac{9x}{9} = \frac{180}{9}$$ Divide both sides by 9.

$$x = 20$$ Simplify.

$$m\angle VWZ = 3x° = (3 \cdot 20)° = 60°$$

YOUR TURN

Find each angle measure.

5. $m\angle GDE =$ _____

6. $m\angle BEF =$ _____

7. $m\angle CDG =$ _____

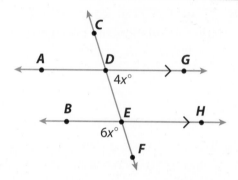

Guided Practice

Use the figure for Exercises 1–4. (Explore Activity 1 and Example 1)

1. $\angle UVY$ and _____ are a pair of corresponding angles.

2. $\angle WVY$ and $\angle VWT$ are _____ angles.

3. Find $m\angle SVW$. _____

4. Find $m\angle VWT$. _____

5. Vocabulary When two parallel lines are cut by a transversal,

_____ angles are supplementary. (Explore Activity 1)

? ESSENTIAL QUESTION CHECK-IN

6. What can you conclude about the interior angles formed when two parallel lines are cut by a transversal?

_____

_____

Name _____ Class _____ Date _____

11.1 Independent Practice

Personal Math Trainer

Online Practice and Help

my.hrw.com

Vocabulary Use the figure for Exercises 7–10.

7. Name all pairs of corresponding angles.

_____

8. Name both pairs of alternate exterior angles.

_____

9. Name the relationship between ∠3 and ∠6.

_____

10. Name the relationship between ∠4 and ∠6.

_____

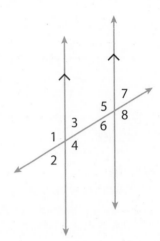

Find each angle measure.

11. m∠AGE when m∠FHD = 30° _____

12. m∠AGH when m∠CHF = 150° _____

13. m∠CHF when m∠BGE = 110° _____

14. m∠CHG when m∠HGA = 120° _____

15. m∠BGH = _____

16. m∠GHD = _____

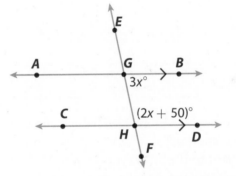

17. The Cross Country Bike Trail follows a straight line where it crosses 350th and 360th Streets. The two streets are parallel to each other. What is the measure of the larger angle formed at the intersection of the bike trail and 360th Street? Explain.

_____

_____

_____

18. **Critical Thinking** How many different angles would be formed by a transversal intersecting three parallel lines? How many different angle measures would there be?

_____

_____

19. Communicate Mathematical Ideas In the diagram at the right, suppose m∠6 = 125°. Explain how to find the measures of each of the other seven numbered angles.

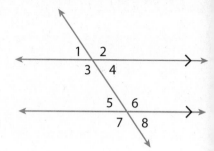

_____

_____

_____

_____

_____

_____

H.O.T. FOCUS ON HIGHER ORDER THINKING

Work Area

20. Draw Conclusions In a diagram showing two parallel lines cut by a transversal, the measures of two same-side interior angles are both given as $3x°$. Without writing and solving an equation, can you determine the measures of both angles? Explain. Then write and solve an equation to find the measures.

_____

_____

_____

21. Make a Conjecture Draw two parallel lines and a transversal. Choose one of the eight angles that are formed. How many of the other seven angles are congruent to the angle you selected? How many of the other seven angles are supplementary to your angle? Will your answer change if you select a different angle?

_____

22. Critique Reasoning In the diagram at the right, ∠2, ∠3, ∠5, and ∠8 are all congruent, and ∠1, ∠4, ∠6, and ∠7 are all congruent. Aiden says that this is enough information to conclude that the diagram shows two parallel lines cut by a transversal. Is he correct? Justify your answer.

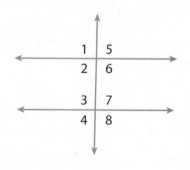

_____

_____

_____

_____

LESSON 11.2 Angle Theorems for Triangles

CA CC 8.G.5
Use informal arguments to establish facts about the angle sum and exterior angle of triangles, about the angles created when parallel lines are cut by a transversal, and the angle-angle criterion for similarity of triangles. *Also 8.EE.7, 8.EE.7b*

ESSENTIAL QUESTION

What can you conclude about the measures of the angles of a triangle?

EXPLORE ACTIVITY 1 CA CC 8.G.5

Sum of the Angle Measures in a Triangle

There is a special relationship between the measures of the interior angles of a triangle.

A Draw a triangle and cut it out. Label the angles *A*, *B*, and *C*.

B Tear off each "corner" of the triangle. Each corner includes the vertex of one angle of the triangle.

C Arrange the vertices of the triangle around a point so that none of your corners overlap and there are no gaps between them.

D What do you notice about how the angles fit together around a point?

_____

E What is the measure of a straight angle? _____

F Describe the relationship among the measures of the angles of △*ABC*.

_____

The Triangle Sum Theorem states that for △*ABC*, m∠*A* + m∠*B* + m∠*C* = _____.

Reflect

1. Justify Reasoning Can a triangle have two right angles? Explain.

_____

_____

_____

2. Analyze Relationships Describe the relationship between the two acute angles in a right triangle. Explain your reasoning.

_____

_____

_____

Justifying the Triangle Sum Theorem

You can use your knowledge of parallel lines intersected by a transversal to informally justify the Triangle Sum Theorem.

Follow the steps to informally prove the Triangle Sum Theorem. You should draw each step on your own paper. The figures below are provided for you to check your work.

A Draw a triangle and label the angles as ∠1, ∠2, and ∠3 as shown.

B Draw line *a* through the base of the triangle.

C The Parallel Postulate states that through a point not on a line ℓ, there is exactly one line parallel to line ℓ. Draw line *b* parallel to line *a*, through the vertex opposite the base of the triangle.

D Extend each of the non-base sides of the triangle to form transversal *s* and transversal *t*. Transversals *s* and *t* intersect parallel lines *a* and *b*.

E Label the angles formed by line *b* and the transversals as ∠4 and ∠5.

F Because ∠4 and _____ are alternate interior

angles, they are _____.

Label ∠4 with the number of the angle to which it is congruent.

G Because ∠5 and _____ are alternate interior angles,

they are _____.

Label ∠5 with the number of the angle to which it is congruent.

H The three angles that lie along line *b* at the vertex of the triangle are ∠1, ∠4, and ∠5. Notice that these three angles lie along a line.

So, m∠1 + m∠4 + m∠5 = _____.

Because angles 2 and 4 are congruent and angles 3 and 5 are congruent, you can substitute m∠2 for m∠4 and m∠3 for m∠5 in the equation above.

So, m∠1 + m∠2 + m∠3 = _____.

This shows that the sum of the angle measures in a triangle is

always _____.

Reflect

3. **Analyze Relationships** How can you use the fact that $m\angle 4 + m\angle 1 + m\angle 5 = 180°$ to show that $m\angle 2 + m\angle 1 + m\angle 3 = 180°$?

_____

_____

_____

Finding Missing Angle Measures in Triangles

If you know the measures of two angles in a triangle, you can use the Triangle Sum Theorem to find the measure of the third angle.

EXAMPLE 1

 CA CC 8.EE.7

My Notes

Find the missing angle measure.

STEP 1 Write the Triangle Sum Theorem for this triangle.

$$m\angle D + m\angle E + m\angle F = 180°$$

STEP 2 Substitute the given angle measures.

$$55° + m\angle E + 100° = 180°$$

STEP 3 Solve the equation for $m\angle E$.

$$55° + m\angle E + 100° = 180°$$

$$\begin{aligned} 155° + m\angle E &= 180° \quad \text{Simplify.} \\ -155° \qquad\quad &\; -155° \quad \text{Subtract } 155° \text{ from both sides.} \\ m\angle E &= 25° \end{aligned}$$

So, $m\angle E = 25°$.

YOUR TURN

Find the missing angle measure.

4.

$m\angle K = $ _____

5.

$m\angle R = $ _____

Exterior Angles and Remote Interior Angles

An **interior angle** of a triangle is formed by two sides of the triangle. An **exterior angle** is formed by one side of the triangle and the extension of an adjacent side. Each exterior angle has two remote interior angles. A **remote interior angle** is an interior angle that is not adjacent to the exterior angle.

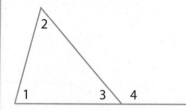

- ∠1, ∠2, and ∠3 are interior angles.

- ∠4 is an exterior angle.

- ∠1 and ∠2 are remote interior angles to ∠4.

There is a special relationship between the measure of an exterior angle and the measures of its remote interior angles.

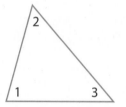

A Extend the base of the triangle and label the exterior angle as ∠4.

B The Triangle Sum Theorem states:

m∠1 + m∠2 + m∠3 = _____.

C ∠3 and ∠4 form a _____,

so m∠3 + m∠4 = _____.

D Use the equations in **B** and **C** to complete the following equation:

m∠1 + m∠2 + _____ = _____ + m∠4

E Use properties of equality to simplify the equation in **D** :

_____

The Exterior Angle Theorem states that the measure of an _____ angle

is equal to the sum of its _____ angles.

Reflect

6. Sketch a triangle and draw all of its exterior angles. How many exterior angles does a triangle have at each vertex?

_____

7. How many total exterior angles does a triangle have?

_____

Using the Exterior Angle Theorem

You can use the Exterior Angle Theorem to find the measures of the interior angles of a triangle.

EXAMPLE 2

Find m∠A and m∠B.

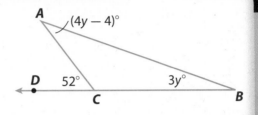

STEP 1 Write the Exterior Angle Theorem as it applies to this triangle.

$$m\angle A + m\angle B = m\angle ACD$$

STEP 2 Substitute the given angle measures.

$$(4y - 4)° + 3y° = 52°$$

Math Talk
Mathematical Practices

Describe two ways to find m∠ACB.

STEP 3 Solve the equation for y.

$$(4y - 4)° + 3y° = 52°$$

$4y° - 4° + 3y° = 52°$	Remove parentheses.
$7y° - 4° = 52°$	Simplify.
$\underline{+4°} \qquad \underline{+4°}$	Add 4° to both sides.
$7y° = 56°$	Simplify.
$\dfrac{7y°}{7} = \dfrac{56°}{7}$	Divide both sides by 7.
$y = 8$	Simplify.

STEP 4 Use the value of y to find m∠A and m∠B.

$$m\angle A = 4y - 4 \qquad\qquad m\angle B = 3y$$
$$= 4(8) - 4 \qquad\qquad = 3(8)$$
$$= 32 - 4 \qquad\qquad = 24$$
$$= 28$$

So, m∠A = 28° and m∠B = 24°.

YOUR TURN

8. Find m∠M and m∠N.

m∠M = _____

m∠N = _____

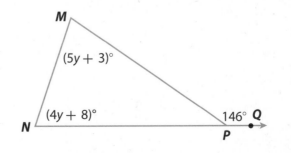

Guided Practice

Find each missing angle measure. (Explore Activity 1 and Example 1)

1.

m∠M = _____

2.

m∠Q = _____

Use the Triangle Sum Theorem to find the measure of each angle in degrees. (Explore Activity 2 and Example 1)

3.

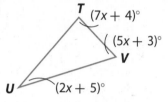

m∠T = _____, m∠U = _____,

m∠V = _____

4.

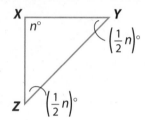

m∠X = _____, m∠Y = _____,

m∠Z = _____

Use the Exterior Angle Theorem to find the measure of each angle in degrees. (Explore Activity 3 and Example 2)

5.

m∠C = _____, m∠D = _____,

m∠DEC = _____

6.

m∠L = _____, m∠M = _____,

m∠LKM = _____

? ESSENTIAL QUESTION CHECK-IN

7. Describe the relationships among the measures of the angles of a triangle.

_____

_____

_____

11.2 Independent Practice

CA CC 8.EE.7, 8.EE.7b, 8.G.5

Personal Math Trainer

Online Practice and Help

my.hrw.com

Find the measure of each angle.

8.

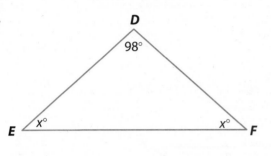

m∠E = _____

m∠F = _____

9.

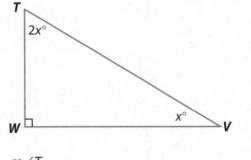

m∠T = _____

m∠V = _____

10.

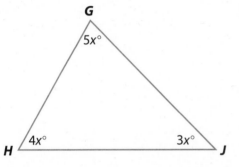

m∠G = _____

m∠H = _____

m∠J = _____

11.

m∠Q = _____

m∠P = _____

m∠QRP = _____

12.

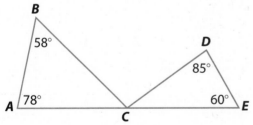

m∠ACB = _____

m∠BCD = _____

m∠DCE = _____

13.

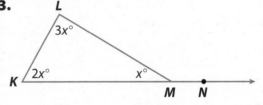

m∠K = _____

m∠L = _____

m∠KML = _____

m∠LMN = _____

14. Multistep The second angle in a triangle is five times as large as the first. The third angle is two-thirds as large as the first. Find the angle measures. _____

15. Analyze Relationships Can a triangle have two obtuse angles? Explain.

_____

_____

_____

_____

Work Area

16. Critical Thinking Explain how you can use the Triangle Sum Theorem to find the measures of the angles of an equilateral triangle.

_____

_____

_____

_____

17. a. Draw Conclusions Find the sum of the measures of the angles in quadrilateral *ABCD*. (Hint: Draw diagonal $\overline{AC}$. How can you use the figures you have formed to find the sum?)

Sum = _____

b. Make a Conjecture Write a "Quadrilateral Sum Theorem." Explain why you think it is true.

_____

_____

_____

_____

_____

_____

18. Communicate Mathematical Ideas Describe two ways that an exterior angle of a triangle is related to one or more of the interior angles.

_____

_____

_____

_____

LESSON
11.3 Angle-Angle Similarity

 CA CC 8.G.5

Use informal arguments to establish facts about the angle sum and exterior angle of triangles, about the angles created when parallel lines are cut by a transversal, and the angle-angle criterion for similarity of triangles. *Also 8.EE.6, 8.EE.7*

ESSENTIAL QUESTION

How can you determine when two triangles are similar?

EXPLORE ACTIVITY 1 **CA CC** 8.G.5

Discovering Angle-Angle Similarity

Similar figures have the same shape but may have different sizes. Two triangles are **similar** if their corresponding angles are congruent and the lengths of their corresponding sides are proportional.

A Use your protractor and a straightedge to draw a triangle. Make one angle measure 45° and another angle measure 60°.

B Compare your triangle to those drawn by your classmates. How are the triangles the same?

_____

How are they different?

_____

C Use the Triangle Sum Theorem to find the measure of the third angle of your triangle.

_____

Reflect

1. If two angles in one triangle are congruent to two angles in another triangle, what do you know about the third pair of angles?

_____

2. **Make a Conjecture** Are two pairs of congruent angles enough information to conclude that two triangles are similar? Explain.

_____

_____

_____

_____

Using the AA Similarity Postulate

Angle-Angle (AA) Similarity Postulate

If two angles of one triangle are congruent to two angles of another triangle, then the triangles are similar.

EXAMPLE 1

CA CC 8.G.5

Explain whether the triangles are similar.

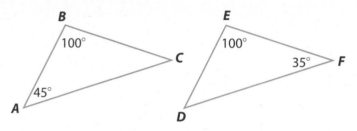

The figure shows only one pair of congruent angles. Find the measure of the third angle in each triangle.

Math Talk
Mathematical Practices

Are all right triangles similar? Why or why not?

$$45° + 100° + m\angle C = 180°$$

$$145° + m\angle C = 180°$$

$$145° + m\angle C - 145° = 180° - 145°$$

$$m\angle C = 35°$$

$$100° + 35° + m\angle D = 180°$$

$$135° + m\angle D = 180°$$

$$135° + m\angle D - 135° = 180° - 135°$$

$$m\angle D = 45°$$

Because two angles in one triangle are congruent to two angles in the other triangle, the triangles are similar.

YOUR TURN

3. **Explain whether the triangles are similar.**

_____

_____

_____

Finding Missing Measures in Similar Triangles

Because corresponding angles are congruent and corresponding sides are proportional in similar triangles, you can use similar triangles to solve real-world problems.

EXAMPLE 2   CA CC 8.EE.7

While playing tennis, Matt is 12 meters from the net, which is 0.9 meter high. He needs to hit the ball so that it just clears the net and lands 6 meters beyond the base of the net. At what height should Matt hit the tennis ball?

My Notes

Both triangles contain ∠A and a right angle, so △ABC and △ADE are similar.

In similar triangles, corresponding side lengths are proportional.

$$\frac{AD}{AB} = \frac{DE}{BC} \longrightarrow \frac{6+12}{6} = \frac{h}{0.9}$$ Substitute the lengths from the figure.

$$0.9 \times \frac{18}{6} = \frac{h}{0.9} \times 0.9$$ Use properties of equality to get *h* by itself.

$$0.9 \times 3 = h$$ Simplify.

$$2.7 = h$$ Multiply.

Matt should hit the ball at a height of 2.7 meters.

Reflect

4. **What If?** Suppose you set up a proportion so that each ratio compares parts of one triangle, as shown below.

$$\begin{array}{ll} \text{height of } △ABC \longrightarrow \\ \text{base of } △ABC \longrightarrow \end{array} \frac{BC}{AB} = \frac{DE}{AD} \begin{array}{ll} \longleftarrow \text{height of } △ADE \\ \longleftarrow \text{base of } △ADE \end{array}$$

Show that this proportion leads to the same value for *h* as in Example 2.

YOUR TURN

5. Rosie is building a wheelchair ramp that is 24 feet long and 2 feet high. She needs to install a vertical support piece 8 feet from the end of the ramp. What is the length of the support piece in inches?

h ft

8 ft

24 ft

2 ft

6. The lower cable meets the tree at a height of 6 feet and extends out 16 feet from the base of the tree. If the triangles are similar, how tall is the tree?

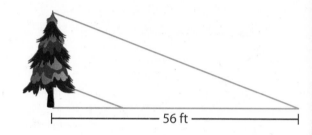

56 ft

EXPLORE ACTIVITY 2 🐻 **CA CC** 8.EE.6

Using Similar Triangles to Explain Slope

You can use similar triangles to show that the slope of a line is constant.

A Draw a line ℓ that is not a horizontal line. Label four points on the line as *A*, *B*, *C*, and *D*.

You need to show that the slope between points *A* and *B* is the same as the slope between points *C* and *D*.

B Draw the rise and run for the slope between points *A* and *B*. Label the intersection as point *E*. Draw the rise and run for the slope between points *C* and *D*. Label the intersection as point *F*.

C Write expressions for the slope between *A* and *B* and between *C* and *D*.

Slope between *A* and *B*: $\dfrac{BE}{\boxed{}}$ Slope between *C* and *D*: $\dfrac{\boxed{}}{CF}$

D Extend $\overleftrightarrow{AE}$ and $\overleftrightarrow{CF}$ across your drawing. $\overleftrightarrow{AE}$ and $\overleftrightarrow{CF}$ are both horizontal lines, so they are parallel.

Line ℓ is a _____ that intersects parallel lines.

E Complete the following statements:

$\angle BAE$ and _____ are corresponding angles and are _____.

$\angle BEA$ and _____ are right angles and are _____.

F By Angle–Angle Similarity, $\triangle ABE$ and _____ are similar triangles.

G Use the fact that the lengths of corresponding sides of similar triangles are proportional to complete the following ratios: $\dfrac{BE}{DF} = \dfrac{\boxed{}}{CF}$

H Recall that you can also write the proportion so that the ratios compare parts of the same triangle: $\dfrac{\boxed{}}{AE} = \dfrac{DF}{\boxed{}}$.

I The proportion you wrote in step **H** shows that the ratios you wrote in **C** are equal. So, the slope of line ℓ is constant.

Reflect

7. **What If?** Suppose that you label two other points on line ℓ as *G* and *H*. Would the slope between these two points be different than the slope you found in the Explore Activity? Explain.

_____

_____

_____

1. Explain whether the triangles are similar. Label the angle measures in the figure. (Explore Activity 1 and Example 1)

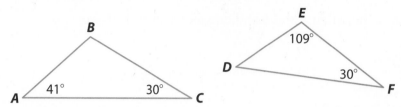

△ABC has angle measures _____ and △DEF has angle

measures _____. Because _____ in one

triangle are congruent to _____ in the other triangle, the

triangles are _____.

2. A flagpole casts a shadow 23.5 feet long. At the same time of day, Mrs. Gilbert, who is 5.5 feet tall, casts a shadow that is 7.5 feet long. How tall in feet is the flagpole? Round your answer to the nearest tenth. (Example 2)

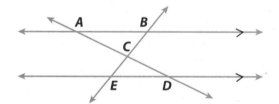

$$\frac{5.5}{\boxed{}} = \frac{h}{\boxed{}}$$

$h =$ _____ feet

3. Two transversals intersect two parallel lines as shown. Explain whether △ABC and △DEC are similar. (Example 1)

∠BAC and ∠EDC are _____ since they are _____.

∠ABC and ∠DEC are _____ since they are _____.

By _____, △ABC and △DEC are _____.

? ESSENTIAL QUESTION CHECK-IN

4. How can you determine when two triangles are similar?

_____

_____

_____

11.3 Independent Practice

CA CC 8.EE.6, 8.EE.7, 8.G.5

Personal
Math Trainer

Online Practice
and Help

my.hrw.com

Use the diagrams for Exercises 5–7.

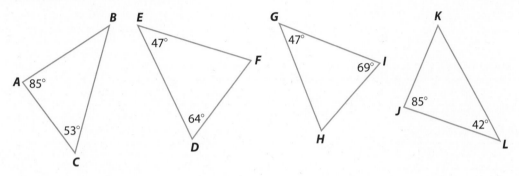

5. Find the missing angle measures in the triangles.

_____

6. Which triangles are similar?

_____

7. Analyze Relationships Determine which angles are congruent to the angles in △ABC.

_____

8. Multistep A tree casts a shadow that is 20 feet long. Frank is 6 feet tall, and while standing next to the tree he casts a shadow that is 4 feet long.

a. How tall is the tree? _____

b. How much taller is the tree than Frank? _____

4 ft

6 ft

20 ft

9. Represent Real-World Problems Sheila is climbing on a ladder that is attached against the side of a jungle gym wall. She is 5 feet off the ground and 3 feet from the base of the ladder, which is 15 feet from the wall. Draw a diagram to help you solve the problem. How high up the wall is the top of the ladder?

_____

10. Justify Reasoning Are two equilateral triangles always similar? Explain.

_____

_____

_____

11. Critique Reasoning Ryan calculated the missing measure in the diagram shown. What was his mistake?

$$\frac{3.4}{6.5} = \frac{h}{19.5}$$

$$19.5 \times \frac{3.4}{6.5} = \frac{h}{19.5} \times 19.5$$

$$\frac{66.3}{6.5} = h$$

$$10.2 \text{ cm} = h$$

_____

_____

_____

 FOCUS ON HIGHER ORDER THINKING

Work Area

12. Communicate Mathematical Ideas For a pair of triangular earrings, how can you tell if they are similar? How can you tell if they are congruent?

_____

_____

_____

_____

13. Critical Thinking When does it make sense to use similar triangles to measure the height and length of objects in real life?

_____

_____

_____

14. Justify Reasoning Two right triangles on a coordinate plane are similar but not congruent. Each of the legs of both triangles are extended by 1 unit, creating two new right triangles. Are the resulting triangles similar? Explain using an example.

_____

_____

_____

_____

_____

Ready to Go On?

Personal
Math Trainer

Online Practice
and Help

my.hrw.com

11.1 Parallel Lines Cut by a Transversal

In the figure, line $p \parallel$ line q. Find the measure of each angle if $m\angle 8 = 115°$.

1. $m\angle 7 =$ _____

2. $m\angle 6 =$ _____

3. $m\angle 1 =$ _____

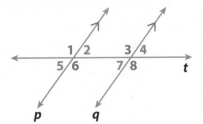

11.2 Angle Theorems for Triangles

Find the measure of each angle.

4. $m\angle A =$ _____

5. $m\angle B =$ _____

6. $m\angle BCA =$ _____

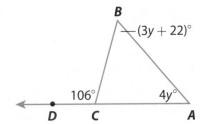

11.3 Angle-Angle Similarity

Triangle FEG is similar to triangle IHJ. Find the missing values.

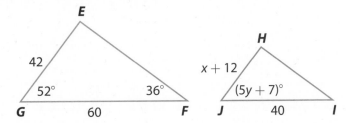

7. $x =$ _____

8. $y =$ _____

9. $m\angle H =$ _____

? **ESSENTIAL QUESTION**

10. How can you use similar triangles to solve real-world problems?

_____

_____

_____

MODULE 11
MIXED REVIEW

Assessment Readiness

Personal
Math Trainer

Online Practice
and Help

my.hrw.com

1. In the diagram, lines a and b are parallel and lines p and q are parallel. Look at each pair of angles. Are the angles congruent?

   Select Yes or No for A–C.

   A. $\angle 1$ and $\angle 2$ ○ Yes   ○ No
   B. $\angle 3$ and $\angle 4$ ○ Yes   ○ No
   C. $\angle 5$ and $\angle 6$ ○ Yes   ○ No

2. The variables x and y are related proportionally, and when $x = 18$, $y = 12$.

   Choose True or False for each statement.

   A. When $x = 3$, $y = 5$.   ○ True   ○ False
   B. When $x = 27$, $y = 18$.   ○ True   ○ False
   C. When $x = 63$, $y = 42$.   ○ True   ○ False

3. An artist is designing a triangular pane of glass for a stained glass window, as shown in the diagram. Given that $\angle ABC$ is an exterior angle, what is the measure of each interior angle of the triangle? Explain your reasoning.

4. The diagram shows several of the boards that form part of the frame of a roof. Is $\triangle JKN$ similar to $\triangle JLM$? Explain how you know.

The Pythagorean Theorem

 ESSENTIAL QUESTION

How can you use the Pythagorean Theorem to solve real-world problems?

Real-World Video

The sizes of televisions are usually described by the length of the diagonal of the screen. To find this length of the diagonal of a rectangle, you can use the Pythagorean Theorem.

🔘 my.hrw.com

GO DIGITAL

my.hrw.com

my.hrw.com

Go digital with your write-in student edition, accessible on any device.

Math On the Spot

Scan with your smart phone to jump directly to the online edition, video tutor, and more.

Animated Math

Interactively explore key concepts to see how math works.

Personal Math Trainer

Get immediate feedback and help as you work through practice sets.

Are YOU Ready?

Complete these exercises to review skills you will need for this module.

Find the Square of a Number

EXAMPLE Find the square of 2.7.

$$\begin{array}{r} 2.7 \\ \times\, 2.7 \\ \hline 189 \\ 54 \\ \hline 7.29 \end{array}$$

Multiply the number by itself.

So, $2.7^2 = 7.29$.

Find the square of each number.

1. 5 _____ **2.** 16 _____ **3.** −11 _____ **4.** $\frac{2}{7}$ _____

Order of Operations

EXAMPLE $\sqrt{(5-2)^2 + (8-4)^2}$ First, operate within parentheses.

$\sqrt{(3)^2 + (4)^2}$ Next, simplify exponents.

$\sqrt{9 + 16}$ Then add and subtract left to right.

$\sqrt{25}$ Finally, take the square root.

5

Evaluate each expression.

5. $\sqrt{(6+2)^2 + (3+3)^2}$ _____ **6.** $\sqrt{(9-4)^2 + (5+7)^2}$ _____

7. $\sqrt{(10-6)^2 + (15-12)^2}$ _____ **8.** $\sqrt{(6+9)^2 + (10-2)^2}$ _____

Simplify Numerical Expressions

EXAMPLE $\frac{1}{2}(2.5)^2(4) = \frac{1}{2}(6.25)(4)$ Simplify the exponent.

$= 12.5$ Multiply from left to right.

Simplify each expression.

9. $5(8)(10)$ _____ **10.** $\frac{1}{2}(6)(12)$ _____ **11.** $\frac{1}{3}(3)(12)$ _____

12. $\frac{1}{2}(8)^2(4)$ _____ **13.** $\frac{1}{4}(10)^2(15)$ _____ **14.** $\frac{1}{3}(9)^2(6)$ _____

Reading Start-Up

Visualize Vocabulary

Use the ✔ words to complete the graphic.

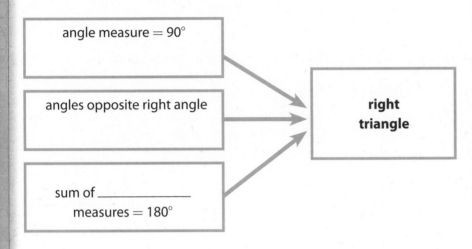

| angle measure = 90° |
| angles opposite right angle |
| sum of _____ measures = 180° |

→ **right triangle**

Vocabulary

Review Words
✔ acute angles *(ángulos agudos)*
✔ angles *(ángulos)*
  area *(área)*
  ordered pair *(par ordenado)*
✔ right angle *(ángulo recto)*
✔ right triangle *(triángulo recto)*
  square root *(raíz cuadrada)*
  x-coordinate *(coordenada x)*
  y-coordinate *(coordenada y)*

Preview Words
  hypotenuse *(hipotenusa)*
  legs *(catetos)*
  theorem *(teorema)*
  vertex *(vértice)*

Understand Vocabulary

Match the term on the left to the correct expression on the right.

1. hypotenuse

2. theorem

3. legs

A. An idea that has been demonstrated as true.

B. The two sides that form the right angle of a right triangle.

C. The side opposite the right angle in a right triangle.

Active Reading

Booklet Before beginning the module, create a booklet to help you learn about the Pythagorean Theorem. Write the main idea of each lesson on each page of the booklet. As you study each lesson, write important details that support the main idea, such as vocabulary and formulas. Refer to your finished booklet as you work on assignments and study for tests.

The Pythagorean Theorem

Understanding the standards and the vocabulary terms in the standards will help you know exactly what you are expected to learn in this module.

 CA CC 8.G.7

Apply the Pythagorean Theorem to determine unknown side lengths in right triangles in real-world and mathematical problems in two and three dimensions.

Key Vocabulary

Pythagorean Theorem
(Teorema de Pitágoras)
In a right triangle, the square of the length of the hypotenuse is equal to the sum of the squares of the lengths of the legs.

What It Means to You

You will find a missing length in a right triangle, or use side lengths to see whether a triangle is a right triangle.

EXAMPLE 8.G.7

Mark and Sarah start walking at the same point, but Mark walks 50 feet north while Sarah walks 75 feet east. How far apart are Mark and Sarah when they stop?

$$a^2 + b^2 = c^2 \qquad \text{Pythagorean Theorem}$$
$$50^2 + 75^2 = c^2 \qquad \text{Substitute.}$$
$$2500 + 5625 = c^2$$
$$8125 = c^2$$
$$90.1 \approx c$$

Mark and Sarah are approximately 90.1 feet apart.

CA CC 8.G.8

Apply the Pythagorean Theorem to find the distance between two points in a coordinate system.

Key Vocabulary

coordinate plane
(plano cartesiano)
A plane formed by the intersection of a horizontal number line called the *x*-axis and a vertical number line called the *y*-axis.

What It Means to You

You can use the Pythagorean Theorem to find the distance between two points.

EXAMPLE 8.G.8

Find the distance between points *A* and *B*.

$$(AC)^2 + (BC)^2 = (AB)^2$$
$$(4 - 1)^2 + (6 - 2)^2 = (AB)^2$$
$$3^2 + 4^2 = (AB)^2$$
$$9 + 16 = (AB)^2$$
$$25 = (AB)^2$$
$$5 = AB$$

The distance is 5 units.

 Visit **my.hrw.com** to see all **CA Common Core Standards** explained.

 my.hrw.com

The Pythagorean Theorem

CA CC 8.G.7

Apply the Pythagorean Theorem to determine unknown side lengths in right triangles in real-world and mathematical problems in two and three dimensions. *Also 8.G.6*

ESSENTIAL QUESTION

How can you prove the Pythagorean Theorem and use it to solve problems?

EXPLORE ACTIVITY CA CC 8.G.6

Proving the Pythagorean Theorem

In a right triangle, the two sides that form the right angle are the **legs**. The side opposite the right angle is the **hypotenuse**.

Leg   Hypotenuse

Leg

The Pythagorean Theorem

In a right triangle, the sum of the squares of the lengths of the legs is equal to the square of the length of the hypotenuse.

If a and b are legs and c is the hypotenuse, $a^2 + b^2 = c^2$.

A Draw a right triangle on a piece of paper and cut it out. Make one leg shorter than the other.

B Trace your triangle onto another piece of paper four times, arranging them as shown. For each triangle, label the shorter leg a, the longer leg b, and the hypotenuse c.

C What is the area of the unshaded square?

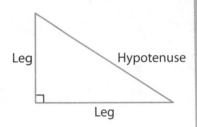

_____

Label the unshaded square with its area.

D Trace your original triangle onto a piece of paper four times again, arranging them as shown. Draw a line outlining a larger square that is the same size as the figure you made in **B**.

E What is the area of the unshaded square at the top right of the figure in **D**? at the top left?

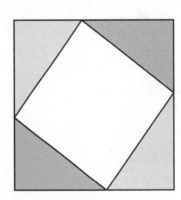

_____

Label the unshaded squares with their areas.

F What is the total area of the unshaded regions in **D**?

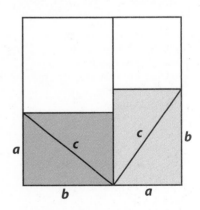

_____

Reflect

1. Explain whether the figures in **B** and **D** have the same area.

   _____

2. Explain whether the unshaded regions of the figures in **B** and **D** have the same area.

   _____

   _____

   _____

3. **Analyze Relationships** Write an equation relating the area of the unshaded region in step **B** to the unshaded region in **D**.

   _____

Math On the Spot
⏻ my.hrw.com

Animated Math
⏻ my.hrw.com

Math Talk
Mathematical Practices

If you are given the length of the hypotenuse and one leg, does it matter whether you solve for *a* or *b*? Explain.

Using the Pythagorean Theorem

You can use the Pythagorean Theorem to find the length of a side of a right triangle when you know the lengths of the other two sides.

EXAMPLE 1

CA CC 8.G.7

Find the length of the missing side.

A

7 in.

24 in.

$a^2 + b^2 = c^2$

$24^2 + 7^2 = c^2$ Substitute into the formula.

$576 + 49 = c^2$ Simplify.

$625 = c^2$ Add.

$25 = c$ Take the square root of both sides.

The length of the hypotenuse is 25 inches.

B

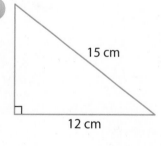

15 cm

12 cm

$a^2 + b^2 = c^2$

$a^2 + 12^2 = 15^2$ Substitute into the formula.

$a^2 + 144 = 225$ Simplify.

$a^2 = 81$ Use properties of equality to get a^2 by itself.

$a = 9$ Take the square root of both sides.

The length of the leg is 9 centimeters.

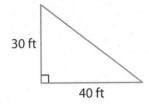

YOUR TURN

Find the length of the missing side.

4.

30 ft

40 ft

_____

5.

41 in.

40 in.

_____

Pythagorean Theorem in Three Dimensions

You can use the Pythagorean Theorem to solve problems in three dimensions.

EXAMPLE 2   CA CC 8.G.7

A box used for shipping narrow copper tubes measures 6 inches by 6 inches by 20 inches. What is the length of the longest tube that will fit in the box, given that the length of the tube must be a whole number of inches?

$h = 6$ in.

$w = 6$ in.

$l = 20$ in.

r

s

STEP 1 You want to find r, the length from a bottom corner to the opposite top corner. First, find s, the length of the diagonal across the bottom of the box.

$$w^2 + l^2 = s^2$$

$6^2 + 20^2 = s^2$ Substitute into the formula.

$36 + 400 = s^2$ Simplify.

$436 = s^2$ Add.

STEP 2 Use your expression for s to find r.

$$h^2 + s^2 = r^2$$

$6^2 + 436 = r^2$ Substitute into the formula.

$472 = r^2$ Add.

$\sqrt{472} = r$ Take the square root of both sides.

$21.7 \approx r$ Use a calculator to round to the nearest tenth.

The length of the longest tube that will fit in the box is 21 inches.

Math Talk
Mathematical Practices

Looking at Step 2, why did the calculations in Step 1 stop before taking the square root of both sides of the final equation?

YOUR TURN

6. Tina ordered a replacement part for her desk. It was shipped in a box that measures 4 in. by 4 in. by 14 in. What is the greatest length in whole inches that the part could have been?

Guided Practice

1. Find the length of the missing side of the triangle. (Explore Activity 1 and Example 1)

$$a^2 + b^2 = c^2 \rightarrow 24^2 + \boxed{} = c^2 \rightarrow \boxed{} = c^2$$

The length of the hypotenuse is $\boxed{}$ feet.

10 ft

24 ft

2. Mr. Woo wants to ship a fishing rod that is 42 inches long to his son. He has a box with the dimensions shown. (Example 2)

$h = 10$ in.

$w = 10$ in.

$l = 40$ in.

a. Find the square of the length of the diagonal across the bottom of the box. _____

b. Find the length from a bottom corner to the opposite top corner to the nearest tenth. Will the fishing rod fit? _____

? ESSENTIAL QUESTION CHECK-IN

3. State the Pythagorean Theorem and tell how you can use it to solve problems.

_____

_____

_____

_____

12.1 Independent Practice

CA CC 8.G.6, 8.G.7

Find the length of the missing side of each triangle. Round your answers to the nearest tenth.

4.

8 cm
4 cm

_____

5.

14 in.
8 in.

_____

6. The diagonal of a rectangular big-screen TV screen measures 152 cm. The length measures 132 cm. What is the height of the screen?   _____

7. Dylan has a square piece of metal that measures 10 inches on each side. He cuts the metal along the diagonal, forming two right triangles. What is the length of the hypotenuse of each right triangle to the nearest tenth of an inch?   _____

8. **Represent Real-World Problems** A painter has a 24-foot ladder that he is using to paint a house. For safety reasons, the ladder must be placed at least 8 feet from the base of the side of the house. To the nearest tenth of a foot, how high can the ladder safely reach?   _____

9. What is the longest flagpole (in whole feet) that could be shipped in a box that measures 2 ft by 2 ft by 12 ft?

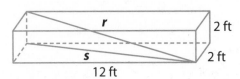
r
2 ft
s
2 ft
12 ft

_____

10. **Sports** American football fields measure 100 yards long between the end zones, and are $53\frac{1}{3}$ yards wide. Is the length of the diagonal across this field more or less than 120 yards? Explain.

_____

11. **Justify Reasoning** A tree struck by lightning broke at a point 12 ft above the ground as shown. What was the height of the tree to the nearest tenth of a foot? Explain your reasoning.

12 ft
39 ft

_____

_____

_____

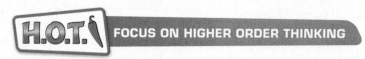

Work Area

12. Multistep Main Street and Washington Avenue meet at a right angle. A large park begins at this corner. Joe's school lies at the opposite corner of the park. Usually Joe walks 1.2 miles along Main Street and then 0.9 miles up Washington Avenue to get to school. Today he walked in a straight path across the park and returned home along the same path. What is the difference in distance between the two round trips? Explain.

_____

_____

_____

13. Analyze Relationships An isosceles right triangle is a right triangle with congruent legs. If the length of each leg is represented by x, what algebraic expression can be used to represent the length of the hypotenuse? Explain your reasoning.

_____

_____

14. Persevere in Problem Solving A square hamburger is centered on a circular bun. Both the bun and the burger have an area of 16 square inches.

a. How far, to the nearest hundredth of an inch, does each corner of the burger stick out from the bun? Explain.

_____

_____

_____

_____

_____

b. How far does each bun stick out from the center of each side of the burger?

_____

c. Are the distances in part **a** and part **b** equal? If not, which sticks out more, the burger or the bun? Explain.

_____

_____

_____

Converse of the Pythagorean Theorem

🐻 CA CC 8.G.6

Explain a proof of the Pythagorean Theorem and its converse.

ESSENTIAL QUESTION

How can you test the converse of the Pythagorean Theorem and use it to solve problems?

EXPLORE ACTIVITY 🐻 CA CC 8.G.6

Testing the Converse of the Pythagorean Theorem

The Pythagorean Theorem states that if a triangle is a right triangle, then $a^2 + b^2 = c^2$.

The *converse* of the Pythagorean Theorem states that if $a^2 + b^2 = c^2$, then the triangle is a right triangle.

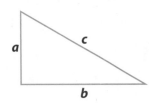

Decide whether the converse of the Pythagorean Theorem is true.

A Verify that the following sets of lengths make the equation $a^2 + b^2 = c^2$ true. Record your results in the table.

a	b	c	Is $a^2 + b^2 = c^2$ true?	Makes a right triangle?
3	4	5		
5	12	13		
7	24	25		
8	15	17		
20	21	29		

B For each set of lengths in the table, cut strips of grid paper with a width of one square and lengths that correspond to the values of a, b, and c.

C For each set of lengths, use the strips of grid paper to try to form a right triangle. An example using the first set of lengths is shown. Record your findings in the table.

Reflect

1. **Draw Conclusions** Based on your observations, explain whether you think the converse of the Pythagorean Theorem is true.

_____

_____

My Notes

Identifying a Right Triangle

The converse of the Pythagorean Theorem gives you a way to tell if a triangle is a right triangle when you know the side lengths.

EXAMPLE 1

 CA CC 8.G.6

Tell whether each triangle with the given side lengths is a right triangle.

A 9 inches, 40 inches, and 41 inches

Let $a = 9$, $b = 40$, and $c = 41$.

$$a^2 + b^2 = c^2$$

$$9^2 + 40^2 \overset{?}{=} 41^2 \qquad \text{Substitute into the formula.}$$

$$81 + 1600 \overset{?}{=} 1681 \qquad \text{Simpify.}$$

$$1681 = 1681 \qquad \text{Add.}$$

Since $9^2 + 40^2 = 41^2$, the triangle is a right triangle by the converse of the Pythagorean Theorem.

B 8 meters, 10 meters, and 12 meters

Let $a = 8$, $b = 10$, and $c = 12$.

$$a^2 + b^2 = c^2$$

$$8^2 + 10^2 \overset{?}{=} 12^2 \qquad \text{Substitute into the formula.}$$

$$64 + 100 \overset{?}{=} 144 \qquad \text{Simpify.}$$

$$164 \neq 144 \qquad \text{Add.}$$

Since $8^2 + 10^2 \neq 12^2$, the triangle is not a right triangle by the converse of the Pythagorean Theorem.

YOUR TURN

Tell whether each triangle with the given side lengths is a right triangle.

2. 14 cm, 23 cm, and 25 cm

3. 16 in., 30 in., and 34 in.

_____

4. 27 ft, 36 ft, 45 ft

5. 11 mm, 18 mm, 21 mm

_____

Using the Converse of the Pythagorean Theorem

You can use the converse of the Pythagorean Theorem to solve real-world problems.

EXAMPLE 2

 CA CC 8.G.6

Katya is buying edging for a triangular flower garden she plans to build in her backyard. If the lengths of the three pieces of edging that she purchases are 13 feet, 10 feet, and 7 feet, will the flower garden be in the shape of a right triangle?

Use the converse of the Pythagorean Theorem. Remember to use the longest length for c.

Let $a = 7$, $b = 10$, and $c = 13$.

$$a^2 + b^2 = c^2$$

$$7^2 + 10^2 \overset{?}{=} 13^2 \qquad \text{Substitute into the formula.}$$

$$49 + 100 \overset{?}{=} 169 \qquad \text{Simpify.}$$

$$149 \neq 169 \qquad \text{Add.}$$

Since $7^2 + 10^2 \neq 13^2$, the garden will not be in the shape of a right triangle.

Math Talk
Mathematical Practices

To what length, to the nearest tenth, can Katya trim the longest piece of edging to form a right triangle?

YOUR TURN

6. A blueprint for a new triangular playground shows that the sides measure 480 ft, 140 ft, and 500 ft. Is the playground in the shape of a right triangle? Explain.

   _____

   _____

7. A triangular piece of glass has sides that measure 18 in., 19 in., and 25 in. Is the piece of glass in the shape of a right triangle? Explain.

   _____

8. A corner of a fenced yard forms a right angle. Can you place a 12 foot long board across the corner to form a right triangle for which the leg lengths are whole numbers? Explain.

   _____

   _____

Personal Math Trainer

Online Practice and Help

⏻ my.hrw.com

1. Lashandra used grid paper to construct the triangle shown. (Explore Activity)

   a. What are the lengths of the sides of Lashandra's triangle?

   _____units, _____units, _____units

   b. Use the converse of the Pythagorean Theorem to determine whether the triangle is a right triangle.

   $$a^2 + b^2 = c^2$$

   The triangle that Lashandra constructed ┃ **is / is not** ┃ a right triangle.

2. A triangle has side lengths 9 cm, 12 cm, and 16 cm. Tell whether the triangle is a right triangle. (Example 1)

   Let $a =$ _____, $b =$ _____, and $c =$ _____.

   $$a^2 + b^2 = c^2$$

   By the converse of the Pythagorean Theorem, the triangle ┃ **is / is not** ┃ a right triangle.

3. The marketing team at a new electronics company is designing a logo that contains a circle and a triangle. On one design, the triangle's side lengths are 2.5 in., 6 in., and 6.5 in. Is the triangle a right triangle? Explain. (Example 2)

   _____

? **ESSENTIAL QUESTION CHECK-IN**

4. How can you use the converse of the Pythagorean Theorem to tell if a triangle is a right triangle?

   _____

   _____

12.2 Independent Practice

 CA CC 8.G.6

Personal Math Trainer

Online Practice and Help

my.hrw.com

Tell whether each triangle with the given side lengths is a right triangle.

5. 11 cm, 60 cm, 61 cm

_____

6. 5 ft, 12 ft, 15 ft

_____

7. 9 in., 15 in., 17 in.

_____

8. 15 m, 36 m, 39 m

_____

9. 20 mm, 30 mm, 40 mm

_____

10. 20 cm, 48 cm, 52 cm

_____

11. 18.5 ft, 6 ft, 17.5 ft

_____

12. 2 mi, 1.5 mi, 2.5 mi

_____

13. 35 in., 45 in., 55 in.

_____

14. 25 cm, 14 cm, 23 cm

_____

15. The emblem on a college banner consists of the face of a tiger inside a triangle. The lengths of the sides of the triangle are 13 cm, 14 cm, and 15 cm. Is the triangle a right triangle? Explain.

_____

16. Kerry has a large triangular piece of fabric that she wants to attach to the ceiling in her bedroom. The sides of the piece of fabric measure 4.8 ft, 6.4 ft, and 8 ft. Is the fabric in the shape of a right triangle? Explain.

_____

17. A mosaic consists of triangular tiles. The smallest tiles have side lengths 6 cm, 10 cm, and 12 cm. Are these tiles in the shape of right triangles? Explain.

_____

18. **History** In ancient Egypt, surveyors made right angles by stretching a rope with evenly spaced knots as shown. Explain why the rope forms a right angle.

_____

_____

_____

19. Justify Reasoning Yoshi has two identical triangular boards as shown. Can he use these two boards to form a rectangle? Explain.

_____

_____

_____

20. Critique Reasoning Shoshanna says that a triangle with side lengths 17 m, 8 m, and 15 m is not a right triangle because $17^2 + 8^2 = 353$, $15^2 = 225$, and $353 \neq 225$. Is she correct? Explain.

_____

_____

 FOCUS ON HIGHER ORDER THINKING

Work Area

21. Make a Conjecture Diondre says that he can take any right triangle and make a new right triangle just by doubling the side lengths. Is Diondre's conjecture true? Test his conjecture using three different right triangles.

_____

_____

_____

_____

22. Draw Conclusions A diagonal of a parallelogram measures 37 inches. The sides measure 35 inches and 1 foot. Is the parallelogram a rectangle? Explain your reasoning.

_____

_____

_____

_____

23. Represent Real-World Problems A soccer coach is marking the lines for a soccer field on a large recreation field. The dimensions of the field are to be 90 yards by 48 yards. Describe a procedure she could use to confirm that the sides of the field meet at right angles.

_____

_____

_____

_____

Distance Between Two Points

CA CC 8.G.8

Apply the Pythagorean Theorem to find the distance between two points in a coordinate system.

ESSENTIAL QUESTION

How can you use the Pythagorean Theorem to find the distance between two points on a coordinate plane?

Pythagorean Theorem in the Coordinate Plane

EXAMPLE 1   CA CC 8.G.8

Math On the Spot
my.hrw.com

The figure shows a right triangle. Approximate the length of the hypotenuse to the nearest tenth using a calculator.

STEP 1 Find the length of each leg.

The length of the vertical leg is 4 units.

The length of the horizontal leg is 2 units.

STEP 2 Let $a = 4$ and $b = 2$. Let c represent the length of the hypotenuse. Use the Pythagorean Theorem to find c.

$$a^2 + b^2 = c^2$$

$$4^2 + 2^2 = c^2 \qquad \text{Substitute into the formula.}$$

$$20 = c^2 \qquad \text{Add.}$$

$$\sqrt{20} = c \qquad \text{Take the square root of both sides.}$$

$$\sqrt{20} \approx 4.5 \qquad \text{Use a calculator and round to the nearest tenth.}$$

STEP 3 Check for reasonableness by finding perfect squares close to 20.

$\sqrt{20}$ is between $\sqrt{16}$ and $\sqrt{25}$, so $4 < \sqrt{20} < 5$.

Since 4.5 is between 4 and 5, the answer is reasonable.

The hypotenuse is about 4.5 units long.

YOUR TURN

1. Approximate the length of the hypotenuse to the nearest tenth without using a calculator.

_____

Personal Math Trainer

Online Practice and Help

my.hrw.com

Finding the Distance Between Any Two Points

The Pythagorean Theorem can be used to find the distance between any two points (x_1, y_1) and (x_2, y_2) in the coordinate plane. The resulting expression is called the Distance Formula.

Distance Formula

In a coordinate plane, the distance d between two points (x_1, y_1) and (x_2, y_2) is

$$d = \sqrt{(x_2 - x_1)^2 + (y_2 - y_1)^2}.$$

Use the Pythagorean Theorem to derive the Distance Formula.

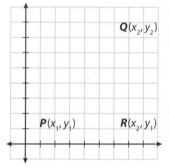

A To find the distance between points P and Q, draw segment $\overline{PQ}$ and label its length d. Then draw horizontal segment $\overline{PR}$ and vertical segment $\overline{QR}$. Label the lengths of these segments a and b. Triangle

     PQR is a _____ triangle, with hypotenuse _____.

B Since $\overline{PR}$ is a horizontal segment, its length, a, is the difference

     between its x-coordinates. Therefore, $a = x_2 -$ _____.

C Since $\overline{QR}$ is a vertical segment, its length, b, is the difference between

     its y-coordinates. Therefore, $b = y_2 -$ _____.

D Use the Pythagorean Theorem to find d, the length of segment $\overline{PQ}$. Substitute the expressions from **B** and **C** for a and b.

     $d^2 = a^2 + b^2$

     $d = \sqrt{a^2 + b^2}$

     $d = \sqrt{\left(\boxed{} - \boxed{}\right)^2 + \left(\boxed{} - \boxed{}\right)^2}$

Math Talk
Mathematical Practices

What do $x_2 - x_1$ and $y_2 - y_1$ represent in terms of the Pythagorean Theorem?

Reflect

2. Why are the coordinates of point R the ordered pair (x_2, y_1)?

_____

_____

_____

Finding the Distance Between Two Points

The Pythagorean Theorem can be used to find the distance between two points in a real-world situation. You can do this by using a coordinate grid that overlays a diagram of the real-world situation.

EXAMPLE 2   CA CC   8.G.8

Francesca wants to find the distance between her house on one side of a lake and the beach on the other side. She marks off a third point forming a right triangle, as shown. The distances in the diagram are measured in meters.

Beach (280, 164)

House (10, 20)   (280, 20)

Use the Pythagorean Theorem to find the straight-line distance from Francesca's house to the beach.

STEP 1   Find the length of the horizontal leg.

The length of the horizontal leg is the absolute value of the difference between the x-coordinates of the points (280, 20) and (10, 20).

$$|280 - 10| = 270$$

The length of the horizontal leg is 270 meters.

STEP 2   Find the length of the vertical leg.

The length of the vertical leg is the absolute value of the difference between the y-coordinates of the points (280, 164) and (280, 20).

$$|164 - 20| = 144$$

The length of the vertical leg is 144 meters.

STEP 3   Let $a = 270$ and $b = 144$. Let c represent the length of the hypotenuse. Use the Pythagorean Theorem to find c.

$$a^2 + b^2 = c^2$$

$$270^2 + 144^2 = c^2 \qquad \text{Substitute into the formula.}$$

$$72{,}900 + 20{,}736 = c^2 \qquad \text{Simplify.}$$

$$93{,}636 = c^2 \qquad \text{Add.}$$

$$\sqrt{93{,}636} = c \qquad \text{Take the square root of both sides.}$$

$$306 = c \qquad \text{Simplify.}$$

The distance from Francesca's house to the beach is 306 meters.

Math Talk
Mathematical Practices

Why is it necessary to take the absolute value of the coordinates when finding the length of a segment?

Reflect

3. Show how you could use the Distance Formula to find the distance from Francesca's house to the beach.

_____

_____

_____

YOUR TURN

4. Camp Sunshine is also on the lake. Use the Pythagorean Theorem to find the distance between Francesca's house and Camp Sunshine to the nearest tenth of a meter.

_____

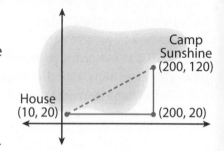

Camp Sunshine
(200, 120)

House
(10, 20)

(200, 20)

Guided Practice

1. Approximate the length of the hypotenuse of the right triangle to the nearest tenth using a calculator. (Example 1)

_____

2. Find the distance between the points (3, 7) and (15, 12) on the coordinate plane. (Explore Activity) _____

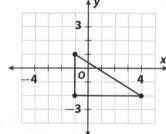

3. A plane leaves an airport and flies due north. Two minutes later, a second plane leaves the same airport flying due east. The flight plan shows the coordinates of the two planes 10 minutes later. The distances in the graph are measured in miles. Use the Pythagorean Theorem to find the distance shown between the two planes.

(Example 2) _____

(1, 80)

Airport
(1, 1)

(68, 1)

❓ ESSENTIAL QUESTION CHECK-IN

4. Describe two ways to find the distance between two points on a coordinate plane.

_____

_____

_____

12.3 Independent Practice

CA CC 8.G.8

Personal
Math Trainer

Online Practice
and Help

my.hrw.com

5. A metal worker traced a triangular piece of sheet metal on a coordinate plane, as shown. The units represent inches. What is the length of the longest side of the metal triangle? Approximate the length to the nearest tenth of an inch using a calculator. Check that your answer is reasonable.

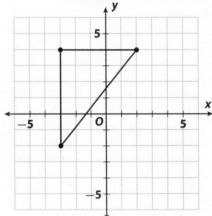

_____

6. When a coordinate grid is superimposed on a map of Harrisburg, the high school is located at (17, 21) and the town park is located at (28, 13). If each unit represents 1 mile, how many miles apart are the high school and the town park? Round your answer to the nearest tenth.

_____

7. The coordinates of the vertices of a rectangle are given by $R(-3, -4)$, $E(-3, 4)$, $C(4, 4)$, and $T(4, -4)$. Plot these points on the coordinate plane at the right and connect them to draw the rectangle. Then connect points E and T to form diagonal $\overline{ET}$.

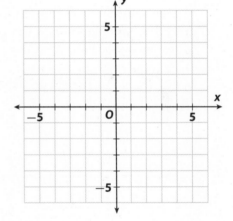

a. Use the Pythagorean Theorem to find the exact length of $\overline{ET}$.

_____

b. How can you use the Distance Formula to find the length of $\overline{ET}$? Show that the Distance Formula gives the same answer.

_____

_____

_____

_____

_____

_____

8. Multistep The locations of three ships are represented on a coordinate grid by the following points: $P(-2, 5)$, $Q(-7, -5)$, and $R(2, -3)$. Which ships are farthest apart?

_____

9. Make a Conjecture Find as many points as you can that are 5 units from the origin. Make a conjecture about the shape formed if all the points 5 units from the origin were connected.

_____

_____

_____

10. Justify Reasoning The graph shows the location of a motion detector that has a maximum range of 34 feet. A peacock at point P displays its tail feathers. Will the motion detector sense this motion? Explain.

_____

_____

_____

H.O.T. FOCUS ON HIGHER ORDER THINKING

Work Area

11. Persevere in Problem Solving One leg of an isosceles right triangle has endpoints (1, 1) and (6, 1). The other leg passes through the point (6, 2). Draw the triangle on the coordinate plane. Then show how you can use the Distance Formula to find the length of the hypotenuse. Round your answer to the nearest tenth.

_____

_____

_____

12. Represent Real-World Problems The figure shows a representation of a football field. The units represent yards. A sports analyst marks the locations of the football from where it was thrown (point A) and where it was caught (point B). Explain how you can use the Pythagorean Theorem to find the distance the ball was thrown. Then find the distance.

_____

_____

_____

_____

_____

Ready to Go On?

12.1 The Pythagorean Theorem

Find the length of the missing side.

1.

35 m

21 m

_____

2.

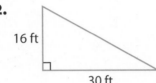

16 ft

30 ft

_____

12.2 Converse of the Pythagorean Theorem

Tell whether each triangle with the given side lengths is a right triangle.

3. 11, 60, 61 _____

4. 9, 37, 40 _____

5. 15, 35, 38 _____

6. 28, 45, 53 _____

7. Keelie has a triangular-shaped card. The lengths of its sides are 4.5 cm, 6 cm, and 7.5 cm. Is the card a right triangle?

_____

12.3 Distance Between Two Points

Find the distance between the given points. Round to the nearest tenth.

8. *A* and *B* _____

9. *B* and *C* _____

10. *A* and *C* _____

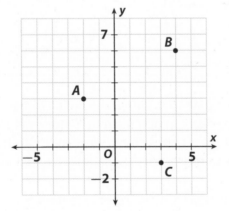

? **ESSENTIAL QUESTION**

11. How can you use the Pythagorean Theorem to solve real-world problems?

_____

_____

_____

MODULE 12
MIXED REVIEW

Assessment Readiness

Personal Math Trainer

Online Practice and Help

my.hrw.com

1. Look at each set of side lengths. Is a triangle with the given side lengths a right triangle? Select Yes or No for A–C.

   A. 2.8 m, 4.5 m, 5.3 m ○ Yes ○ No

   B. 15 in., 17 in., 32 in. ○ Yes ○ No

   C. 21 ft, 28 ft, 35 ft ○ Yes ○ No

2. Consider the set of numbers $\frac{29}{6}$, 4.9, and $\sqrt{24}$.

   Choose True or False for each statement.

   A. 4.9 is to the right of $\frac{29}{6}$ on a number line. ○ True ○ False

   B. $\frac{29}{6}$ is to the left of $\sqrt{24}$ on a number line. ○ True ○ False

   C. $\sqrt{24}$ is to the right of 4.9 on a number line. ○ True ○ False

3. A bald eagle's nest is located 3.2 miles west and 2.6 miles north of the entrance to a national forest. A biologist plans to hike directly from the forest entrance to the nest. Will the biologist hike more than 5 miles to reach the nest? Explain how you know.

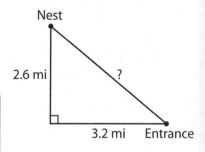

4. Three of the paths in a city park form a right triangle, as shown on the map. Each unit on the map represents 10 meters. The city plans to plant trees along these paths. To the nearest meter, what is the perimeter of the triangle? Explain how you solved this problem.

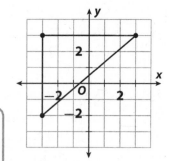

Volume

? ESSENTIAL QUESTION

How can you use volume to solve real-world problems?

Real-World Video

Aquariums are in the shape of cylinders and rectangular prisms. To find out how much water an aquarium holds, you can use formulas for volume.

my.hrw.com

GO DIGITAL
my.hrw.com

my.hrw.com
Go digital with your write-in student edition, accessible on any device.

Math On the Spot
Scan with your smart phone to jump directly to the online edition, video tutor, and more.

Animated Math
Interactively explore key concepts to see how math works.

Personal Math Trainer
Get immediate feedback and help as you work through practice sets.

Are YOU Ready?

Complete these exercises to review skills you will need for this module.

Exponents

> **EXAMPLE** $6^3 = 6 \times 6 \times 6$ Multiply the base (6) by itself the number of times indicated by the exponent (3).
>
> $ = 36 \times 6$ Find the product of the first two terms.
>
> $ = 216$ Find the product of all the terms.

Evaluate each exponential expression.

1. 11^2 _____

2. 2^5 _____

3. $\left(\dfrac{1}{5}\right)^3$ _____

4. $(0.3)^2$ _____

5. 2.1^3 _____

6. 0.1^3 _____

7. $\left(\dfrac{9.6}{3}\right)^2$ _____

8. 100^3 _____

Round Decimals

> **EXAMPLE** Round 43.2685 to the underlined place.
>
> $43.2685 \longrightarrow 43.27$
>
> The digit to be rounded: 6
> The digit to its right is 8.
> 8 is *5 or greater*, so round *up*.
> The rounded number is 43.27.

Round to the underlined place.

9. 2.3<u>7</u>4 _____

10. 12<u>6</u>.399 _____

11. 13.<u>9</u>577 _____

12. 42.6<u>9</u>0 _____

13. 134.<u>9</u>5 _____

14. 2.<u>0</u>486 _____

15. 63.6<u>3</u>52 _____

16. 98.<u>9</u>499 _____

Simplify Numerical Expressions

> **EXAMPLE** $\dfrac{1}{3}(3.14)(4)^2(3) = \dfrac{1}{3}(3.14)(16)(3)$ Simplify the exponent.
>
> $\phantom{\dfrac{1}{3}(3.14)(4)^2(3)} = 50.24$ Multiply from left to right.

Simplify each expression.

17. $3.14\,(5)^2\,(10)$ _____

18. $\dfrac{1}{3}(3.14)(3)^2(5)$ _____

19. $\dfrac{4}{3}(3.14)(3)^3$ _____

20. $\dfrac{4}{3}(3.14)(6)^3$ _____

21. $3.14\,(4)^2\,(9)$ _____

22. $\dfrac{1}{3}(3.14)(9)^2\left(\dfrac{2}{3}\right)$ _____

Reading Start-Up

Visualize Vocabulary

Use the ✔ words to complete the empty columns in the chart. You may use words more than once.

Shape	Distance Around	Attributes	Associated Review Words
circle		r, d	
square		90° corner, sides	
rectangle		90° corner, sides	

Understand Vocabulary

Complete the sentences using the preview words.

1. A three-dimensional figure that has one vertex and one circular base is a _____.

2. A three-dimensional figure with all points the same distance from the center is a _____.

3. A three-dimensional figure that has two congruent circular bases is a _____.

Active Reading

Three-Panel Flip Chart Before beginning the module, create a three-panel flip chart to help you organize what you learn. Label each flap with one of the lesson titles from this module. As you study each lesson, write important ideas like vocabulary, properties, and formulas under the appropriate flap.

Volume

Understanding the standards and the vocabulary terms in the standards will help you know exactly what you are expected to learn in this module.

CA CC 8.G.9

Know the formulas for the volumes of cones, cylinders, and spheres and use them to solve real-world and mathematical problems.

Key Vocabulary

volume *(volumen)*
The number of cubic units needed to fill a given space.

cylinder *(cilindro)*
A three-dimensional figure with two parallel, congruent circular bases connected by a curved lateral surface.

What It Means to You

You will learn the formula for the volume of a cylinder.

EXAMPLE 8.G.9

The Asano Taiko Company of Japan built the world's largest drum in 2000. The drum's diameter is 4.8 meters, and its height is 4.95 meters. Estimate the volume of the drum.

$d = 4.8 \approx 5$ $V = (\pi r^2)h$ *Volume of a cylinder*

$h = 4.95 \approx 5$ $\approx (3)(2.5)^2 \cdot 5$ *Use 3 for π.*

$r = \dfrac{d}{2} \approx \dfrac{5}{2} = 2.5$ $= (3)(6.25)(5)$

                     $= 18.75 \cdot 5$

                     $= 93.75 \approx 94$

The volume of the drum is approximately 94 m³.

CA CC 8.G.9

Know the formulas for the volumes of cones, cylinders, and spheres and use them to solve real-world and mathematical problems.

Key Vocabulary

cone *(cono)*
A three-dimensional figure with one vertex and one circular base.

sphere *(esfera)*
A three-dimensional figure with all points the same distance from the center.

What It Means to You

You will learn formulas for the volume of a cone and a sphere.

EXAMPLE 8.G.9

6 in.

2 in.

Find the volume of the cone. Use 3.14 for π.

$B = \pi(2^2) = 4\pi$ in²

$V = \dfrac{1}{3} \cdot 4\pi \cdot 6$ $V = \dfrac{1}{3}Bh$

$V = 8\pi$ *Use 3.14 for π.*

≈ 25.1 in³

The volume of the cone is approximately 25.1 in³.

The volume of a sphere with the same radius is $V = \dfrac{4}{3}\pi r^3 \approx \dfrac{4}{3}(3)(2)^3 = 32$ in³.

Visit **my.hrw.com** to see all **CA** Common Core Standards unpacked.

my.hrw.com

CA CC 8.G.9

Know the formulas for the volumes of cones, cylinders, and spheres and use them to solve real-world and mathematical problems.

ESSENTIAL QUESTION

How do you find the volume of a cylinder?

EXPLORE ACTIVITY   **CA CC** 8.G.9

Modeling the Volume of a Cylinder

A **cylinder** is a three-dimensional figure that has two congruent circular bases that lie in parallel planes. The volume of any three-dimensional figure is the number of cubic units needed to fill the space taken up by the solid figure.

One cube represents one cubic unit of volume. You can develop the formula for the volume of a cylinder using an empty soup can or other cylindrical container. First, remove one of the bases.

A Arrange centimeter cubes in a single layer at the bottom of the cylinder. Fit as many cubes into the layer as possible. How many cubes are in this layer?

_____

B To find how many layers of cubes fit in the cylinder, make a stack of cubes along the inside of the cylinder. How many layers fit in the cylinder?

_____

C How can you use what you know to find the approximate number of cubes that would fit in the cylinder?

_____

_____

Reflect

1. **Make a Conjecture** Suppose you know the area of the base of a cylinder and the height of the cylinder. How can you find the cylinder's volume?

_____

2. Let the area of the base of a cylinder be *B* and the height of the cylinder be *h*. Write a formula for the cylinder's volume *V*. _____

Finding the Volume of a Cylinder Using a Formula

Finding volumes of cylinders is similar to finding volumes of prisms. You find the volume V of both a prism and a cylinder by multiplying the height h by the area of the base B, so $V = Bh$.

The base of a cylinder is a circle, so for a cylinder, $B = \pi r^2$.

Volume of a Cylinder	
The volume V of a cylinder with radius r is the area of the base B times the height h.	
$V = Bh$ or $V = \pi r^2 h$	

EXAMPLE 1

CA CC 8.G.9

Find the volume of each cylinder. Round your answers to the nearest tenth if necessary. Use 3.14 for π.

A

10 in.

3 in.

$V = \pi r^2 h$

$\approx 3.14 \cdot 3^2 \cdot 10$ Substitute.

$\approx 3.14 \cdot 9 \cdot 10$ Simplify.

≈ 282.6 Multiply.

The volume is about 282.6 in³.

B   6.4 cm   13 cm

Since the diameter is 6.4 cm, the radius is 3.2 cm.

> Recall that the diameter of a circle is twice the radius, so $2r = d$ and $r = \frac{d}{2}$.

$V = \pi r^2 h$

$\approx 3.14 \cdot 3.2^2 \cdot 13$ Substitute.

$\approx 3.14 \cdot 10.24 \cdot 13$ Simplify.

≈ 418 Multiply.

The volume is about 418 cm³.

Reflect

3. **What If?** If you want a formula for the volume of a cylinder that involves the diameter d instead of the radius r, how can you rewrite it?

Find the volume of each cylinder. Round your answers to the nearest tenth if necessary. Use 3.14 for π.

4.

6 in.

10 in.

_____

5.

4 ft
12 ft

_____

Finding the Volume of a Cylinder in a Real-World Context

You can find the volume of a bass drum by using the formula for the volume of a cylinder.

EXAMPLE 2 *Real World*   CA CC 8.G.9

One of the bass drums used in a marching band has a diameter of 18 inches and a depth of 14 inches. Find the volume of the drum to the nearest tenth. Use 3.14 for π.

STEP 1 Find the radius of the drum.

$$r = \frac{d}{2} = \frac{18}{2} = 9 \text{ in.}$$

STEP 2 Find the volume of the drum.

$V = \pi r^2 h$

$\approx 3.14 \cdot 9^2 \cdot 14$ Substitute.

$\approx 3.14 \cdot 81 \cdot 14$ Simplify the exponent.

≈ 3560.76 Multiply.

The volume of the drum is about 3560.8 in³.

YOUR TURN

6. A drum company advertises a snare drum that is 4 inches high and 12 inches in diameter. Find the volume of the drum to the nearest tenth. Use 3.14 for π.

_____

1. **Vocabulary** Describe the bases of a cylinder. (Explore Activity)

   _____

2. Figure 1 shows a view from above of inch cubes on the bottom of a cylinder. Figure 2 shows the highest stack of cubes that will fit inside the cylinder. Estimate the volume of the cylinder. Explain your reasoning. (Explore Activity)

   _____

   _____

   _____

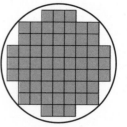

Figure 1   Figure 2

3. Find the volume of the cylinder to the nearest tenth. Use 3.14 for π. (Example 1)

   $V = \pi r^2 h$

   $V = \pi \cdot \boxed{}^2 \cdot \boxed{}$

   $\approx 3.14 \cdot \boxed{} \cdot \boxed{}$

   $\approx \boxed{}$

6 m

15 m

   The volume of the cylinder is approximately _____ m³.

4. A Japanese odaiko is a very large drum that is made by hollowing out a section of a tree trunk. A museum in Takayama City has three odaikos of similar size carved from a single tree trunk. The largest measures about 2.7 meters in both diameter and length, and weighs about 4.5 metric tons. Using the volume formula for a cylinder, approximate the volume of the drum to the nearest tenth. (Example 2)

   The radius of the drum is about _____ m.

   The volume of the drum is about _____ m³.

ESSENTIAL QUESTION CHECK-IN

5. How do you find the volume of a cylinder? Describe which measurements of a cylinder you need to know.

   _____

   _____

   _____

Name _____ Class _____ Date _____

 CA CC 8.G.9

Personal
Math Trainer

Online Practice
and Help

my.hrw.com

Find the volume of each figure. Round your answers to the nearest tenth if necessary. Use 3.14 for π.

6.

1.5 cm
11 cm

7.

4 in.
24 in.

_____

_____

8.

5 m
16 m

9.

10 in.
12 in.

_____

_____

10. A cylinder has a radius of 4 centimeters and a height of 40 centimeters.

_____

11. A cylinder has a radius of 8 meters and a height of 4 meters.

_____

Round your answer to the nearest tenth, if necessary. Use 3.14 for π.

12. The cylindrical Giant Ocean Tank at the New England Aquarium in Boston is 24 feet deep and has a radius of 18.8 feet. Find the volume of the tank.

_____

13. A standard-size bass drum has a diameter of 22 inches and is 18 inches deep. Find the volume of this drum.

_____

14. Grain is stored in cylindrical structures called silos. Find the volume of a silo with a diameter of 11.1 feet and a height of 20 feet.

_____

15. The Frank Erwin Center, or "The Drum," at the University of Texas in Austin can be approximated by a cylinder that is 120 meters in diameter and 30 meters in height. Find its volume.

_____

16. A barrel of crude oil contains about 5.61 cubic feet of oil. How many barrels of oil are contained in 1 mile (5280 feet) of a pipeline that has an inside diameter of 6 inches and is completely filled with oil? How much is "1 mile" of oil in this pipeline worth at a price of $100 per barrel?

_____

17. A pan for baking French bread is shaped like half a cylinder. It is 12 inches long and 3.5 inches in diameter. What is the volume of uncooked dough that would fill this pan?

3.5 in.

12 in.

_____

![H.O.T.] **FOCUS ON HIGHER ORDER THINKING**

18. Explain the Error A student said the volume of a cylinder with a 3-inch diameter is two times the volume of a cylinder with the same height and a 1.5-inch radius. What is the error?

_____

_____

_____

19. Communicate Mathematical Ideas Explain how you can find the height of a cylinder if you know the diameter and the volume. Include an example with your explanation.

_____

_____

_____

_____

_____

_____

20. Analyze Relationships Cylinder A has a radius of 6 centimeters. Cylinder B has the same height and a radius half as long as cylinder A. What fraction of the volume of cylinder A is the volume of cylinder B? Explain.

_____

_____

_____

_____

Work Area

LESSON
13.2 Volume of Cones

CA CC 8.G.9

Know the formulas for the volumes of cones, cylinders, and spheres and use them to solve real-world and mathematical problems.

ESSENTIAL QUESTION

How do you find the volume of a cone?

EXPLORE ACTIVITY   CA CC 8.G.9

Modeling the Volume of a Cone

A **cone** is a three-dimensional figure that has one vertex and one circular base.

To explore the volume of a cone, Sandi does an experiment with a cone and a cylinder that have congruent bases and heights. She fills the cone with popcorn kernels and then pours the kernels into the cylinder. She repeats this until the cylinder is full.

Sandi finds that it takes 3 cones to fill the volume of the cylinder.

STEP 1 What is the formula for the volume V of a cylinder with base area B and height h? _____

STEP 2 What is the area of the base of the cone? _____

STEP 3 Sandi found that, when the bases and height are the same,

_____ times $V_{cone} = V_{cylinder}$.

STEP 4 How does the volume of the cone compare to the volume of the cylinder?

Volume of the cone: $V_{cone} = \dfrac{\square}{\square} \cdot V_{cylinder}$

Reflect

1. Use the conclusion from this experiment to write a formula for the volume of a cone in terms of the height and the radius. Explain.

_____

_____

_____

Finding the Volume of a Cone Using a Formula

The formulas for the volume of a prism and the volume of a cylinder are the same: multiply the height h by the area of the base B, so $V = Bh$.

In the **Explore Activity**, you saw that the volume of a cone is one third the volume of a cylinder with the same base and height.

Volume of a Cone

The volume V of a cone with radius r is one third the area of the base B times the height h.

$$V = \frac{1}{3}Bh \text{ or } V = \frac{1}{3}\pi r^2 h$$

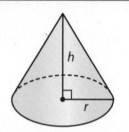

EXAMPLE 1

CA CC 8.G.9

Find the volume of each cone. Round your answers to the nearest tenth. Use 3.14 for π.

A

8 in.

2 in.

$V = \frac{1}{3}\pi r^2 h$

$\approx \frac{1}{3} \cdot 3.14 \cdot 2^2 \cdot 8$ Substitute.

$\approx \frac{1}{3} \cdot 3.14 \cdot 4 \cdot 8$ Simplify.

≈ 33.5 Multiply.

The volume is about 33.5 in³.

Math Talk

Mathematical Practices

How can you estimate the volume of any cone?

B Since the diameter is 8 ft, the radius is 4 ft.

9 ft

8 ft

$V = \frac{1}{3}\pi r^2 h$

$\approx \frac{1}{3} \cdot 3.14 \cdot 4^2 \cdot 9$ Substitute.

$\approx \frac{1}{3} \cdot 3.14 \cdot 16 \cdot 9$ Simplify.

≈ 150.7 Multiply.

The volume is about 150.7 ft³.

Reflect

2. How can you rewrite the formula for the volume of a cone using the diameter d instead of the radius r? _____

Find the volume of each cone. Round your answers to the nearest tenth. Use 3.14 for π.

3.
15 cm
16 cm

4.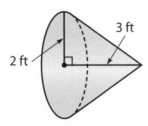
3 ft
2 ft

_____   _____

Personal
Math Trainer

Online Practice
and Help

⏱ my.hrw.com

Finding the Volume of a Volcano

The mountain created by a volcano is often cone–shaped.

EXAMPLE 2 Real World   🐻 CA CC 8.G.9

Math On the Spot

⏱ my.hrw.com

For her geography project, Karen built a clay model of a volcano in the shape of a cone. Her model has a diameter of 12 inches and a height of 8 inches. Find the volume of clay in her model to the nearest tenth. Use 3.14 for π.

STEP 1 Find the radius.

$r = \frac{12}{2} = 6$ in.

STEP 2 Find the volume of clay.

$V = \frac{1}{3}\pi r^2 h$

$\approx \frac{1}{3} \cdot 3.14 \cdot 6^2 \cdot 8$ Substitute.

$\approx \frac{1}{3} \cdot 3.14 \cdot 36 \cdot 8$ Simplify.

≈ 301.44 Multiply.

The volume of the clay is about 301.4 in³.

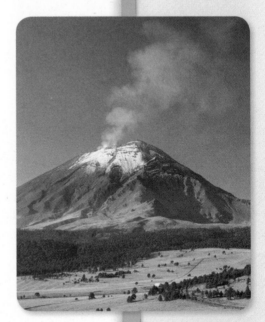

5. The cone of the volcano Parícutin in Mexico had a height of 410 meters and a diameter of 424 meters. Find the volume of the cone to the nearest tenth. Use 3.14 for π.

_____

Personal
Math Trainer

Online Practice
and Help

⏱ my.hrw.com

Guided Practice

1. The area of the base of a cylinder is 45 square inches and its height is 10 inches. A cone has the same area for its base and the same height. What is the volume of the cone? (Explore Activity)

$V_{cylinder} = Bh = $ ⬚ $\cdot$ ⬚ $=$ ⬚

$V_{cone} = \dfrac{1}{3} V_{cylinder}$

$= \dfrac{1}{3}$ ⬚

$=$ ⬚

The volume of the cone is _____ in³.

2. A cone and a cylinder have congruent height and bases. The volume of the cone is 18 m³. What is the volume of the cylinder? Explain. (Explore Activity)

_____

_____

_____

_____

_____

_____

_____

Find the volume of each cone. Round your answer to the nearest tenth if necessary. Use 3.14 for π. (Example 1)

3.

7 ft

6 ft

_____

4.

100 in.

33 in.

_____

5. Gretchen made a paper cone to hold a gift for a friend. The paper cone was 15 inches high and had a radius of 3 inches. Find the volume of the paper cone to the nearest tenth. Use 3.14 for π. (Example 2)

_____

6. A cone-shaped building is commonly used to store sand. What would be the volume of a cone-shaped building with a diameter of 50 meters and a height of 20 meters? Round your answer to the nearest tenth. Use 3.14 for π. (Example 2)

_____

? ESSENTIAL QUESTION CHECK-IN

7. How do you find the volume of a cone?

_____

_____

_____

13.2 Independent Practice

Personal Math Trainer

my.hrw.com Online Practice and Help

Find the volume of each cone. Round your answers to the nearest tenth if necessary. Use 3.14 for π.

8.

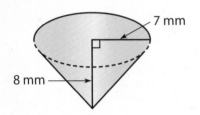

7 mm

8 mm

_____

9.

6 in.

2 in.

_____

10. A cone has a diameter of 6 centimeters and a height of 11.5 centimeters.

_____

11. A cone has a radius of 3 meters and a height of 10 meters.

_____

Round your answers to the nearest tenth if necessary. Use 3.14 for π.

12. Antonio is making mini waffle cones. Each waffle cone is 3 inches high and has a radius of $\frac{3}{4}$ inch. What is the volume of a waffle cone?

_____

13. A snack bar sells popcorn in cone-shaped containers. One container has a diameter of 8 inches and a height of 10 inches. How many cubic inches of popcorn does the container hold?

_____

14. A volcanic cone has a diameter of 300 meters and a height of 150 meters. What is the volume of the cone?

_____

15. **Multistep** Orange traffic cones come in a variety of sizes. Approximate the volume, in cubic inches, of a traffic cone that has a height of 2 feet and a diameter of 10 inches. Use 3.14 for π.

_____

Find the missing measure for each cone. Round your answers to the nearest tenth if necessary. Use 3.14 for π.

16. radius = _____

height = 6 in.

volume = 100.48 in³

17. diameter = 6 cm

height = _____

volume = 56.52 cm³

18. The diameter of a cone-shaped container is 4 inches, and its height is 6 inches. How much greater is the volume of a cylinder-shaped container with the same diameter and height? Round your answer to the nearest hundredth. Use 3.14 for π.

_____

FOCUS ON HIGHER ORDER THINKING

Work Area

19. Alex wants to know the volume of sand in an hourglass. When all the sand is in the bottom, he stands a ruler up beside the hourglass and estimates the height of the cone of sand.

a. What else does he need to measure to find the volume of sand?

_____

_____

b. **Make a Conjecture** If the volume of sand is increasing at a constant rate, is the height increasing at a constant rate? Explain.

_____

_____

_____

20. **Problem Solving** The diameter of a cone is x cm, the height is 18 cm, and the volume is 301.44 cm³. What is x? Use 3.14 for π.

_____

21. **Analyze Relationships** A cone has a radius of 1 foot and a height of 2 feet. How many cones of liquid would it take to fill a cylinder with a diameter of 2 feet and a height of 2 feet? Explain.

_____

_____

_____

22. **Critique Reasoning** Herb knows that the volume of a cone is one third that of a cylinder with the same base and height. He reasons that a cone with the same height as a given cylinder but 3 times the radius should therefore have the same volume as the cylinder, since $\frac{1}{3} \cdot 3 = 1$. Is Herb correct? Explain.

_____

_____

_____

_____

_____

412 Unit 5

13.3 Volume of Spheres

 CA CC 8.G.9

Know the formulas for the volumes of cones, cylinders, and spheres and use them to solve real-world and mathematical problems.

ESSENTIAL QUESTION

How do you find the volume of a sphere?

EXPLORE ACTIVITY CA CC 8.G.9

Modeling the Volume of a Sphere

A **sphere** is a three-dimensional figure with all points the same distance from the center. The **radius** of a sphere is the distance from the center to any point on the sphere.

You have seen that a cone fills $\frac{1}{3}$ of a cylinder of the same radius and height h. If you were to do a similar experiment with a sphere of the same radius, you would find that a sphere fills $\frac{2}{3}$ of the cylinder. The cylinder's height is equal to twice the radius of the sphere.

  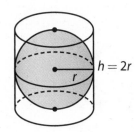

STEP 1 Write the formula $V = Bh$ for each shape. Use $B = \pi r^2$ and substitute the fractions you know for the cone and sphere.

Cylinder	**Cone**	**Sphere**
$V = \pi r^2 h$	$V = \frac{1}{3}\pi r^2 h$	$V = \frac{2}{3}\pi r^2 h$

STEP 2 Notice that a sphere always has a height equal to twice the radius. Substitute $2r$ for h. $V = \frac{2}{3}\pi r^2 (2r)$

STEP 3 Simplify this formula for the volume of a sphere. $V = \boxed{}\pi r^3$

Reflect

1. **Analyze Relationships** A cone has a radius of r and a height of $2r$. A sphere has a radius of r. Compare the volume of the sphere and cone.

   _____

   _____

   _____

Finding the Volume of a Sphere Using a Formula

The Explore Activity illustrates a formula for the volume of a sphere with radius r.

Volume of a Sphere

The volume V of a sphere is $\frac{4}{3}\pi$ times the cube of the radius r.

$$V = \frac{4}{3}\pi r^3$$

EXAMPLE 1

 CA CC 8.G.9

Find the volume of each sphere. Round your answers to the nearest tenth if necessary. Use 3.14 for π.

A

 2.1 cm

$V = \frac{4}{3}\pi r^3$

$\approx \frac{4}{3} \cdot 3.14 \cdot 2.1^3$ Substitute.

$\approx \frac{4}{3} \cdot 3.14 \cdot 9.26$ Simplify.

≈ 38.8 Multiply.

The volume is about 38.8 cm³.

B

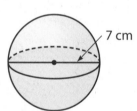 7 cm

Since the diameter is 7 cm, the radius is 3.5 cm.

$V = \frac{4}{3}\pi r^3$

$\approx \frac{4}{3} \cdot 3.14 \cdot 3.5^3$ Substitute.

$\approx \frac{4}{3} \cdot 3.14 \cdot 42.9$ Simplify.

≈ 179.6 Multiply.

The volume is about 179.6 cm³.

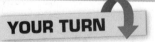 **YOUR TURN**

Find the volume of each sphere. Round your answers to the nearest tenth. Use 3.14 for π.

2. A sphere has a radius of 10 centimeters. _____

3. A sphere has a diameter of 3.4 meters. _____

Finding the Volume of a Sphere in a Real-World Context

Many sports, including golf and tennis, use a ball that is spherical in shape.

EXAMPLE 2 Real World   CA CC 8.G.9

Soccer balls come in several different sizes. One soccer ball has a diameter of 22 centimeters. What is the volume of this soccer ball? Round your answer to the nearest tenth. Use 3.14 for π.

STEP 1 Find the radius.

$$r = \frac{d}{2} = 11 \text{ cm}$$

STEP 2 Find the volume of the soccer ball.

$$V = \frac{4}{3}\pi r^3$$

$$\approx \frac{4}{3} \cdot 3.14 \cdot 11^3 \qquad \text{Substitute.}$$

$$\approx \frac{4}{3} \cdot 3.14 \cdot 1331 \qquad \text{Simplify.}$$

$$\approx 5572.4533 \qquad \text{Multiply.}$$

The volume of the soccer ball is about 5572.5 cm³.

Reflect

4. What is the volume of the soccer ball in terms of π, to the nearest whole number multiple? Explain your answer.

_____

_____

5. **Analyze Relationships** The diameter of a basketball is about 1.1 times that of a soccer ball. The diameter of a tennis ball is about 0.3 times that of a soccer ball. How do the volumes of these balls compare to that of a soccer ball? Explain.

_____

_____

_____

YOUR TURN

6. Val measures the diameter of a ball as 12 inches. How many cubic inches of air does this ball hold, to the nearest tenth? Use 3.14 for π.

_____

Personal Math Trainer

Online Practice and Help

my.hrw.com

1. **Vocabulary** A sphere is a three-dimensional figure with all points

   _____ from the center. (Explore Activity)

2. **Vocabulary** The _____ is the distance from the center
   of a sphere to a point on the sphere. (Explore Activity)

**Find the volume of each sphere. Round your answers to the nearest tenth
if necessary. Use 3.14 for π.** (Example 1)

3.

1 in.

_____

4.

20 cm

_____

5. A sphere has a radius of 1.5 feet. _____

6. A sphere has a diameter of 2 yards. _____

7. A baseball has a diameter of 2.9 inches. Find the volume of the
   baseball. Round your answer to the nearest tenth if necessary.
   Use 3.14 for π. (Example 2)   _____

8. A basketball has a radius of 4.7 inches. What is its volume to the
   nearest cubic inch. Use 3.14 for π. (Example 2)   _____

9. A company is deciding whether to package a ball
   in a cubic box or a cylindrical box. In either case,
   the ball will touch the bottom, top, and sides.
   (Explore Activity)

   a. What portion of the space inside the cylindrical
      box is empty? Explain.

      _____

   b. Find an expression for the volume of the cubic box. _____

   c. About what portion of the space inside the cubic box is empty? Explain.

      _____

      _____

? ESSENTIAL QUESTION CHECK-IN

10. Explain the steps you use to find the volume of a sphere.

    _____

13.3 Independent Practice

 CA CC 8.G.9

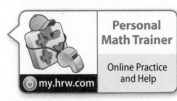

Personal Math Trainer

Online Practice and Help

Find the volume of each sphere. Round your answers to the nearest tenth if necessary. Use 3.14 for π.

11. radius of 3.1 meters _____

12. diameter of 18 inches _____

13. *r* = 6 in. _____

14. *d* = 36 m _____

15.

11 cm

_____

16.

2.5 ft

_____

The eggs of birds and other animals come in many different shapes and sizes. Eggs often have a shape that is nearly spherical. When this is true, you can use the formula for a sphere to find their volume.

17. The green turtle lays eggs that are approximately spherical with an average diameter of 4.5 centimeters. Each turtle lays an average of 113 eggs at one time. Find the total volume of these eggs, to the nearest cubic centimeter.

_____

18. Hummingbirds lay eggs that are nearly spherical and about 1 centimeter in diameter. Find the volume of an egg. Round your answer to the nearest tenth.

_____

19. Fossilized spherical eggs of dinosaurs called titanosaurid sauropods were found in Patagonia. These eggs were 15 centimeters in diameter. Find the volume of an egg. Round your answer to the nearest tenth.

_____

20. **Persevere in Problem Solving** An ostrich egg has about the same volume as a sphere with a diameter of 5 inches. If the eggshell is about $\frac{1}{12}$ inch thick, find the volume of just the shell, not including the interior of the egg. Round your answer to the nearest tenth.

_____

21. **Multistep** Write the steps you would use to find a formula for the volume of the figure at right. Then write the formula.

r
r
r

_____

_____

_____

_____

_____

_____

_____

_____

_____

_____

_____

22. Critical Thinking Explain what happens to the volume of a sphere if you double the radius.

_____

23. Multistep A cylindrical can of tennis balls holds a stack of three balls so that they touch the can at the top, bottom, and sides. The radius of each ball is 1.25 inches. Find the volume inside the can that is not taken up by the three tennis balls.

_____

Work Area

H.O.T. FOCUS ON HIGHER ORDER THINKING

24. Critique Reasoning A sphere has a radius of 4 inches, and a cube-shaped box has an edge length of 7.5 inches. J.D. says the box has a greater volume, so the sphere will fit in the box. Is he correct? Explain.

_____

_____

_____

25. Critical Thinking Which would hold the most water: a bowl in the shape of a hemisphere with radius _r_, a cylindrical glass with radius _r_ and height _r_, or a cone-shaped drinking cup with radius _r_ and height _r_? Explain.

_____

_____

_____

26. Analyze Relationships Hari has models of a sphere, a cylinder, and a cone. The sphere's diameter and the cylinder's height are the same, 2_r_. The cylinder has radius _r_. The cone has diameter 2_r_ and height 2_r_. Compare the volumes of the cone and the sphere to the volume of the cylinder.

_____

_____

_____

27. A spherical helium balloon that is 8 feet in diameter can lift about 17 pounds. What does the diameter of a balloon need to be to lift a person who weighs 136 pounds? Explain.

_____

_____

_____

Ready to Go On?

13.1 Volume of Cylinders

Find the volume of each cylinder. Round your answers to the
nearest tenth if necessary. Use 3.14 for π.

1. 6 ft

8 ft

_____

2. A can of juice has a radius of 4 inches
and a height of 7 inches. What is the
volume of the can?

_____

13.2 Volume of Cones

Find the volume of each cone. Round your answers to the
nearest tenth if necessary. Use 3.14 for π.

3.

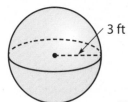

15 cm

6 cm _____

4.

20 in.

12 in. _____

13.3 Volume of Spheres

Find the volume of each sphere. Round your answers to the
nearest tenth if necessary. Use 3.14 for π.

5.

3 ft

_____

6.

13 cm

_____

? ESSENTIAL QUESTION

7. What measurements do you need to know to find the volume of a
cylinder? a cone? a sphere?

_____

_____

MODULE 13
MIXED REVIEW

Assessment Readiness

Personal Math Trainer

Online Practice and Help

my.hrw.com

1. Triangle *JKL* is dilated by a scale factor of 1.5 with the origin as the center of dilation. Look at each ordered pair. Does the ordered pair represent a vertex of the image?

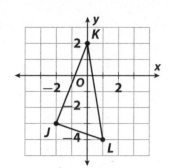

Select Yes or No for A–C.

A. (−3, −4.5)   ◯ Yes   ◯ No

B. (1.5, −6)   ◯ Yes   ◯ No

C. (3, 0)   ◯ Yes   ◯ No

2. A sphere has a radius of 4 inches.

Choose True or False for each statement.

A. A sphere with half the radius has $\frac{1}{8}$ of the volume.   ◯ True   ◯ False

B. A sphere with twice the radius has 6 times the volume.   ◯ True   ◯ False

C. A sphere with 3 times the radius has 27 times the volume.   ◯ True   ◯ False

3. A pile of sand is shaped like a cone with a height of 4 feet and a base diameter of 13 feet. Each cubic foot of sand weighs 90 pounds. Does the pile of sand weigh more than a ton (2000 pounds)? Explain how you know.

4. A cylindrical drinking glass has a base radius of 3.2 centimeters and a height of 14.0 centimeters. Given that 1 cubic centimeter is equivalent to 1 milliliter, how many milliliters of water does the glass hold when it is $\frac{3}{4}$ full? Round to the nearest milliliter.

14.0 cm

3.2 cm

Study Guide Review

Angle Relationships in Parallel Lines and Triangles

Key Vocabulary

alternate exterior angles *(ángulos alternos externos)*

alternate interior angles *(ángulos alternos internos)*

corresponding angles *(ángulos correspondientes (para líneas))*

exterior angle *(ángulo externo)*

interior angle *(ángulos internos)*

remote interior angle *(ángulo interno remoto)*

same-side interior angles *(ángulos internos del mismo lado)*

similar *(semejantes)*

transversal *(transversal)*

? ESSENTIAL QUESTION

How can you solve real-world problems that involve angle relationships in parallel lines and triangles?

EXAMPLE 1

Find each angle measure when $m\angle 6 = 81°$.

A $m\angle 5$

$m\angle 5 = 180° - 81° = 99°$

5 and 6 are supplementary angles.

B $m\angle 1$

$m\angle 1 = 99°$

1 and 5 are corresponding angles.

C $m\angle 3$

$m\angle 3 = 180° - 81° = 99°$

3 and 6 are same-side interior angles.

EXAMPLE 2

Are the triangles similar? Explain your answer.

$y = 180° - (67° + 35°)$

$y = 78°$

$x = 180° - (67° + 67°)$

$x = 46°$

The triangles are not similar, because they do not have 2 or more pairs of corresponding congruent angles.

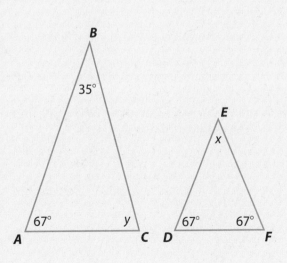

EXERCISES

1. If m∠GHA = 106°, find the measures of the given angles.
(Lesson 11.1)

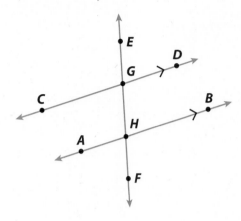

m∠EGC = _____

m∠EGD = _____

m∠BHF = _____

m∠HGD = _____

2. Find the missing angle measures. (Lesson 11.2)

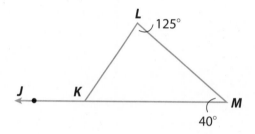

m∠JKL = _____

m∠LKM = _____

3. Is the larger triangle similar to the smaller triangle?
Explain your answer. (Lesson 11.3)

_____

_____

_____

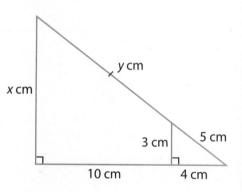

4. Find the value of *x* and *y* in the figure. (Lesson 11.3)

_____

5. If m∠CJI = 132° and m∠EIH = 59°, find the measures of
the given angles. (Lesson 11.1)

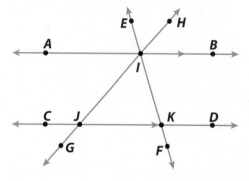

m∠IKJ = _____

m∠HIB = _____

m∠EIJ = _____

m∠AIK = _____

The Pythagorean Theorem

Key Vocabulary
hypotenuse *(hipotenusa)*
legs *(catetos)*
Pythagorean Theorem
(teorema de Pitágoras)

? **ESSENTIAL QUESTION**

How can you use the Pythagorean Theorem to solve real-world problems?

EXAMPLE 1

Find the missing side length.
Round your answer to the nearest tenth.

$$a^2 + b^2 = c^2$$

$$7^2 + b^2 = 18^2$$

$$49 + b^2 = 324$$

$$b^2 = 275$$

$$b = \sqrt{275} \approx 16.6$$

The length of the leg is about 16.6 inches.

EXAMPLE 2

Thomas drew a diagram to represent the location of his house, the school, and his friend Manuel's house. What is the distance from the school to Manuel's house? Round your answer to the nearest tenth.

$$a^2 + b^2 = c^2$$

$$5^2 + 9^2 = c^2$$

$$25 + 81 = c^2$$

$$c^2 = 106$$

$$c = \sqrt{106} \approx 10.3$$

The distance from the school to Manuel's house is about 10.3 miles.

EXERCISES

Find the missing side lengths. Round your answers to the nearest hundredth. (Lesson 12.1)

1.

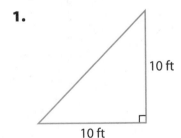

10 ft

10 ft

_____

2.

$h = 10$ cm
r
$w = 10$ cm
s
$\ell = 25$ cm

_____

3. Hye Sun has a modern coffee table whose top is a triangle with the following side lengths: 8 feet, 3 feet, and 5 feet. Is Hye Sun's coffee table top a right triangle? (Lesson 12.2)

_____

4. Find the length of each side of triangle *ABC*. If necessary, round your answers to the nearest hundredth. (Lesson 12.3)

$\overline{AB}$ _____

$\overline{BC}$ _____

$\overline{AC}$ _____

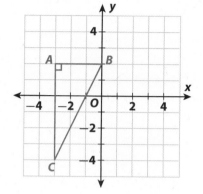

? ESSENTIAL QUESTION

How can you solve real-world problems that involve volume?

EXAMPLE 1

Find the volume of the cistern. Round your answer to the nearest hundredth. Use 3.14 for π.

$V = \pi r^2 h$

$\approx 3.14 \cdot 2.5^2 \cdot 7.5$

$\approx 3.14 \cdot 6.25 \cdot 7.5$

≈ 147.19

The cistern has a volume of approximately 147.19 cubic feet.

EXAMPLE 2

Find the volume of a sphere with a radius of 3.7 cm. Write your answer in terms of π and to the nearest hundredth.

$V = \frac{4}{3}\pi r^3$

$\approx \frac{4}{3} \cdot \pi \cdot 3.7^3$

$\approx \frac{4}{3} \cdot \pi \cdot 50.653$

$\approx 67.54\pi$

$V = \frac{4}{3}\pi r^3$

$\approx \frac{4}{3} \cdot 3.14 \cdot 3.7^3$

$\approx \frac{4}{3} \cdot 3.14 \cdot 50.653$

≈ 212.07

The volume of the sphere is approximately 67.54π cm³, or 212.07 cm³.

EXERCISES

Find the volume of each figure. Round your answers to the nearest hundredth. Use 3.14 for π. (Lessons 13.1, 13.2, 13.3)

1.

12 mm

4 mm

_____

2.

34 in.

50 in.

_____

3.

10 cm

_____

4.

2.2 m

1.4 m

_____

5.

0.8 in.

11.2 in.

_____

6.

10 yd

13.3 yd

_____

7. Find the volume of a ball with a radius of 1.68 inches.

_____

8. A round above-ground swimming pool has a diameter of 15 ft and a height of 4.5 ft. What is the volume of the swimming pool?

_____

9. A paper cup in the shape of a cone has a height of 4.7 inches and a diameter of 3.6 inches. What is the volume of the paper cup?

_____

CA CC 8.G.7

The Wheel of Theodorus

The Wheel of Theodorus is named after Theodorus of Cyrene, who lived at the time of Pythagoras of the Pythagorean theorem. For this project you will draw and decorate a Wheel of Theodorus.

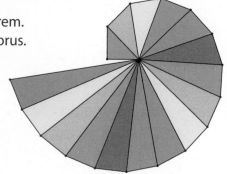

You'll need a large piece of paper, a right angle, and a ruler.

- Begin with a right triangle that has both legs 1 unit long.
- Next, draw a second right triangle so that the hypotenuse of the first triangle is one of the legs of the second triangle and the other leg is 1 unit long, as shown in the diagram.
- Draw a third right triangle beginning with the hypotenuse of the second triangle as one leg of the third triangle and a 1-unit leg as the other leg.
- Continue drawing right triangles in this manner until you have 16 triangles.
- Decorate your Wheel of Theodorus.
- Calculate the lengths of the hypotenuses of the 16 triangles.
- Write a brief report on Theodorus of Cyrene.

Use the space below to write down any questions you have or important information from your teacher.

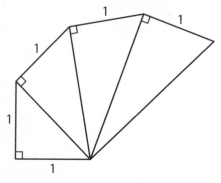

This Wheel of Theodorus shows the first four triangles.

MATH IN CAREERS | ACTIVITY

Hydrologist A hydrologist needs to determine if an underground aquifer, which is roughly cylindrical in shape, is totally filled with water. The diameter of the aquifer is 70 meters, and its depth is 9 meters. The mass of the water in it is 2.7×10^7 kilograms. One cubic meter of water has a mass of about 1000 kilograms. Is the aquifer totally filled with water? Explain how you determined your answer.

UNIT 5
MIXED REVIEW

Assessment Readiness

Personal
Math Trainer

Online Practice
and Help

my.hrw.com

1. Consider the system of equations $\begin{cases} 3x + 3y = 6 \\ 6x - y = -16 \end{cases}$.

   Will the solution method eliminate a variable from the system?

   Select Yes or No.

   A. Multiply the first equation by
   2 and subtract the equations.   ◯ Yes   ◯ No

   B. Multiply the second equation by
   3 and add the equations.   ◯ Yes   ◯ No

   C. Multiply the first equation by 6
   and the second equation by 3
   and add the equations.   ◯ Yes   ◯ No

2. Angle ABC is an exterior angle of $\angle BCD$.

   Choose True or False for each statement.

   A. m$\angle D = 40°$ ◯ True   ◯ False

   B. m$\angle ABC = 110°$ ◯ True   ◯ False

   C. m$\angle CBD = 70°$ ◯ True   ◯ False

   C
   62°
   $(3x - 10)°$ $(x + 8)°$
   A   *B*   *D*

3. A straight road connects the towns of Winridge and Upper Lansbury. On
   a map on which each unit represents 10 miles, the coordinates of Winridge
   are (8, 4) and the coordinates of Upper Lansbury are (6, 10). If Ty drives from
   Winridge to Upper Lansbury at an average speed of 40 miles per hour, will
   the trip take more than an hour? Explain your reasoning.

4. Earth has a radius of 6371 kilometers, and the Moon has a radius of
   1737 kilometers. How many times larger is Earth's volume than the Moon's
   volume? Explain how you determined the answer.

Performance Tasks

★**5.** A paper cup is shaped like a cone. The radius of the opening is 4.6 centimeters, and the slant height is 12.8 centimeters.

    a. What is the height h of the cup to the nearest tenth of a centimeter? Explain how you determined the answer.

    b. What is the volume of the cup to the nearest cubic centimeter?

★★**6.** An architect uses drafting software to draw $\triangle ABC$ to model the patio of a house.

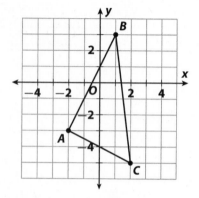

    a. Determine the exact length of each side of the triangle in the drawing.

    b. Is the triangle a right triangle? Justify your answer.

    c. The architect uses the software to determine that $\angle C$ measures 56.3°. What are the measures of the other two angles of the triangle? Explain how you determined the answers.

★★★**7.** The diagram shows how several steel beams intersect to form part of the structure of a building. In the diagram line p is parallel to line q. What is the length of the beam with endpoints at A and B? Justify each step of your work. (*Hint:* First show similar triangles.)

UNIT 6
Statistics

MODULE 14
Scatter Plots
 CA CC 8.SP.1, 8.SP.2, 8.SP.3

MODULE 15
Two-Way Tables
CA CC 8.SP.4

MATH IN CAREERS

Psychologist A psychologist investigates the physical, mental, emotional, and social aspects of human behavior. Psychologists use math to evaluate and interpret data about human activities and the human mind. They create and use mathematical models to predict behavior of humans, both individually and in groups.

If you are interested in a career in psychology, you should study the following mathematical subjects:
- Algebra
- Trigonometry
- Probability and Statistics
- Calculus

Research other careers that require the analysis of data and use of mathematical models.

ACTIVITY At the end of the unit, check out how **psychologists** use math.

Unit Project Preview

Altitude or Latitude?

The Unit Project at the end of this unit asks you to collect data on the temperatures, latitudes, and elevations of a number of American cities. You will then analyze the data to decide which, if either, has a greater effect on the temperature of a city: latitude or elevation. To successfully complete the Unit Project you'll need to master these skills:

- Draw scatter plots.
- Analyze scatter plots.
- Draw trend lines.
- Use trend lines to make predictions.

1. How does the elevation of a city—its distance above sea level—affect its temperature?

_____

_____

_____

_____

2. How does the latitude of a city—its distance north of the equator—affect its temperature?

_____

_____

_____

_____

Tracking Your Learning Progression

This unit addresses important California Common Core Standards in the Critical Area of understanding bivariate data.

Domain 8.SP Statistics and Probability

    Cluster Investigate patterns of association in bivariate data.

Scatter Plots

ESSENTIAL QUESTION

How can you use scatter plots to solve real-world problems?

Real-World Video

An anthropologist measures dinosaur bones. To estimate a dinosaur's height based on the length of a bone, he can make a scatter plot comparing bone length and height of several dinosaurs.

⏻ my.hrw.com

GO DIGITAL

my.hrw.com

my.hrw.com

Go digital with your write-in student edition, accessible on any device.

Math On the Spot

Scan with your smart phone to jump directly to the online edition, video tutor, and more.

Animated Math

Interactively explore key concepts to see how math works.

Personal Math Trainer

Get immediate feedback and help as you work through practice sets.

Are YOU Ready?

Complete these exercises to review skills you will need for this module.

Evaluate Expressions

> **EXAMPLE**   Evaluate $4x + 3$ for $x = 5$.
>
> $4x + 3 = 4(5) + 3$ Substitute the given value for x.
>
> $ = 20 + 3$ Multiply.
>
> $ = 23$ Add.

Evaluate each expression for the given value of x.

1. $6x - 5$ for $x = 4$

2. $-2x + 7$ for $x = 2$

3. $5x - 6$ for $x = 3$

_____ _____ _____

4. $0.5x + 8.4$ for $x = -1$

5. $\frac{3}{4}x - 9$ for $x = -20$

6. $1.4x + 3.5$ for $x = -4$

_____ _____ _____

Solve Two-Step Equations

> **EXAMPLE** $5x + 3 = -7$
>
> $\underline{ -3 = -3}$ Subtract 3 from both sides.
>
> $5x = -10$
>
> $\dfrac{5x}{5} = \dfrac{-10}{5}$ Divide both sides by 5.
>
> $x = -2$

Solve for x.

7. $3x + 4 = 10$

8. $5x - 11 = 34$

9. $-2x + 5 = -9$

10. $8x + 13 = -11$

_____ _____ _____ _____

11. $4x - 7 = -27$

12. $\frac{1}{2}x + 16 = 39$

13. $\frac{2}{3}x - 16 = 12$

14. $0.5x - 1.5 = -6.5$

_____ _____ _____ _____

Reading Start-Up

Visualize Vocabulary

Use the ✔ words to complete the right column of the chart.

Reviewing Slope	
Mathematical Representation	**Review Word**
$y = mx + b$	
y	
m	
x	
b	

Understand Vocabulary

Match the term on the left to the correct expression on the right.

1. cluster

2. outlier

3. trend line

A. A data point that is very different from the rest of the data in a set

B. A straight line that comes closest to the points on a scatter plot.

C. A set of closely grouped data.

Vocabulary

Review Words
  bivariate data
  (datos bivariados)
  data (datos)
✔ linear equation (ecuación lineal)
✔ slope (pendiente)
✔ slope-intercept form of an equation (forma pendiente-intersección)
✔ x-coordinate (coordenada x)
✔ y-coordinate (coordenada y)
✔ y-intercept (intersección con el eje y)

Preview Words
  cluster (agrupación)
  outlier (valor extremo)
  scatter plot (diagrama de dispersión)
  trend line (línea de tendencia)

Active Reading

Two-Panel Flip Chart Create a two-panel flip chart, to help you understand the concepts in this module. Label each flap with the title of one of the lessons in the module. As you study each lesson, write important ideas under the appropriate flap. Include any sample problems or equations that will help you remember the concepts later when you look back at your notes.

Scatter Plots

Understanding the standards and the vocabulary terms in the standards will help you know exactly what you are expected to learn in this module.

CA CC 8.SP.1

Construct and interpret scatter plots for bivariate measurement data to investigate patterns of association between two quantities. Describe patterns such as clustering, outliers, positive or negative association, linear association, and nonlinear association.

What It Means to You

You will describe how the data in a scatter plot are related.

EXAMPLE 8.SP.1

The scatter plot shows Bob's height at various ages. Describe the type(s) of association between Bob's age and his height. Explain.

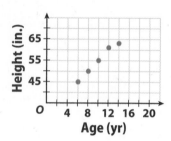

As Bob gets older, his height increases roughly along a straight line on the graph, so the association is positive and basically linear.

CA CC 8.SP.2

Know that straight lines are widely used to model relationships between two quantitative variables. For scatter plots that suggest a linear association, informally fit a straight line, and informally assess the model fit by judging the closeness of the data points to the line.

What It Means to You

You will use a trend line to show the relationship between two quantities.

EXAMPLE 8.SP.2

Joyce is training for a 10K race. For each of her training runs, she recorded the distance she ran and the time she ran. She made a scatter plot of her data and drew a trend line. Use the trend line to predict how long it would take Joyce to run 4.5 miles.

Distance (mi)	Time (min)
4	38
2	25
1	7
2	16
3	26
5	55
2	20
4	45
3	31

For a distance of 4.5 miles, the trend line shows a time of 45 minutes. So, it will take Joyce about 45 minutes to run 4.5 miles.

Scatter Plots and Association

CA CC 8.SP.1
Construct and interpret scatter plots.... Describe patterns such as clustering, outliers, positive or negative association, linear association, and nonlinear association. (For the full text of the standard, see the table at the front of the book beginning on page CA2.)

ESSENTIAL QUESTION

How can you construct and interpret scatter plots?

EXPLORE ACTIVITY 1   **CA CC** 8.SP.1

Making a Scatter Plot

Recall that a set of bivariate data involves two variables. Bivariate data are used to explore the relationship between two variables. You can graph bivariate data on a *scatter plot*. A **scatter plot** is a graph with points plotted to show the relationship between two sets of data.

The final question on a math test reads, "How many hours did you spend studying for this test?" The teacher records the number of hours each student studied and the grade the student received on the test.

Hours Spent Studying	Test Grade
0	75
0.5	80
1	80
1	85
1.5	85
1.5	95
2	90
3	100
4	90

A Make a prediction about the relationship between the number of hours spent studying and test grades.

_____

_____

_____

B Make a scatter plot. Graph hours spent studying as the independent variable and test grades as the dependent variable.

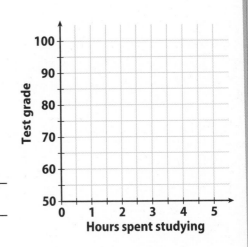

Reflect

1. What trend do you see in the data?

_____

_____

2. **Justify Reasoning** Do you think the grade associated with studying for 10 hours would follow this trend?

_____

_____

Interpreting Clusters and Outliers

A **cluster** is a set of closely grouped data. Data may cluster around a point or along a line. An **outlier** is a data point that is very different from the rest of the data in the set.

A scientist gathers information about the eruptions of Old Faithful, a geyser in Yellowstone National Park. She uses the data to create a scatter plot. The data show the length of time between eruptions (interval) and how long the eruption lasts (duration).

A Describe any clusters you see in the scatter plot.

_____

_____

B What do the clusters tell you about eruptions of Old Faithful?

_____

_____

C Describe any outliers you see in the scatter plot.

_____

_____

Math Talk
Mathematical Practices

If the point (20, 1) appeared on the scatter plot, would it be an outlier? Explain.

Reflect

3. Suppose the geyser erupts for 2.2 minutes after a 75-minute interval. Would this point lie in one of the clusters? Would it be an outlier? Explain your answer.

_____

_____

_____

4. Suppose the geyser erupts after an 80-minute interval. Give a range of possible duration times for which the point on the scatter plot would not be considered an outlier. Explain your reasoning.

_____

_____

Determining Association

Association describes how sets of data are related. A *positive* association means that both data sets increase together. A *negative* association means that as one data set increases, the other decreases. *No* association means that there is no relationship between the two data sets.

Positive association

Negative association

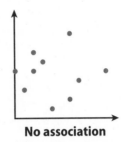
No association

Data that show a positive or negative association and lie basically along a line exhibit a *linear* association. Data that show a positive or negative association but do not lie basically along a line exhibit a *nonlinear* association.

EXAMPLE 1

CA CC 8.SP.1

Susan asked 20 people if they would buy a new product she developed at each of several prices. The scatter plot shows how many of the 20 said "yes" at a given price. Describe the association between price and the number of buyers.

As price increases, the number of buyers decreases. So, there is a negative association. Because the data points do not lie along a line, the association is nonlinear.

Animated Math
my.hrw.com

Reflect

5. **What If?** Based on the association shown in the scatter plot, what might happen if Susan increased the price to $14?

_____

YOUR TURN

6. The plot shows the reading level and height for 16 students in a district. Describe the association and give a possible reason for it.

_____

_____

_____

Personal Math Trainer
Online Practice and Help
my.hrw.com

Bob recorded his height at different ages. The table below shows his data.

Age (years)	6	8	10	12	14
Height (inches)	45	50	55	61	63

1. Make a scatter plot of Bob's data. (Explore Activity 1)

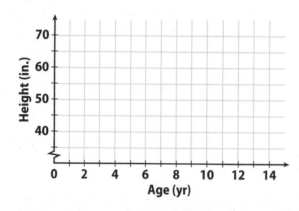

2. Describe the association between Bob's age and his height. Explain the association. (Example 1)

_____

_____

_____

3. The scatter plot shows the basketball shooting results for 14 players. Describe any clusters you see in the scatter plot. Identify any outliers. (Explore Activity 2)

_____

_____

_____

Basketball Shooting

? **ESSENTIAL QUESTION CHECK-IN**

4. Explain how you can make a scatter plot from a set of bivariate data.

_____

_____

_____

_____

14.1 Independent Practice

CA CC 8.SP.1

Personal Math Trainer

Online Practice and Help

my.hrw.com

Sports Use the scatter plot for 5–8.

Olympic Men's Long Jump Winning Distances

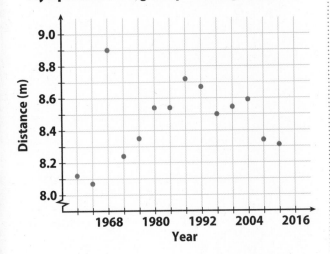

5. Describe the association between the year and the distance jumped for the years 1960 to 1988.

_____

_____

_____

_____

6. Describe the association between the year and the distance jumped for the years after 1988.

_____

_____

_____

_____

_____

7. For the entire scatter plot, is the association between the year and the distance jumped linear or nonlinear?

_____

_____

_____

_____

_____

8. Identify the outlier and interpret its meaning.

_____

_____

_____

_____

_____

9. **Communicate Mathematical Ideas** Compare a scatter plot that shows no association to one that shows negative association.

_____

_____

_____

_____

_____

_____

For 10–11, describe a set of real-world bivariate data that the given scatter plot could represent. Define the variable represented on each axis.

10.

_____

_____

_____

11.

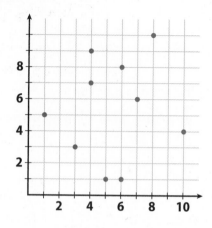

_____

_____

_____

H.O.T. FOCUS ON HIGHER ORDER THINKING

Work Area

12. **Multiple Representations** Describe what you might see in a table of bivariate data that would lead you to conclude that the scatter plot of the data would show a cluster.

_____

_____

13. **Justify Reasoning** Is it possible for a scatter plot to have a positive or negative association that is not linear? Explain.

_____

_____

_____

14. **Critical Thinking** To try to increase profits, a theater owner increases the price of a ticket by $25 every month. Describe what a scatter plot might look like if x represents the number of months and y represents the profits. Explain your reasoning.

_____

_____

_____

_____

_____

LESSON 14.2

Trend Lines and Predictions

CA CC 8.SP.3

Use the equation of a linear model to solve problems in the context of bivariate measurement data, interpreting the slope and intercept. *Also 8.SP.1, 8.SP.2*

ESSENTIAL QUESTION

How can you use a trend line to make a prediction from a scatter plot?

EXPLORE ACTIVITY 1 **CA CC** 8.SP.2, 8.SP.1

Drawing a Trend Line

When a scatter plot shows a linear association, you can use a line to model the relationship between the variables. A **trend line** is a straight line that comes closest to the points on a scatter plot.

Joyce is training for a 10K race. For some of her training runs, she records the distance she ran and how many minutes she ran.

A Make a scatter plot of Joyce's running data.

Distance (mi)	Time (min)
4	38
2	25
1	7
2	16
3	26
5	55
2	20
4	45
3	31

B To draw a trend line, use a straight edge to draw a line that has about the same number of points above and below it. Ignore any outliers.

C Use your trend line to predict how long it would take Joyce to run 4.5 miles.

_____

Reflect

1. How well does your trend line fit the data? Explain.

_____

_____

2. Do you think you can use a scatter plot that shows no association to make a prediction? Explain your answer.

_____

_____

Math On the Spot

⏻ my.hrw.com

Finding the Equation of a Trend Line

You can use two points on a trend line to write an equation in slope-intercept form for the trend line.

EXAMPLE 1 *Real World*

CA CC 8.SP.3

The scatter plot and trend line show the relationship between the number of chapters and the total number of pages for several books. Write an equation for the trend line.

STEP 1 Find the slope of the trend line. The line passes through points (5, 50) and (17, 170).

$$m = \frac{y_2 - y_1}{x_2 - x_1}$$ Use the slope formula.

$$m = \frac{170 - 50}{17 - 5}$$ Substitute (5, 50) for (x_1, y_1) and (17, 170) for (x_2, y_2).

$$m = \frac{120}{12} = 10$$ Simplify.

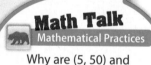

Math Talk
Mathematical Practices

Why are (5, 50) and (17, 170) the best points to use to draw the trend line?

STEP 2 Find the *y*-intercept of the trend line.

$$y = mx + b$$ Slope-intercept form

$$50 = 10 \cdot 5 + b$$ Substitute 50 for y, 10 for m, and 5 for x.

$$50 = 50 + b$$ Simplify.

$$50 - 50 = 50 - 50 + b$$ Subtract 50 from both sides.

$$0 = b$$ Simplify.

STEP 3 Use your slope and *y*-intercept values to write the equation.

$$y = mx + b$$ Slope-intercept form

$$y = 10x + 0$$ Substitute 10 for m and 0 for y.

The equation for the trend line is $y = 10x$.

Reflect

3. What type(s) of association does the scatter plot show?

_____

4. What is the meaning of the slope in this situation?

_____

5. What is the meaning of the *y*-intercept in this situation?

_____

YOUR TURN

6. The scatter plot and trend line show the relationship between the number of rainy days in a month and the number of umbrellas sold each month. Write an equation for the trend line.

_____

_____

Number of rainy days

Personal Math Trainer

Online Practice and Help

⏻ my.hrw.com

EXPLORE ACTIVITY 2 *Real World*   🐻 **CA CC** 8.SP.3

Making Predictions

When you use a trend line or its equation to predict a value between data points that you already know, you *interpolate* the predicted value. When you make a prediction that is outside the data that you know, you *extrapolate* the predicted value.

Use the equation of the trend line in Example 1 to predict how many pages would be in a book with 26 chapters.

Is this prediction an example of interpolation or extrapolation? _____

$y =$ ▢   Write the equation for your trend line.

$y =$ ▢   Substitute the number of chapters for x.

$y =$ ▢   Simplify.

I predict that a book with 26 chapters will have _____ pages.

Reflect

7. **Make a Prediction** Predict how many pages would be in a book with 14 chapters. Is this prediction an example of interpolation or extrapolation?

_____

8. Do you think that extrapolation or interpolation is more accurate? Explain.

_____

_____

_____

Guided Practice

Angela recorded the price of different weights of several bulk grains. She made a scatter plot of her data. Use the scatter plot for 1–4.

1. Draw a trend line for the scatter plot. (Explore Activity 1)

2. How do you know whether your trend line is a good fit for the data? (Explore Activity 1)

_____

_____

_____

3. Write an equation for your trend line. (Example 1) _____

4. Use the equation for your trend line to interpolate the price of 7 ounces and extrapolate the price of 50 ounces.

(Explore Activity 2) _____

? ESSENTIAL QUESTION CHECK-IN

5. A trend line passes through two points on a scatter plot. How can you use the trend line to make a prediction between or outside the given data points?

_____

_____

_____

14.2 Independent Practice

CA CC 8.SP.1, 8.SP.2, 8.SP.3

Personal
Math Trainer

Online Practice
and Help

my.hrw.com

Use the data in the table for Exercises 6–10.

Apparent Temperature Due to Wind at 15 °F						
Wind speed (mi/h)	10	20	30	40	50	60
Wind chill (°F)	2.7	−2.3	−5.5	−7.9	−9.8	−11.4

**Apparent Temperature
Due to Wind at 15 °F**

Wind speed (mi/h)

6. Make a scatter plot of the data and draw a trend line.

7. What type of association does the trend line show?

_____

8. Write an equation for your trend line. _____

9. **Make a Prediction** Use the trend line to predict the wind chill at these wind speeds.

   a. 36 mi/h _____ **b.** 100 mi/h _____

10. What is the meaning of the slope of the line?

_____

_____

Use the data in the table for Exercises 11–14.

Apparent Temperature Due to Humidity at a Room Temperature of 72 °F						
Humidity (%)	0	20	40	60	80	100
Apparent temperature (°F)	64	67	70	72	74	76

**Apparent Temperature at a
Room Temperature of 72 °F**

Humidity (%)

11. Make a scatter plot of the data and draw a trend line.

12. Write an equation for your trend line.

_____

13. **Make a Prediction** Use the trend line to predict the apparent

    temperature at 70% humidity. _____

14. What is the meaning of the y-intercept of the line?

_____

15. Communicate Mathematical Ideas Is it possible to draw a trend line on a scatter plot that shows no association? Explain.

_____

_____

_____

16. Critique Reasoning Sam drew a trend line that had about the same number of data points above it as below it, but did not pass through any data points. He then picked two data points to write the equation for the line. Is this a correct way to write the equation? Explain.

_____

_____

_____

_____

17. Marlene wanted to find a relationship between the areas and populations of counties in Texas. She plotted x (area in square miles) and y (population) for two counties on a scatter plot:

Kent County (903, 808)   Edwards County (2118, 2002)

She concluded that the population of Texas counties is approximately equal to their area in square miles and drew a trend line through her points.

a. Critique Reasoning Do you agree with Marlene's method of creating a scatter plot and a trend line? Explain why or why not.

_____

_____

_____

b. Counterexamples Harris County has an area of 1778 square miles and a population of about 4.3 million people. Dallas County has an area of 908 square miles and a population of about 2.5 million people. What does this data show about Marlene's conjecture that the population of Texas counties is approximately equal to their area?

_____

_____

_____

_____

Ready to Go On?

14.1 Scatter Plots and Association

An auto store is having a sale on motor oil. The chart shows the price per quart as the number of quarts purchased increases. Use the data for Exs. 1–2.

Number of quarts	1	2	3	4	5	6
Price per quart ($)	2	1.50	1.25	1.10	1	0.95

1. Use the given data to make a scatter plot.

2. Describe the association you see between the number of quarts purchased and the price per quart. Explain.

_____

_____

_____

14.2 Trend Lines and Predictions

The scatter plot below shows data comparing wind speed and wind chill for an air temperature of 20°F. Use the scatter plot for Exs. 3–5.

3. Draw a trend line for the scatter plot.

4. Write an equation for your trend line.

_____

5. Use your equation to predict the wind chill to the nearest degree for a wind speed of 60 mi/h.

_____

Wind Chill for 20°F

ESSENTIAL QUESTION

6. How can you use scatter plots to solve real-world problems?

_____

_____

MODULE 14
MIXED REVIEW

Assessment Readiness

Personal
Math Trainer

Online Practice
and Help

my.hrw.com

CALIFORNIA

1. Consider the equation of each function. Is the function a linear function?

   Select Yes or No for A–C.

   A. $y = \frac{8}{x}$ ○ Yes ○ No

   B. $y = x - 5$ ○ Yes ○ No

   C. $y = -4x + 1$ ○ Yes ○ No

2. The scatter plot shows the relationship between the sizes and costs of the televisions at an appliance store.

   Choose True or False for each statement.

   A. There is a cluster of data points near (55, 650).

   ○ True ○ False

   B. The point at (50, 1000) appears to be an outlier.

   ○ True ○ False

   C. There is a positive association between size and price.

   ○ True ○ False

3. Draw a trend line on the scatter plot from Item 2. How well does your trend line fit the data? Explain.

4. The scatter plot shows the relationship between the number of laps Claudia swims and the time needed to swim those laps. Write the equation of the trend line, and explain what the slope of the trend line represents in this situation.

Two-Way Tables

LESSON 15.1

Two-Way Frequency Tables

 CA CC 8.SP.4

LESSON 15.2

Two-Way Relative Frequency Tables

CA CC 8.SP.4

ESSENTIAL QUESTION

How can you use two-way frequency tables to solve real-world problems?

Real-World Video

Two-way tables can help identify and compare probabilities for non-numerical data, such as the probability that girls will like one of two sports teams more than boys will.

my.hrw.com

GO DIGITAL

my.hrw.com

my.hrw.com

Go digital with your write-in student edition, accessible on any device.

Math On the Spot

Scan with your smart phone to jump directly to the online edition, video tutor, and more.

Animated Math

Interactively explore key concepts to see how math works.

Personal Math Trainer

Get immediate feedback and help as you work through practice sets.

Are YOU Ready?

Complete these exercises to review skills you will need for this module.

Personal Math Trainer

Online Practice and Help

my.hrw.com

Simplify Fractions

EXAMPLE   Simplify $\frac{18}{30}$.

$$\frac{1, 2, 3, 6, 9, 18}{1, 2, 3, 5, 6, 10, 30}$$

$$\frac{18 \div 6}{30 \div 6} = \frac{3}{5}$$

List all the factors of the numerator and denominator.

Find the greatest common factor (GCF). Divide the numerator and denominator by the GCF.

Write each fraction in simplest form.

1. $\frac{25}{30}$ _____   **2.** $\frac{27}{36}$ _____   **3.** $\frac{14}{16}$ _____   **4.** $\frac{15}{45}$ _____

5. $\frac{27}{63}$ _____   **6.** $\frac{45}{75}$ _____   **7.** $\frac{8}{27}$ _____   **8.** $\frac{16}{28}$ _____

Fractions, Decimals, Percents

EXAMPLE   Write $\frac{13}{20}$ as a decimal and a percent.

$$
\begin{array}{r}
0.65 \\
20\overline{)13.00} \\
12\ 0 \\
\hline
100 \\
-100 \\
\hline
0
\end{array}
$$

$0.65 = 65\%$

Write the fraction as a division problem. Write a decimal point and zeros in the dividend.

Place a decimal point in the quotient.

Write the decimal as a percent.

Write each fraction as a decimal and a percent.

9. $\frac{7}{8}$ _____   **10.** $\frac{4}{5}$ _____   **11.** $\frac{5}{4}$ _____

12. $\frac{3}{10}$ _____   **13.** $\frac{19}{20}$ _____   **14.** $\frac{7}{25}$ _____

Find the Percent of a Number

EXAMPLE   6.5% of 24 = ?

$6.5\% = 0.065$

$$
\begin{array}{r}
24 \\
\times\, 0.065 \\
\hline
1.560
\end{array}
$$

Write the percent as a decimal.

Multiply.

Find each percent of a number.

15. 4% of 40 _____   **16.** 7% of 300 _____   **17.** 4.3% of 1,200 _____

18. 2.9% of 780 _____   **19.** 1.6% of 75.20 _____   **20.** 3.56% of 3,200 _____

Reading Start-Up

Visualize Vocabulary

Use the ✔ words to complete the chart.

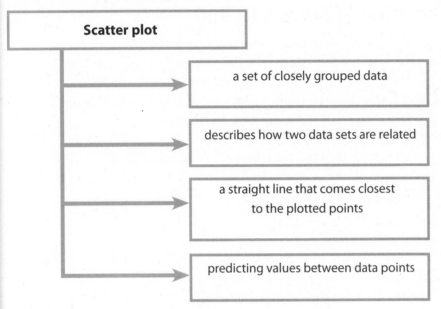

Scatter plot

→ a set of closely grouped data

→ describes how two data sets are related

→ a straight line that comes closest to the plotted points

→ predicting values between data points

Understand Vocabulary

Complete the sentences using preview words.

1. The _____ is the number of times an event occurs.

2. A _____ shows the frequencies of data that is categorized two ways.

3. _____ is the ratio of the number of times an event occurs to the total number of events.

Vocabulary

Review Words
- ✔ association *(asociación)*
- ✔ cluster *(grupo)*
- data *(datos)*
- ✔ interpolation *(interpolación)*
- extrapolation *(extrapolación)*
- outlier *(parte aislada)*
- scatter plot *(gráfico de dispersión)*
- ✔ trend line *(la línea de tendencia)*

Preview Words
- conditional relative frequency *(frecuencia relativa condicional)*
- frequency *(frecuencia)*
- joint relative frequency *(frecuencia relativa conjunta)*
- marginal relative frequency *(frecuencia relativa marginal)*
- relative frequency *(frecuencia relativa)*
- two-way table *(de dos vías mesa)*
- two-way relative frequency table *(dos vías tabla de frecuencias relativas)*

Active Reading

Tri-Fold Before beginning the module, create a tri-fold to help you learn the concepts and vocabulary in this module. Fold the paper into three sections. Label the columns "What I Know," "What I Want to Know," and "What I Learned." Complete the first two columns before you read. After studying the module, complete the third column.

GETTING READY FOR

Two-Way Tables

Understanding the standards and the vocabulary terms in the standards will help you know exactly what you are expected to learn in this module.

CA CC 8.SP.4

Understand that patterns of association can also be seen in bivariate categorical data by displaying frequencies and relative frequencies in a two-way table. Construct and interpret a two-way table summarizing data on two categorical variables collected from the same subjects.

Key Vocabulary

two-way table *(tabla de doble entrada)* A table that shows the frequencies of data categorized in two ways.

CA CC 8.SP.4

Understand ... frequencies and relative frequencies in a two-way table. Construct and interpret a two-way table .... Use relative frequencies calculated for rows or columns to describe possible association between the two variables.

Key Vocabulary

conditional relative frequency *(frecuencia relativa condicional)* The ratio of a joint relative frequency to a related marginal relative frequency in a two-way table.

What It Means to You

You will use two-way tables to find relative frequencies.

EXAMPLE 8.SP.4

Soojinn counted the vehicles in the school parking lot and recorded the data in the two-way table shown.

	During School Day	**After School Day**	**Total**
Cars	36	14	50
Trucks	19	6	25
Total	55	20	75

What percent of the vehicles parked after school were trucks?

$$\frac{\text{trucks after school}}{\text{total vehicles after school}} = \frac{6}{20} = 0.3, \text{ or } 30\%$$

30% of the vehicles in the school parking lot after school were trucks.

What It Means to You

You will use two-way tables to find conditional relative frequencies.

EXAMPLE 8.SP.4

Soojinn determined the gender of the driver for each of the 55 vehicles parked in the school parking lot during the day.

	Male	**Female**	**Total**
Cars	8	25	33
Trucks	15	7	22
Total	23	32	55

What is the conditional relative frequency that a driver is female given that the vehicle is a car?

$$\frac{\text{female car drivers}}{\text{total cars}} = \frac{25}{33} \approx 0.758, \text{ or about } 76\%$$

There is a 76% likelihood that a driver is female given that the vehicle is a car.

CA CC 8.SP.4

Understand that patterns ... can be seen in bivariate categorical data by displaying frequencies in a two-way table. Construct and interpret a two-way table .... Use relative frequencies ... to describe possible association .... (For the full text of the standard, see the table at the front of the book beginning on page CA2.)

ESSENTIAL QUESTION

How can you construct and interpret two-way frequency tables?

EXPLORE ACTIVITY   CA CC 8.SP.4

Making a Two-Way Table

The **frequency** is the number of times an event occurs. A **two-way table** shows the frequencies of data that is categorized two ways. The rows indicate one categorization and the columns indicate another.

A poll of 120 town residents found that 40% own a bike. Of those who own a bike, 75% shop at the farmer's market. Of those who do not own a bike, 25% shop at the farmer's market.

	Farmer's Market	No Farmer's Market	TOTAL
Bike			
No Bike			
TOTAL			

A Start in the bottom right cell of the table. Enter the total number of people polled.

B **Fill in the right column.** 40% of 120 people polled own a bike.

The remaining people polled do not own a bike.

C **Fill in the top row.** 75% of those who own a bike also shop at the market.

The remaining bike owners do not shop at the market.

D **Fill in the second row.** 25% of those who do not own a bike shop at the market.

The remaining people without bikes do not shop at the market.

E **Fill in the last row.** In each column, add the numbers in the first two rows to find the total number of people who shop at the farmer's market and who do not shop at the farmer's market.

Reflect

1. How can you check that your table is completed correctly?

_____

_____

Math On the Spot

 my.hrw.com

Animated Math

 my.hrw.com

Deciding Whether There Is an Association

Relative frequency is the ratio of the number of times an event occurs to the total number of events. In the Explore Activity, the relative frequency of bike owners who shop at the farmer's market is $\frac{36}{120} = 0.30 = 30\%$. You can use relative frequencies to decide if there is an association between two variables or events.

EXAMPLE 1 **CA CC** 8.SP.4

Determine whether there is an association between the events.

A One hundred teens were polled about whether they are required to do chores and whether they have a curfew. Is there an association between having a curfew and having to do chores?

	Curfew	No Curfew	TOTAL
Chores	16	4	20
No Chores	16	64	80
TOTAL	32	68	100

Math Talk

Mathematical Practices

What is the difference between frequency and relative frequency?

STEP 1 **Find the relative frequency of having to do chores.**

Total who have to do chores → $\frac{20}{100} = 0.20 = 20\%$
Total number of teens polled →

STEP 2 **Find the relative frequency of having to do chores among those who have a curfew.**

Number with a curfew who have chores → $\frac{16}{32} = 0.50 = 50\%$
Total number with a curfew →

STEP 3 **Compare the relative frequencies.** Students who have a curfew are more likely to have to do chores than the general population. There is an association. The relative frequencies show that students who have a curfew are more likely to have to do chores than the general population of teens polled in the survey.

B Data from 200 flights were collected. The flights were categorized as domestic or international and late or not late. Is there an association between international flights and a flight being late?

	Late	Not Late	TOTAL
Domestic	30	120	150
International	10	40	50
TOTAL	40	160	200

 STEP 1 **Find the relative frequency of a flight being late.**

Total flights that are late → $\dfrac{40}{200} = 0.20 = 20\%$
Total number of flights →

 STEP 2 **Find the relative frequency of a flight being late among international flights.**

Number of international flights that are late → $\dfrac{10}{50} = 0.20 = 20\%$
Total number of international flights →

 STEP 3 **Compare the relative frequencies.** International flights are no more likely to be late than flights in general. There is no association. The relative frequencies show that international flights are just as likely to be late as any other flight.

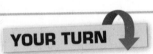

2. Data from 200 middle school and high school students were collected. Students were asked whether or not they had visited at least one national park. Is there an association between being a high school student and visiting a national park? Explain.

	Have Visited a National Park	Have NOT Visited a National Park	TOTAL
Middle School	25	55	80
High School	80	40	120
TOTAL	105	95	200

_____

_____

_____

_____

_____

Personal Math Trainer

Online Practice and Help

my.hrw.com

1. In a survey of 50 students, 60% said that they have a cat. Of the students who have a cat, 70% also have a dog. Of the students who do not have a cat, 75% have a dog. Complete the two-way table. (Explore Activity)

	Dog	No Dog	TOTAL
Cat			
No Cat			
TOTAL			

   a. Enter the total number of students surveyed in the bottom right cell of the table.

   b. Fill in right column.

   c. Fill in top row.

   d. Fill in second row.

   e. Fill in last row.

2. The results of a survey at a school are shown. Is there an association between being a boy and being left-handed? Explain. (Example 1)

	Left-handed	Right-handed	TOTAL
Boys	14	126	140
Girls	10	90	100
TOTAL	24	216	240

_____

_____

_____

? ESSENTIAL QUESTION CHECK-IN

3. Voters were polled to see whether they supported Smith or Jones. Can you construct a two-way table of the results? Why or why not?

_____

_____

_____

15.1 Independent Practice

 CA CC 8.SP.4

Personal Math Trainer

Online Practice and Help

my.hrw.com

4. **Represent Real-World Problems** One hundred forty students were asked about their language classes. Out of 111 who take French, only 31 do not take Spanish. Twelve take neither French nor Spanish. Use this information to make a two-way table.

	Take French	Do NOT Take French	TOTAL
Take Spanish			
Do NOT Take Spanish			
TOTAL			

5. **Represent Real-World Problems** Seventh- and eighth-grade students were asked whether they preferred science or math.

a. Complete the two-way table.

	Prefer Science	Prefer Math	TOTAL
Seventh Grade		72	96
Eighth Grade	32		
TOTAL			176

b. Is there an association between being in eighth grade and preferring math? Explain.

_____

_____

_____

_____

6. **Persevere in Problem Solving** The table gives partial information on the number of men and women who play in the four sections of the Metro Orchestra.

a. Complete the table.

	Strings	Brass	Woodwinds	Percussion	TOTAL
Men	13	7		5	33
Women			10		
TOTAL	55			9	98

b. Is there an association between being a woman and playing strings? Explain.

_____

_____

_____

 FOCUS ON HIGHER ORDER THINKING

7. Multi-Step The two-way table below shows the results of a survey of Florida teenagers who were asked whether they preferred surfing or snorkeling.

a. To the right of the number in each cell, write the relative frequency of the number compared to the total for the *row* the number is in. Round to the nearest percent.

	Prefer Surfing	Prefer Snorkeling	TOTAL
Ages 13–15	52 _____ ; _____	78 _____ ; _____	130 100%
Ages 16–18	52 _____ ; _____	28 _____ ; _____	80 _____
TOTAL	104 _____ ; _____	106 _____ ; _____	210 _____

b. Explain the meaning of the relative frequency you wrote beside 28.

_____

_____

_____

c. To the right of each number you wrote in part a, write the relative frequency of each number compared to the total for the *column* the number is in. Are the relative frequencies the same? Why or why not?

_____

_____

_____

d. Explain the meaning of the relative frequency you wrote beside 28.

_____

_____

_____

LESSON
15.2 Two-Way Relative Frequency Tables

 CA CC 8.SP.4

Understand that patterns . . . can be seen in bivariate categorical data by displaying frequencies in a two-way table. Construct and interpret a two-way table . . . . Use relative frequencies calculated for rows or columns to describe possible association . . . . (For the full text of the standard, see the table at the front of the book beginning on page CA2.)

ESSENTIAL QUESTION

How can categorical data be organized and analyzed?

EXPLORE ACTIVITY 1 **CA CC** 8.SP.4

Creating a Relative Frequency Table

The frequency table below shows the results of a survey that Maria took at her school. She asked 50 randomly selected students whether they preferred dogs, cats, or other pets. Convert this table to a *relative frequency* table that uses decimals as well as one that uses percents.

Preferred Pet	Dog	Cat	Other	TOTAL
Frequency	22	15	13	50

A Divide the numbers in the frequency table by the total to obtain relative frequencies as decimals. Record the results in the table below.

Preferred Pet	Dog	Cat	Other	TOTAL
Relative Frequency	$\frac{22}{50} = 0.44$			

B Write the decimals as percents in the table below.

Preferred Pet	Dog	Cat	Other	TOTAL
Relative Frequency	44%			

Reflect

1. How can you check that you have correctly converted frequencies to relative frequencies?

_____

_____

2. Explain why the number in the Total column of a relative frequency table is always 1 or 100%.

_____

_____

Lesson 15.2 **459**

Creating a Two-Way Frequency Table

In the previous Explore Activity, the categorical variable was pet preference, and the variable had three possible data values: dog, cat, and other. The frequency table listed the frequency for each value of that single variable. If you have two categorical variables whose values have been paired, you list the frequencies of the paired values in a **two-way frequency table.**

For her survey, Maria also recorded the gender of each student. The results are shown in the two-way frequency table below. Each entry is the frequency of students who prefer a certain pet *and* are a certain gender. For instance, ten girls prefer dogs as pets. Complete the table.

Preferred Pet / Gender	Dog	Cat	Other	TOTAL
Girl	10	9	3	
Boy	12	6	10	
TOTAL				

A Find the total for each gender by adding the frequencies in each row.

B Find the total for each pet by adding the frequencies in each column.

C Find the grand total, which is the sum of the row totals as well as the sum of the column totals. Write this in the lower-right corner.

Reflect

3. Where have you seen the numbers in the Total row before?

_____

_____

4. In terms of Maria's survey, what does the grand total represent?

_____

5. What does the number 28 in the last column represent?

_____

6. What does the number 9 represent in the frequency table?

_____

Two-Way Relative Frequency Tables

You can obtain *relative* frequencies from a two-way frequency table:

- A **joint relative frequency** is found by dividing a frequency that is not in the Total row or the Total column by the grand total.
- A **marginal relative frequency** is found by dividing a row total or a column total by the grand total.
- A **two-way relative frequency table** displays both joint relative frequencies and marginal relative frequencies.

Math Talk
Mathematical Practices

What is the relationship between joint relative frequency and marginal relative frequency?

Create a two-way relative frequency table for Maria's data.

A Divide each number in the two-way frequency table from the previous Explore Activity by the grand total. Write the quotients as decimals.

Preferred Pet / Gender	Dog	Cat	Other	TOTAL
Girl	$\frac{10}{50} = 0.2$	$\frac{9}{50} = 0.18$	$\frac{3}{50} = 0.06$	$\frac{22}{50} = 0.44$
Boy	$\frac{12}{50} = 0.24$			
TOTAL	$\frac{22}{50} = 0.44$			$\frac{50}{50} = 1$

B Check by adding the joint relative frequencies in a row or column to see if the sum equals that row's or column's marginal relative frequency.

Boy row: $0.24 +$ _____ $+$ _____ $=$ _____

Cat column: $0.18 +$ _____ $=$ _____

Other column: $0.06 +$ _____ $=$ _____

Reflect

7. A joint relative frequency tells you what portion of the entire data set falls into the intersection of a column and a row. What is the joint relative frequency of students surveyed who are boys and prefer cats as pets?

_____

8. A marginal relative frequency tells you what portion of the entire data set represents just one column or row. What is the marginal relative frequency of students surveyed who are boys?

_____

Calculating Conditional Relative Frequencies

One other type of relative frequency that you can obtain from a two-way frequency table is a *conditional relative frequency*. A **conditional relative frequency** is found by dividing a frequency that is not in the Total row or the Total column by the frequency's row total or column total.

EXAMPLE 1

 CA CC 8.SP.4

From Maria's two-way frequency table you know that 22 students are girls and 15 students prefer cats. You also know that 9 students are girls who prefer cats. Use this to find each conditional relative frequency.

Ⓐ Find the conditional relative frequency that a student surveyed prefers cats as pets, given that the student is a girl.

Divide the number of girls who prefer cats by the number of girls. Express your answer as a decimal and as a percent.

$\frac{9}{22} = 0.409$, or 40.9%

Ⓑ Find the conditional relative frequency that a student surveyed is a girl, given that the student prefers cats as pets.

Divide the number of girls who prefer cats by the number of students who prefer cats. Express your answer as a decimal and as a percent.

$\frac{9}{15} = 0.6$, or 60%

Reflect

9. When calculating a conditional relative frequency, why do you divide by a row total or a column total and not by the grand total?

_____

_____

_____

_____

YOUR TURN

10. You can obtain conditional relative frequencies from a two-way relative frequency table. Find the conditional relative frequency that a student prefers cats as pets, given that the student is a girl.

_____

Finding Possible Associations Between Variables

You can use conditional relative frequency to see if there is an association between two variables.

EXAMPLE 2   CA CC 8.SP.4

Maria conducted a survey that asked the question "For students at my school, is there a gender-specific difference in pet preference?" If there is no gender-specific difference, then the distribution of gender within each subgroup of pet preference should roughly equal the distribution of gender within the whole group. Use the results of Maria's survey to investigate possible differences in pet preference between genders.

STEP 1 Identify the percent of all students surveyed who are girls: 44%

STEP 2 Determine each conditional relative frequency.

Of the 22 students who prefer dogs as pets, 10 are girls.
Percent who are girls, given a preference for dogs as pets: 45%

Of the 15 students who prefer cats as pets, 9 are girls.
Percent who are girls, given a preference for cats as pets: 60%

Of the 13 students who prefer other pets. 3 are girls.
Percent who are girls, given a preference for other pets: 23%

STEP 3 Interpret the results by comparing each conditional relative frequency to the percent of all students surveyed who are girls.

The percent of girls among students who prefer dogs is close to 44%, so there does not appear to be a gender-specific preference for dogs.

The percent of girls among students who prefer cats is much greater than 44%, so girls are more likely than boys to prefer cats.

The percent of girls among students who prefer other pets is much less than 44%, so girls are less likely than boys to prefer other pets.

YOUR TURN

11. Suppose you analyzed the data by focusing on boys rather than girls. How would the percent in Step 1 change? How would the percents in Step 2 change? How would the conclusions in Step 3 change?

_____

_____

_____

Guided Practice

1. In a class survey, students were asked to choose their favorite vacation destination. The results are displayed by gender in the two-way frequency table. (Explore Activities 1–3)

Vacation Spot / Gender	Seashore	Mountains	Other	TOTAL
Girl	7	3	2	
Boy	5	2	6	
TOTAL				

a. Find the total for each gender by adding the frequencies in each row. Write the row totals in the Total column.

b. Find the total for each preferred vacation spot by adding the frequencies in each column. Write the column totals in the Total row.

c. Write the grand total (the sum of the row totals or the column totals) in the lower-right corner of the table.

d. Create a two-way relative frequency table by dividing each number in the above table by the grand total. Write the quotients as decimals.

Vacation Spot / Gender	Seashore	Mountains	Other	TOTAL
Girl				
Boy				
TOTAL				

e. Use the table to find the joint relative frequency of students surveyed who are boys and who prefer vacationing in the mountains. _____

f. Use the table to find the marginal relative frequency of students surveyed who prefer vacationing at the seashore. _____

g. Find the conditional relative frequency that a student surveyed prefers vacationing in the mountains, given that the student is a girl.

Interpret this result. (Examples 1–2) _____

_____

ESSENTIAL QUESTION CHECK-IN

2. How can you use a two-way frequency table to learn more about its data?

_____

_____

Name _____ Class _____ Date _____

15.2 Independent Practice

CA CC 8.SP.4

Personal Math Trainer

Online Practice and Help

my.hrw.com

Stefan surveyed 75 of his classmates about their participation in school activities as well as whether they have a part-time job. The results are shown in the two-way frequency table. Use the table for Exercises 3–6.

Job \ Activity	Clubs Only	Sports Only	Both	Neither	TOTAL
Yes		12		9	51
No	5		10		
TOTAL	15	18			75

3. a. Complete the table.

  b. Explain how you found the correct data to enter in the table.

  _____

  _____

  _____

  _____

4. Create a two-way relative frequency table using decimals. Round to the nearest hundredth.

Job \ Activity	Clubs Only	Sports Only	Both	Neither	TOTAL
Yes					
No					
TOTAL					

5. Give each relative frequency as a percent.

  a. the joint relative frequency of students surveyed who participate in

  school clubs only and have part-time jobs _____

  b. the marginal frequency of students surveyed who do not have a

  part-time job _____

  c. the conditional relative frequency that a student surveyed participates in both school clubs and sports, given that the student

  has a part-time job _____

6. Discuss possible associations between having a part-time job and participation in school activities. Support your response with an analysis of the data.

_____

_____

_____

_____

The head of quality control for a chair manufacturer collected data on the quality of two types of wood that the company grows on its tree farm. The table shows the acceptance and rejection data. Use the table for Exercises 7 and 8.

Accept/Reject Wood	Accepted	Rejected	TOTAL
White Oak	245	105	350
Redwood	140	110	250
TOTAL	385	215	600

Work Area

7. Critique Reasoning To create a two-way relative frequency table for this data, the head of quality control divided each number in each row by the row total. Is this correct? Explain.

Accept/Reject Wood	Accepted	Rejected	TOTAL
White Oak	0.7	0.3	1
Redwood	0.56	0.44	1
TOTAL	0.64	0.36	1

_____

_____

8. Draw Conclusions Are any of the data the head of quality control entered into the two-way relative frequency table correct? If so, which is and which isn't? Explain.

_____

_____

_____

_____

Ready to Go On?

Personal
Math Trainer

Online Practice
and Help

my.hrw.com

15.1 Two-Way Frequency Tables

Martin collected data from students about whether they played a musical instrument. The table shows his results. Use the table for Exercises 1–4.

	Instrument	No Instrument	TOTAL
Boys	42	70	112
Girls	48		88
Total	90	110	200

1. Of the students surveyed, how many played an instrument? _____

2. How many girls surveyed did NOT play an instrument? _____

3. What is the relative frequency of a student playing an instrument? Write the answer as a percent. _____

4. What is the relative frequency of playing an instrument among boys? Write the answer as a decimal. _____

15.2 Two-Way Relative Frequency Tables

Students were asked how they traveled to school. The two-way relative frequency table shows the results. Use the table for Exercises 5–7. Write answers as decimals rounded to the nearest hundredth.

	Method			
School	Car	Bus	Other	TOTAL
Middle School	0.18	0.14	0.10	0.42
High School	0.38	0.12	0.08	0.58
TOTAL	0.56	0.26	0.18	1.00

5. What is the joint relative frequency of high school students who ride the bus? _____

6. What is the marginal relative frequency of students surveyed who are in middle school? _____

7. What is the conditional relative frequency that a student rides the bus, given that the student is in middle school? _____

? ESSENTIAL QUESTION

8. How can you use two-way tables to solve real-world problems?

_____

_____

MODULE 15
MIXED REVIEW

Assessment Readiness

Personal Math Trainer

Online Practice and Help

my.hrw.com

1. Which expression(s) below are equivalent to 3^6? Select all that apply.

○ $3^2 \cdot 3^3$ ○ $\dfrac{3^8}{3^2}$

○ $(3^3)^3$ ○ $3^7 \cdot 3^{-1}$

Kathy asked 80 randomly selected students whether they play school sports and whether they are in the school band. Her results are shown in the two-way frequency table. Use the table for Items 2–4.

Band \\ Sports	Yes	No	TOTAL
Yes	5	10	15
No	40	25	65
TOTAL	45	35	80

2. Choose True or False for each statement.

A. The joint relative frequency of students who play sports but are not in band is 50%.   ○ True   ○ False

B. The marginal relative frequency of students who are in the band is about 33%.   ○ True   ○ False

C. The marginal relative frequency of students who do not play sports is about 44%.   ○ True   ○ False

3. Find the conditional relative frequency of a student who does not play sports, given the student is in the band. Explain how you solved this problem.

4. Is a student who plays sports less likely than most students to be in the band? Justify your answer.

Scatter Plots

? ESSENTIAL QUESTION

How can you use scatter plots to solve real-world problems?

EXAMPLE 1

As part of a research project, a researcher made a table of test scores and the number of hours of sleep a person got the night before the test. Make a scatter plot of the data. Does the data show a positive association, negative association, or no association?

Sleep (hours)	Test score
4	30
5	40
6	50
6	70
8	100
9	90
10	100

The data show a positive association. Generally, as the number of hours of sleep increases, so do the test scores.

EXAMPLE 2

Write an equation for a trend line of the data shown on the graph.

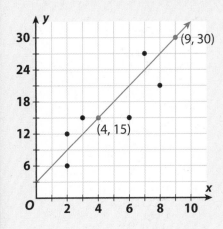

$m = \dfrac{30 - 15}{9 - 4} = 3$ Find the slope.

$15 = 3(4) + b$ Find the y-intercept.

$b = 3$

$y = 3x + 3$ Use the slope and y-intercept to write the equation.

EXERCISES

1. The table shows the income of 8 households, in thousands of dollars, and the number of televisions in each household. (Lesson 14.1)

Income ($1000)	20	20	30	30	40	60	70	90
Number of televisions	4	0	1	2	2	3	3	4

a. Make a scatter plot of the data.

b. Describe the association between income and number of televisions. Are any of the values outliers?

_____

_____

_____

_____

_____

_____

_____

_____

2. The scatter plot shows the relationship between the price of a product and the number of potential buyers. (Lesson 14.2)

a. Draw a trend line for the scatter plot.

b. Write an equation for your trend line.

_____

c. When the price of the product is $3.50, the number of potential buyers will be

about _____.

d. When the price of the product is $5.50, the number of potential buyers will be

about _____.

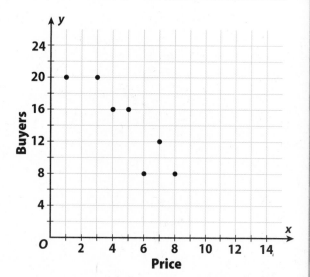

Two-Way Tables

Key Vocabulary
conditional relative frequency
 (frecuencia relativa condicional)
frequency *(frecuencia)*
joint relative frequency
 (frecuencia relativa común)
marginal relative frequency
 (frecuencia relativa marginal)
relative frequency *(frecuencia relativa)*
two-way frequency table
 (de dos vías frecuencia mesa)
two-way relative frequency table *(dos vías tabla de frecuencias relativas)*
two-way table *(de dos vías mesa)*

ESSENTIAL QUESTION

How can you use two-way tables to solve real-world problems?

EXAMPLE

A movie theater kept a record of patrons who bought tickets for a particular movie for two different times. The results are shown in the two-way frequency table. Create a two-way relative frequency table of these data.

	5:00 P.M. Showing	8:00 P.M. Showing	Total
Adults	22	39	61
Children	40	25	65
Total	62	64	126

Step 1: Divide each entry by the total number of patrons. Round to the nearest hundredth.

	5:00 P.M. Showing	8:00 P.M. Showing	Total
Adults	$\frac{22}{126} \approx 0.17$	$\frac{39}{126} \approx 0.31$	$\frac{61}{126} \approx 0.48$
Children	$\frac{40}{126} \approx 0.32$	$\frac{25}{126} \approx 0.20$	$\frac{65}{126} \approx 0.52$
Total	$\frac{62}{126} \approx 0.49$	$\frac{64}{126} \approx 0.51$	$\frac{126}{126} \approx 1.00$

Step 2: Convert decimals to percents.

	5:00 P.M. Showing	8:00 P.M. Showing	Total
Adults	17%	31%	48%
Children	32%	20%	52%
Total	49%	51%	100%

EXERCISES

Use the tables in the Example to answer each question.

1. What is the joint relative frequency of patrons who are adults and attended the 8:00 P.M. showing? _____

2. What is the marginal relative frequency of patrons who went to the 8:00 P.M. showing? _____

3. What is the conditional relative frequency that a patron is an adult, given that the patron attends the 8:00 P.M. showing? _____

Altitude or Latitude?

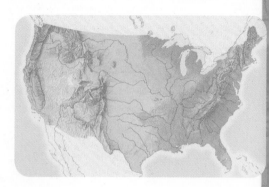

The elevation of a city affects its average temperature. Generally speaking, the greater the elevation, the cooler the city. A similar relationship holds for a city's latitude. The farther north a city is, the cooler it is. But which influences temperature more: elevation or latitude?

In this project, you will attempt to answer that question by collecting data and analyzing the data. Create a presentation that includes the following:

- The latitude, the elevation, and the average annual temperature of at least 20 United States cities, NOT including Denver
- Two scatter plots of the data you collect, with trend lines: (1) Latitude vs. Temperature and (2) Elevation vs. Temperature
- Your conclusion about which influences temperature more
- Your prediction of Denver's latitude and elevation, based on the average annual temperature of 50 °F. State whether your predictions were accurate.

Use the space below to write down any questions you have or important information from your teacher.

MATH IN CAREERS | ACTIVITY

Psychologist A psychologist gave a test to 15 women of different ages to measure their short-term memory. The test score scale goes from 0 to 24, and a higher score means that the participant has a better short-term memory. The scatter plot shows the results of this study. Use a line of best fit to describe the rate of change in test scores over increasing age.

UNIT 6
MIXED REVIEW

Assessment Readiness

Personal
Math Trainer

Online Practice
and Help

my.hrw.com

---

1. Jeremy surveyed 90 randomly selected 7th and 8th graders about whom they plan to vote for in the election for student council president. The two-way frequency table shows the results. Consider each number below. Does the number belong in the cell that matches the letter?

Select Yes or No.

A. 20   ◯ Yes   ◯ No

B. 58   ◯ Yes   ◯ No

C. 34   ◯ Yes   ◯ No

Grade \ Candidate	Walsh	Neil	Total
7th	28	A	B
8th	28	14	42
Total	56	C	90

2. The scatter plot shows the relationship between the number of floors and the heights of the tallest skyscrapers in a city.

Choose True or False for each statement.

A. The scatter plot shows a positive association.   ◯ True   ◯ False

B. There is a cluster of data near (22, 330).   ◯ True   ◯ False

C. The slope of the trend line represents the typical height in feet of a skyscraper.   ◯ True   ◯ False

3. The trend line on the scatter plot in Item 2 passes through the points (22, 298) and (40, 478). What is the equation of the trend line? Predict the height of a skyscraper with 50 floors, and explain how you made your prediction.

4. The bases of a baseball field form a square with a side length of 90 feet. To the nearest foot, what is the distance d between 3rd base and 1st base? Explain how you solved this problem.

Unit 6 **473**

Performance Tasks

★**5.** The scatter plot shows how the population of bacteria in a test tube changes over time. Describe any trends or associations you observe in the scatterplot.

★★**6.** Of the males who attended a movie, 50 liked the movie and 33 disliked it. Of the females who attended the movie, 58 liked it and 39 disliked it.

	Liked	Disliked	TOTAL
Male			
Female			
TOTAL			

   a. Complete the two-way frequency table for the data.

   b. Create a two-way relative frequency table for the data.

   c. Is there an association between a person's gender and whether he or she liked the movie? Justify your reasoning.

★★★**7.** The table shows how the winning times in the men's Olympic 1500-meter race have changed over time. Based on the data, predict the winning time in the men's 1500-meter race in the 2048 Olympics. Explain how you made your prediction. Be sure to include a scatter plot and a trend line in your explanation.

Year	Winning Time (s)
1900	246
1912	237
1924	234
1936	228
1948	230
1960	216
1972	216
1984	213
1996	216
2008	213
2012	214

MODULE 1

LESSON 1.1

Your Turn

1. $0.\overline{45}$ **2.** 0.125 **3.** $2.\overline{3}$ **4.** $\frac{3}{25}$ **5.** $\frac{19}{33}$
6. $1\frac{2}{5}$ **7.** $x = \pm 14$ **8.** $x = \pm\frac{3}{16}$
9. $x = 8$ **10.** $x = \frac{4}{7}$

Guided Practice

1. 0.4 **2.** $0.\overline{8}$ **3.** 3.75 **4.** 0.7
5. 2.375 **6.** $0.8\overline{3}$ **7.** $\frac{27}{40}$ **8.** $5\frac{3}{5}$ **9.** $\frac{11}{25}$
10. $4.\overline{4}$; $0.\overline{4}$; 9; 4; $\frac{4}{9}$ **11.** $26.\overline{26}$; $0.\overline{26}$;
99; 26; $\frac{26}{99}$ **12.** $325.\overline{325}$; $0.\overline{325}$; 999;
325; $\frac{325}{999}$ **13.** 17; 4.1 **14.** $\frac{25}{289}$; $\pm\frac{5}{17}$
15. 216; 6 **16.** 2.2 **17.** 1.7
18. 3.2

Independent Practice

21. $0.1\overline{6}$ **23.** $98.\overline{6}$
25. $26\frac{1}{5}$ mi **27.** $\frac{101}{200}$ cent
29. $x = \pm\sqrt{14} \approx \pm 3.7$
31. $x = \pm\sqrt{144} = \pm 12$ **33.** His
estimate is low because 15 is very
close to 16, so $\sqrt{15}$ is very close to
$\sqrt{16}$, or 4. A better estimate would
be 3.8 or 3.9.
35. 3 feet
37. $\sqrt{\frac{4}{25}} = \frac{2}{5} = \frac{\sqrt{4}}{\sqrt{25}}$; $\sqrt{\frac{16}{81}} = \frac{4}{9} = \frac{\sqrt{16}}{\sqrt{81}}$;
$\sqrt{\frac{36}{49}} = \frac{6}{7} = \frac{\sqrt{36}}{\sqrt{49}}$; $\frac{\sqrt{a}}{\sqrt{b}} = \sqrt{\frac{a}{b}}$;
$\sqrt{a} \cdot \sqrt{b} = \sqrt{a \cdot b}$

LESSON 1.2

Your Turn

1. rational, real **2.** irrational,
real **3.** False. Every integer is a
rational number, but not every
rational number is an integer.
Rational numbers such as $\frac{3}{5}$
and $-\frac{5}{2}$ are not integers.
4. False. Real numbers are either
rational or irrational numbers.
Integers are rational numbers,
so no integers are irrational
numbers. **5.** Real numbers; the
amount can be any number
greater than 0. **6.** Rational

numbers; a person's weight can
be a decimal such as 83.5 pounds.

Guided Practice

1. rational, real **2.** whole, integer,
rational, real **3.** irrational, real
4. rational, real **5.** whole, integer,
rational, real **6.** integer, rational,
real **7.** rational, real **8.** integer,
rational, real **9.** True. Whole
numbers are a subset of the set
of rational numbers and can
be written as a ratio of the
whole number to 1. **10.** True.
Whole numbers are rational
numbers. **11.** Integers; the
change can be a whole dollar
amount and can be positive,
negative, or zero. **12.** Rational
numbers; the ruler is marked
every $\frac{1}{16}$th inch.

Independent Practice

15. whole, integer, rational,
real **17.** rational, real **19.** whole,
integer, rational, real **21.** Integers;
the scores are counting numbers,
their opposites, and zero.
23. Whole; the diameter is $\frac{\pi}{\pi} =$
1 mile. **25.** rational number
27. Sample answer: If the
calculator shows a terminating
decimal, the number is rational.
Otherwise, you cannot tell
because you see only a few digits.

LESSON 1.3

Your Turn

3. $>$ **4.** $<$ **5.** $\sqrt{3}, \sqrt{5}, 2.5$

6. $\sqrt{75}, \pi^2, 10$

7. $3\frac{1}{2}$ mi, $3.\overline{45}$ mi, $\frac{10}{3}$ mi, $\sqrt{10}$ mi

Guided Practice

1. $<$ **2.** $>$ **3.** $<$ **4.** $<$ **5.** $>$
6. $<$ **7.** $>$ **8.** $>$ **9.** 1.7; 1.8; 1.75;
6.28; 1.5; $\sqrt{3}$; 2π **10.** $\left(1 + \frac{\pi}{2}\right)$ km,
2.5 km, $\frac{12}{5}$ km, $(\sqrt{17} - 2)$ km

Independent Practice

13. π, $\sqrt{10}$, 3.5 **15.** -3.75, $\frac{9}{4}$, $\sqrt{8}$, 3
17a. $\sqrt{60} \approx 7.75$, $\frac{58}{8} = 7.25$,
$7.\overline{3} \approx 7.33$, $7\frac{3}{5} = 7.60$, so the
average is 7.4825 km. **b.** They
are nearly identical. $\sqrt{56}$ is
approximately 7.4833...
19. Sample answer: $\sqrt{31}$
21a. between $\sqrt{7} \approx 2.65$ and
$\sqrt{8} \approx 2.83$ **b.** between $\sqrt{9} = 3$
and $\sqrt{10} \approx 3.16$ **23.** 2 points;
A rational number and an
irrational number cannot be
represented by the same point on
the number line.

MODULE 2

LESSON 2.1

Your Turn

10. 5 **11.** $63\frac{15}{16}$

Guided Practice

1. $\frac{1}{8}$ **2.** $\frac{1}{36}$ **3.** 1 **4.** 100 **5.** 625
6. $\frac{1}{32}$ **7.** $\frac{1}{1024}$ **8.** 1 **9.** $\frac{1}{1331}$ **10.** 4^3
11. $2^2 \cdot 2^3 = 2^5$ **12.** 6^2
13. $8^{12-9} = 8^3$ **14.** 5^{12} **15.** 7^{13}
16. $6^2 \cdot {}^4 = 6^8$ **17.** $8^3 \cdot 12^3$ **18.** $\frac{1}{6}$
19. 10,000 **20.** 1168 **21.** 343
22. When multiplying powers
with the same base, you add the
exponents. When dividing powers
with the same base, you subtract
the exponents. When raising a
product to a power, you raise each
factor to that power. When raising
a power to a power, you multiply
the exponents.

Independent Practice

23. 125 **25.** 1125 **27.** 36
29. 69 **31.** $\frac{1}{100}$ **33.** 216
37. The exponents cannot be

added because the bases are not the same. **39.** Earth to Neptune; 22^3, or 10,648, times greater. **41.** -3 **43.** 19 **45.** 10^3 kg, or 1000 kg **47.** Both expressions equal x^5, so $x^7 \cdot x^{-2} = \frac{x^7}{x^2}$. When multiplying powers with the same base, you add exponents; $7 + (-2) = 5$. When dividing powers with the same base, you subtract exponents; $7 - 2 = 5$. In cases like this, $x^n \cdot x^{-m} = \frac{x^n}{x^m}$. **49.** 3^6; 3^3

LESSON 2.2

Your Turn

3. 6.4×10^3 **4.** 5.7×10^{11} **5.** 9.461×10^{12} km **8.** 7,034,000,000 **9.** 236,000 **10.** 5,000,000 g

Guided Practice

1. 5.8927×10^4 **2.** 1.304×10^9 **3.** 6.73×10^6 **4.** 1.33×10^4 **5.** 9.77×10^{22} **6.** 3.84×10^5 **7.** 400,000 **8.** 1,849,900,000 **9.** 6410 **10.** 84,560,000 **11.** 800,000 **12.** 90,000,000,000 **13.** 54,000 s **14.** 7,600,000 cans

Independent Practice

17. 2.2×10^5 lb **19.** 4×10^4 lb **21.** 5×10^4 lb **23.** $108\frac{1}{3}$ hours or 108 hours and 20 minutes **25.** 4.6×10^3 lb **27a.** None of the girls has the correct answer. **b.** Polly and Samantha have the decimal in the wrong place; Esther miscounted the number of places the decimal moved. **29.** The speed of a car because it is likely to be less than 100. **31.** Is the first factor greater than 1 and less than 10? Is the second factor a power of 10?

LESSON 2.3

Your Turn

4. 8.29×10^{-5} **5.** 3.02×10^{-7} **6.** 7×10^{-6} m **9.** 0.000001045 **10.** 0.000099 **11.** 0.01 m

Guided Practice

1. 4.87×10^{-4} **2.** 2.8×10^{-5} **3.** 5.9×10^{-5} **4.** 4.17×10^{-2} **5.** 2×10^{-5} **6.** 1.5×10^{-5} **7.** 0.00002 **8.** 0.000003582 **9.** 0.00083 **10.** 0.0297 **11.** 0.0000906 **12.** 0.00004 **13.** 1×10^{-4} **14.** 0.000000000000000000000000017

Independent Practice

17. 1.3×10^{-3} cm **19.** 4.5×10^{-3} cm **21.** 8×10^{-4} cm **23.** 7 cm $= 0.07$ m, 7 cm $= 7 \times 10^0$ cm; 0.07 m $= 7 \times 10^{-2}$ m The first factors are the same; the exponents differ by 2. **25.** If the exponent on 10 is nonnegative, the number is greater than or equal to 1. **27.** Negative, because a ladybug would weigh less than 1 ounce. **29.** 0.000000000125 **31.** 71,490,000 **33.** 3,397,000 **35.** 5.85×10^{-3} m, 1.5×10^{-2} m, 2.3×10^{-2} m, 9.6×10^{-1} m, 1.2×10^2 m **37.** The result will be greater than the number with the positive exponent because the divisor is less than 1.

LESSON 2.4

Your Turn

1. 7.62×10^7 more people **2.** 8.928×10^8 miles **3.** 3.14×10^2 minutes **4.** 7.5E5 **5.** 3E–7 **6.** 2.7E13 **7.** 4.5×10^{-1} **8.** 5.6×10^{12} **9.** 6.98×10^{-8}

Guided Practice

1. 0.225; 10^6; 0.225; 2.8; 7.225×10^6 **2.** 0.10; 10^3; 8.5; 5.3; 0.10; 3.1×10^3 **3.** 5×10^2 **4.** 5.9381×10^5 **5.** 1.206×10^{22} **6.** 1.73×10^8 **7.** 1.69×10^{19} **8.** 2×10^7 **9.** 3.6E11 **10.** 7.25E–5 **11.** 8E–1 **12.** 7.6×10^{-4} **13.** 1.2×10^{16} **14.** 9×10^1

Independent Practice

17. about 2000 as many **19.** 5.025×10^7 tons **21.** Plastics **23.** about 7 people per square mile **25.** 13 years, 3 months, 22.5 days **27.** about 3×10^4, or $30,000 per person **29.** The student is off by a power of 10. The correct product is 40×10^{15}, or 4.0×10^{16}.

MODULE **3**

LESSON 3.1

Your Turn

3. $y = 15x$ **4.** 6 miles hiked in 5 hours **5.** $y = \frac{6}{5}x$

Guided Practice

1. is **2.** constant of proportionality **3a.** The pairs (weeks, days) are (2, 14), (4, 28), (8, 56), (10, 70). **b.** the time in weeks; the time in days; $y = 7x$ **4.** The pairs (oxygen atoms, hydrogen atoms) are (5, 10), (17, 34), (120, 240); $y = 2x$ **5.** $y = 30x$

Independent Practice

7. No; the ratios of the numbers in each column are not equal.
9a. Sample answer: The account had a balance of $100 to begin with. **b.** Sample answer: Have Ralph open the account with no money to begin with and then put $20 in every month. **11.** $y = 105$
13a. The pairs (time, distance) are (1, 10), (2, 20), (3, 30), (4, 40), (5, 50). **b.** $y = 10x$, where y is the distance in inches and x is the time in minutes. **c.** 8.5 minutes **15.** For $S = 1, P = 4$ and $A = 1$; For $S = 2$, $P = 8$ and $A = 4$; For $S = 3, P = 12$ and $A = 9$; For $S = 4, P = 16$ and $A = 16$; For $S = 5, P = 20$ and $A = 25$. **a.** Yes. The ratio of the perimeter of a square to its side length is always 4. **b.** No. The ratio of the area of a square to its side length is not constant.

LESSON 3.2

Your Turn

1. 36, 13, −10; variable **4.** +3; +4; $\frac{3}{4}$

Guided Practice

1. constant **2.** variable **3.** variable **4.** constant **5.** 200; 1;

200; 1; 200 **6.** 200 ft per min
7. −2 **8.** $\frac{3}{2}$

Independent Practice

11. 15 miles per hour
13a. 1 gallon every 5 minutes, or 0.2 gal/min **b.** 25 minutes
15.

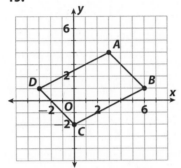

a. slope $\overline{AB} = -1$; slope $\overline{BC} = \frac{1}{2}$; slope $\overline{CD} = -1$; slope $\overline{DA} = \frac{1}{2}$
b. The slopes of the opposite sides are the same. **c.** Yes; opposite sides still have the same slope. **17.** Sample answer: One line has a positive slope and one has a negative slope. The lines are equally steep, but one slants upward left to right and the other slants downward left to right. The lines cross at the origin.

LESSON 3.3

Your Turn

2. His unit rate and the slope of a graph of the ride both equal $\frac{2}{3}$ mi/min.

Tomas's Ride

4. A: 375, 375 mi/h; B: 425, 425 mi/h; B is flying faster.

Guided Practice

1. slope = unit rate = $\frac{5}{6}$ mi/h
2. slope = unit rate = $\frac{5}{4}$ mi/h
3. Clark is faster. From the equation, Henry's rate is equal to 0.5, or $\frac{1}{2}$ mile per hour. Clark's rate is the slope of the line, which is $\frac{3}{2}$, or 1.5 miles per hour.
4. $y = 15x$ **5.** $y = \frac{3}{8}x$

Independent Practice

7a. The pairs (time, distance) are (4, 3), (8, 6), (12, 9), (16, 12), (20, 15).
b.

Migration Flight

c. $\frac{3}{4}$; The unit rate of migration of the goose and the slope of the graph both equal $\frac{3}{4}$ mi/min.
9a. Machine 1: slope = unit rate = $\frac{0.6}{1}$ = 0.6 gal/s; Machine 2: slope = unit rate = $\frac{3}{4}$ = 0.75 gal/s
b. Machine 2 is working at a faster rate since 0.75 > 0.6. **11.** slope = unit rate = 4.75. If the graph of a proportional relationship passes through the point (1, r), then r equals the slope and the unit rate, which is $4.75/min. **13.** 243 gallons; Sample answer: The unit rate is $\frac{36}{2}$ = 18 gal/min. So, $1\frac{1}{2}$ min after 12 min, an additional $18 \times 1\frac{1}{2}$ = 27 gal will be pumped in. The total is 216 + 27 = 243 gal.

MODULE 4

LESSON 4.1

Your Turn

1. Sample answer: (2, 20), (3, 32), (4, 44), (5, 56) **3.** (−1, 3), (0, 1), (1, −1), (2, −3)

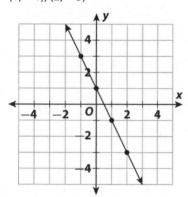

Guided Practice

1. (−2,1), (−1, 3), (0, 5), (1, 7), (2, 9)
2. (−8, −8), (0, −5), (8, −2), (16, 1), (24, 4) **3.** Undefined, 3.5, 2.75, 2.5, 2.375; The ratio $\frac{y}{x}$ is not constant. **4.** The graph is a line, but it does not pass through the origin. **5.** (−2, −3), (−1, −2), (0, −1), (1, 0), (2, 1)

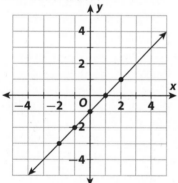

Independent Practice

7. Set of unconnected points; you cannot buy a fractional part of a lunch. **9a.** Sample answer: For (*x, y*) where *x* is number of years renewed and *y* is total cost in dollars: (0, 12), (1, 20), (2, 28), (3, 36), (4, 44)

b.

Magazine Subscription Costs

c. The graph does not include the origin. Also, the ratio of the total cost and number of years is not constant. **d.** No; the number of years must be a whole number, so total cost goes up in $8 increments. **11.** Sample answer: In a table, the ratios $\frac{y}{x}$ will not be equal; a graph will not pass through the origin; an equation will be in the form $y = mx + b$, where $b \neq 0$. **13.** At most one. A line representing a proportional relationship must pass through the origin. A line parallel to it cannot also pass through the origin.

LESSON 4.2

Your Turn

1. $m = 5; b = 12$ **2.** $m = 7; b = 1$

Guided Practice

1. −2; 1 **2.** 5; −15 **3.** $\frac{3}{2}$; −2
4. −3; 9 **5.** 3; 1 **6.** −4; 140

Independent Practice

9a. $5 to park; $12 per hour
b. $23.50; (3.5 hours × $12 per hour + $5) ÷ 2 = $23.50
11. Rate of change is constant from 1 to 2 to 3, but not from 3 to 4. **13.** Express the slope *m* between a random point (*x, y*) on the line and the point (0, *b*) where the line crosses the *y*-axis. Then solve the equation for *y*.

15. After parking 61 cars; John earns a fixed weekly salary of $300 plus $5 for each car he parks. He earns the same in fees as his fixed salary for parking 300 ÷ 5 = 60 cars.

LESSON 4.3

Your Turn

2.

3.

4.

5. The new graph has the same *y*-intercept but a slope of −200 instead of −300.
6. The calories left to burn will decrease more slowly with each hour of exercise, so it will take longer for Ken to meet his goal.
7. The *y*-intercept would not change, but the slope would become −600, which is much steeper. The line would intersect the *x*-axis when *x* = 4 hours.

Guided Practice

1. $\frac{1}{2}$; -3

2. -3; 2

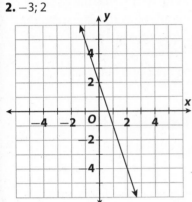

3a. Slope $= 4$; y-intercept $= 2$; you start with 2 cards and add 4 cards each week.

b. The points with coordinates that are not whole numbers; you will not buy part of a baseball card and you are buying only once a week.

Independent Practice

5a.

b. The slope, 0.75, means that the spring stretches by 0.75 inch with each additional pound of weight. The y-intercept, 0.25, is the unstretched length of the spring in inches. **c.** 1.75 inches; no; the length with a 4-pound weight is 3.25 in., not 3.5 in. **7.** (0, 8), (1, 7), (2, 6), (3, 5) **9.** (0, -3), (1, -1.5), (2, 0), (3, 1.5) **11.** (0, -5), (3, -3), (6, -1), (9, 1) **13a.** Yes; since the horizontal and vertical gridlines each represent 25 units, moving up 3 gridlines and right 1 gridline represents a slope of $\frac{75}{25}$, or 3. **b.** $m = 3$ so $3 is the charge per visit; $b = 50$ so the membership fee is $50.

c. 50 visits **15.** Yes; plot the point and use the slope to find a second point. Then draw a line through the two points.

LESSON 4.4

Your Turn

1. nonproportional
2. proportional
5. proportional
6. nonproportional

7. nonproportional
8. nonproportional
9. nonproportional
10. proportional
11. Test-Prep Center A's charges are proportional, but B's are not. Center B offers a coupon for an initial credit, but its hourly rate, $25, is higher than Center A's hourly rate of $20. So, Center B will cost more in the long run.

Guided Practice

1. Proportional; the line includes the origin. **2.** Nonproportional; the line does not include the origin. **3.** Nonproportional; when the equation is written in the form $y = mx + b$, the value of b is not 0. **4.** Proportional; when the equation is written in the form $y = mx + b$, the value of b is 0. **5.** Proportional; the quotient of y and x is constant, 4, for every number pair. **6.** No; the quotient of y and x is not constant for every number pair. **7.** Sample answer: The rating is proportional to the number of households watching: the quotient of the rating and the number of households is always 0.0000008.

Independent Practice

9a. Nonproportional; the graph does not pass through the origin, so $b \neq 0$. **b.** $m = 0.5$, $b = 10$; each cup of sports drink weighs a half pound. The empty cooler weighs 10 pounds. **11.** Proportional; this equation has the form $y = mx + b$, where $b = 0$.

15a. No; from Equation B, the y-intercept is 273.15, not 0, so the graph does not include the origin. From Table C, the quotient of K and C is not constant.
b. No; Equation A is in the form $y = mx + b$, with F instead of y and C instead of x. The value of b is 32, not 0, so the relationship is not proportional.

UNIT 2 Selected Answers (cont'd)

LESSON 5.1

Your Turn

3. $y = -2.5x + 25$ **5.** $y = 0.5x + 10$

Guided Practice

1a. the length of the necklace in inches **b.** the total number of beads in the necklace **c.** $y = 5x + 27$ **2.** $\frac{0 - 300}{5 - 0} = \frac{-300}{5} = -60$; 300; $y = -60x + 300$ **3.** temperature; chirps per minute; $\frac{100 - 76}{65 - 59} = \frac{24}{6} = 4$; $100 = 4 \cdot 65$; -160; $y = 4x - 160$

Independent Practice

5. $y = 30x$ **7.** $m = 0.125$; the diver ascends at a rate of 0.125 m/s **9.** $y = 0.125x - 10$ **11.** $y = 20x + 12$ **13.** $m = 500$; $b = 1000$ **15.** The amount of money in the savings account increases by $500 each month. **17.** The rate of change would not be constant. Using different pairs of points in the slope formula would give different results.

LESSON 5.2

Your Turn

1. $m = 15{,}000$; $b = 0$; $y = 15{,}000x$

Water Released from Hoover Dam

4. $p = 75n + 250$ **5.** $c = 0.50d + 40$

Guided Practice

1. $m = -1.25$; $b = 20$; $y = -1.25x + 20$

Bus Pass Balance

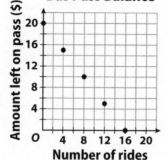

2. $m = \frac{51 - 59}{2000 - 0} = \frac{-8}{2000} = -0.004$
3. $b = 59$ **4.** $y = -0.004x + 59$
5. $y = -0.004(5000) + 59 = 39°F$

Independent Practice

7. $m = 2$; $b = 8$; $C = 2t + 8$
9a. $y = -1.5x + 30$ **b.** The number of dollars left decreases as the number of car washes increases. **c.** 20; after 20 washes there is no money left on the card.
11. $y = -2x + 6$ **13a.** No, the change between weeks is constant, but the change in the amount of rain is not constant. **b.** No; there is no apparent pattern in the table. **15.** 0; Jaíme's graph contained (0, 0). Since Jayla's data were the same, but with x and y switched, her graph also contained (0, 0).

LESSON 5.3

Your Turn

1. $y = 4x + 20$ **2.** $y = 240x$
6. $30 **7.** $48.75 **8.** $600

Guided Practice

1. $y = 30x$ **2.** $y = 2.5x + 2$ **3.** $y = 20x + 30$; $140 **4.** Yes, because the graph has a constant rate of change. **5.** No, because the graph does not have a constant rate of change.

Independent Practice

7. Yes, because the rate of change is constant. **9.** Linear; the rate of change is the cost of a DVD, which is constant. **11.** Not linear;

the rate of change in the area of a square increases as the side length increases. **13.** The relationship is linear; the equation of the linear relationship is $y = 0.125x$, so the Mars Rover would travel 7.5 feet in 60 seconds. **15.** Sample answer: Because $x = 6$ lies halfway between $x = 4$ and $x = 8$, the y-value should lie halfway between the corresponding y-values. **17.** Find the equation of the linear relationship using the slope and given point, and then insert any x-value to find a y-value on the graph of the line.

LESSON 6.1

Your Turn

4. Function; each input value is paired with only one output value. **5.** Not a function; the input value is paired with more than one output value. **7.** Function; each input value is paired with only one output value. **8.** Not a function; the input value 8 is paired with more than one output value.
10. Not a function; input values are paired with more than one output value; (70, 165) and (70, 174)

Guided Practice

1. $20x$; 200 **2.** $\frac{x}{2}$; 15 **3.** $2.25x$; 27.00 **4.** Function; each input value is paired with only one output value **5.** Not a function; the input value 4 is paired with more than one output value.
6. Yes; each input value is paired with only one output value.

Independent Practice

9. Not a function; the input value 5 is paired with more than one output value. **11a.** There is only one number of bacteria for each number of hours, so each input is paired with only one output.

b. Yes. Each input value would still be paired with only one output value. **13.** Yes. Each input value (the weight) is paired with only one output value (the price). **15.** It does not represent a function. For the input values to be paired with all four output values, at least one of the input values would be paired with more than one output value.

LESSON 6.2

Your Turn
2. proportional

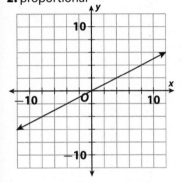

3. $(x, y) = (0, 0), (3, 2), (6, 4), (9, 6)$; linear; proportional

Making Soda

Guided Practice
1. $(-1, 7), (1, 3), (3, -1), (5, -5)$; linear

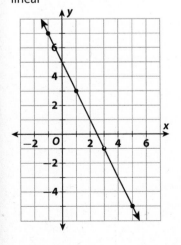

2. $(-2, -2), (-1, 1), (0, 2), (1, 1),$ $(2, -2)$; nonlinear

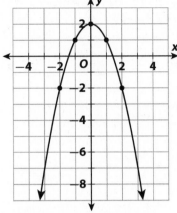

3. No; the equation cannot be written in the form $y = mx + b$, and the graph of the solutions is not a line. **4.** Yes; the equation can be written in the form $y = mx + b$, and the graph of the solutions is a line.

Independent Practice
7. No. The relationship is not linear because x is squared, so it will not be proportional. **9a.** Yes. The solutions lie in a line.

Drill Team Uniforms

b. $720
11. Disagree; the equation can be written in the form $y = mx + b$ where m is 0, and the graph of the solutions is a horizontal line. **13.** The relationship is linear if the points all lie on the same line and proportional if it is linear and a line through the points passes through the origin. **15.** Applying the Distributive Property gives $y + 3 = 6x + 3$, or $y = 6x$. This is in the form $y = mx + b$ with $b = 0$, so it is linear and proportional.

LESSON 6.3

Your Turn
1. Buying at the bookstore is more expensive.

Guided Practice
1. The second method (159 bpm vs. 150 bpm) gives the greater heart rate. **2.** Heart rate and age are nonproportional for each method. **3.** Students pay a $40 fee and $5 per hour.
4.

Tutoring Fees

5. With both plans, it costs $60 for 4 hours of tutoring. **6.** Plan 2 ($90 vs. $150) is cheaper for 10 hours of tutoring. **7.** Cost and time are proportional for Plan 1 and nonproportional for Plan 2.

Independent Practice
9. Scooter B (15 gallons vs. 18 gallons) uses fewer gallons of gas. **11.** the first plan **13.** The camera at the second store; the cost at the first store is $290 and the cost at the second store is $260. **15.** Since the rate per visit is the same, the monthly cost of Gym A is always more than that of Gym B. **17.** $y = -24x + 8$ is changing more quickly because even though -24 is less than -21, the absolute value of -24 is greater than the absolute value of -21.

LESSON 6.4

Guided Practice

1. The graph is increasing quickly. This shows a period of rapid growth.

2. The number of bacteria is decreasing.

3. Graph 2 **4.** Graph 3

5.

Distance from Edge of Pool

6. increasing where surfacing; decreasing where diving; linear where walking and swimming; nonlinear where diving

Independent Practice

9. Graph 1

11. Regina left the rental shop and rode for an hour. She took a half-hour rest and then started back. She changed her mind and continued for another half hour. She took a half-hour break and then returned to the rental shop.

13.

15. 3:23 to 3:24

17.

MODULE 7

LESSON 7.1

Your Turn
2. 64 weeks

Guided Practice
1. $x = -4$ **2.** $x = 5$ **3.** $b = 9$
4. $h = -4$ **5.** $x = -2$ **6.** $a = 6$
7. $n = 8$ **8.** $p = 3$ **9.** 4 personal training sessions **10.** 16 hours
11. Sample answer: Xavier has $100 in his lunch account. He spends $6 for lunch each day. Zack has $160 in his lunch account. He spends $10 each day. After how many days will the boys have the same amount in their accounts?

Independent Practice
13a. $12 + 5x = 18 + 3x$; $x = 3$; 3 hours **b.** Darlene's Dog Sitting; the cost would be $33, as opposed to $37 at Derrick's Dog Sitting.
15. $3x - 2 = x + 10$; $x = 6$ **17.** $8x - 20 = x + 15$; $x = 5$ **19.** $9x + 3 = 7x + 19$; $x = 8$; 75 chairs **21.** $3x + 6 = 5x + 2$; $x = 2$; 6 laps

LESSON 7.2

Your Turn
3. $k = -35$ **4.** $y = -\frac{9}{16}$
5. $1.9x = 1.3x + 37.44$; 62.4 lb

Guided Practice
1a. $60 + 50.45x = 57.95x$ **b.** $x = 8$; 8 months **2.** $n = 28$ **3.** $b = 60$
4. $m = 33$ **5.** $t = -0.8$ **6.** $w = 12$
7. $p = -2$

Independent Practice
11. 60 tiles **13a.** 100 mi
b. $80 **17.** $C = 1.8C + 32$; $-40°F = -40°C$

LESSON 7.3

Your Turn
1. $y = -1$ **2.** $x = 6$ **3.** $b = -4$
4. $t = 7$ **5.** $46,000

Guided Practice
1. 4; 32; 4; 28; 6; 28; 6; 6; 6; 6; 6; 6; $x = 1$ **2.** 3; 3; 2; -15; 18; 2; -60; $+$; 15; -13; -78; -13; -78; -13; -13; $x = 6$ **3.** $x = 3$ **4.** $x = 7$ **5.** $x = -1$
6. $x = 3$ **7.** $x = 9$ **8.** $x = -2$
9. $x = 10$ **10.** $x = -8$
11. $0.12(x + 3{,}000) = 4{,}200$;
$32,000

Independent Practice
13. a. $x + 14$ **b.** Joey's age in 5 years: $x + 5$; Martina's age in 5 years: $x + 19$ **c.** $3(x + 5) = x + 19$ **d.** Joey: 2 years old; Martina: 16 years old
15. It is not necessary. In this case, distributing the fractions directly results in whole number coefficients and constants.
17. Table first row: 0.25, $0.25x$; table second row: $100 - x$, 0.15, $0.15(100 - x)$; table third row: 0.19, 19 **a.** The milliliters of acid in the 25% solution plus the milliliters of acid in the 15% solution equals the milliliters of acid in the mixture. **b.** $0.25x + 0.15(100 - x) = 19$ **c.** The chemist used 40 ml of the 25% solution and 60 ml of the 15% solution.
19. Use the Distributive Property to distribute both 3 and 2 inside the square parentheses on the left side. Combine like terms inside the square parentheses. Then use the Distributive Property again to distribute 5. Combine like terms on the left side and use inverse operations to solve the equation.
$x = 1$

LESSON 7.4

Your Turn
2. $x = 3$; one solution
3. $7 = 7$; infinitely many solutions **4.** $-9 = 5$; no solution
5. You started with a false

statement and performed balanced operations on both sides of the equation. This does not change the true or false nature of the original statement.
6. Sample answer: 6 **7.** 4

Guided Practice
1. $x = 3$; true
2. $-4 = 1$; false
3. none
4. Any value of x will result in a true statement; infinitely many solutions
5. One solution
6. Infinitely many solutions
7. true; same variable; same constant; like; 10; $10 + x$; $10 + x + 5$; $15 + x = 15 + x$

Independent Practice
11. $0 = 0$; infinitely many solutions
13. $2 = 6$; no solution **15.** $x + 1$
17a. Yes; because the perimeters are equal, you get the equation $(2x - 2) + (x + 1) + x + (x + 1) = (2x - 9) + (x + 1) + (x + 8) + x$, or $5x = 5x$. Since $5x = 5x$ is a true statement, there are an infinite number of values for x.
b. The condition was that the two perimeters are to be equal. However, a specific number was not given, so there are an infinite number of possible perimeters.
c. 12; Sample answer: I used the trapezoid and wrote the equation $(2x - 2) + (x + 1) + x + (x + 1) = 60$. Solving this gives $x = 12$.
19. No; setting the expressions equal to each other and solving gives $100 + 35x = 50 + 35x$, or $100 = 50$, which is false.
21. Matt is incorrect. He applied the Distributive Property to the right side incorrectly. Correctly simplified, the equation is $0 = -7$, which is false, meaning no solution.

Selected Answers

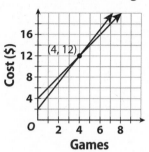

LESSON 8.1

Your Turn

3. $(-1, 3)$

4. $(1, 3)$

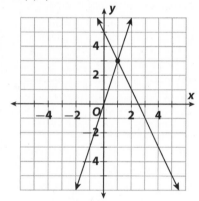

6a. $x + y = 6$ and $2x + 4y = 20$;
$y = -x + 6$ and $y = -0.5x + 5$

b.

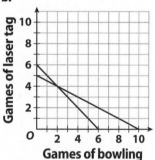

c. Marquis will bowl 2 games and play 4 games of laser tag.

Guided Practice

1. $(3, 5)$

2. $(2, 0)$

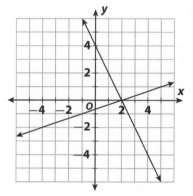

3a. $y = -x + 15$ **b.** $y = -0.5x + 10$

c.

d. 10 spelling questions and 5 vocabulary questions

Independent Practice

5. system of equations

7a. $y = 2.50x + 2$; $y = 2x + 4$
b. The solution is $(4, 12)$. The cost at both alleys will be the same for 4 games bowled, $12.

Cost of Bowling

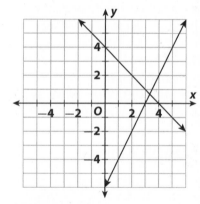

11. Infinitely many; rearranging the left side of the 2nd equation and subtracting $3a$ from both sides gives $-ax + ay = -3a$. Dividing both sides by $-a$ gives $x - y = 3$. The equations describe the same line.

LESSON 8.2

Your Turn

4. $(2, 5)$ **5.** $(-6, 4)$ **6.** $(-9, -7)$

7.

Estimate: $(3, 1)$
Solution: $\left(\frac{10}{3}, \frac{2}{3}\right)$
The solution is reasonable because $\frac{10}{3}$ is close to the estimate of 3 and $\frac{2}{3}$ is close to the estimate of 1.

8. Carlos: $4x + 160y = 120$
Vanessa: $x + 240y = 80$
$(20, 0.25)$; 20 represents the cost per day: $20; 0.25 represents the cost per mile: $0.25

Guided Practice

1. $(5, 3)$ **2.** $(3, -1)$ **3.** $(2, 1)$ **4.** $(4, 1)$
5. Estimate: $(1, -4)$;
Solution: $\left(\frac{7}{5}, -\frac{22}{5}\right)$

6. Estimate: $(-1, 5)$;
Solution: $\left(-1, \frac{9}{2}\right)$
7. Estimate: $(3, -6)$;
Solution: $\left(\frac{13}{4}, -\frac{23}{4}\right)$
8. Estimate: $(-2, 1)$;
Solution: $\left(-\frac{9}{5}, \frac{4}{5}\right)$
9. a. Hensons' cost: $3x + y = 163$;
Garcias' cost: $2x + 3y = 174$
b. adult ticket price: $45; child
ticket price: $28

Independent Practice
11.

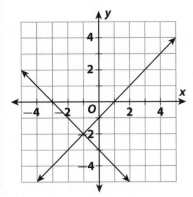

The graph shows that the
x-coordinate of the solution is
negative, so Zach's solution is not
reasonable.
13. 120 nickels and 80 dimes
15. $\left(\frac{8}{3}, -\frac{10}{3}\right)$
17. The substitution method has
the advantage of always giving an
exact answer. Graphing produces
an exact answer only if the
solution is an ordered pair whose
coordinates are integers.

LESSON 8.3

Your Turn
3. $(3, -4)$ **4.** $(2, -3)$ **5.** $(-1, 2)$
8. $(0, -2)$ **9.** $(7, -3)$ **10.** $\left(7, \frac{1}{2}\right)$
11. bag of roasted almonds: $1.95;
juice drink: $1.25

Guided Practice
1. Step 1: 0; -10; y; -10; -2; 5.
Step 2: 3; $(-2, 3)$ **2.** $(2, -2)$
3. $(6, 5)$ **4.** $(7, -7)$ **5.** $(-3, 8)$
6. $(2, 3)$ **7.** $(-5, -2)$
8. a. Tony: $2x + 3.5y = 355$;
Rae: $2x + 3y = 320$
b. Minimum speed limit: 55 mi/h;
maximum speed limit: 70 mi/h

11. Guppy: 3 inches; platy:
2 inches
13. Labor fee: $14.95; quart of oil:
$1.50
15. 407 adult tickets; 839 student
tickets
17. a. Jenny substituted her
expression for y into the same
equation she used to find y. She
should substitute her expression
into the other equation. **b.** Yes;
adding the equations would have
resulted in $3x = 9$, easily giving
$x = 3$ after dividing each side by 3.
Substitution requires many more
steps.

LESSON 8.4

Your Turn
4. $(-8, 15)$ **5.** $(-1, 5)$ **6.** $\left(\frac{1}{2}, -1\right)$
7. $(3, 1)$ **8.** $(-4, -1)$
9. $\left(\frac{1}{3}, 6\right)$ **10.** Contestants run
0.75 hour and bike 0.5 hour.

Guided Practice
1. Step 1: 12; 4; 32; 20; y; 2; 10.
Step 2: -2; $(2, -2)$ **2.** $(6, -1)$
3. $(-3, 8)$ **4.** $\left(\frac{7}{2}, \frac{7}{4}\right)$ **5.** $(3, -3)$
6. $(4, -1)$ **7.** $(-2, 4)$
8. a. First store: $0.64x + 0.45y = 5.26$; second store: $0.32x + 0.39y = 3.62$ **b.** Number of apples:
4; number of pears: 6

Independent Practice
11. a. $\begin{cases} 79x + 149y = 1456 \\ x + y = 14 \end{cases}$
b. Multiply the second equation
by 79. Subtract the new equation
from the first one and solve
the resulting equation for y.
c. Solve the second equation for
x. Substitute the expression for x
in the first equation and solve the
resulting equation for y.
d. 9 polyester-fill, 5 down-fill
13. 21 pies, 16 jars of applesauce
15. a. Multiply the first equation
by 1.5 and subtract. This would
be less than ideal because you
would introduce decimals into the
solution process. **b.** Yes; multiply
the first equation by 3 and the

second equation by 2. Both x-term
coefficients would be 6. Solve
by eliminating the x-terms using
subtraction. **c.** $(9, -4)$

LESSON 8.5

Your Turn
6. no solution **7.** $(10, -2)$; one
solution **8.** infinitely many
solutions

Guided Practice
1. Step 1: are parallel; intersect;
are the same line Step 2: no; 1;
infinitely many **2.** infinitely
many solutions **3.** no solution
4. $(-3, -4)$; one solution

Independent Practice
9.

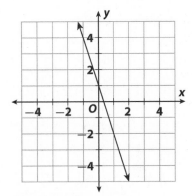

infinitely many solutions
11. one solution **13.** one solution
15. one solution
17. No; although the lines do
not intersect on the graph, they
intersect at a point that is not on
the graph. To prove that a system
has no solution, you must do so
algebraically.
19. No; both Juan and Tory run
at the same rate, so the lines
representing the distances each
has run are parallel. There is no
solution to the system.
21. A, B, and C must all be the
same multiple of 3, 5, and 8,
respectively. The two equations
represent a single line, so the
coefficients and constants of one
equation must be a multiple of
the other.

UNIT 4 **Selected Answers**

LESSON 9.1

Your Turn

4.

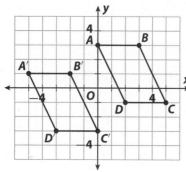

Guided Practice

1. transformation **2.** preimage; image **3.** The orientation will be the same. **4.** They are congruent.

5.

Independent Practice

7a.

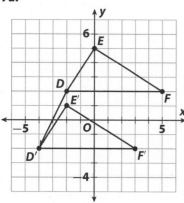

b. The translation moved the triangle 2 units to the left and 4 units down. **c.** They are congruent.

9.

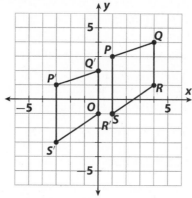

11. The hot air balloon was translated 4 units to the right and 5 units up.

13a.–c.

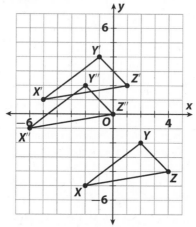

d. The original triangle was translated 4 units up and 4 units to the left.

LESSON 9.2

Your Turn

4.

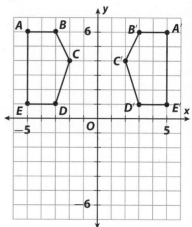

Guided Practice

1. line of reflection

2a.

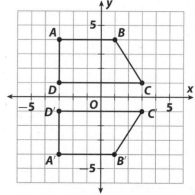

b. They are congruent. **c.** The orientation would be reversed horizontally: the figure from left to right in the preimage would match the figure from right to left in the image.

Independent Practice

5. C and D **7.** Sample answer: Since each triangle is either a reflection or translation of triangle C, they are all congruent. **9.** Yes; if the point lies on the line of reflection, then the image and the preimage will be the same point.

11a.–c.

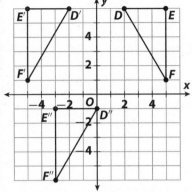

d. Sample answer: Translate triangle *DEF* 7 units down and 2 units to the left. Then reflect the image across the *y*-axis.

LESSON 9.3

Your Turn

6.–7.

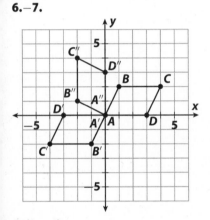

8. (2, −4)

Guided Practice

1. point   **2.** Each leg in the preimage is perpendicular to its corresponding leg in the image.
3. Yes, the figures are congruent.
4.

5.

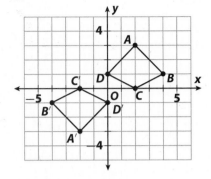

Independent Practice

7a. *ABC* was rotated 90° counterclockwise about the origin.   **b.** *A'* (3, 1); *B'* (2, 3); *C'* (−1, 4)
9. 180° rotation about the origin
11. 90° clockwise   **13.** 90° clockwise
15.

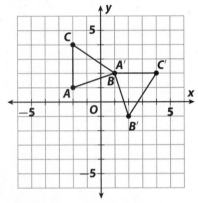

17. 2 times; 1 time; 4 times
19. Sample answer: If *A* is at the origin, then so is *A'* for any rotation about the origin. Otherwise, *A'* is on the *x*-axis for 90° and 270° rotations and on the *y*-axis for a 180° rotation.

LESSON 9.4

Your Turn

1. (−6, −5), (−6, 0), (−3, −5), and (−3, 0); the rectangle is translated 6 units to the left and 3 units down.   **2.** *A'*(−2, −6), *B'*(0, −5), and *C'*(3, 1)   **4.** *J'*(4, −2), *K'*(−5, 1), and *L'*(−2, 2)

Guided Practice
1. *X'*(3, −2), *Y'*(5, 0), and *Z'*(7, −6)

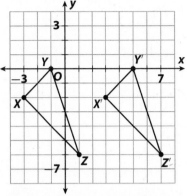

2. The *x*-coordinate remains the same, while the *y*-coordinate changes sign.   **3.** The triangle is rotated 90° clockwise about the origin.

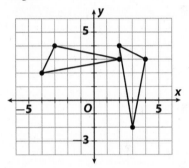

Independent Practice
5. $(x, y) \rightarrow (x − 2, y − 5)$; translation of 2 units to the left and 5 units down   **7.** $(x, y) \rightarrow (x − 3.2, y + 1)$; *Y'*(4.3, 6), *Z'*(4.8, 5)
9. The rectangle is translated 2 units to the left and 4 units down.

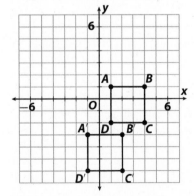

11. $(x, y) \rightarrow (x + 0.5, y − 0.25)$
13a. (−5, −5); *x* and *y* are equal, so switching *x* and *y* has no effect on the coordinates.   **b.** $y = x$ **c.** The triangle is reflected across the line $y = x$.

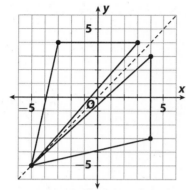

15a. A"(1, 0), B"(0, 3), and C"(4, 3)
b. $(x, y) \rightarrow (x + 3, y + 2)$

LESSON 9.5

Your Turn

3. Rotation 90° clockwise about the origin, translation 5 units down; $(x, y) \rightarrow (y, -x)$, $(x, y) \rightarrow (x, y - 5)$

Guided Practice

1.

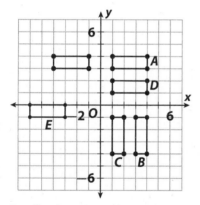

2. reflection across the y-axis
3. translation 3 units right and 4 units down
4. $(x, y) \rightarrow (-x, y)$, $(x, y) \rightarrow (x + 3, y - 4)$
5. The figures have the same size and the same shape.

Independent Practice

7.

Different orientation

9.

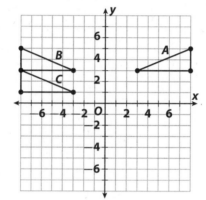

Different orientation

11. Sample answer: translation 2 units right and 4 units down, reflection across y-axis; size: no; orientation: yes

13. No; the point (1, 2) translated 2 units to the right becomes (3, 2), rotated 90° clockwise about the origin, it becomes (2, −3). The point (1, 2) rotated 90° clockwise around the origin becomes (2, −1), translated 2 units to the right, it becomes (4, −1), which is not the same.

MODULE 10

LESSON 10.1

Your Turn

5. The scale factor is 0.5.

Guided Practice

1. 2; 2 **2.** equal; equal **3.** 2
4. congruent **5.** 2

Independent Practice

7. No; the ratios of the lengths of the corresponding sides are not equal. **9.** Yes; a dilation produces an image similar to the original figure. **11.** Yes; each coordinate of triangle U'V'W' is $\frac{3}{4}$ times the corresponding coordinate of triangle UVW. **13.** changed; same; same **15.** same; changed; same
17. 3 **19.** Locate the corresponding vertices of the triangles and draw lines connecting each pair. The lines will intersect at the center of dilation.

LESSON 10.2

Your Turn

5. $(x, y) \rightarrow \left(\frac{1}{3}x, \frac{1}{3}y\right)$

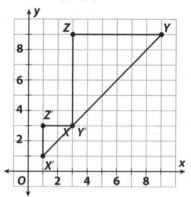

Guided Practice

1.

PreImage	Image
(2, 0)	(3, 0)
(0, 2)	(0, 3)
(−2, 0)	(−3, 0)
(0, −2)	(0, −3)

2.

$(x, y) \rightarrow (1.5x, 1.5y)$

3.

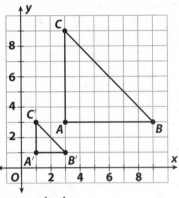

$(x, y) \rightarrow (\frac{1}{3}x, \frac{1}{3}y)$

Independent Practice

5. Green square: $(x, y) \rightarrow (2x, 2y)$; Purple square $(x, y) \rightarrow (\frac{1}{2}x, \frac{1}{2}y)$
7. $(x, y) \rightarrow (\frac{2}{3}x, \frac{2}{3}y)$ **9a.** The scale factor is 48. **b.** 48 inches or 4 feet **c.** $(x, y) \rightarrow (48x, 48y)$

d. $Q'(2.5, 2.5)$, $R'(8.75, 2.5)$, $S'(8.75, 6.25)$, and $T'(2.5, 6.25)$
e. Dimensions on blueprint: 6.25 in. by 3.75 in. Dimensions in house: 25 ft by 15 ft **11.** The crewmember's calculation is incorrect. The scale factor is $\frac{1}{20}$, not $\frac{1}{12}$. **13.** The figure is dilated by a factor of 2, but the orientation of the figure is rotated 180°.

LESSON 10.3

Your Turn

3. Sample answer: $(x, y) \rightarrow (x + 7, y - 12)$; rotation 90° clockwise about the origin; $(x, y) \rightarrow (x + 5, y + 3)$; $(x, y) \rightarrow (3x, 3y)$

Guided Practice

1.

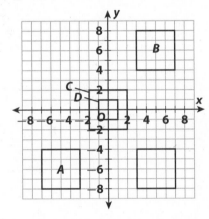

2. $(x, y) \rightarrow (x, -y)$; $(x, y) \rightarrow (x + 5, y - 6)$
3. $(x, y) \rightarrow (x, y + 6)$; rotate 90° counterclockwise
4. $(x, y) \rightarrow (1.5x, 1.5y)$; $(x, y) \rightarrow (x + 3, y + 5)$

Independent Practice

7. Dilate the image by a scale factor of $\frac{1}{3}$ and reflect it back across the x-axis; $(x, y) \rightarrow (\frac{1}{3}x, \frac{1}{3}y)$, $(x, y) \rightarrow (x, -y)$.
9. Rotate the image 90° counterclockwise and dilate it by a factor of $\frac{1}{5}$; $(x, y) \rightarrow (-y, x)$, $(x, y) \rightarrow (\frac{1}{5}x, \frac{1}{5}y)$.

11. There can be an even number of dilations in pairs where each has the opposite effect.

UNIT 5 Selected Answers

LESSON 11.1

Your Turn
5. 72° **6.** 108° **7.** 108°

Guided Practice
1. $\angle VWZ$ **2.** alternate interior
3. 80° **4.** 100° **5.** same-side interior

Independent Practice
7. $\angle 1$ and $\angle 5$, $\angle 2$ and $\angle 6$, $\angle 3$ and $\angle 7$, $\angle 4$ and $\angle 8$ **9.** alternate interior angles **11.** 30°
13. 110° **15.** 78° **17.** 132°; the 48° angle is supplementary to the larger angle because the two angles are same-side interior angles. **19.** $\angle 6$ and $\angle 2$ are corr., so m$\angle 2 = 125°$. $\angle 6$ and $\angle 3$ are alt. int., so m$\angle 3 = 125°$. $\angle 3$ and $\angle 7$ are corr., so m$\angle 7 = 125°$. $\angle 6$ and $\angle 4$ are same-side int., so m$\angle 4 = 180° - 125°$, or 55°. $\angle 4$ and $\angle 8$ are corr., so m$\angle 8 = 55°$. $\angle 4$ and $\angle 5$ are alt. int., so m$\angle 5 = 55°$. $\angle 1$ and $\angle 5$ are corr., so m$\angle 1 = 55°$.
21. 3 angles; 4 angles; no

LESSON 11.2

Your Turn
4. 53° **5.** 90° **8.** 78°; 68°

Guided Practice
1. 71° **2.** 30° **3.** 88°; 29°; 63°
4. 90°; 45°; 45° **5.** 40°; 76°; 64°
6. 129°; 32°; 19°

Independent Practice
9. 60°; 30° **11.** 98°; 55°; 27°
13. 60°; 90°; 30°; 150° **15.** No; the measure of an obtuse angle is greater than 90°. If a triangle had two obtuse angles, the sum of their measures would be greater than 180°, the sum of the angle measures of a triangle. **17a.** 360° **b.** The sum of the angle measures of a quadrilateral is 360°.

Sample answer: Any quadrilateral can be divided into two triangles, so the sum of its angle measures is $2 \times 180° = 360°$.

LESSON 11.3

Your Turn
3. The triangles are not similar, because only one angle is congruent. The angle measures of the triangles are 70°, 58°, and 52° and 70°, 61°, and 49°. **5.** 8 inches
6. 21 ft

Guided Practice
1. 41°, 109°, and 30°; 41°, 109°, and 30°; two angles; two angles; similar **2.** 7.5; 23.5; 17.2
3. congruent; alternate interior angles; congruent; alternate interior angles; AA Similarity; similar

Independent Practice
5. m$\angle B = 42°$, m$\angle F = 69°$, m$\angle H = 64°$, m$\angle K = 53°$ **7.** $\angle J \cong \angle A$, $\angle L \cong \angle B$, and $\angle K \cong \angle C$ **9.** 25 feet
11. In the first line, Ryan should have added 19.5 and 6.5 to get a denominator of 26 for the expression on the right side to get the correct value of 13.6 cm for h.

LESSON 12.1

Your Turn
4. 50 ft **5.** 9 in. **6.** $r = \sqrt{228}$, so the greatest length is 15 in.

Guided Practice
1. 10^2, 676, 26 **2a.** 1700
2b. 42.4 in.; yes

Independent Practice
5. 11.5 in. **7.** 14.1 in. **9.** 12 feet
11. 52.8 ft; $12^2 + 39^2 = c^2$, so $144 + 1521 = c^2$, $1665 = c^2$, and $40.8 \approx c$. Adding this to the height of the bottom of the tree: $40.8 + 12 = 52.8$ ft. **13.** $\sqrt{x^2 + x^2}$ (or $\sqrt{2x^2}$ or $x\sqrt{2}$); if $a = x$ and $b = x$, then $x^2 + x^2 = c^2$. Thus, $c = \sqrt{x^2 + x^2}$.

LESSON 12.2

Your Turn
2. not a right triangle **3.** right triangle **4.** right triangle **5.** not a right triangle **6.** Yes; $140^2 + 480^2 = 250{,}000$; $500^2 = 250{,}000$; $250{,}000 = 250{,}000$ **7.** No; $18^2 + 19^2 = 685$, $25^2 = 625$, $685 \neq 625$ **8.** No; there are no pairs of whole numbers whose squares add to $12^2 = 144$.

Guided Practice
1a. 6; 8, 10 **b.** 6, 8, 10; 36, 64, 100; 100, 100; is **2.** 9, 12, 16; 9, 12, 16; 81, 144, 256; 225, 256; is not **3.** Yes; $2.5^2 + 6^2 = 42.25$, $6.5^2 = 42.25$, $42.25 = 42.25$

Independent Practice
5. right triangle **7.** not a right triangle **9.** not a right triangle **11.** right triangle **13.** not a right triangle **15.** No; $13^2 + 14^2 = 365$, $15^2 = 225$, and $365 \neq 225$.
17. No; $6^2 + 10^2 = 136$, $12^2 = 144$, and $136 \neq 144$. **19.** Yes; since $0.75^2 + 1^2 = 1.25^2$, the triangles are right triangles. Adjoining them at their hypotenuses will form a rectangle with sides 1 m and 0.75 m. **21.** Yes

LESSON 12.3

Your Turn
1. 6.4 units **4.** approximately 214.7 meters

Guided Practice
1. 5.8 units **2.** 13 units
3. 103.6 miles

Independent Practice

7a. $ET = \sqrt{113}$ units **b.** Let (x_1, y_1) = $(-3, 4)$ and $(x_2, y_2) = (4, -4)$. Substitute the coordinates into the Distance Formula and then simplify. **9.** $(5, 0)$, $(4, 3)$, $(3, 4)$, $(0, 5)$, $(-3, 4)$, $(-4, 3)$, $(-5, 0)$, $(-4, -3)$, $(-3, -4)$, $(0, -5)$, $(3, -4)$, $(4, -3)$; The points would form a circle.

11.

Let $(x_1, y_1) = (6, 6)$, and $(x_2, y_2) =$ $(1, 1)$. Use the Distance Formula to show that hypotenuse = $\sqrt{50} \approx 7.1$.

LESSON 13.1

Your Turn

4. 471 in³ **5.** 602.9 ft³ **6.** 452.2 in³

Guided Practice

1. two congruent circles that lie in parallel planes **2.** Sample answer: 427 in³; there are 61 cubes on the bottom of the cylinder. The height is 7 cubes. $V = 61 \times 7 = 427$ in³ **3.** 6; 15; 36; 15; 1695.6; 1695.6 **4.** 1.35; 15.5

Independent Practice

7. 1205.8 in³ **9.** 942 in³ **11.** 803.8 m³ **13.** 6838.9 in³ **15.** 339,120 m³ **17.** 57.7 in³ **19.** Divide the diameter by 2 to find the radius. Substitute the volume and radius in $V = \pi r^2 h$ and solve for h.

LESSON 13.2

Your Turn

3. 942 cm³ **4.** 12.6 ft³ **5.** 19,286,968.5 m³

Guided Practice

1. 45; 10; 450; 450; 150; 150 **2.** 54 m³; the volume of a cylinder is 3 times the volume of a cone with a congruent base and height. **3.** 65.9 ft³ **4.** 113,982 in³ **5.** 141.3 in³ **6.** 13,083.3 m³

Independent Practice

9. 25.1 in³ **11.** 94.2 m³ **13.** 167.5 in³ **15.** 628 in³ **17.** 6 cm **19a.** either the diameter or the radius of the base **b.** No; the cone is tapered from top to bottom. An equal volume of sand has a smaller radius and a greater height as the sand rises. **21.** Since the radius and height of the cones and cylinder are the same, it will take 3 cones to equal the volume of the cylinder.

LESSON 13.3

Your Turn

2. 4186.7 cm³ **3.** 20.6 m³ **6.** 904.3 in³

Guided Practice

1. the same distance **2.** radius **3.** 4.2 in³ **4.** 4,186.7 cm³ **5.** 14.1 ft³ **6.** 4.2 yd³ **7.** 12.8 in³ **8.** 435 in³ **9a.** $\frac{1}{3}$; the ball takes up $\frac{2}{3}$ of the space, so $\frac{1}{3}$ is empty. **b.** $(2r)^3 = 8r^3$ **c.** Almost $\frac{1}{2}$; the empty space is $8r^3 - \frac{4}{3}\pi r^3$, or about $3.81r^3$, and $\frac{3.81}{8} \approx 0.48$.

Independent Practice

11. 124.7 m³ **13.** 904.3 in³ **15.** 5572.5 cm³ **17.** 5389 cm³ **19.** 1766.3 cm³ **21.** Divide $V = \frac{4}{3}\pi r^3$ by 2 to find the volume of the hemisphere: $V = \frac{2}{3}\pi r^3$. Add the volume of the cylinder, $V = \pi r^2 h = \pi r^3$: $V = \frac{2}{3}\pi r^3 + \pi r^3 = \frac{5}{3}\pi r^3$. **23.** 12.3 in³ **25.** The cylindrical glass; the cylinder has a volume of πr^3, the hemisphere's volume is $\frac{2}{3}\pi r^3$, and the cone's volume is $\frac{1}{3}\pi r^3$. **27.** About 16 feet; 136 is 8 times 17, so the volume must be 8 times as big. Because $2^3 = 8$, this means the radius, and thus the diameter, must be twice as big.

MODULE 14

LESSON 14.1

Your Turn

6. Positive and basically linear: older students would be taller and read at a higher level.

Guided Practice

1.

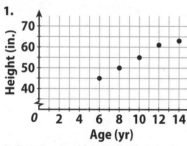

2. Positive and basically linear; the plot shows Bob's height increasing as he gets older. **3.** There is a cluster for 20−23 shots attempted and a lesser one for 7−14 shots attempted; (35, 18) is an outlier.

Independent Practice

5. A generally positive linear association: as the year increases, so does the winning distance. **7.** Nonlinear; the points generally rise up to 1988 and then fall from 1988 to 2012, so there is no overall linear pattern. **13.** Yes; for example, the points may appear to lie along a rising or falling curve, or may generally rise or fall, but not in a way that suggests a linear association.

LESSON 14.2

Your Turn

6. Sample answer: $y = \frac{9}{10}x$

Guided Practice

Answers for 1–4 may vary slightly.

1.

2. Most data points are close to the trend line, with about the same number of points above and below the line. **3.** $y = 0.09x$
4. \$0.63; \$4.50

Independent Practice

Answers for 6–14 may vary slightly.

7. negative; basically linear
9a. about −6°F **b.** about −22°F
11.

13. about 73°F **17a.** No; two data points are not enough to create a scatter plot or trend line. A random sample of many counties should be used. **b.** Sample answer: Marlene's conjecture is incorrect. Harris and Dallas counties are counterexamples to Marlene's original conclusion.

MODULE 15

LESSON 15.1

Your Turn

2. Yes; the relative frequency of visiting a park $= \frac{105}{200} = 0.525 = 52.5\%$; relative frequency of visiting a park among high school students $= \frac{80}{120} \approx 0.667 = 66.7\%$; $66.7\% > 52.5\%$, so being in high school improves the likelihood that a student has visited a national park.

Guided Practice

1.

	Dog	No Dog	TOTAL
Cat	21	9	30
No Cat	15	5	20
TOTAL	36	14	50

2. No; the relative frequency of being left-handed ($\frac{24}{240} = 10\%$) is the same as the relative frequency of being left-handed among boys ($\frac{14}{140} = 10\%$).

Independent Practice

5.a.

	Prefer Science	Prefer Math	TOTAL
Seventh Grade	24	72	96
Eighth Grade	32	48	80
TOTAL	56	120	176

b. No; the relative frequency of preferring math is $\frac{120}{176} \approx 68\%$, and the relative frequency of preferring math among eighth graders is $\frac{48}{80} = 60\%$, so eighth graders are slightly less likely to prefer math than the general population of students polled.

7. a.

	Prefer Surfing	Prefer Snorkeling	TOTAL
Ages 13–15	52 40%; 50%	78 60%; 74%	130 100%
Ages 16–18	52 65%; 50%	28 35%; 26%	80 100%
TOTAL	104 50%; 100%	106 50%; 100%	210 100%

b. It is the relative frequency of teenagers who are 16 to 18 years old and who prefer snorkeling to all 16- to 18-year-olds who were surveyed.

c. No; the total numbers in the last column (ages) are not the same as the total numbers in the last row (preferences), so the relative frequencies are different.

d. It is the relative frequency of teenagers who are 16 to 18 years old and who prefer snorkeling to all of those surveyed who prefer snorkeling.

LESSON 15. 2

Your Turn

10. $\frac{0.18}{0.44} \approx 0.409$, or 40.9%

11. Step1: 44% becomes 56%; Step 2: 45% becomes 55%, 60% becomes 40%, and 23% becomes 77%; Step 3: conclusions would not change.

Guided Practice

1. a-c. TOTAL row: 12, 5, 8, 25; TOTAL column: 12, 13, 25

d.

Gender \ Preferred Pet	Seashore	Mountains	Other	TOTAL
Girl	0.28	0.12	0.08	0.48
Boy	0.2	0.08	0.24	0.52
TOTAL	0.48	0.2	0.32	1.00

e. 0.08, or 8% **f.** 0.48, or 48%

g. 0.25, or 25%; 1 in 4 girls surveyed prefer the mountains; girls are more likely than boys to prefer the mountains.

Independent Practice

3. a. first row: 10, 20; second row: 6, 3, 24; third row: 30, 12

b. Sample answer: I worked backward from the given data, using the fact that the sum of the entries in each row and each column must equal the total for that row or column.

5. a. 13% **b.** 32% **c.** about 40%

7. No; each data value should have been divided by the grand total, 600, not by the row total.

8. Yes, the data in the Total row, the marginal relative frequencies of each column, are correct. The joint relative frequencies and their marginal relative frequencies in the Total column are incorrect.

Glossary/Glosario

ENGLISH	SPANISH	EXAMPLES
absolute value The distance of a number from zero on a number line; shown by | |.	**valor absoluto** Distancia a la que está un número de 0 en una recta numérica. El símbolo del valor absoluto es | |.	$\|-5\| = 5$
accuracy The closeness of a given measurement or value to the actual measurement or value.	**exactitud** Cercanía de una medida o un valor a la medida o el valor real.	
acute angle An angle that measures greater than 0° and less than 90°.	**ángulo agudo** Ángulo que mide mas de 0° y menos de 90°.	
acute triangle A triangle with all angles measuring less than 90°.	**triángulo acutángulo** Triángulo en el que todos los ángulos miden menos de 90°.	
Addition Property of Equality The property that states that if you add the same number to both sides of an equation, the new equation will have the same solution.	**Propiedad de igualdad de la suma** Propiedad que establece que puedes sumar el mismo número a ambos lados de una ecuación y la nueva ecuación tendrá la misma solución.	$\begin{aligned} 14 - 6 &= 8 \\ +6 \quad & +6 \\ \hline 14 &= 14 \end{aligned}$
Addition Property of Opposites The property that states that the sum of a number and its opposite equals zero.	**Propiedad de la suma de los opuestos** Propiedad que establece que la suma de un número y su opuesto es cero.	$12 + (-12) = 0$
additive inverse The opposite of a number; one of two numbers whose sum is 0.	**inverso aditivo** El opuesto de un número; uno de dos números cuya suma es 0.	The additive inverse of 5 is -5.
adjacent angles Angles in the same plane that have a common vertex and a common side.	**ángulos adyacentes** Ángulos en el mismo plano que comparten un vértice y un lado.	
algebraic expression An expression that contains at least one variable.	**expresión algebraica** Expresión que contiene al menos una variable.	$x + 8$ $4(m - b)$
algebraic inequality An inequality that contains at least one variable.	**desigualdad algebraica** Desigualdad que contiene al menos una variable.	$x + 3 > 10$ $5a > b + 3$

ENGLISH	SPANISH	EXAMPLES
alternate exterior angles For two lines intersected by a transversal, a pair of angles that lie on opposite sides of the transversal and outside the other two lines.	**ángulos alternos externos** Dadas dos rectas cortadas por una transversal, par de ángulos no adyacentes ubicados en los lados opuestos de la transversal y fuera de las otras dos rectas.	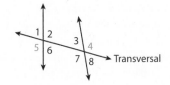 ∠4 and ∠5 are alternate exterior angles.
alternate interior angles For two lines intersected by a transversal, a pair of nonadjacent angles that lie on opposite sides of the transversal and between the other two lines.	**ángulos alternos internos** Dadas dos rectas cortadas por una transversal, par de ángulos no adyacentes ubicados en los lados opuestos de la transversal y entre de las otras dos rectas.	 ∠3 and ∠6 are alternate interior angles.
angle A figure formed by two rays with a common endpoint called the vertex.	**ángulo** Figura formada por dos rayos con un extremo común llamado vértice.	
angle bisector A line, segment, or ray that divides an angle into two congruent angles.	**bisectriz de un ángulo** Línea, segmento o rayo que divide un ángulo en dos ángulos congruentes.	 $\overrightarrow{MP}$ is an angle bisector.
arc An unbroken part of a circle.	**arco** Parte continua de un círculo.	
area The number of square units needed to cover a given surface.	**área** El número de unidades cuadradas que se necesitan para cubrir una superficie dada.	
arithmetic sequence An ordered list of numbers in which the difference between consecutive terms is always the same.	**sucesión aritmética** Lista ordenada de números en la que la diferencia entre términos consecutivos es siempre la misma.	The sequence 2, 5, 8, 11, 14 … is an arithmetic sequence.
association A description of how data sets are related.	**asociación** Descripción de cómo se relaciona un conjunto de datos.	
Associative Property (of Addition) The property that states that for all real numbers a, b, and c, the sum is always the same, regardless of their grouping.	**Propiedad asociativa (de la suma)** Propiedad que establece que para todos los números reales a, b y c, la suma siempre es la misma sin importar cómo se agrupen.	$a + b + c = (a + b) + c = a + (b + c)$

ENGLISH	SPANISH	EXAMPLES
Associative Property (of Multiplication) The property that states that for all real numbers *a, b,* and *c,* their product is always the same, regardless of their grouping.	**Propiedad asociativa (de la multiplicación)** Propiedad que establece que para todos los números reales *a, b* y *c,* el producto siempre es el mismo, sin importar cómo se agrupen.	$a \cdot b \cdot c = (a \cdot b) \cdot c = a \cdot (b \cdot c)$
average The sum of a set of data divided by the number of items in the data set; also called *mean.*	**promedio** La suma de los elementos de un conjunto de datos dividida entre el número de elementos del conjunto. También se llama media.	Data set: 4, 6, 7, 8, 10 Average: $\frac{4+6+7+8+10}{5}$ $= \frac{35}{5} = 7$

B

back-to-back stem-and-leaf plot A stem-and-leaf plot that compares two sets of data by displaying one set of data to the left of the stem and the other to the right.	**diagrama doble de tallo y hojas** Diagrama de tallo y hojas que compara dos conjuntos de datos presentando uno de ellos a la izquierda del tallo y el otro a la derecha.	Data set A: 9, 12, 14, 16, 23, 27 Data set B: 6, 8, 10, 13, 15, 16, 21 Set A | | Set B 9 | 0 | 6 8 6 4 2 | 1 | 0 3 5 6 7 3 | 2 | 1 Key: |2| 1 means 21 7 |2| means 27
bar graph A graph that uses vertical or horizontal bars to display data.	**gráfica de barras** Gráfica en la que se usan barras verticales u horizontales para presentar datos.	
base When a number is raised to a power, the number that is used as a factor is the base.	**base** Cuando un número es elevado a una potencia, el número que se usa como factor es la base.	$3^5 = 3 \cdot 3 \cdot 3 \cdot 3 \cdot 3$; 3 is the base.
base (of a polygon or three-dimensional figure) A side of a polygon; a face of a three-dimensional figure by which the figure is measured or classified.	**base (de un polígono o figura tridimensional)** Lado de un polígono; cara de una figura tridimensional según la cual se mide o se clasifica la figura.	 Bases of Bases of a cylinder a prism Base of Base of a cone a pyramid

Sunlight's Travel Time to Planets

(Bar graph: Earth 500, Mars 760, Jupiter 2600, Saturn 4800; Time (s) vs. Planet)

Glossary/Glosario

ENGLISH	SPANISH	EXAMPLES
biased question A question that leads people to give a certain answer.	**pregunta tendenciosa** pregunta que lleva a las personas a dar una respuesta determinada	
biased sample A sample that does not fairly represent the population.	**muestra no representativa** Muestra que no representa adecuadamente la población.	
binomial A polynomial with two terms.	**binomio** Polinomio con dos términos.	$x + y$ $2a^2 - 3$ $4m^3n^2 + 6mn^4$
bisect To divide into two congruent parts.	**trazar una bisectriz** Dividir en dos partes congruentes.	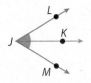 $\overrightarrow{JK}$ bisects $\angle LJM$.
bivariate data A set of data that is made of two paired variables.	**datos bivariados** Conjunto de datos compuesto de dos variables apareadas.	
boundary line The set of points where the two sides of a two-variable linear inequality are equal.	**línea de límite** Conjunto de puntos donde los dos lados de una desigualdad lineal con dos variables son iguales.	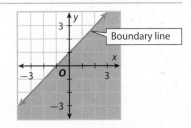
box-and-whisker plot A graph that shows how data are distributed by using the median, quartiles, least value, and greatest value; also called a *box plot*.	**gráfica de mediana y rango** Gráfica para demostrar la distribución de datos utilizando la mediana, los cuartiles y los valores menos y más grande; también llamado gráfica de caja.	
break (graph) A zigzag on a horizontal or vertical scale of a graph that indicates that some of the numbers on the scale have been omitted.	**discontinuidad (gráfica)** Zig-zag en la escala horizontal o vertical de una gráfica que indica la omisión de algunos de los números de la escala.	

capacity The amount a container can hold when filled.	**capacidad** Cantidad que cabe en un recipiente cuando se llena.	A large milk container has a capacity of 1 gallon.
Celsius A metric scale for measuring temperature in which 0 °C is the freezing point of water and 100 °C is the boiling point of water; also called *centigrade*.	**Celsius** Escala métrica para medir la temperatura, en la que 0 °C es el punto de congelación del agua y 100 °C es el punto de ebullición. También se llama *centígrado*.	

ENGLISH	SPANISH	EXAMPLES
center (of a circle) The point inside a circle that is the same distance from all the points on the circle.	**centro (de un círculo)** Punto interior de un círculo que se encuentra a la misma distancia de todos los puntos de la circunferencia.	
center of dilation The point of intersection of lines through each pair of corresponding vertices in a dilation.	**centro de una dilatación** Punto de intersección de las líneas que pasan a través de cada par de vértices correspondientes en una dilatación.	
center of rotation The point about which a figure is rotated.	**centro de una rotación** Punto alrededor del cual se hace girar una figura.	
central angle An angle formed by two radii with its vertex at the center of a circle.	**ángulo central de un círculo** Ángulo formado por dos radios cuyo vértice se encuentra en el centro de un círculo.	
chord A segment with its endpoints on a circle.	**cuerda** Segmento de recta cuyos extremos forman parte de un círculo.	
circle The set of all points in a plane that are the same distance from a given point called the center.	**círculo** Conjunto de todos los puntos en un plano que se encuentran a la misma distancia de un punto dado llamado centro.	
circle graph A graph that uses sectors of a circle to compare parts to the whole and parts to other parts.	**gráfica circular** Gráfica que usa secciones de un círculo para comparar partes con el todo y con otras partes.	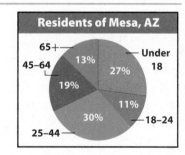
circuit A path in a graph that begins and ends at the same vertex.	**circuito** Una trayectoria en una gráfica que empieza y termina en el mismo vértice.	
circumference The distance around a circle.	**circunferencia** Distancia alrededor de un círculo.	

ENGLISH	SPANISH	EXAMPLES
clockwise A circular movement in the direction shown.	**en el sentido de las manecillas del reloj** Movimiento circular en la dirección que se indica.	
cluster A set of closely grouped data.	**agrupación** Conjunto de datos bien agrupados.	
clustering A condition that occurs when data points in a scatter plot are grouped more in one part of the graph than another.	**arracimando** Una condición que ocurre cuando los datos están apiñando en una parte de una diagrama de dispersión mas que en otras partes.	
coefficient The number that is multiplied by the variable in an algebraic expression.	**coeficiente** Número que se multiplica por la variable en una expresión algebraica.	5 is the coefficient in $5b$.
combination An arrangement of items or events in which order does not matter.	**combinación** Agrupación de objetos o sucesos en la que el orden no es importante.	For objects A, B, C, and D, there are 6 different combinations of 2 objects: AB, AC, AD, BC, BD, CD.
commission A fee paid to a person for making a sale.	**comisión** Pago que recibe una persona por realizar una venta.	
commission rate The fee paid to a person who makes a sale expressed as a percent of the selling price.	**tasa de comisión** Pago que recibe una persona por hacer una venta, expresado como un porcentaje del precio de venta.	A commission rate of 5% on a sale of $10,000 results in a commission of $500.
common denominator A denominator that is the same in two or more fractions.	**denominador común** Denominador que es común a dos o más fracciones.	The common denominator of $\frac{5}{8}$ and $\frac{2}{8}$ is 8.
common factor A number that is a factor of two or more numbers.	**factor común** Número que es factor de dos o más números.	8 is a common factor of 16 and 40.
common multiple A number that is a multiple of each of two or more numbers.	**múltiplo común** Número que es múltiplo de dos o más números.	15 is a common multiple of 3 and 5.
common ratio The ratio each term is multiplied by to produce the next term in a geometric sequence.	**razón común** Razón por la que se multiplica cada término para obtener el siguiente término de una sucesión geométrica.	In the geometric sequence 32, 16, 8, 4, 2, …, the common ratio is $\frac{1}{2}$.
Commutative Property (of Addition) The property that states that two or more numbers can be added in any order without changing the sum.	**Propiedad conmutativa (de la suma)** Propiedad que establece que sumar dos o más números en cualquier orden no altera la suma.	$8 + 20 = 20 + 8; a + b = b + a$

ENGLISH	SPANISH	EXAMPLES
Commutative Property (of Multiplication) The property that states that two or more numbers can be multiplied in any order without changing the product.	**Propiedad conmutativa (de la multiplicación)** Propiedad que establece que multiplicar dos o más números en cualquier orden no altera el producto.	$6 \cdot 12 = 12 \cdot 6;\ a \cdot b = b \cdot a$
compatible numbers Numbers that are close to the given numbers that make estimation or mental calculation easier.	**números compatibles** Números que están cerca de los números dados y hacen más fácil la estimación o el cálculo mental.	To estimate $7{,}957 + 5{,}009$, use the compatible numbers 8,000 and 5,000: $8{,}000 + 5{,}000 = 13{,}000$
complement The set of all outcomes in the sample space that are not the event.	**complemento** La serie de resultados que no están en el suceso.	Experiment: rolling a number cube Sample space: {1, 2, 3, 4, 5, 6} Event: rolling a 1, 3, 4, or 6 Complement: rolling a 2 or 5
complementary angles Two angles whose measures add to 90°.	**ángulos complementarios** Dos ángulos cuyas medidas suman 90°.	The complement of a 53° angle is a 37° angle.
composite figure A figure made up of simple geometric shapes.	**figura compuesta** Figura formada por figuras geométricas simples.	
composite number A number greater than 1 that has more than two whole-number factors.	**número compuesto** Número mayor que 1 que tiene más de dos factores que son números cabales.	4, 6, 8, and 9 are composite numbers.
compound interest Interest earned or paid on principal and previously earned or paid interest.	**interés compuesto** Interés que se gana o se paga sobre el capital y los intereses previamente ganados o pagados.	If $100 is put into an account with an interest rate of 5% compounded monthly, then after 2 years, the account will have $100\left(1 + \frac{0.05}{12}\right)^{12\cdot2} =$ $110.49
conditional relative frequency The ratio of a joint relative frequency to a related marginal relative frequency in a two-way table.	**frecuencia relativa condicional** Razón de una frecuencia relativa conjunta a una frecuencia relativa marginal en una tabla de doble entrada.	
cone A three-dimensional figure with one vertex and one circular base.	**cono** Figura tridimensional con un vértice y una base circular.	
congruence transformation A transformation that results in an image that is the same shape and the same size as the original figure.	**transformación de congruencia** Una transformación que resulta en una imagen que tiene la misma forma y el mismo tamaño como la figura original.	

Glossary/Glosario

ENGLISH	SPANISH	EXAMPLES
congruent Two plane or solid figures are congruent if one can be obtained from the other by rigid motion (a sequence of rotations, reflections, and translations).	**congruentes** Dos figuras planas o dos cuerpos geométricos son congruentes si de una figura se obtiene la otra mediante un movimiento rígido (una secuencia de rotaciones, reflexiones y traslaciones).	$PQRS \cong WXYZ$
congruent angles Angles that have the same measure.	**ángulos congruentes** Ángulos que tienen la misma medida.	$\angle ABC \cong \angle DEF$
congruent figures See *congruent*.	**figuras congruentes** Vea *congruentes*.	
congruent segments Segments that have the same length.	**segmentos congruentes** Segmentos que tienen la misma longitud.	$\overline{PQ} \cong \overline{SR}$
conjecture A statement believed to be true.	**conjetura** Enunciado que se supone verdadero.	
constant A value that does not change.	**constante** Valor que no cambia.	$3, 0, \pi$
constant of variation The constant k in direct and inverse variation equations.	**constante de variación** La constante k en ecuaciones de variación directa e inversa.	$y = 5x$ ↑ Constant of variation
continuous graph A graph made up of connected lines or curves.	**gráfica continua** Gráfica compuesta por líneas rectas o curvas conectadas.	
convenience sample A sample based on members of the population that are readily available.	**muestra de conveniencia** Una muestra basada en miembros de la población que están fácilmente disponibles.	
conversion factor A fraction whose numerator and denominator represent the same quantity but use different units; the fraction is equal to 1 because the numerator and denominator are equal.	**factor de conversión** Fracción cuyo numerador y denominador representan la misma cantidad pero con unidades distintas; la fracción es igual a 1 porque el numerador y el denominador son iguales.	$\frac{24 \text{ hours}}{1 \text{ day}}$ and $\frac{1 \text{ day}}{24 \text{ hours}}$
coordinate One of the numbers of an ordered pair that locate a point on a coordinate graph.	**coordenada** Uno de los números de un par ordenado que ubica un punto en una gráfica de coordenadas.	The coordinates of *B* are (−2, 3).

coordinate plane A plane formed by the intersection of a horizontal number line called the *x*-axis and a vertical number line called the *y*-axis.

plano cartesiano Plano formado por la intersección de una recta numérica horizontal llamada eje *x* y otra vertical llamada eje *y*.

---

correlation The description of the relationship between two data sets.

correlación Descripción de la relación entre dos conjuntos de datos.

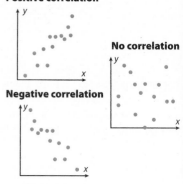

Positive correlation

No correlation

Negative correlation

---

correspondence The relationship between two or more objects that are matched.

correspondencia La relación entre dos o más objetos que coinciden.

∠*A* and ∠*D* are corresponding angles.

$\overline{AB}$ and $\overline{DE}$ are corresponding sides.

---

corresponding angles (for lines) For two lines intersected by a transversal, a pair of angles that lie on the same side of the transversal and on the same sides of the other two lines.

ángulos correspondientes (en líneas) Dadas dos rectas cortadas por una transversal, el par de ángulos ubicados en el mismo lado de la transversal y en los mismos lados de las otras dos rectas.

Transversal

∠1 and ∠3 are corresponding angles.

---

corresponding angles (of polygons) Angles in the same relative position in polygons with an equal number of sides.

ángulos correspondientes (en polígonos) Ángulos en la misma posición formaron cuando una tercera línea interseca dos líneas.

∠*A* and ∠*D* are corresponding angles.

---

corresponding sides Matching sides of two or more polygons.

lados correspondientes Lados que se ubican en la misma posición relativa en dos o más polígonos.

$\overline{AB}$ and $\overline{DE}$ are corresponding sides.

---

counterclockwise A circular movement in the direction shown.

en sentido contrario a las manecillas del reloj Movimiento circular en la dirección que se indica.

Glossary/Glosario

ENGLISH	SPANISH	EXAMPLES
counterexample An example that proves that a conjecture or statement is false.	**contraejemplo** Ejemplo que demuestra que una conjetura o enunciado es falso.	
cube (geometric figure) A rectangular prism with six congruent square faces.	**cubo (figura geométrica)** Prisma rectangular con seis caras cuadradas congruentes.	
cube (in numeration) A number raised to the third power.	**cubo (en numeración)** Número elevado a la tercera potencia.	$2^3 = 2 \cdot 2 \cdot 2 = 8$ 8 is the cube of 2.
cube root A number, written as $\sqrt[3]{x}$, whose cube is x.	**raíz cúbica** Número, expresado como $\sqrt[3]{x}$, cuyo cubo es x.	$\sqrt[3]{8} = \sqrt[3]{2 \cdot 2 \cdot 2} = 2$ 2 is the cube root of 8.
cumulative frequency The sum of successive data items.	**frecuencia acumulativa** La suma de datos sucesivos.	
customary system of measurement The measurement system often used in the United States.	**sistema usual de medidas** El sistema de medidas que se usa comúnmente en Estados Unidos.	inches, feet, miles, ounces, pounds, tons, cups, quarts, gallons
cylinder A three-dimensional figure with two parallel, congruent circular bases connected by a curved lateral surface.	**cilindro** Figura tridimensional con dos bases circulares paralelas y congruentes, unidas por una superficie lateral curva.	

D

decagon A polygon with ten sides.	**decágono** Polígono de diez lados.	
degree The unit of measure for angles or temperature.	**grado** Unidad de medida para ángulos y temperaturas.	
degree of a polynomial The highest power of the variable in a polynomial.	**grado de un polinomio** La potencia más alta de la variable en un polinomio.	The polynomial $4x^5 - 6x^2 + 7$ has degree 5.
denominator The bottom number of a fraction that tells how many equal parts are in the whole.	**denominador** Número que está abajo en una fracción y que indica en cuántas partes iguales se divide el entero.	In the fraction $\frac{2}{5}$, 5 is the denominator.
Density Property The property that states that between any two real numbers there is always another real number.	**Propiedad de densidad** Propiedad según la cual entre dos números reales cualesquiera siempre hay otro número real.	

ENGLISH	SPANISH	EXAMPLES
dependent events Events for which the outcome of one event affects the probability of the other.	**sucesos dependientes** Dos sucesos son dependientes si el resultado de uno afecta la probabilidad del otro.	A bag contains 3 red marbles and 2 blue marbles. Drawing a red marble and then drawing a blue marble without replacing the first marble is an example of dependent events.
dependent variable The output of a function; a variable whose value depends on the value of the input, or independent variable.	**variable dependiente** Salida de una función; variable cuyo valor depende del valor de la entrada, o variable independiente.	For $y = 2x + 1$, y is the dependent variable. input: x output: y
diagonal A line segment that connects two nonadjacent vertices of a polygon.	**diagonal** Segmento de recta que une dos vértices no adyacentes de un polígono.	
diameter A line segment that passes through the center of a circle and has endpoints on the circle, or the length of that segment.	**diámetro** Segmento de recta que pasa por el centro de un círculo y tiene sus extremos en la circunferencia, o bien la longitud de ese segmento.	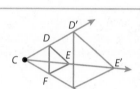
dilation A transformation that moves each point along the ray through the point emanating from a fixed center, and multiplies distances from the center by a common scale factor.	**dilatación** Transformación que mueve cada punto de la semirrecta a través del punto que emana de un centro fijo y multiplica la distancia desde el centro por un factor de escala común.	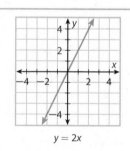
dimensions (geometry) The length, width, or height of a figure.	**dimensiones (geometría)** Longitud, ancho o altura de una figura.	
dimensions (of a matrix) The number of horizontal rows and vertical columns in a matrix.	**dimensiones (de una matriz)** Número de filas y columnas que hay en una matriz.	
direct variation A linear relationship between two variables, x and y, that can be written in the form $y = kx$, where k is a nonzero constant.	**variación directa** Relación lineal entre dos variables, x e y, que puede expresarse en la forma $y = kx$, donde k es una constante distinta de cero.	 $y = 2x$
discount The amount by which the original price is reduced.	**descuento** Cantidad que se resta del precio original de un artículo.	
discrete graph A graph made up of unconnected points.	**gráfica discreta** Gráfica compuesta de puntos no conectados.	

ENGLISH	SPANISH	EXAMPLES
disjoint events See *mutually exclusive*.	**sucesos disjuntos** Vea *mutuamente excluyentes*.	
Distributive Property For all real numbers a, b, and c, $a(b + c) = ab + ac$, and $a(b - c) = ab - ac$.	**Propiedad distributiva** Dados los números reales a, b, y c, $a(b + c) = ab + ac$, y $a(b - c) = ab - ac$.	$5 \cdot 21 = 5(20 + 1) =$ $(5 \cdot 20) + (5 \cdot 1)$
dividend The number to be divided in a division problem.	**dividendo** Número que se divide en un problema de división.	In $8 \div 4 = 2$, 8 is the dividend.
divisible Can be divided by a number without leaving a remainder.	**divisible** Que se puede dividir entre un número sin dejar residuo.	18 is divisible by 3.
Division Property of Equality The property that states that if you divide both sides of an equation by the same nonzero number, the new equation will have the same solution.	**Propiedad de igualdad de la división** Propiedad que establece que puedes dividir ambos lados de una ecuación entre el mismo número distinto de cero, y la nueva ecuación tendrá la misma solución.	
divisor The number you are dividing by in a division problem.	**divisor** El número entre el que se divide en un problema de división.	In $8 \div 4 = 2$, 4 is the divisor.
dodecahedron A polyhedron with 12 faces.	**dodecaedro** Poliedro de 12 caras.	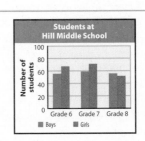
domain The set of all possible input values of a function.	**dominio** Conjunto de todos los posibles valores de entrada de una función.	The domain of the function $y = x^2 + 1$ is all real numbers.
double-bar graph A bar graph that compares two related sets of data.	**gráfica de doble barra** Gráfica de barras que compara dos conjuntos de datos relacionados.	**Students at Hill Middle School**

ENGLISH	SPANISH	EXAMPLES

double-line graph A line graph that shows how two related sets of data change over time.

gráfica de doble línea Gráfica lineal que muestra cómo cambian con el tiempo dos conjuntos de datos relacionados.

E

edge The line segment along which two faces of a polyhedron intersect.

arista Segmento de recta donde se intersecan dos caras de un poliedro.

endpoint A point at the end of a line segment or ray.

extremo Un punto ubicado al final de un segmento de recta o rayo.

enlargement An increase in size of all dimensions in the same proportions.

agrandamiento Aumento de tamaño de todas las dimensiones en las mismas proporciones.

entries (of a matrix) Individual entries in a matrix.

elementos (de una matriz) Entradas individuales de una matriz.

equally likely Outcomes that have the same probability.

resultados igualmente probables Resultados que tienen la misma probabilidad de ocurrir.

When tossing a coin, the outcomes "heads" and "tails" are equally likely.

equation A mathematical sentence that shows that two expressions are equivalent.

ecuación Enunciado matemático que indica que dos expresiones son equivalentes.

$x + 4 = 7$
$6 + 1 = 10 - 3$

equilateral triangle A triangle with three congruent sides.

triángulo equilátero Triángulo con tres lados congruentes.

equivalent Having the same value.

equivalentes Que tienen el mismo valor.

equivalent expressions Expressions that have the same value for all values of the variables.

expresiones equivalentes Las expresiones equivalentes tienen el mismo valor para todos los valores de las variables.

$4x + 5x$ and $9x$ are equivalent expressions.

equivalent fractions Fractions that name the same amount or part.

fracciones equivalentes Fracciones que representan la misma cantidad o parte.

$\frac{1}{2}$ and $\frac{2}{4}$ are equivalent fractions.

Glossary/Glosario

ENGLISH	SPANISH	EXAMPLES
equivalent ratios Ratios that name the same comparison.	**razones equivalentes** Razones que representan la misma comparación.	$\frac{1}{2}$ and $\frac{2}{4}$ are equivalent ratios.
estimate (*n*) An answer that is close to the exact answer and is found by rounding or other methods. (*v*) To find such an answer.	**estimación** Una solución aproximada a la respuesta exacta que se halla mediante el redondeo u otros métodos. **estimar** Hallar una solución aproximada a la respuesta exacta.	500 is an estimate for the sum $98 + 287 + 104$.
evaluate To find the value of a numerical or algebraic expression.	**evaluar** Hallar el valor de una expresión numérica o algebraica.	Evaluate $2x + 7$ for $x = 3$. $2x + 7$ $2(3) + 7$ $6 + 7$ 13
event An outcome or set of outcomes of an experiment or situation.	**suceso** Un resultado o una serie de resultados de un experimento o una situación.	When rolling a number cube, the event "an odd number" consists of the outcomes 1, 3, and 5.
expanded form A multi-digit number is expressed in expanded form when it is written as a sum of single-digit multiples of powers of ten.	**forma desarrollada** Un número de varios dígitos se expresa en forma desarrollada cuando se escribe como la suma de múltiplos de un dígito de potencias de diez.	236,536 written in expanded form is $200{,}000 + 30{,}000 + 6{,}000 + 500 + 30 + 6$.
experiment (probability) In probability, any activity based on chance (such as tossing a coin).	**experimento (probabilidad)** En probabilidad, cualquier actividad basada en la posibilidad, como lanzar una moneda.	Tossing a coin 10 times and noting the number of "heads"
experimental probability The ratio of the number of times an event occurs to the total number of trials, or times that the activity is performed.	**probabilidad experimental** Razón del número de veces que ocurre un suceso al número total de pruebas o al número de que se realiza el experimento.	Kendra attempted 27 free throws and made 16 of them. Her experimental probability of making a free throw is $\frac{\text{number made}}{\text{number attempted}} = \frac{16}{27} \approx 0.59$.
exponent The number that indicates how many times the base is used as a factor.	**exponente** Número que indica cuántas veces se usa la base como factor.	$2^3 = 2 \times 2 \times 2 = 8;$ 3 is the exponent.
exponential decay An exponential function of the form $f(x) = a \cdot r^x$ in which $0 < r < 1$.	**decremento exponencial** Función exponencial del tipo $f(x) = a \cdot r^x$ en la cual $0 < r < 1$.	
exponential form A number written with a base and an exponent.	**forma exponencial** Se dice que un número está en forma exponencial cuando se escribe con una base y un exponente.	4^2 is the exponential form for $4 \cdot 4$.
exponential function A nonlinear function in which the variable is in the exponent.	**función exponencial** Función no lineal en la que la variable está en el exponente.	$f(x) = 4^x$
exponential growth An exponential function of the form $f(x) = a \cdot r^x$ in which $r > 1$.	**crecimiento exponencial** Función exponencial del tipo $f(x) = a \cdot r^x$ en la cual $r > 1$.	

expression A mathematical phrase that contains operations, numbers, and/or variables.

expresión Enunciado matemático que contiene operaciones, números y/o variables.

$6x + 1$

exterior angle (of a polygon) An angle formed by one side of a polygon and the extension of an adjacent side.

ángulo extreno de un polígono Ángulo formado por un lado de un polígono y la prolongación del lado adyacente.

F

face A flat surface of a polyhedron.

cara Superficie plana de un poliedro.

Face

factor A number that is multiplied by another number to get a product.

factor Número que se multiplica por otro para hallar un producto.

7 is a factor of 21 since $7 \cdot 3 = 21$.

factorial The product of all whole numbers except zero that are less than or equal to a number.

factorial El producto de todos los números cabales, excepto cero, que son menores que o iguales a un número.

$4 \text{ factorial} = 4! = 4 \cdot 3 \cdot 2 \cdot 1$

Fahrenheit A temperature scale in which 32 °F is the freezing point of water and 212 °F is the boiling point of water.

Fahrenheit Escala de temperatura en la que 32° F es el punto de congelación del agua y 212° F es el punto de ebullición.

fair When all outcomes of an experiment are equally likely, the experiment is said to be fair.

justo Se dice de un experimento donde todos los resultados posibles son igualmente probables.

When tossing a coin, heads and tails are equally likely, so it is a fair experiment.

Fibonacci sequence The infinite sequence of numbers (1, 1, 2, 3, 5, 8, 13,…); starting with the third term, each number is the sum of the two previous numbers; it is named after the thirteenth-century mathematician Leonardo Fibonacci.

sucesión de Fibonacci La sucesión infinita de números (1, 1, 2, 3, 5, 8, 13…); a partir del tercer término, cada número es la suma de los dos anteriores. Esta sucesión lleva el nombre de Leonardo Fibonacci, un matemático del siglo XIII.

1, 1, 2, 3, 5, 8, 13, . . .

first differences A sequence formed by subtracting each term of a sequence from the next term.

primeras diferencias Sucesión que se forma al restar cada término de una sucesión del término siguiente.

For the sequence 4, 7, 10, 13, 16, . . ., the first differences are all 3.

first quartile The median of the lower half of a set of data; also called *lower quartile*.

primer cuartil La mediana de la mitad inferior de un conjunto de datos. También se llama *cuartil inferior*.

Glossary/Glosario

ENGLISH	SPANISH	EXAMPLES

FOIL An acronym for the terms used when multiplying two binomials: the First, Outer, Inner, and Last terms.

FOIL Sigla en inglés de los términos que se usan al multiplicar dos binomios: los primeros, los externos, los internos y los últimos (First, Outer, Inner, Last).

$(x + 2)(x - 3) = x^2 - 3x + 2x - 6$
$= x^2 - x - 6$

---

formula A rule showing relationships among quantities.

fórmula Regla que muestra relaciones entre cantidades.

$A = \ell w$ is the formula for the area of a rectangle.

---

fractal A structure with repeating patterns containing shapes that are like the whole but are of different sizes throughout.

fractal Estructura con patrones repetidos que contiene figuras similares al patrón general pero de diferente tamaño.

---

fraction A number expressible in the form $\frac{a}{b}$ where a is a whole number and b is a positive whole number.

fracción Número que se puede expresar en la forma $\frac{a}{b}$, donde a es un número entero y b es un número entero positivo.

$\frac{2}{3}$

---

frequency The number of times the value appears in the data set.

frecuencia Cantidad de veces que aparece el valor en un conjunto de datos.

Data set: 5, 6, 6, 7, 8, 9
The data value 6 has a frequency of 2.

---

frequency table A table that lists items together according to the number of times, or frequency, that the items occur.

tabla de frecuencia Una tabla en la que se organizan los datos de acuerdo con el número de veces que aparece cada valor (o la frecuencia).

Data set: 1, 1, 2, 2, 3, 5, 5, 5
Frequency table:

Data	Frequency
1	2
2	2
3	1

---

function An input-output relationship that has exactly one output for each input.

función Regla que relaciona dos candidates de forma que a cada valor de entrada corresponde exactamente un valor de salida.

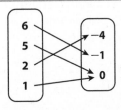

---

function notation The notation used to describe a function.

notación de función Notación que se usa para describir una función.

Equation: $y = 2x$
Function notation: $f(x) = 2x$

---

function table A table of ordered pairs that represent solutions of a function.

tabla de función Tabla de pares ordenados que representan soluciones de una función.

x	3	4	5	6
y	7	9	11	13

Fundamental Counting Principle If one event has m possible outcomes and a second event has n possible outcomes after the first event has occurred, then there are $m \cdot n$ total possible outcomes for the two events.

Principio fundamental de conteo Si un suceso tiene m resultados posibles y otro suceso tiene n resultados posibles después de ocurrido el primer suceso, entonces hay $m \cdot n$ resultados posibles en total para los dos sucesos.

There are 4 colors of shirts and 3 colors of pants. There are $4 \cdot 3 = 12$ possible outfits.

Glossary/Glosario

geometric probability A form of theoretical probability determined by a ratio of geometric measures such as lengths, areas, or volumes.

probabilidad geométrica Método para calcular probabilidades basado en una medida geométrica como la longitud o el área.

The probability of the pointer landing on red is $\frac{80}{360}$, or $\frac{2}{9}$.

geometric sequence An ordered list of numbers that has a common ratio between consecutive terms.

sucesión geométrica Lista ordenada de números que tiene una razón común entre términos consecutivos.

The sequence 2, 4, 8, 16 . . . is a geometric sequence.

graph of an equation A graph of the set of ordered pairs that are solutions of the equation.

gráfica de una ecuación Gráfica del conjunto de pares ordenados que son soluciones de la ecuación.

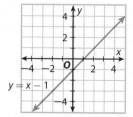

$y = x - 1$

great circle A circle on a sphere such that the plane containing the circle passes through the center of the sphere.

círculo máximo Círculo de una esfera tal que el plano que contiene el círculo pasa por el centro de la esfera.

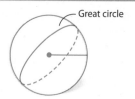

Great circle

greatest common factor (GCF) The largest common factor of two or more given numbers.

máximo común divisor (MCD) El mayor de los factores comunes compartidos por dos o más números dados.

The GCF of 27 and 45 is 9.

height In a pyramid or cone, the perpendicular distance from the base to the opposite vertex.

altura En una pirámide o cono, la distancia perpendicular desde la base al vértice opuesto.

In a triangle or quadrilateral, the perpendicular distance from the base to the opposite vertex or side.

En un triángulo o cuadrilátero, la distancia perpendicular desde la base de la figura al vértice o lado opuesto.

In a prism or cylinder, the perpendicular distance between the bases.

En un prisma o cilindro, la distancia perpendicular entre las bases.

ENGLISH	SPANISH	EXAMPLES
hemisphere A half of a sphere.	**hemisferio** La mitad de una esfera.	
heptagon A seven-sided polygon.	**heptágono** Polígono de siete lados.	
hexagon A six-sided polygon.	**hexágono** Polígono de seis lados.	
histogram A bar graph that shows the frequency of data within equal intervals.	**histograma** Gráfica de barras que muestra la frecuencia de los datos en intervalos iguales.	
hypotenuse In a right triangle, the side opposite the right angle.	**hipotenusa** En un triángulo rectángulo, el lado opuesto al ángulo recto.	Hypotenuse

Identity Property Addition The property that states the sum of zero and any number is that number.	**Propiedad de identidad de la suma** Propiedad que establece que la suma de cero y cualquier número es ese número.	$4 + 0 = 4$ $-3 + 0 = -3$
Identity Property Multiplication The property that states that the product of 1 and any number is that number.	**Propiedad de identidad de la multiplicación** Propiedad que establece que el producto de 1 y cualquier número es ese número.	$4 \cdot 1 = 4$ $-3 \cdot 1 = -3$
image A figure resulting from a transformation.	**imagen** Figura que resulta de una transformación.	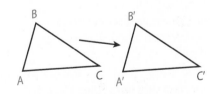 A'B'C' is the image of ABC.
improper fraction A fraction in which the numerator is greater than or equal to the denominator.	**fracción impropia** Fracción cuyo numerador es mayor que o igual al denominador.	$\frac{17}{5}, \frac{3}{3}$

	ENGLISH	SPANISH	EXAMPLES

independent events Events for which the outcome of one event does not affect the probability of the other.

sucesos independientes Dos sucesos son independientes si el resultado de uno no afecta la probabilidad del otro.

A bag contains 3 red marbles and 2 blue marbles. Drawing a red marble, replacing it, and then drawing a blue marble is an example of independent events.

---

independent variable The input of a function; a variable whose value determines the value of the output, or dependent variable.

variable independiente Entrada de una función; variable cuyo valor determina el valor de la salida, o variable dependiente.

For $y = 2x + 1$, x is the independent variable.
input: x output: y

---

indirect measurement The technique of using similar figures and proportions to find a measure.

medición indirecta La técnica de usar figuras semejantes y proporciones para hallar una medida.

---

inductive reasoning Using a pattern to make a conclusion.

razonamiento inductivo Uso de un patrón para sacar una conclusión.

---

inequality A mathematical sentence that shows the relationship between quantities that are not equivalent.

desigualdad Enunciado matemático que muestra una relación entre cantidades que no son equivalentes.

$5 < 8$
$5x + 2 \geq 12$

---

input The value substituted into an expression or function.

valor de entrada Valor que se usa para sustituir una variable en una expresión o función.

For the function $y = 6x$, the input 4 produces an output of 24.

---

inscribed angle An angle formed by two chords with its vertex on a circle.

ángulo inscrito Ángulo formado por dos cuerdas cuyo vértice está en un círculo.

---

integers The set of whole numbers and their opposites.

enteros Conjunto de todos los números cabales y sus opuestos.

$\ldots -3, -2, -1, 0, 1, 2, 3, \ldots$

---

interest The amount of money charged for borrowing or using money.

interés Cantidad de dinero que se cobra por el préstamo o uso del dinero.

---

interior angles Angles on the inner sides of two lines cut by a transversal.

ángulos internos Ángulos en los lados internos de dos líneas intersecadas por una transversal.

$\angle 1$ is an interior angle.

---

interquartile range (IQR) The difference of the third (upper) and first (lower) quartiles in a data set, representing the middle half of the data.

rango intercuartil (RIC) Diferencia entre el tercer cuartil (superior) y el primer cuartil (inferior) de un conjunto de datos, que representa la mitad central de los datos.

Interquartile range:
$36 - 23 = 13$

---

intersecting lines Lines that cross at exactly one point.

líneas secantes Líneas que se cruzan en un solo punto.

ENGLISH	SPANISH	EXAMPLES
interval The space between marked values on a number line or the scale of a graph.	**intervalo** El espacio entre los valores marcados en una recta numérica o en la escala de una gráfica.	
inverse operations Operations that undo each other: addition and subtraction, or multiplication and division.	**operaciones inversas** Operaciones que se cancelan mutuamente: suma y resta, o multiplicación y división.	Addition and subtraction are inverse operations: $5 + 3 = 8; 8 - 3 = 5$ Multiplication and division are inverse operations: $2 \cdot 3 = 6; 6 \div 3 = 2$
inverse variation A relationship in which one variable quantity increases as another variable quantity decreases; the product of the variables is a constant.	**variación inversa** Relación en la que una cantidad variable aumenta a medida que otra cantidad variable disminuye; el producto de las variables es una constante.	$xy = 7, y = \frac{7}{x}$
irrational number A number that cannot be expressed as a ratio of two integers or as a repeating or terminating decimal.	**número irracional** Número que no se puede expresar como una razón de dos enteros ni como un decimal periódico o finito.	$\sqrt{2}, \pi$
isolate the variable To get a variable alone on one side of an equation or inequality in order to solve the equation or inequality.	**despejar la variable** Dejar sola la variable en un lado de una ecuación o desigualdad para resolverla.	$\begin{aligned} x + 7 &= 22 \\ \underline{-7} &\underline{-7} \\ x &= 15 \end{aligned}$ $\begin{aligned} \frac{12}{3} &= \frac{3x}{3} \\ 4 &= x \end{aligned}$
isometric drawing A representation of a three-dimensional figure that is drawn on a grid of equilateral triangles.	**dibujo isométrico** Representación de una figura tridimensional que se dibuja sobre una cuadrícula de triángulos equiláteros.	
isosceles triangle A triangle with at least two congruent sides.	**triángulo isósceles** Triángulo que tiene al menos dos lados congruentes.	

| **joint relative frequency** The ratio of the frequency in a particular category divided by the total number of data values. | **frecuencia relativa conjunta** La razón de la frecuencia en una determinada categoría dividida entre el número total de valores. | |

| **lateral area** The sum of the areas of the lateral faces of a prism or pyramid, or the area of the lateral surface of a cylinder or cone. | **área lateral** Suma de las áreas de las caras laterales de un prisma o pirámide, o área de la superficie lateral de un cilindro o cono. |
Lateral area = area of the 5 rectangular faces |

lateral face In a prism or a pyramid, a face that is not a base.

cara lateral En un prisma o pirámide, una cara que no es la base.

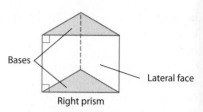

Bases

Lateral face

Right prism

---

lateral surface In a cylinder, the curved surface connecting the circular bases; in a cone, the curved surface that is not a base.

superficie lateral En un cilindro, superficie curva que une las bases circulares; en un cono, la superficie curva que no es la base.

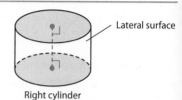

Lateral surface

Right cylinder

---

least common denominator (LCD) The least common multiple of two or more denominators.

mínimo común denominador (mcd) El mínimo común múltiplo más pequeño de dos o más denominadores.

The LCD of $\frac{3}{4}$ and $\frac{5}{6}$ is 12.

---

least common multiple (LCM) The smallest whole number, other than zero, that is a multiple of two or more given numbers.

mínimo común múltiplo (mcm) El menor de los números cabales, distinto de cero, que es múltiplo de dos o más números dados.

The LCM of 6 and 10 is 30.

---

legs In a right triangle, the sides that include the right angle; in an isosceles triangle, the pair of congruent sides.

catetos En un triángulo rectángulo, los lados adyacentes al ángulo recto. En un triángulo isósceles, el par de lados congruentes.

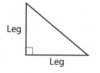

Leg

Leg

---

like fractions Fractions that have the same denominator.

fracciones semejantes Fracciones que tienen el mismo denominador.

$\frac{5}{12}$ and $\frac{7}{12}$ are like fractions.

---

like terms Terms that have the same variable raised to the same exponents.

términos semejantes Términos que contienen las mismas variables elevada a las mismas exponentes.

In the expression $3a^2 + 5b + 12a^2$, $3a^2$ and $12a^2$ are like terms.

---

line A straight path that has no thickness and extends forever.

línea Un trazo recto que no tiene grosor y se extiende infinitamente.

---

line graph A graph that uses line segments to show how data changes.

gráfica lineal Gráfica que muestra cómo cambian los datos mediante segmentos de recta.

Marlon's Video Game Scores

---

line of best fit A straight line that comes closest to the points on a scatter plot.

línea de mejor ajuste La línea recta que más se aproxima a los puntos de un diagrama de dispersión.

Glossary/Glosario

ENGLISH	SPANISH	EXAMPLES
line of reflection A line that a figure is flipped across to create a mirror image of the original figure.	**línea de reflexión** Línea sobre la cual se invierte una figura para crear una imagen reflejada de la figura original.	
line of symmetry A line that divides a figure into two congruent reflected halves.	**eje de simetría** Línea que divide una figura en dos mitades reflejas.	
line plot A number line with marks or dots that show frequency.	**diagrama de acumulación** Recta numérica con marcas o puntos que indican la frecuencia.	
line segment A part of a line consisting of two endpoints and all points between them.	**segmento de recta** Parte de una línea que consiste en dos extremos y todos los puntos entre éstos.	
line symmetry A figure has line symmetry if one half is a mirror image of the other half.	**simetría axial** Una figura tiene simetría axial si una de sus mitades es la imagen reflejada de la otra.	
linear equation An equation whose solutions form a straight line on a coordinate plane.	**ecuación lineal** Ecuación cuyas soluciones forman una línea recta en un plano cartesiano.	$y = 2x + 1$
linear function A function whose graph is a straight line.	**función lineal** Función cuya gráfica es una línea recta.	$y = x - 1$
linear inequality A mathematical sentence using $<$, $>$, $\leq$, or $\geq$ whose graph is a region with a straight-line boundary.	**desigualdad lineal** Enunciado matemático en que se usan los símbolos $<$, $>$, $\leq$, o $\geq$ y cuya gráfica es una región con una línea de límite recta.	
literal equation An equation that contains two or more variables.	**ecuación literal** Ecuación que contiene dos o más variables.	$d = rt$ $A = bh$

major arc An arc that is more than half of a circle.

arco mayor Arco que es más de la mitad de un círculo.

$\overset{\frown}{ADC}$ is a major arc of the circle.

---

marginal relative frequency The sum of the joint relative frequencies in a row or column of a two-way table.

frecuencia relativa marginal La suma de las frecuencias relativas conjuntas en una fila o columna de una tabla de doble entrada.

---

matrix A rectangular arrangement of data enclosed in brackets.

matriz Arreglo rectangular de datos encerrado entre corchetes.

$$\begin{bmatrix} 1 & 0 & 3 \\ -2 & 2 & -5 \\ 7 & -6 & 3 \end{bmatrix}$$

---

mean The sum of a set of data divided by the number of items in the data set; also called *average*.

media La suma de todos los elementos de un conjunto de datos dividida entre el número de elementos del conjunto. También se llama promedio.

Data set: 4, 6, 7, 8, 10
Mean:
$$\frac{4+6+7+8+10}{5} = \frac{35}{5} = 7$$

---

mean absolute deviation (MAD) The mean distance between each data value and the mean of the data set.

desviación absoluta media (DAM) Distancia media entre cada dato y la media del conjunto de datos.

---

measure of center A measure used to describe the middle of a data set; the mean, median, and mode are measures of center. Also called *measure of central tendency*.

medida de tendencia dominante Medida que describe la parte media de un conjunto de datos; la media, la mediana y la moda son medidas de tendencia dominante.

---

median The middle number, or the mean (average) of the two middle numbers, in an ordered set of data.

mediana El número intermedio o la media (el promedio) de los dos números intermedios en un conjunto ordenado de datos.

Data set: 4, 6, 7, 8, 10
Median: 7

---

metric system of measurement A decimal system of weights and measures that is used universally in science and commonly throughout the world.

sistema métrico de medición Sistema decimal de pesos y medidas empleado universalmente en las ciencias y de uso común en todo el mundo.

centimeters, meters, kilometers, grams, kilograms, milliliters, liters

---

midpoint The point that divides a line segment into two congruent line segments.

punto medio El punto que divide un segmento de recta en dos segmentos de recta congruentes.

```
A        B        C
•────┼────•────┼────•
```
B is the midpoint of $\overline{AC}$.

---

minor arc An arc that is less than half of a circle.

arco menor Arco que es menor que la mitad de un círculo.

$\overset{\frown}{AC}$ is the minor arc of the circle.

ENGLISH	SPANISH	EXAMPLES
mixed number A number made up of a whole number that is not zero and a fraction.	**número mixto** Número compuesto por un número cabal distinto de cero y una fracción.	$4\frac{1}{8}$
mode The number or numbers that occur most frequently in a set of data; when all numbers occur with the same frequency, we say there is no mode.	**moda** Número o números más frecuentes en un conjunto de datos; si todos los números aparecen con la misma frecuencia, no hay moda.	Data set: 3, 5, 8, 8, 10 Mode: 8
monomial A number or a product of numbers and variables with exponents that are whole numbers.	**monomio** Un número o un producto de números y variables con exponentes que son números cabales.	$3x^2y^4$
Multiplication Property of Equality The property that states that if you multiply both sides of an equation by the same number, the new equation will have the same solution.	**Propiedad de igualdad de la multiplicación** Propiedad que establece que puedes multiplicar ambos lados de una ecuación por el mismo número y la nueva ecuación tendrá la misma solución.	$3 \cdot 4 = 12$ $3 \cdot 4 \cdot 2 = 12 \cdot 2$ $24 = 24$
Multiplication Property of Zero The property that states that for all real numbers a, $a \cdot 0 = 0$ and $0 \cdot a = 0$.	**Propiedad de multiplicación del cero** Propiedad que establece que para todos los números reales a, $a \cdot 0 = 0$ y $0 \cdot a = 0$.	
multiplicative inverse A number times its multiplicative inverse is equal to 1; also called *reciprocal*.	**inverso multiplicativo** Un número multiplicado por su inverso multiplicativo es igual a 1. También se llama *recíproco*.	The multiplicative inverse of $\frac{4}{5}$ is $\frac{5}{4}$.
multiple The product of any number and a nonzero whole number is a multiple of that number.	**múltiplo** El producto de cualquier número y un número cabal distinto de cero es un múltiplo de ese número.	
mutually exclusive Two events are mutually exclusive if they cannot occur in the same trial of an experiment.	**mutuamente excluyentes** Dos sucesos son mutuamente excluyentes cuando no pueden ocurrir en la misma prueba de un experimento.	When rolling a number cube once, rolling a 3 and rolling an even number are mutually exclusive events.

N

ENGLISH	SPANISH	EXAMPLES
negative correlation Two data sets have a negative correlation if one set of data values increases while the other decreases.	**correlación negativa** Dos conjuntos de datos tienen correlación negativa si los valores de un conjunto aumentan a medida que los valores del otro conjunto disminuyen.	
negative integer An integer less than zero.	**entero negativo** Entero menor que cero.	-2 is a negative integer.

ENGLISH	SPANISH	EXAMPLES

net An arrangement of two-dimensional figures that can be folded to form a polyhedron.

plantilla Arreglo de figuras bidimensionales que se doblan para formar un poliedro.

---

network A set of points and the line segments or arcs that connect the points.

red Conjunto de puntos y los segmentos de recta o arcos que los conectan.

---

no correlation Two data sets have no correlation when there is no relationship between their data values.

sin correlación Caso en que los valores de dos conjuntos no muestran ninguna relación.

---

nonlinear function A function whose graph is not a straight line.

función no lineal Función cuya gráfica no es una línea recta.

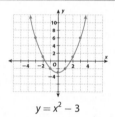

$y = x^2 - 3$

---

nonlinear relationship A relationship between two variables in which the data do not increase or decrease together at the same rate.

relación no lineal Relación entre dos variables en la cual los datos no aumentan o disminuyen al mismo tiempo a una tasa constante.

---

nonterminating decimal A decimal that never ends.

decimal infinito Decimal que nunca termina.

$0.\overline{3}$

---

numerator The top number of a fraction that tells how many parts of a whole are being considered.

numerador El número de arriba de una fracción; indica cuántas partes de un entero se consideran.

$\frac{4}{5}$ ⟵ numerator

---

numerical expression An expression that contains only numbers and operations.

expresión numérica Expresión que incluye sólo números y operaciones.

$(2 \cdot 3) + 1$

Ⓞ

---

obtuse angle An angle whose measure is greater than 90° but less than 180°.

ángulo obtuso Ángulo que mide más de 90° y menos de 180°.

---

obtuse triangle A triangle containing one obtuse angle.

triángulo obtusángulo Triángulo que tiene un ángulo obtuso.

---

octagon An eight-sided polygon.

octágono Polígono de ocho lados.

Glossary/Glosario

odds A comparison of the number of ways an event can occur and the number of ways an event can *not* occur.

probabilidades Comparación del número de las maneras que puede ocurrir un suceso y el número de maneras que no puede ocurrir el suceso.

---

odds against The ratio of the number of unfavorable outcomes to the number of favorable outcomes.

probabilidades en contra Razón del número de resultados no favorables al número de resultados favorables.

The odds against rolling a 3 on a number cube are 5:1.

---

odds in favor The ratio of the number of favorable outcomes to the number of unfavorable outcomes.

probabilidades a favor Razón del número de resultados favorables al número de resultados no favorables.

The odds in favor of rolling a 3 on a number cube are 1:5.

---

opposites Two numbers that are an equal distance from zero on a number line; also called *additive inverse*.

opuestos Dos números que están a la misma distancia de cero en una recta numérica. También se llaman *inversos aditivos*.

5 and −5 are opposites.

---

order of operations A rule for evaluating expressions: First perform the operations in parentheses, then compute powers and roots, then perform all multiplication and division from left to right, and then perform all addition and subtraction from left to right.

orden de las operaciones Regla para evaluar expresiones: primero se hacen las operaciones entre paréntesis, luego se hallan las potencias y raíces, después todas las multiplicaciones y divisiones de izquierda a derecha, y por último, todas las sumas y restas de izquierda a derecha.

$4^2 + 8 \div 2$ Evaluate the power.
$16 + 8 \div 2$ Divide.
$16 + 4$ Add.
20

---

ordered pair A pair of numbers that can be used to locate a point on a coordinate plane.

par ordenado Par de números que sirven para ubicar un punto en un plano cartesiano.

The coordinates of B are (−2, 3).

---

origin The point where the *x*-axis and *y*-axis intersect on the coordinate plane; (0, 0).

origen Punto de intersección entre el eje *x* y el eje *y* en un plano cartesiano: (0, 0).

---

orthogonal views A drawing that shows the top, bottom, front, back, and side views of a three-dimensional object.

vista ortogonal Un dibujo que muestra la vista superior, inferior, frontal, posterior y lateral de un objeto de tres dimensiones.

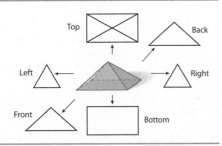

---

outcome (probability) A possible result of a probability experiment.

resultado (en probabilidad) Posible resultado de un experimento de probabilidad.

When rolling a number cube, the possible outcomes are 1, 2, 3, 4, 5, and 6.

ENGLISH	SPANISH	EXAMPLES
outlier A value much greater or much less than the others in a data set.	**valor extremo** Un valor mucho mayor o menor que los demás valores de un conjunto de datos.	Most of data · Mean · Outlier
output The value that results from the substitution of a given input into an expression or function.	**valor de salida** Valor que resulta después de sustituir una variable por un valor de entrada determinado en una expresión o función.	For the function $y = 6x$, the input 4 produces an output of 24.

parabola The graph of a quadratic function.	**parábola** Gráfica de una función cuadrática.	
parallel lines Lines in a plane that do not intersect.	**líneas paralelas** Líneas que se encuentran en el mismo plano pero que nunca se intersecan.	
parallelogram A quadrilateral with two pairs of parallel sides.	**paralelogramo** Cuadrilátero con dos pares de lados paralelos.	
pentagon A five-sided polygon.	**pentágono** Polígono de cinco lados.	
percent A ratio comparing a number to 100.	**porcentaje** Razón que compara un número con el número 100.	$45\% = \frac{45}{100}$
percent change The amount stated as a percent that a number increases or decreases.	**porcentaje de cambio** Cantidad en que un número aumenta o disminuye, expresada como un porcentaje.	
percent decrease A percent change describing a decrease in a quantity.	**porcentaje de disminución** Porcentaje de cambio en que una cantidad disminuye.	An item that costs \$8 is marked down to \$6. The amount of the decrease is \$2, and the percent decrease is $\frac{2}{8} = 0.25 = 25\%$.
percent increase A percent change describing an increase in a quantity.	**porcentaje de incremento** Porcentaje de cambio en que una cantidad aumenta.	The price of an item increases from \$8 to \$12. The amount of the increase is \$4, and the percent increase is $\frac{4}{8} = 0.5 = 50\%$.
perfect cube A cube of a whole number.	**cubo perfecto** El cubo de un número cabal.	$2^3 = 8$, so 8 is a perfect cube.
perfect square A square of a whole number.	**cuadrado perfecto** El cuadrado de un número cabal.	$5^2 = 25$, so 25 is a perfect square.
perimeter The distance around a polygon.	**perímetro** Distancia alrededor de un polígono.	18 ft / 6 ft perimeter $= 18 + 6 + 18 + 6 = 48$ ft

Glossary/Glosario

permutation An arrangement of items or events in which order is important.

permutación Arreglo de objetos o sucesos en el que el orden es importante.

For objects *A*, *B*, and *C*, there are 6 different permutations: *ABC*, *ACB*, *BAC*, *BCA*, *CAB*, *CBA*.

---

perpendicular bisector A line that intersects a segment at its midpoint and is perpendicular to the segment.

mediatriz Línea que cruza un segmento en su punto medio y es perpendicular al segmento.

---

perpendicular lines Lines that intersect to form right angles.

líneas perpendiculares Líneas que al intersecarse forman ángulos rectos.

---

pi (π) The ratio of the circumference of a circle to the length of its diameter; $\pi \approx 3.14$ or $\frac{22}{7}$.

pi (π) Razón de la circunferencia de un círculo a la longitud de su diámetro; $\pi \approx 3.14$ ó $\frac{22}{7}$.

---

plane A flat surface that has no thickness and extends forever.

plano Superficie plana que no tiene ningún grueso y que se extiende por siempre.

---

point An exact location that has no size.

punto Ubicación exacta que no tiene ningún tamaño.

$P \bullet$

---

point-slope form The equation of a line in the form of $y - y_1 = m(x - x_1)$, where *m* is the slope and (x_1, y_1) is a specific point on the line.

forma de punto y pendiente Ecuación lineal del tipo $y - y_1 = m(x - x_1)$, donde *m* es la pendiente y (x_1, y_1) es un punto específico de la línea.

$y - 3 = 2(x - 3)$

---

polygon A closed plane figure formed by three or more line segments that intersect only at their endpoints (vertices).

polígono Figura plana cerrada, formada por tres o más segmentos de recta que se intersecan sólo en sus extremos (vértices).

---

polyhedron A three-dimensional figure in which all the surfaces or faces are polygons.

poliedro Figura tridimensional cuyas superficies o caras tiene forma de polígonos.

---

polynomial One monomial or the sum or difference of monomials.

polinomio Un monomio o la suma o la diferencia de monomios.

$2x^2 + 3xy - 7y^2$

---

population The entire group of objects or individuals considered for a survey.

población Grupo completo de objetos o individuos que se desea estudiar.

In a survey about study habits of middle school students, the population is all middle school students.

Glossary/Glosario

positive correlation Two data sets have a positive correlation when their data values increase or decrease together.

correlación positiva Dos conjuntos de datos tienen una correlación positiva cuando los valores de ambos conjuntos aumentan o disminuyen al mismo tiempo.

---

positive integer An integer greater than zero.

entero positivo Entero mayor que cero.

2 is a positive integer.

---

power A number produced by raising a base to an exponent.

potencia Número que resulta al elevar una base a un exponente.

$2^3 = 8$, so 2 to the 3rd power is 8.

---

preimage The original figure in a transformation.

imagen original Figura original en una transformación.

---

prime factorization A number written as the product of its prime factors.

factorización prima Un número escrito como el producto de sus factores primos.

$10 = 2 \cdot 5$,
$24 = 2^3 \cdot 3$

---

prime number A whole number greater than 1 that has exactly two factors, itself and 1.

número primo Número cabal mayor que 1 que sólo es divisible entre 1 y él mismo.

5 is prime because its only factors are 5 and 1.

---

principal The initial amount of money borrowed or saved.

principal Cantidad inicial de dinero depositada o recibida en préstamo.

---

principal square root The nonnegative square root of a number.

raíz cuadrada principal Raíz cuadrada no negativa de un número.

$\sqrt{25} = 5$; the principal square root of 25 is 5.

---

prism A polyhedron that has two congruent, polygon-shaped bases and other faces that are all parallelograms.

prisma Poliedro con dos bases congruentes con forma de polígono y caras con forma de paralelogramo.

---

probability A number from 0 to 1 (or 0% to 100%) that describes how likely an event is to occur.

probabilidad Un número entre 0 y 1 (ó 0% y 100%) que describe qué tan probable es un suceso.

A bag contains 3 red marbles and 4 blue marbles. The probability of randomly choosing a red marble is $\frac{3}{7}$.

---

proper fraction A fraction in which the numerator is less than the denominator.

fracción propia Fracción en la que el numerador es menor que el denominador.

$\frac{3}{4}, \frac{1}{12}, \frac{7}{8}$

---

proportion An equation that states that two ratios are equivalent.

proporción Ecuación que establece que dos razones son equivalentes.

$\frac{2}{3} = \frac{4}{6}$

---

proportional relationship A relationship between two quantities in which the ratio of one quantity to the other quantity is constant.

relación proporcional Relación entre dos cantidades en que la razón de una cantidad a la otra es constante.

Glossary/Glosario

ENGLISH	SPANISH	EXAMPLES
protractor A tool for measuring angles.	**transportador** Instrumento para medir ángulos.	
pyramid A polyhedron with a polygon base and triangular sides that all meet at a common vertex.	**pirámide** Poliedro cuya base es un polígono; tiene caras triangulares que se juntan en un vértice común.	
Pythagorean Theorem In a right triangle, the square of the length of the hypotenuse is equal to the sum of the squares of the lengths of the legs.	**Teorema de Pitágoras** En un triángulo rectángulo, la suma de los cuadrados de los catetos es igual al cuadrado de la hipotenusa.	$5^2 + 12^2 = 13^2$ $25 + 144 = 169$
Pythagorean triple A set of three positive integers a, b, and c such that $a^2 + b^2 = c^2$.	**Tripleta de Pitágoras** Conjunto de tres números enteros positivos de cero a, b y c tal que $a^2 + b^2 = c^2$.	3, 4, 5 because $3^2 + 4^2 = 5^2$

quadrant The x- and y-axes divide the coordinate plane into four regions. Each region is called a quadrant.	**cuadrante** El eje x y el eje y dividen el plano cartesiano en cuatro regiones. Cada región recibe el nombre de cuadrante.	
quadratic function A function of the form $y = ax^2 + bx + c$, where $a \neq 0$.	**función cuadrática** Función del tipo $y = ax^2 + bx + c$, donde $a \neq 0$.	$y = x^2 - 6x + 8$
quadrilateral A four-sided polygon.	**cuadrilátero** Polígono de cuatro lados.	
quarterly Four times a year.	**trimestral** Cuatro veces al año.	
quartile Three values, one of which is the median, that divide a data set into fourths.	**cuartil** Cada uno de tres valores, uno de los cuales es la mediana, que dividen en cuartos un conjunto de datos.	
quotient The result when one number is divided by another.	**cociente** Resultado de dividir un número entre otro.	In $8 \div 4 = 2$, 2 is the quotient.

R

radical symbol The symbol $\sqrt{}$ used to represent the nonnegative square root of a number.

símbolo de radical El símbolo $\sqrt{}$ con que se representa la raíz cuadrada no negativa de un número.

radius A line segment with one endpoint at the center of the circle and the other endpoint on the circle, or the length of that segment.

radio Segmento de recta con un extremo en el centro de un círculo y el otro en la circunferencia, o bien se llama radio a la longitud de ese segmento.

Radius

random numbers In a set of random numbers, each number has an equal chance of appearing.

muestra aleatoria Muestra en la que cada individuo u objeto de la población tiene la misma posibilidad de ser elegido.

random sample A sample in which each individual or object in the entire population has an equal chance of being selected.

números aleatorios En un conjunto de números aleatorios, todos los números tienen la misma probabilidad de ser seleccionados.

range (in statistics) The difference between the greatest and least values in a data set.

rango (en estadística) Diferencia entre los valores máximo y mínimo de un conjunto de datos.

Data set: 3, 5, 7, 7, 12
Range: $12 - 3 = 9$

range (of a function) The set of all possible output values of a function.

rango (en una función) El conjunto de todos los valores posibles de una función.

The range of $y = |x|$ is $y \geq 0$.

rate A ratio that compares two quantities measured in different units.

tasa Una razón que compara dos cantidades medidas en diferentes unidades.

The speed limit is 55 miles per hour or 55 mi/h.

rate of change A ratio that compares the amount of change in a dependent variable to the amount of change in an independent variable.

tasa de cambio Razón que compara la cantidad de cambio de la variable dependiente con la cantidad de cambio de la variable independiente.

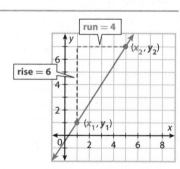

Rate of change $= \dfrac{\text{change in } y}{\text{change in } x} = \dfrac{6}{4} = \dfrac{3}{2}$

rate of interest The percent charged or earned on an amount of money; see *simple interest*.

tasa de interés Porcentaje que se cobra por una cantidad de dinero prestada o que se gana por una cantidad de dinero ahorrada; ver *interés simple*.

ENGLISH	SPANISH	EXAMPLES
ratio A comparison of two quantities by division.	**razón** Comparación de dos cantidades mediante una división.	12 to 25, 12:25, $\frac{12}{25}$
rational number Any number that can be expressed as a ratio of two integers.	**número racional** Número que se puede escribir como una razón de dos enteros.	6 can be expressed as $\frac{6}{1}$. 0.5 can be expressed as $\frac{1}{2}$.
ray A part of a line that starts at one endpoint and extends forever in one direction.	**rayo** Parte de una línea que comienza en un extremo y se extiende de manera infinitamente en una dirección.	*D*
real number A rational or irrational number.	**número real** Número racional o irracional.	
reciprocal One of two numbers whose product is 1; also called *multiplicative inverse*.	**recíproco** Uno de dos números cuyo producto es igual a 1. También se llama *inverso multiplicativo*.	The reciprocal of $\frac{2}{3}$ is $\frac{3}{2}$.
rectangle A parallelogram with four right angles.	**rectángulo** Paralelogramo con cuatro ángulos rectos.	
rectangular prism A polyhedron whose bases are rectangles and whose other faces are parallelograms.	**prisma rectangular** Poliedro cuyas bases son rectángulos y cuyas caras tienen forma de paralelogramo.	
reduction A decrease in the size of all dimensions.	**reducción** Disminución de tamaño en todas las dimensiones de una figura.	
reflection A transformation of a figure that flips the figure across a line.	**reflexión** Transformación que ocurre cuando se invierte una figura sobre una línea.	
regular polygon A polygon with congruent sides and angles.	**polígono regular** Polígono con lados y ángulos congruentes.	
regular pyramid A pyramid whose base is a regular polygon and whose lateral faces are all congruent.	**pirámide regular** Pirámide que tiene un polígono regular como base y caras laterales congruentes.	
relation A set of ordered pairs.	**relación** Conjunto de pares ordenados.	(0, 5), (0, 4), (2, 3), (4, 0)
relative frequency The frequency of a specific data value divided by the total number of data values in the set.	**frecuencia relativa** La frecuencia de un valor dividido por el número total de los valores en el conjunto.	

ENGLISH	SPANISH	EXAMPLES
relatively prime Two numbers are relatively prime if their greatest common factor (GCF) is 1.	**primo relativo** Dos números son primos relativos si su máximo común divisor (MCD) es 1.	8 and 15 are relatively prime.
remote interior angle An interior angle of a polygon that is not adjacent to the exterior angle.	**ángulo interno remoto** Ángulo interno de un polígono que no es adyacente al ángulo externo.	
repeating decimal A decimal in which one or more digits repeat infinitely.	**decimal periódico** Decimal en el que uno o más dígitos se repiten infinitamente.	$0.757575\ldots = 0.\overline{75}$
rhombus A parallelogram with all sides congruent.	**rombo** Paralelogramo en el que todos los lados son congruentes.	
right angle An angle that measures 90°.	**ángulo recto** Ángulo que mide exactamente 90°.	
right cone A cone in which a perpendicular line drawn from the base to the tip (vertex) passes through the center of the base.	**cono regular** Cono en el que una línea perpendicular trazada de la base a la punta (vértice) pasa por el centro de la base.	Right cone
right triangle A triangle containing a right angle.	**triángulo rectángulo** Triángulo que tiene un ángulo recto.	
rise The vertical change when the slope of a line is expressed as the ratio $\frac{rise}{run}$, or "rise over run."	**distancia vertical** El cambio vertical cuando la pendiente de una línea se expresa como la razón $\frac{distancia\ vertical}{distancia\ horizontal}$, o "distancia vertical sobre distancia horizontal".	For the points $(3, -1)$ and $(6, 5)$, the rise is $5 - (-1) = 6$.
rotation A transformation in which a figure is turned around a point.	**rotación** Transformación que ocurre cuando una figura gira alrededor de un punto.	
rotational symmetry A figure has rotational symmetry if it can be rotated less than 360° around a central point and coincides with the original figure.	**simetría de rotación** Ocurre cuando una figura gira menos de 360° alrededor de un punto central sin dejar de ser congruente con la figura original.	90° 90° 90° 90°

ENGLISH	SPANISH	EXAMPLES
run The horizontal change when the slope of a line is expressed as the ratio $\frac{rise}{run}$, or "rise over run."	**distancia horizontal** El cambio horizontal cuando la pendiente de una línea se expresa como la razón $\frac{distancia\ vertical}{distancia\ horizontal}$, o "distancia vertical sobre distancia horizontal".	For the points $(3, -1)$ and $(6, 5)$, the run is $6 - 3 = 3$.

ENGLISH	SPANISH	EXAMPLES
sales tax A percent of the cost of an item that is charged by governments to raise money.	**impuesto sobre la venta** Porcentaje del costo de un artículo que los gobiernos cobran para recaudar fondos.	
same-side interior angles A pair of angles on the same side of a transversal and between two lines intersected by the transversal.	**ángulo internos del mismo lado** Dadas dos rectas cortadas por una transversal, par de ángulos ubicados en el mismo lado de la transversal y entre las dos rectas.	
sample A part of the population.	**muestra** Una parte de la población.	
sample space All possible outcomes of an experiment.	**espacio muestral** Conjunto de todos los resultados posibles de un experimento.	When rolling a number cube, the sample space is 1, 2, 3, 4, 5, 6.
scale The ratio between two sets of measurements.	**escala** La razón entre dos conjuntos de medidas.	1 cm : 5 mi
scale drawing A drawing that uses a scale to make an object smaller than (a reduction) or larger than (an enlargement) the real object.	**dibujo a escala** Dibujo en el que se usa una escala para que un objeto se vea menor (reducción) o mayor (agrandamiento) que el objeto real al que representa.	A blueprint is an example of a scale drawing.
scale factor The ratio used to enlarge or reduce similar figures.	**factor de escala** Razón empleada para agrandar o reducir figuras semejantes.	
scale model A proportional model of a three-dimensional object.	**modelo a escala** Modelo proporcional de un objeto tridimensional.	
scalene triangle A triangle with no congruent sides.	**triángulo escaleno** Triángulo que no tiene lados congruentes.	
scatter plot A graph with points plotted to show a possible relationship between two sets of data.	**diagrama de dispersión** Gráfica de puntos que muestra una posible relación entre dos conjuntos de datos.	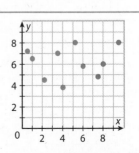

ENGLISH	SPANISH	EXAMPLES
scientific notation A method of writing very large or very small numbers by using powers of 10.	**notación científica** Método que se usa para escribir números muy grandes o muy pequeños mediante potencias de 10.	$12,560,000,000,000 = 1.256 \times 10^{13}$
second quartile The median of a set of data.	**segundo cuartil** Mediana de un conjunto de datos.	Data set: 4, 6, 7, 8, 10 Second quartile: 7
segment A part of a line between two endpoints.	**segmento** Parte de una línea entre dos extremos.	
self-selected sample A sample in which members choose to be in the sample.	**muestra auto-seleccionada** Una muestra en la que los miembros eligen participar.	A store provides survey cards for customers who choose to fill them out.
sequence An ordered list of numbers.	**sucesión** Lista ordenada de números.	2, 4, 6, 8, 10, …
side A line bounding a geometric figure; one of the faces forming the outside of an object.	**lado** Línea que delimita las figuras geométricas; una de las caras que forman la parte exterior de un objeto.	
similar Figures with the same shape but not necessarily the same size.	**semejantes** Figuras que tienen la misma forma, pero no necesariamente el mismo tamaño.	
similarity transformation A transformation that results in an image that is the same shape, but not necessarily the same size, as the original figure.	**transformación de semejanza** Una transformación que resulta en una imagen que tiene la misma forma, pero no necesariamente el mismo tamaño como la figura original.	
simple interest A fixed percent of the principal. It is found using the formula $I = Prt$, where P represents the principal, r the rate of interest, and t the time.	**interés simple** Un porcentaje fijo del capital. Se calcula con la fórmula $I = Cit$, donde C representa el capital, i, la tasa de interés y t, el tiempo.	$100 is put into an account with a simple interest rate of 5%. After 2 years, the account will have earned $I = 100 \cdot 0.05 \cdot 2 = \$10$.
simplest form A fraction in which the numerator and denominator have no common factors other than 1.	**mínima expresión** Una fracción está en su mínima expresión cuando el numerador y el denominador no tienen más factor común que 1.	Fraction: $\frac{8}{12}$ Simplest form: $\frac{2}{3}$
simplify To write a fraction or expression in simplest form.	**simplificar** Escribir una fracción o expresión numérica en su mínima expresión.	
simulation A model of an experiment, often one that would be too difficult or too time-consuming to actually perform.	**simulación** Representación de un experimento, por lo general, de uno cuya realización sería demasiado difícil o llevaría mucho tiempo.	

Glossary/Glosario

ENGLISH	SPANISH	EXAMPLES

slant height (of a regular pyramid) The distance from the vertex of a regular pyramid to the midpoint of an edge of the base.

altura inclinada (de una pirámide) Distancia desde el vértice de una pirámide hasta el punto medio de una arista de la base.

Regular pyramid

---

slant height (of a right cone) The distance from the vertex of a right cone to a point on the edge of the base.

altura inclinada (de un cono recto) Distancia desde el vértice de un cono recto hasta un punto en el borde de la base.

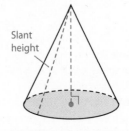

---

slope A measure of the steepness of a line on a graph; the rise divided by the run.

pendiente Medida de la inclinación de una línea en una gráfica. Razón de la distancia vertical a la distancia horizontal.

Slope $= \frac{\text{rise}}{\text{run}} = \frac{3}{4}$

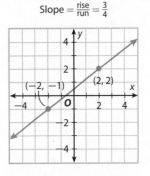

---

slope-intercept form A linear equation written in the form $y = mx + b$, where m represents slope and b represents the y-intercept.

forma de pendiente-intersección Ecuación lineal escrita en la forma $y = mx + b$, donde m es la pendiente y b es la intersección con el eje y.

$y = 6x - 3$

---

solution of an equation A value or values that make an equation true.

solución de una ecuación Valor o valores que hacen verdadera una ecuación.

Equation: $x + 2 = 6$
Solution: $x = 4$

---

solution of an inequality A value or values that make an inequality true.

solución de una desigualdad Valor o valores que hacen verdadera una desigualdad.

Inequality: $x + 3 \geq 10$
Solution: $x \geq 7$

---

solution of a system of equations A set of values that make all equations in a system true.

solución de un sistema de ecuaciones Conjunto de valores que hacen verdaderas todas las ecuaciones de un sistema.

System: $\begin{cases} x + y = -1 \\ -x + y = -3 \end{cases}$
Solution: $(1, -2)$

---

solution set The set of values that make a statement true.

conjunto solución Conjunto de valores que hacen verdadero un enunciado.

Inequality: $x + 3 \geq 5$
Solution set: $x \geq 2$

-4 -3 -2 -1 0 1 2 3 4 5 6

---

solve To find an answer or a solution.

resolver Hallar una respuesta o solución.

ENGLISH	SPANISH	EXAMPLES
sphere A three-dimensional figure with all points the same distance from the center.	**esfera** Figura tridimensional en la que todos los puntos están a la misma distancia del centro.	
square A rectangle with four congruent sides.	**cuadrado** Rectángulo con cuatro lados congruentes.	
square (numeration) A number raised to the second power.	**cuadrado (en numeración)** Número elevado a la segunda potencia.	In 5^2, the number 5 is squared.
square root A number that is multiplied by itself to form a product is called a square root of that product.	**raíz cuadrada** El número que se multiplica por sí mismo para formar un producto se denomina la raíz cuadrada de ese producto.	A square root of 16 is 4, because $4^2 = 4 \cdot 4 = 16$. Another square root of 16 is -4 because $(-4)^2 = (-4)(-4) = 16$.
stem-and-leaf plot A graph used to organize and display data so that the frequencies can be compared.	**diagrama de tallo y hojas** Gráfica que muestra y ordena los datos, y que sirve para comparar las frecuencias.	Stem | Leaves 3 | 2 3 4 4 7 9 4 | 0 1 5 7 7 7 8 5 | 1 2 2 3 *Key: 3|2 means 3.2*
straight angle An angle that measures 180°.	**ángulo llano** Ángulo que mide exactamente 180°.	
substitute To replace a variable with a number or another expression in an algebraic expression.	**sustituir** Reemplazar una variable por un número u otra expresión en una expresión algebraica.	Substituting 3 for m in the expression $5m - 2$ gives $5(3) - 2 = 15 - 2 = 13$.
Subtraction Property of Equality The property that states that if you subtract the same number from both sides of an equation, the new equation will have the same solution.	**Propiedad de igualdad de la resta** Propiedad que establece que puedes restar el mismo número de ambos lados de una ecuación y la nueva ecuación tendrá la misma solución.	$14 - 6 = 8$ $\underline{ - 6 = -6}$ $14 - 12 = 2$
supplementary angles Two angles whose measures have a sum of 180°.	**ángulos suplementarios** Dos ángulos cuyas medidas suman 180°.	
surface area The sum of the areas of the faces, or surfaces, of a three-dimensional figure.	**área total** Suma de las áreas de las caras, o superficies, de una figura tridimensional.	 Surface area $= 2(8)(12) + 2(8)(6) + 2(12)(6) = 432$ cm^2

system of equations A set of two or more equations that contain two or more variables.

sistema de ecuaciones Conjunto de dos o más ecuaciones que contienen dos o más variables.

$$\begin{cases} x + y = -1 \\ -x + y = -3 \end{cases}$$

---

systematic sample A sample of a population that has been selected using a pattern.

muestra sistemática Muestra de una población, que ha sido elegida mediante un patrón.

To conduct a phone survey, every tenth name is chosen from the phone book.

---

term (in an expression) A part of an expression that is added or subtracted.

término (en una expresión) Las partes de una expresión que se suman o se restan.

$$3x^2 \quad + \quad 6x \quad - \quad 8$$

Term   Term   Term

---

term (in a sequence) An element or number in a sequence.

término (en una sucesión) Elemento o número de una sucesión.

5 is the third term in the sequence 1, 3, 5, 7, 9, …

---

terminating decimal A decimal is called terminating if its repeating digit is 0.

decimal finito Un decimal es finito si el dígito que se repite es 0.

6.75

---

tessellation A repeating pattern of plane figures that completely cover a plane with no gaps or overlaps.

teselado Patrón repetido de figuras planas que cubren totalmente un plano sin superponerse ni dejar huecos.

---

theoretical probability The ratio of the number of ways an event can occur to the number of equally likely outcomes.

probabilidad teórica Razón del número de las maneras que puede ocurrir un suceso al numero total de resultados igualmente probables.

When rolling a number cube, the theoretical probability of rolling a 4 is $\frac{1}{6}$.

---

third quartile The median of the upper half of a set of data; also called *upper quartile*.

tercer cuartil La mediana de la mitad superior de un conjunto de datos. También se llama *cuartil superior*.

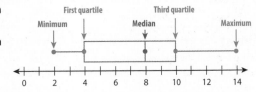

---

transformation A change in the size or position of a figure.

transformación Cambio en el tamaño o la posición de una figura.

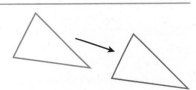

---

translation A movement (slide) of a figure along a straight line.

traslación Desplazamiento de una figura a lo largo de una línea recta.

ENGLISH	SPANISH	EXAMPLES

transversal A line that intersects two or more lines.

transversal Línea que cruza dos o más líneas.

trapezoid A quadrilateral with exactly one pair of parallel sides.

trapecio Cuadrilátero con un par de lados paralelos.

tree diagram A branching diagram that shows all possible combinations or outcomes of an event.

diagrama de árbol Diagrama ramificado que muestra todas las posibles combinaciones o resultados de un suceso.

trend line A line on a scatter plot that helps show the correlation between data sets more clearly.

línea de tendencia Línea en un diagrama de dispersión que sirve para mostrar la correlación entre conjuntos de datos más claramente. *ver también* línea de mejor ajuste.

trial Each repetition or observation of an experiment.

prueba Una sola repetición u observación de un experimento.

When rolling a number cube, each roll is one trial.

Triangle Inequality Theorem The theorem that states that the sum of the lengths of any two sides of a triangle is greater than the length of the third side.

Teorema de desigualdad de triángulos El teorema dice que la suma de cualquier dos lados de un triangulo es mayor que la longitud del lado tercero.

Can form a triangle   Cannot form a triangle

Triangle Sum Theorem The theorem that states that the measures of the angles in a triangle add up to 180°.

Teorema de la suma del triángulo Teorema que establece que las medidas de los ángulos de un triángulo suman 180°.

triangular prism A polyhedron whose bases are triangles and whose other faces are parallelograms.

prisma triangular Poliedro cuyas bases son triángulos y cuyas demás caras tienen forma de paralelogramo.

trinomial A polynomial with three terms.

trinomio Polinomio con tres términos.

$4x^2 + 3xy - 5y^2$

two-way relative frequency table A two-way table that displays relative frequencies.

tabla de frecuencia relativa de doble entrada Una tabla de doble entrada que muestran las frecuencias relativas.

two-way table A table that displays two-variable data by organizing it into rows and columns.

tabla de doble entrada Una tabla que muestran los datos de dos variables por organizándolos en columnas y filas.

		Preference		
		Inside	**Outside**	*Total*
Pet	**Cats**	35	15	50
	Dogs	20	30	50
	Total	55	45	100

unit conversion The process of changing one unit of measure to another.	**conversión de unidades** Proceso que consiste en cambiar una unidad de medida por otra.	
unit conversion factor A fraction used in unit conversion in which the numerator and denominator represent the same amount but are in different units.	**factor de conversión de unidades** Fracción que se usa para la conversión de unidades, donde el numerador y el denominador representan la misma cantidad pero están en unidades distintas.	$\frac{60 \text{ min}}{1 \text{ h}}$ or $\frac{1 \text{ h}}{60 \text{ min}}$
unit price A unit rate used to compare prices.	**precio unitario** Tasa unitaria que sirve para comparar precios.	Cereal costs $0.23 per ounce.
unit rate A rate in which the second quantity in the comparison is one unit.	**tasa unitaria** Una tasa en la que la segunda cantidad de la comparación es la unidad.	10 cm per minute

variability The spread of values in a set of data.	**variabilidad** Amplitud de los valores de un conjunto de datos.	The data set {1, 5, 7, 10, 25} has greater variability than the data set {8, 8, 9, 9, 9}.
variable A symbol used to represent a quantity that can change.	**variable** Símbolo que representa una cantidad que puede cambiar.	In the expression $2x + 3$, x is the variable.
Venn diagram A diagram that is used to show relationships between sets.	**diagrama de Venn** Diagrama que muestra las relaciones entre conjuntos.	
vertex On an angle or polygon, the point where two sides intersect; on a polyhedron, the intersection of three or more faces; on a cone or pyramid, the top point.	**vértice** En un ángulo o polígono, el punto de intersección de dos lados; en un poliedro, el punto de intersección de tres o más caras; en un cono o pirámide, la punta.	*A* is the vertex of $\angle CAB$.
vertical angles A pair of opposite congruent angles formed by intersecting lines.	**ángulos opuestos por el vértice** Par de ángulos opuestos congruentes formados por líneas secantes.	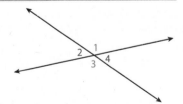 $\angle 1$ and $\angle 3$ are vertical angles.

Glossary/Glosario

ENGLISH	SPANISH	EXAMPLES

vertical line test A test used to determine whether a relation is a function. If any vertical line crosses the graph of a relation more than once, the relation is not a function.

prueba de la línea vertical Prueba utilizada para determinar si una relación es una función. Si una línea vertical corta la gráfica de una relación más de una vez, la relación no es una función.

Function   Not a function

volume The number of cubic units needed to fill a given space.

volumen Número de unidades cúbicas que se necesitan para llenar un espacio.

4 ft
3 ft
12 ft

Volume = $3 \cdot 4 \cdot 12 = 144 \text{ ft}^3$

W

weighted average A mean that is calculated by multiplying each data value by a weight, and dividing the sum of these products by the sum of the weights.

promedio ponderado Promedio que se calcula por multiplicando cada valor de datos por un peso, y dividiendo la suma de estos productos por la suma de los pesos.

If the data values 0, 5, and 10 are assigned the weights 0.1, 0.2, and 0.7, respectively, the weighted average is:

$$\frac{0(0.1) + 5(0.2) + 10(0.7)}{0.1 + 0.2 + 0.7} = \frac{8}{1}$$

X

x-axis The horizontal axis on a coordinate plane.

eje x El eje horizontal del plano cartesiano.

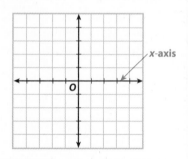

x-axis

O

x-coordinate The first number in an ordered pair; it tells the distance to move right or left from the origin (0, 0).

coordenada x El primer número de un par ordenado; indica la distancia que debes moverte hacia la izquierda o la derecha desde el origen, (0, 0).

5 is the x-coordinate in (5, 3).

x-intercept The x-coordinate of the point where the graph of a line crosses the x-axis.

intersección con el eje x Coordenada x del punto donde la gráfica de una línea cruza el eje x.

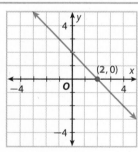

(2, 0)

The x-intercept is 2.

y-axis The vertical axis on a coordinate plane.

eje y El eje vertical del plano cartesiano.

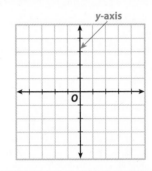

y-coordinate The second number in an ordered pair; it tells the distance to move up or down from the origin (0, 0).

coordenada y El segundo número de un par ordenado; indica la distancia que debes avanzar hacia arriba o hacia abajo desde el origen, (0, 0).

3 is the y-coordinate in (5, 3).

y-intercept The y-coordinate of the point where the graph of a line crosses the y-axis.

intersección con el eje y Coordenada y del punto donde la gráfica de una línea cruza el eje y.

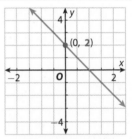

The y-intercept is 2.

zero pair A number and its opposite, which add to 0.

par nulo Un número y su opuesto, cuya suma es 0.

18 and −18

Glossary/Glosario

Index

Index

Index

W

weight, 57
What If?, 86, 111, 116, 137, 140, 143, 156, 161,
    180, 205, 231, 247, 290, 365, 367, 402, 437
Wheel of Theodorus, 344
whole numbers, 15

X

x-intercept, 79

Y

Yellowstone National Park, 436

y-intercept, 103
    defined, 96, 103
    in graphing, 109–114
    slope-intercept form of equations, 103–114

Z

zeros, in scientific notation, 42, 43

Index

ASSESSMENT REFERENCE SHEET

TABLE OF MEASURES

Length

1 inch = 2.54 centimeters

1 meter ≈ 39.37 inches

1 mile = 5,280 feet

1 mile = 1,760 yards

1 mile ≈ 1.609 kilometers

1 kilometer ≈ 0.62 mile

Mass/Weight

1 pound = 16 ounces

1 pound ≈ 0.454 kilogram

1 kilogram ≈ 2.2 pounds

1 ton = 2,000 pounds

Capacity

1 cup = 8 fluid ounces

1 pint = 2 cups

1 quart = 2 pints

1 gallon = 4 quarts

1 gallon ≈ 3.785 liters

1 liter ≈ 0.264 gallon

1 liter = 1000 cubic centimeters

FORMULAS

Area

Parallelogram	$A = bh$
Circle	$A = \pi r^2$
Triangle	$A = \frac{1}{2} bh$

Volume

General Prisms	$V = Bh$
Cylinder	$V = \pi r^2 h$
Sphere	$V = \frac{4}{3} \pi r^3$
Cone	$V = \frac{1}{3} \pi r^2 h$

Circumference

Circle	$C = \pi d$ or $C = 2\pi r$

Other

Pythagorean Theorem	$a^2 + b^2 = c^2$